Takeshi Obata ART

Tsugumi Ohba STORY

PLATINUM END

14

D1289980

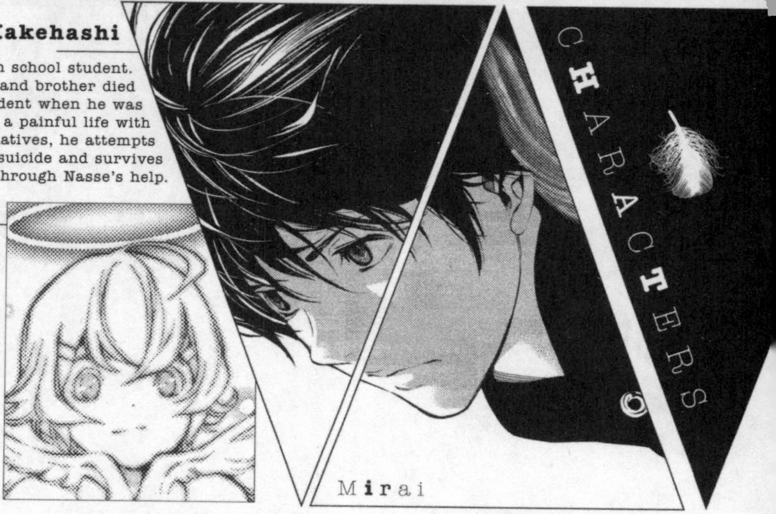
CHARACTERS
Mirai

Mirai Kakehashi

First-year high school student. His parents and brother died in an accident when he was seven. After a painful life with his abusive relatives, he attempts to commit suicide and survives through Nasse's help.

Nasse

A special-rank angel who wants to bring happiness to Mirai's life. Bright and bubbly.

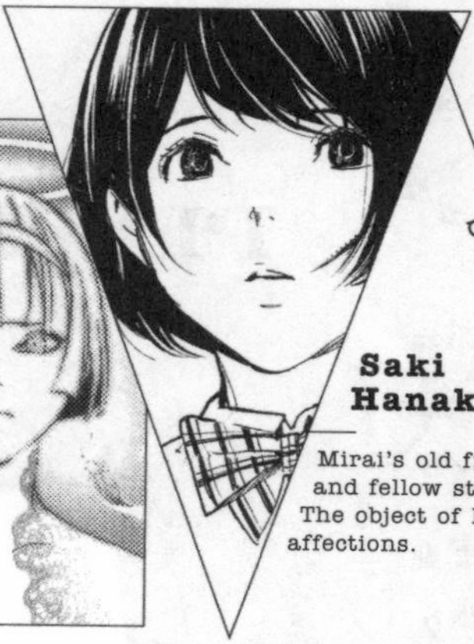
Saki

Saki Hanakago

Mirai's old friend and fellow student. The object of his affections.

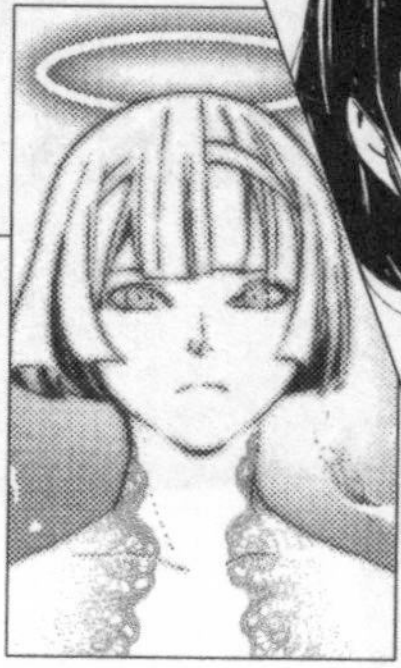

Revel

Promoted to the first-rank Angel of Emotion.

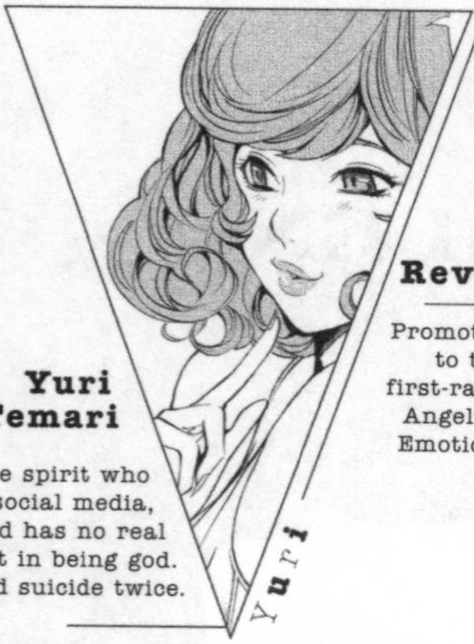
Yuri

Yuri Temari

Free spirit who enjoys social media, and has no real interest in being god. Attempted suicide twice.

Story

"My time has come. I leave the seat of god to the next human.
To a younger, fresher power.

The next god shall be chosen from the 13 humans chosen by you 13 angels. When the chosen human is made the next god, your [redacted]

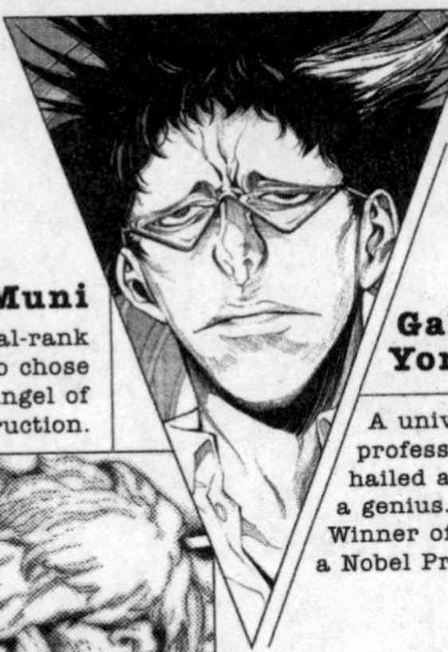

GAKU

Gaku Yoneda

A university professor hailed as a genius. Winner of a Nobel Prize.

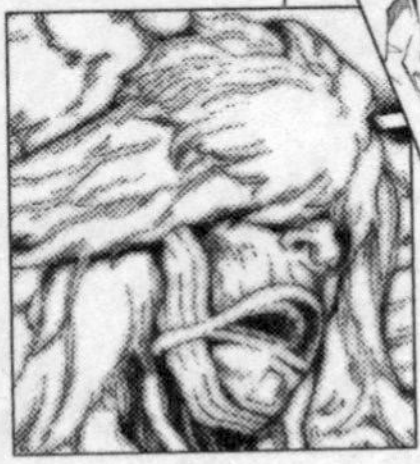

Muni

The special-rank angel who chose Yoneda. Angel of Destruction.

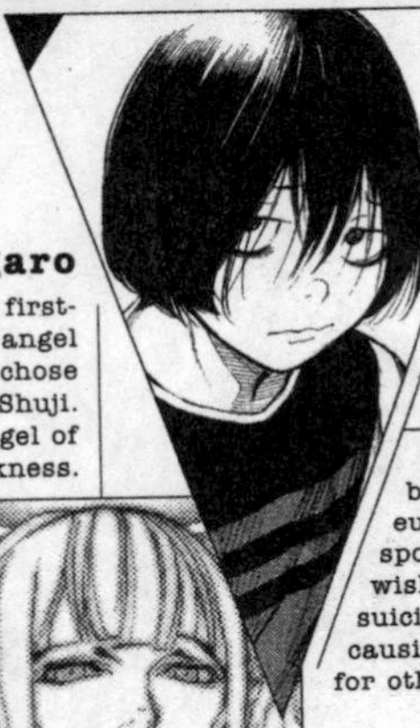

Shuji

Shuji Nakaumi

A boy who believes in euthanasia and spoke of his own wish to commit suicide. Hates causing trouble for others.

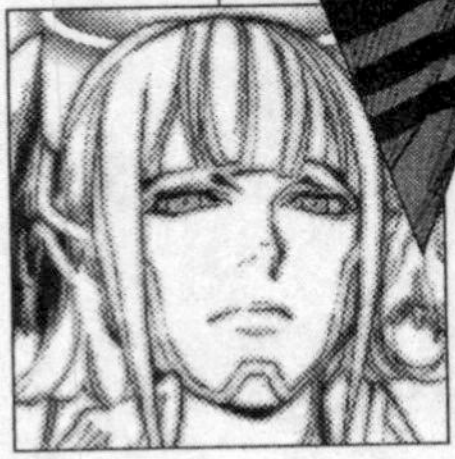

Ogaro

The first-rank angel who chose Shuji. Angel of Darkness.

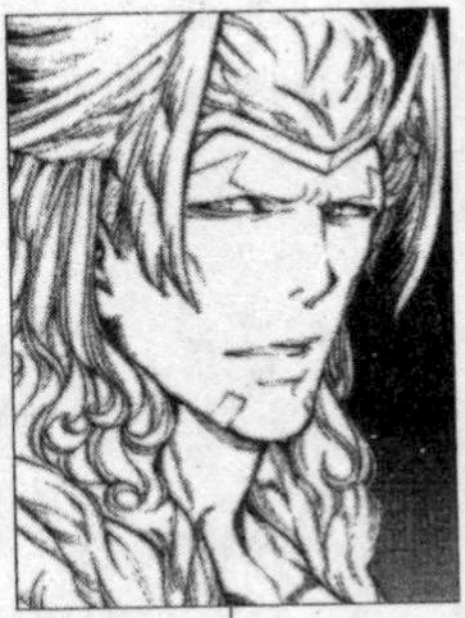

Yazeli

The second-rank angel who chose Yuri. Angel of Truth.

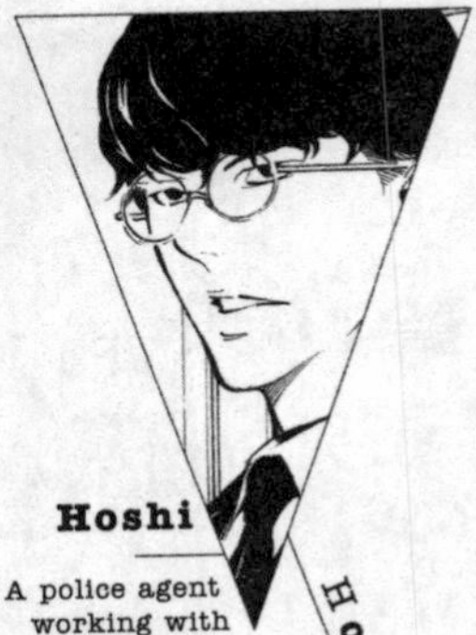

Hoshi

Hoshi

A police agent working with Yumiki to help Mirai's group without telling the government.

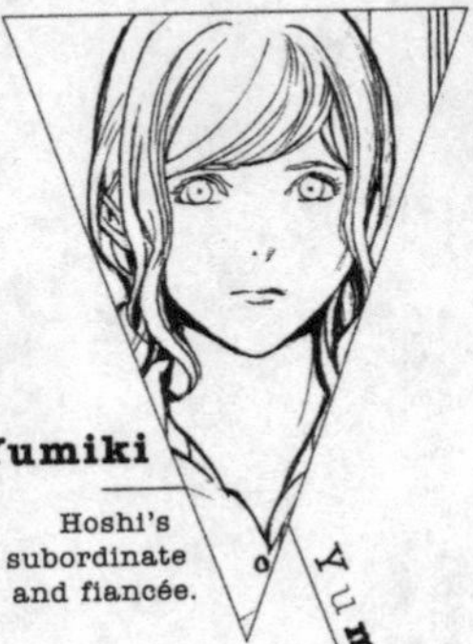

Yumiki

Yumiki

Hoshi's subordinate and fiancée.

Story

HUMANITY'S FUTURE

Yoneda predicts the end of humanity. Mirai says he'll be god. The two decide to have a dialogue.

THE BOY'S TRAP

The others leave to allow Mirai and Yoneda to be alone, but Shuji holds them hostage with white arrows.

WINGS OF SALVATION

With the women captured, Yoneda unleashes a white arrow on Mirai. But a moment later, Saki appears and rescues Mirai.

CONTENTS

14

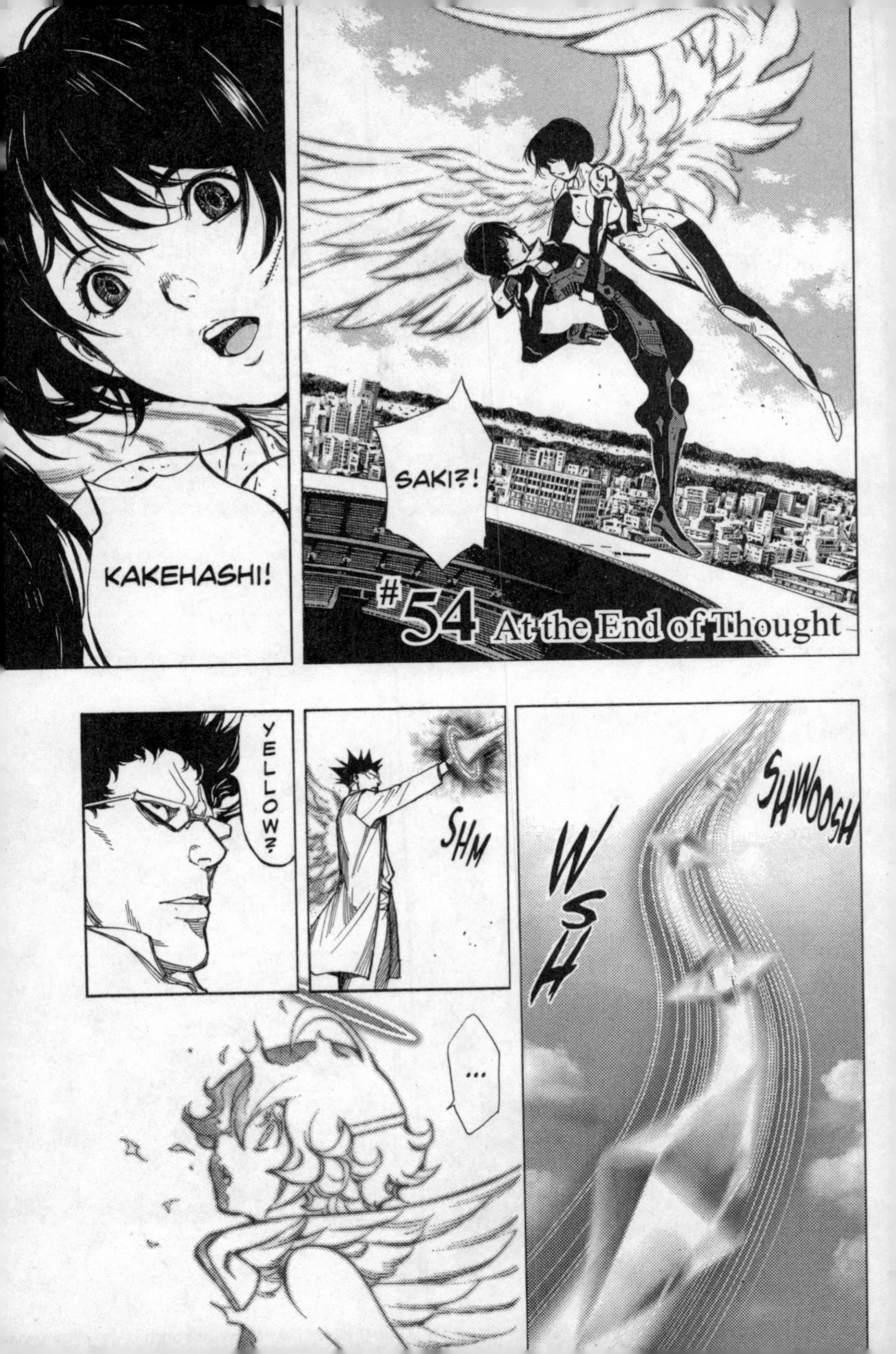
SAKI?!
#54 At the End of Thought
KAKEHASHI!
SHWOOSH
WSH
SHM
YELLOW?
...

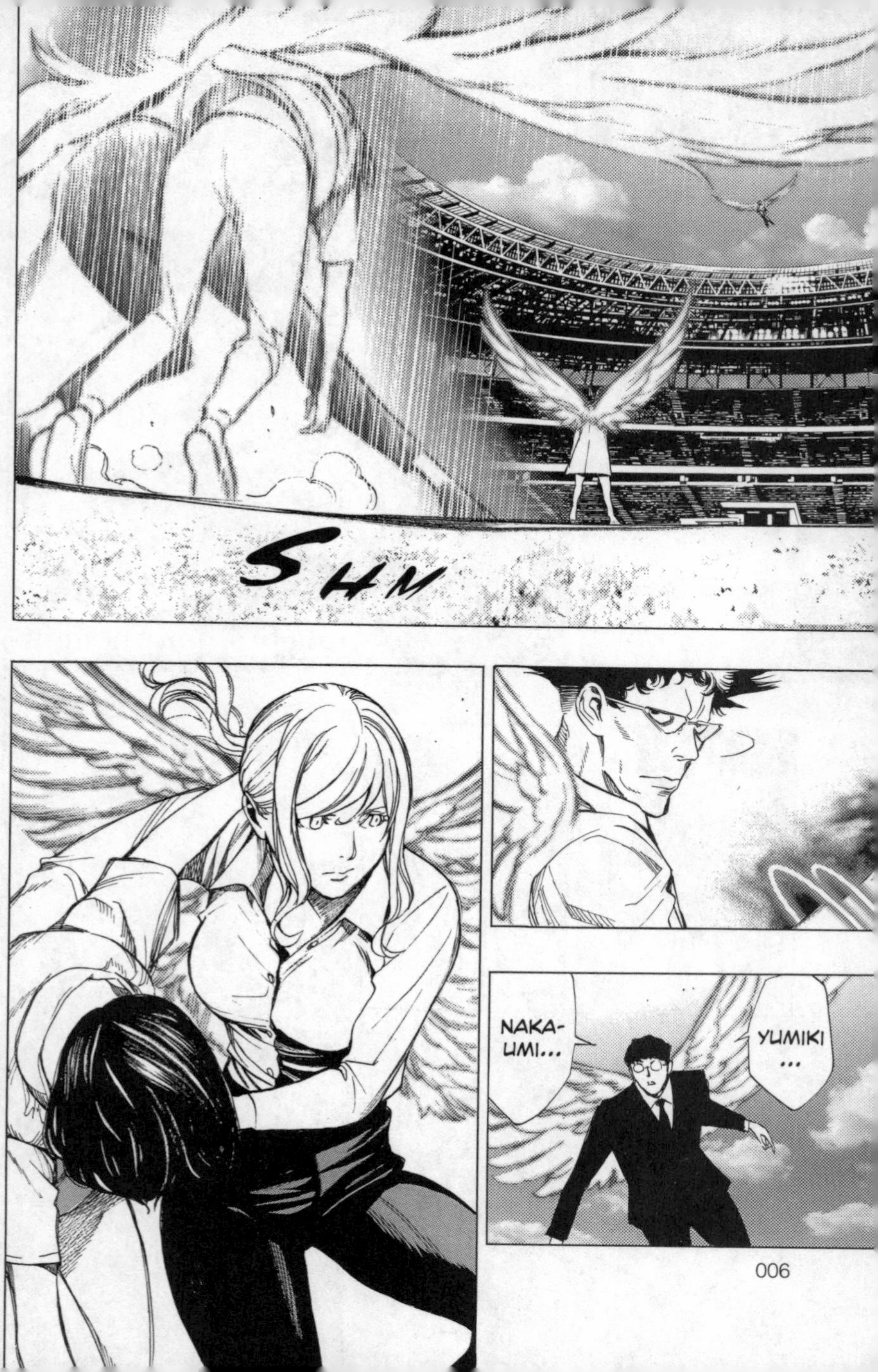
SHM
YUMIKI ...
NAKA-UMI...

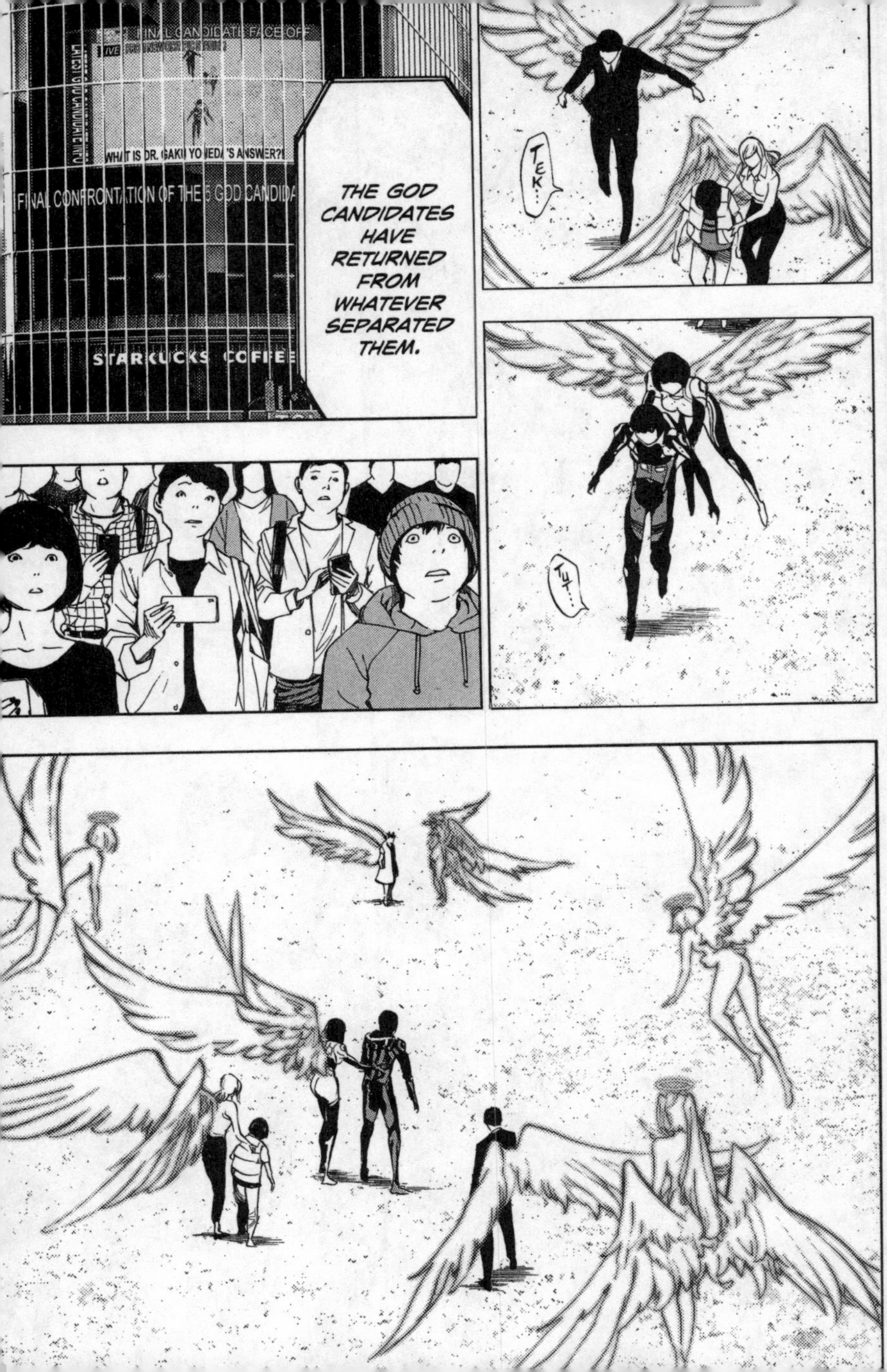
TEK...
FINAL CANDIDATE FACE-OFF
LIVE
LATEST GOD CANDIDATE INFO
WHAT IS DR. GAKU YONEDA'S ANSWER?!
FINAL CONFRONTATION OF THE 5 GOD CANDIDA
STARKUCKS COFFEE
THE GOD CANDIDATES HAVE RETURNED FROM WHATEVER SEPARATED THEM.
TUT...

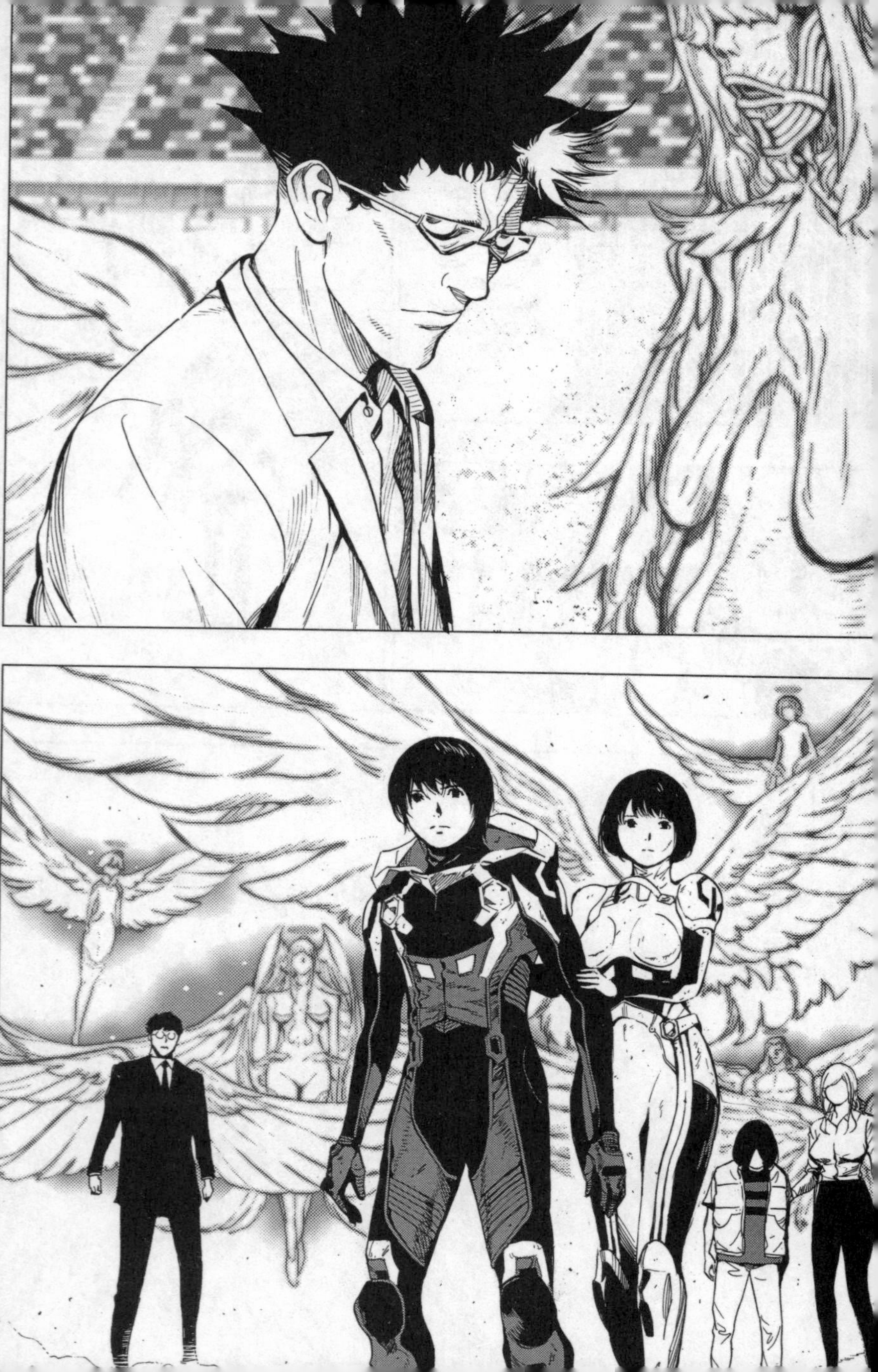

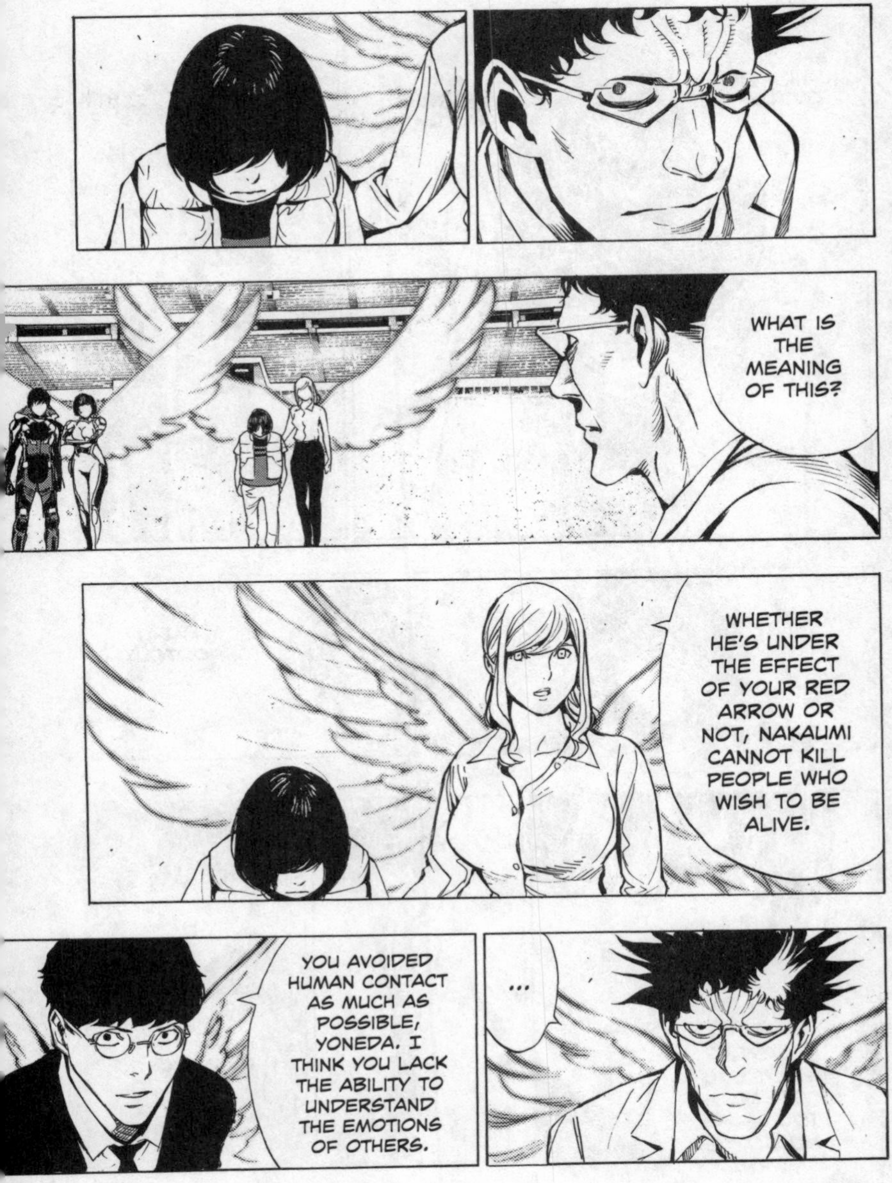
WHAT IS THE MEANING OF THIS?
WHETHER HE'S UNDER THE EFFECT OF YOUR RED ARROW OR NOT, NAKAUMI CANNOT KILL PEOPLE WHO WISH TO BE ALIVE.
...
YOU AVOIDED HUMAN CONTACT AS MUCH AS POSSIBLE, YONEDA. I THINK YOU LACK THE ABILITY TO UNDERSTAND THE EMOTIONS OF OTHERS.

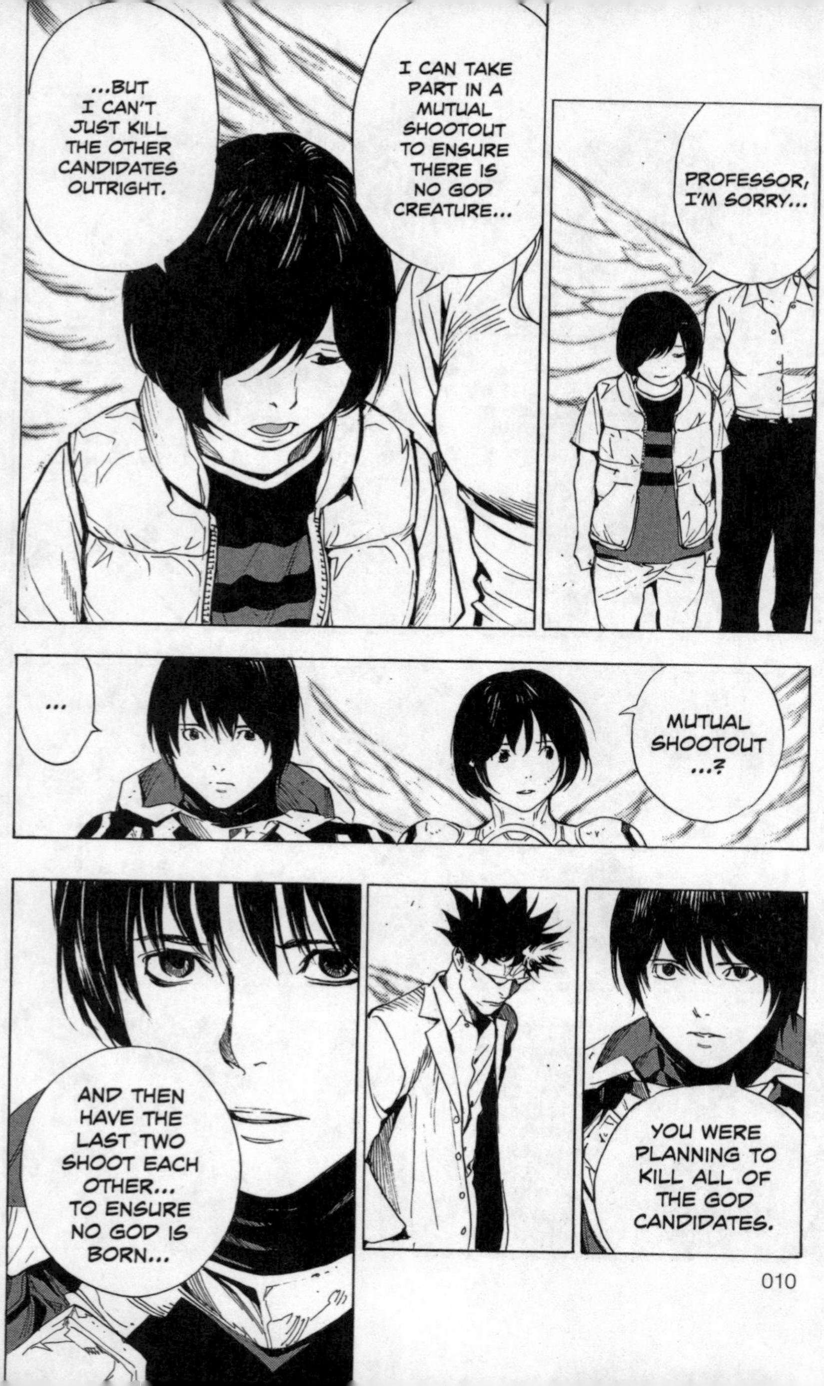
PROFESSOR, I'M SORRY...
I CAN TAKE PART IN A MUTUAL SHOOTOUT TO ENSURE THERE IS NO GOD CREATURE...
...BUT I CAN'T JUST KILL THE OTHER CANDIDATES OUTRIGHT.
MUTUAL SHOOTOUT ...?
...
YOU WERE PLANNING TO KILL ALL OF THE GOD CANDIDATES.
AND THEN HAVE THE LAST TWO SHOOT EACH OTHER... TO ENSURE NO GOD IS BORN...

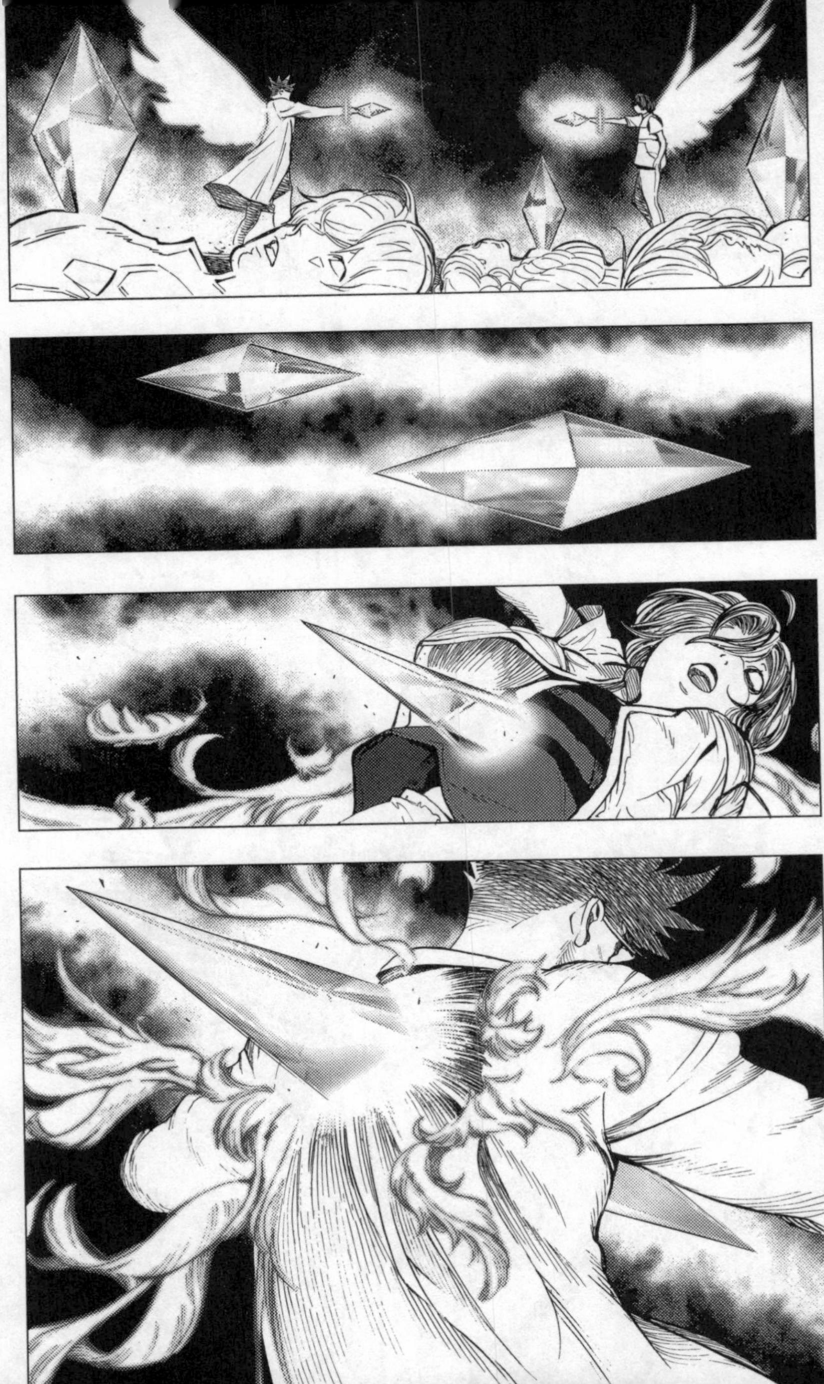

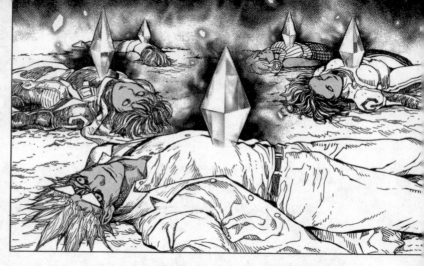

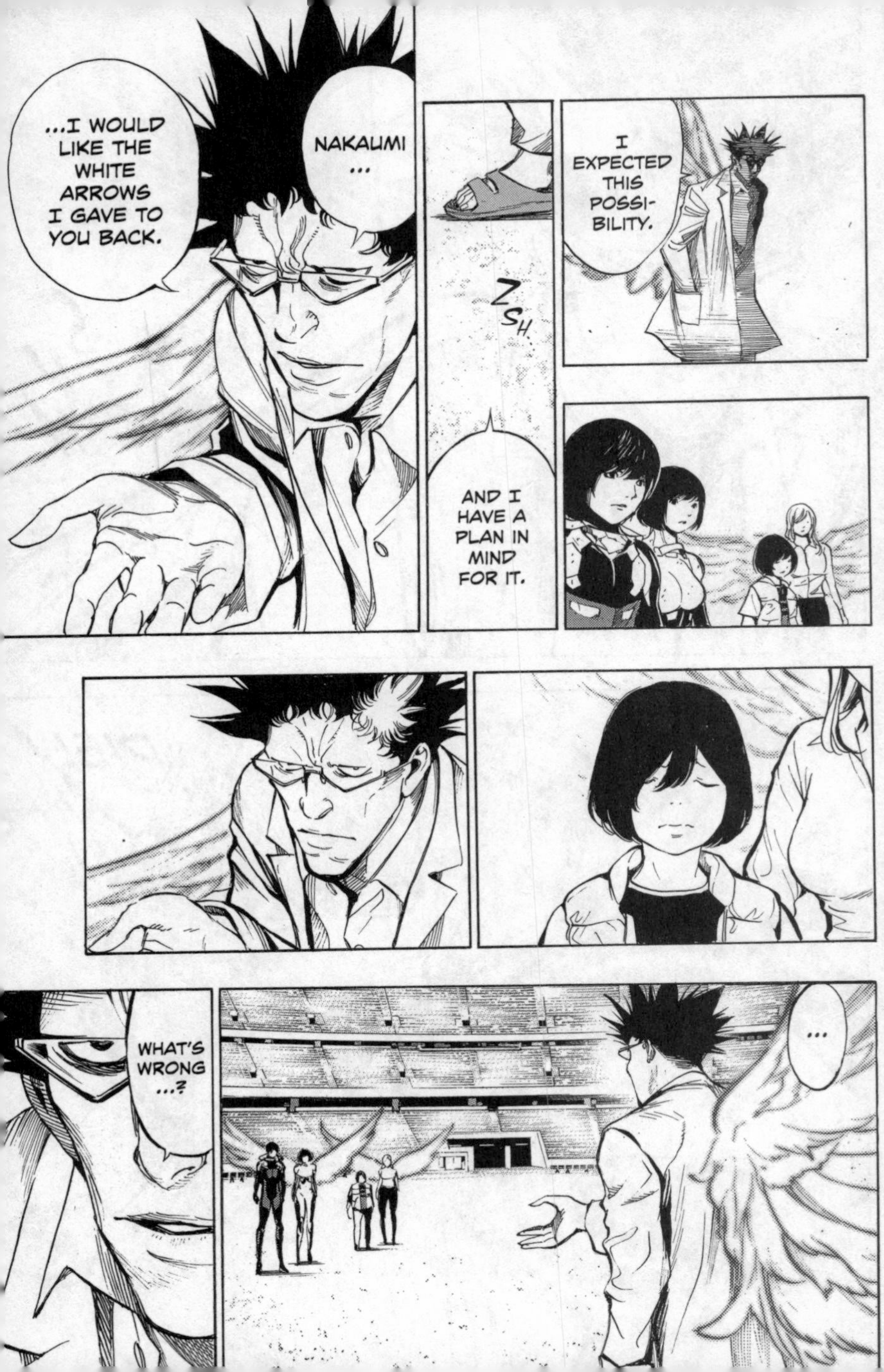
I EXPECTED THIS POSSIBILITY.
ZSH
AND I HAVE A PLAN IN MIND FOR IT.
NAKAUMI ...
...I WOULD LIKE THE WHITE ARROWS I GAVE TO YOU BACK.
...
WHAT'S WRONG ...?

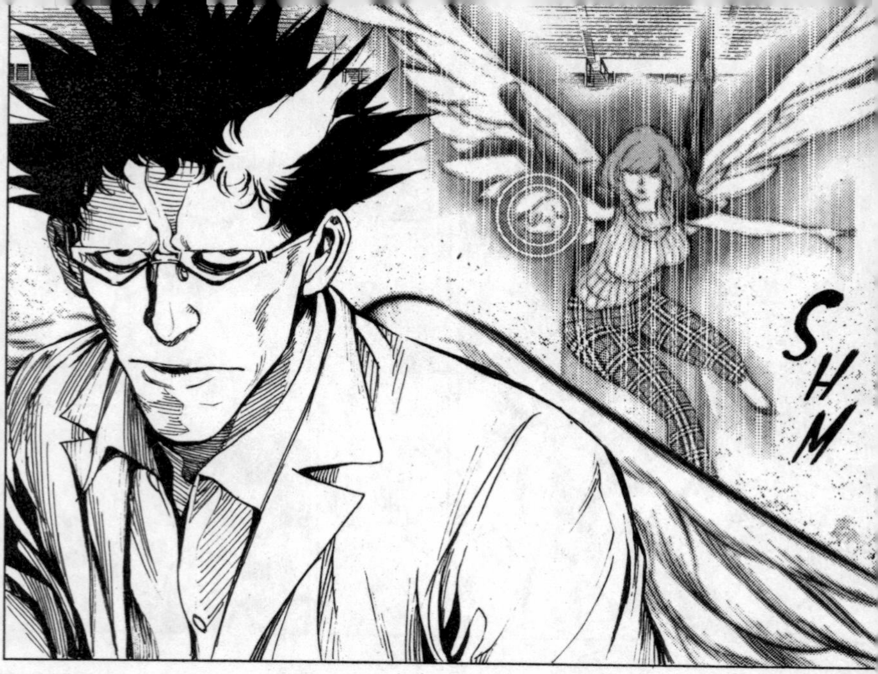
SHM
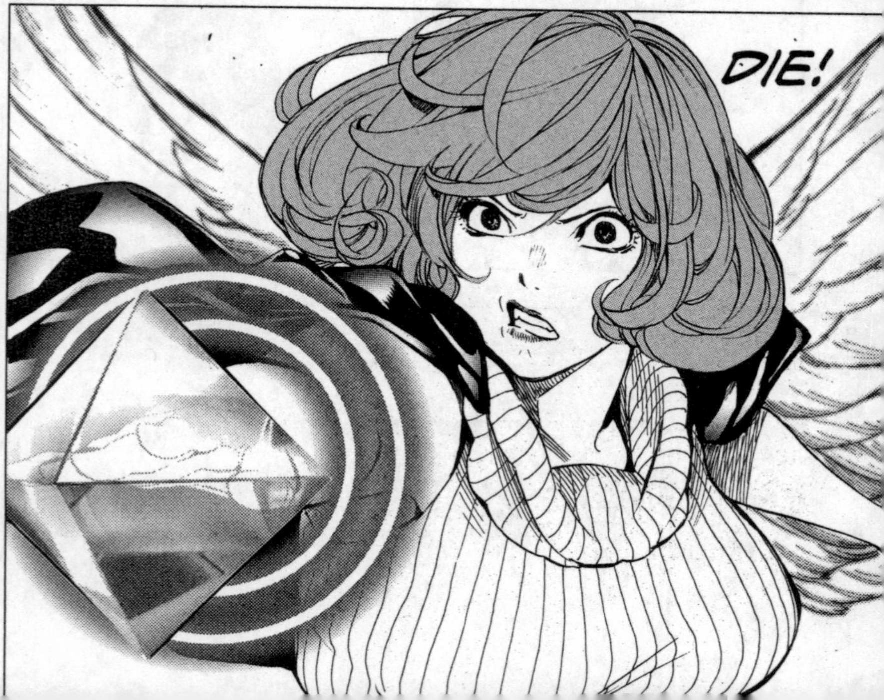
DIE!

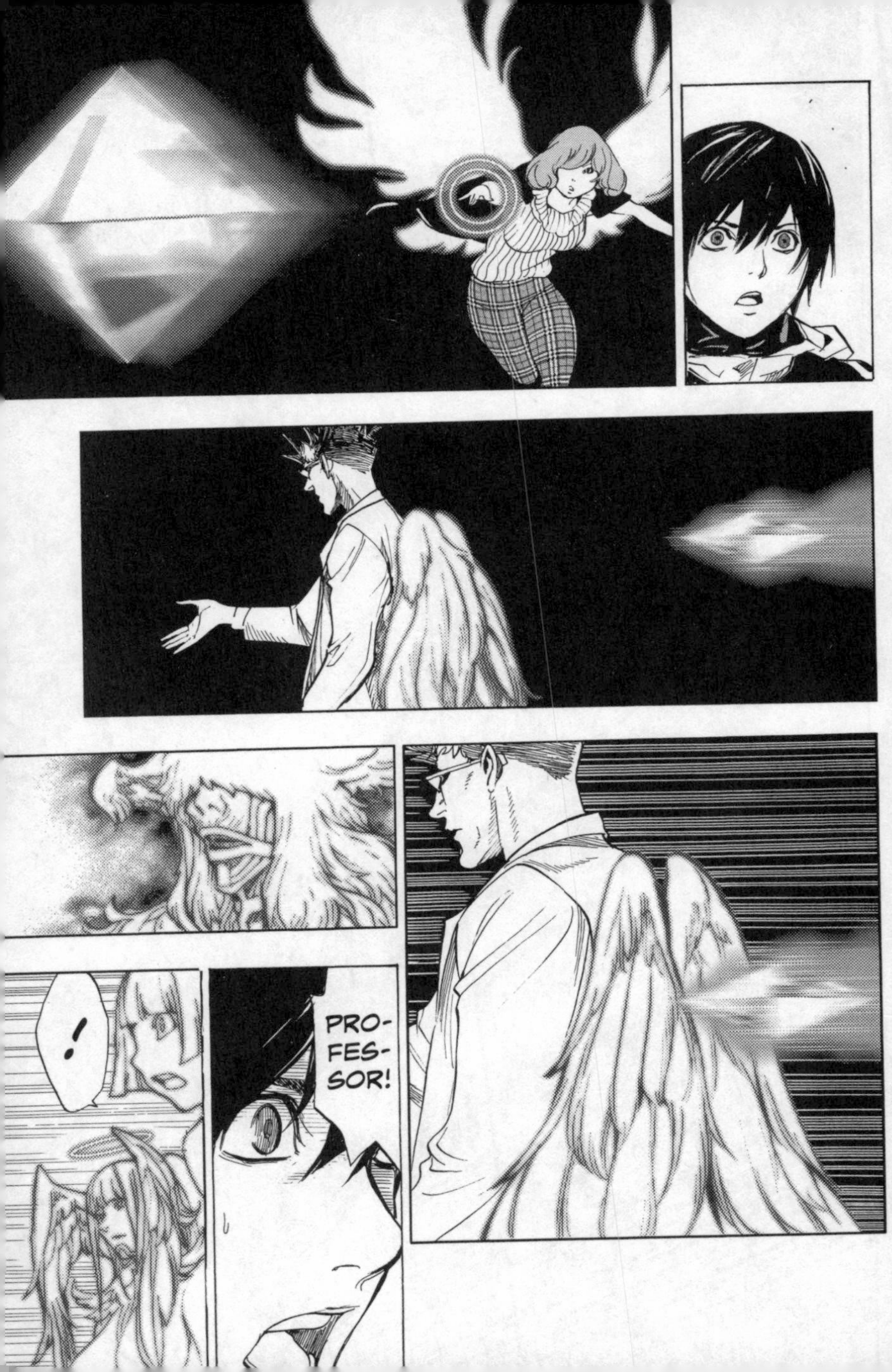
PRO-
FES-
SOR!
!

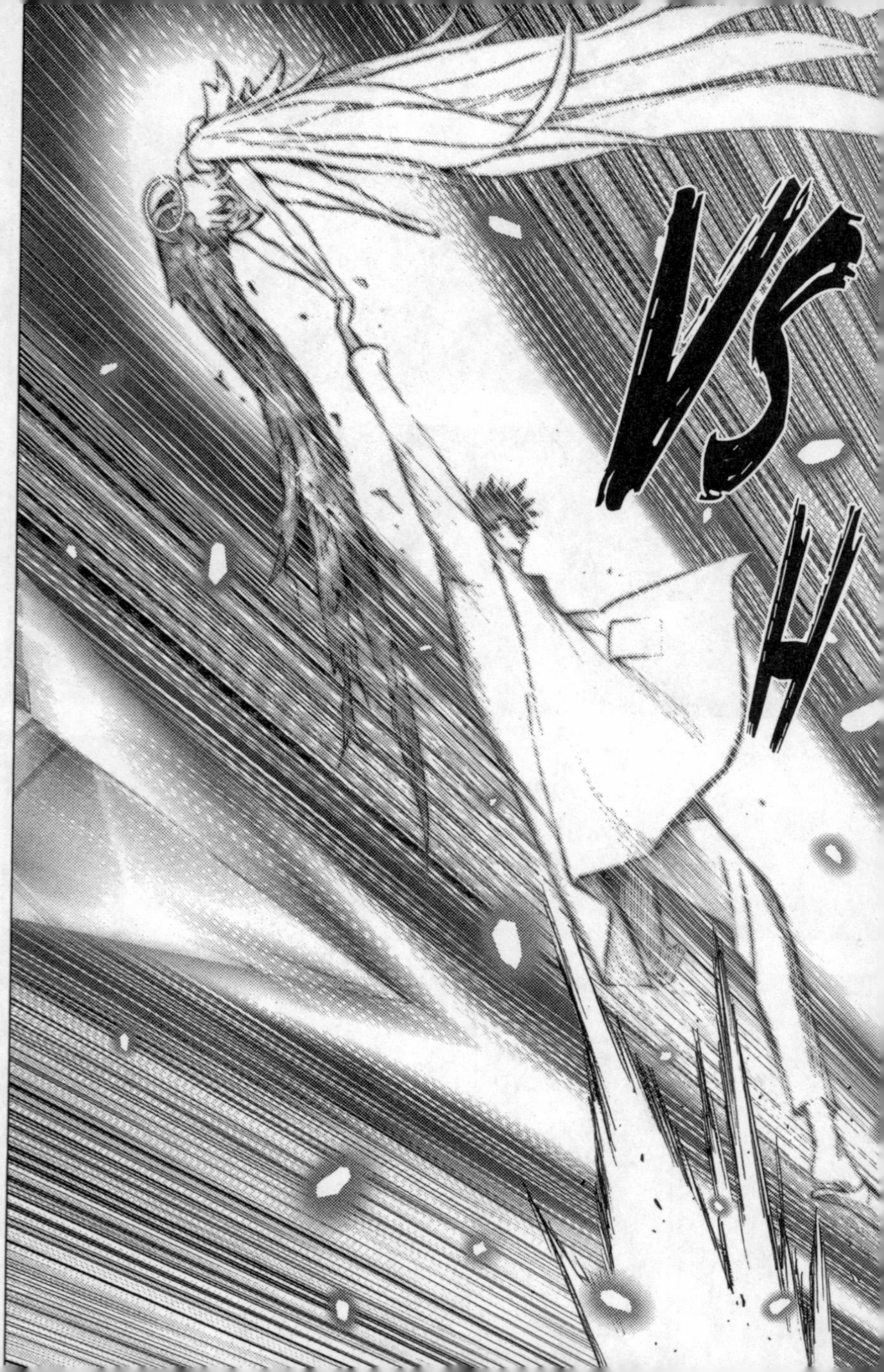
VSHH

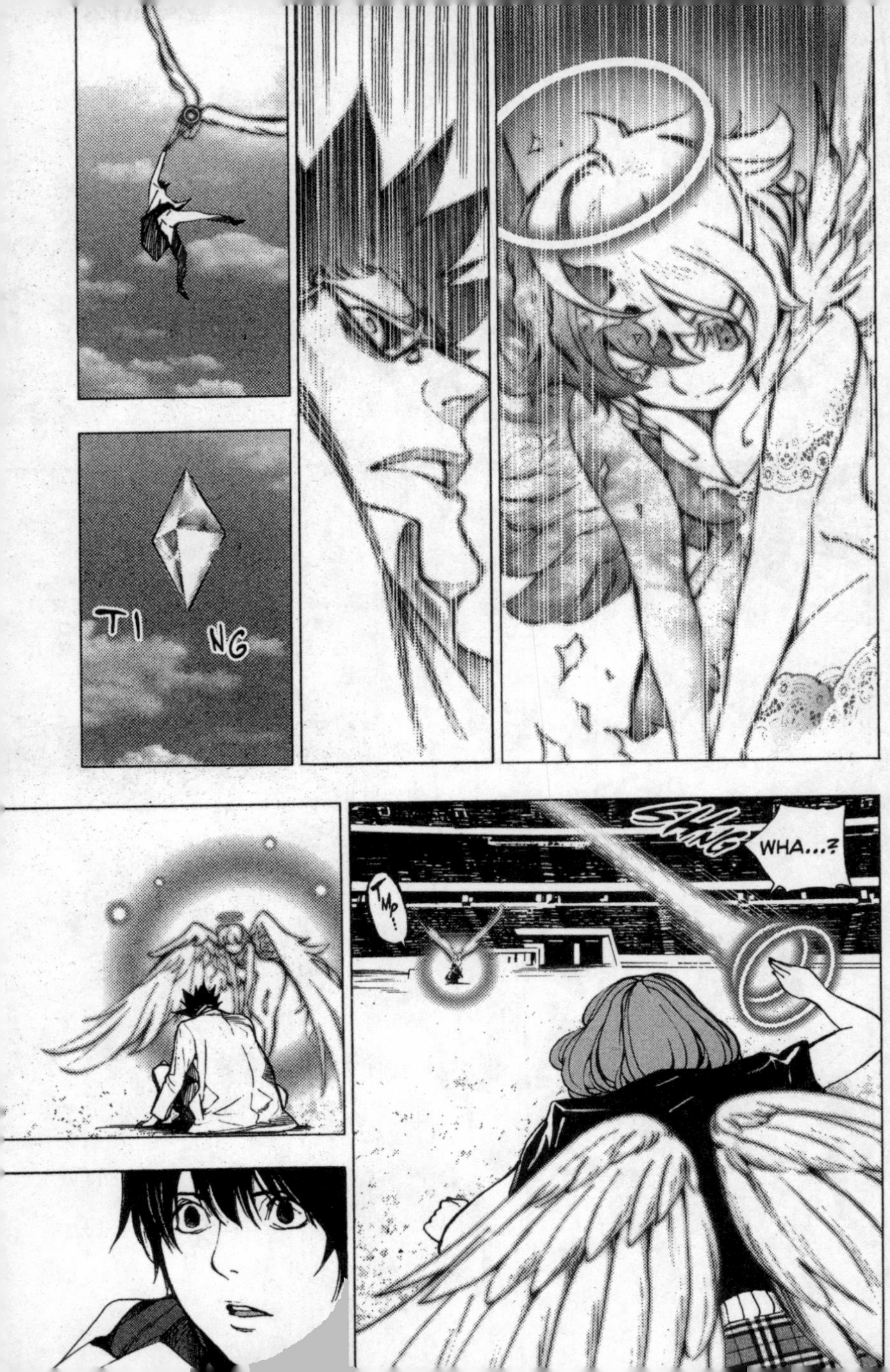
TI NG
WHA...?
TMP...

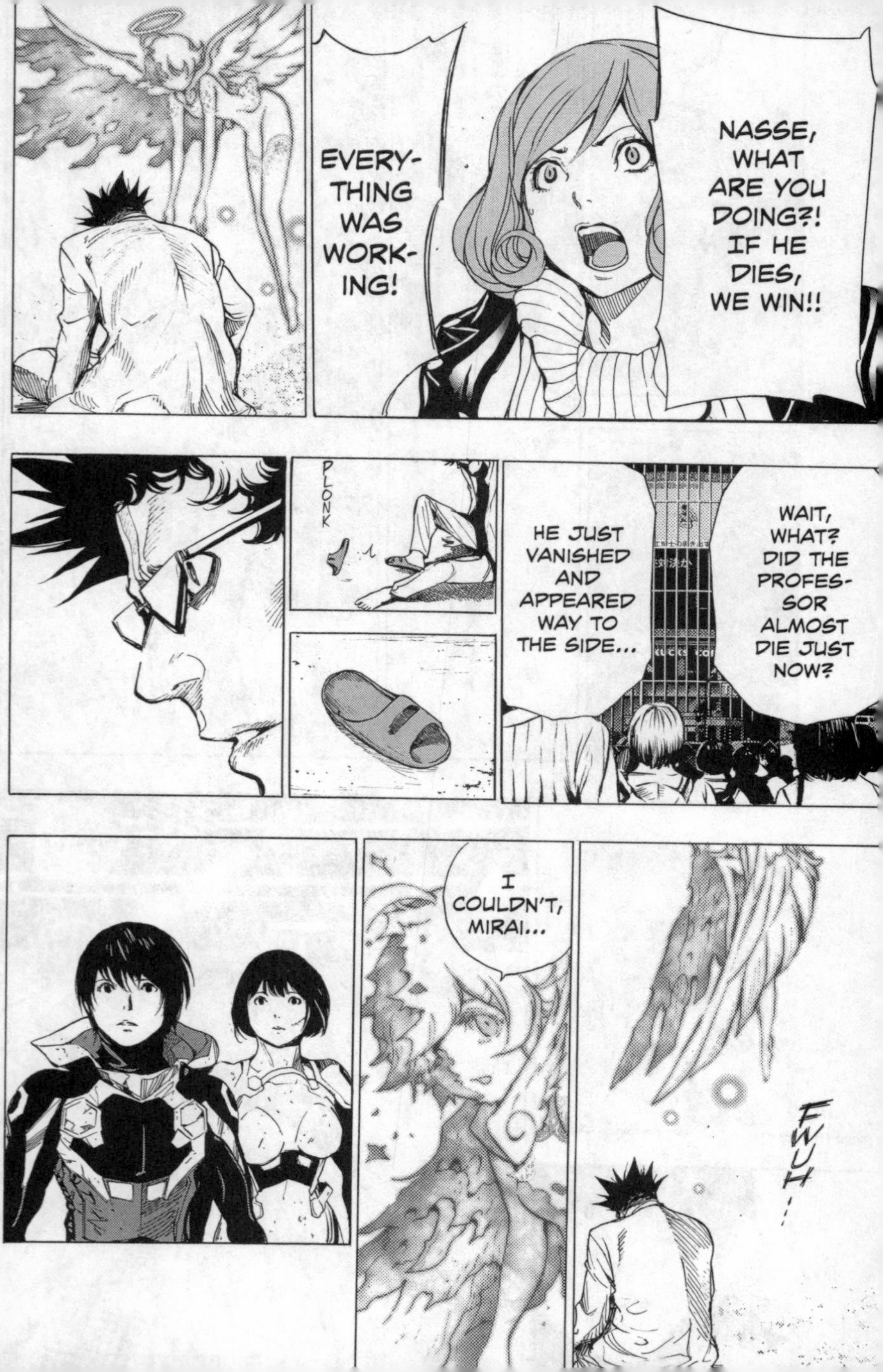
NASSE, WHAT ARE YOU DOING?! IF HE DIES, WE WIN!!
EVERY-THING WAS WORK-ING!
WAIT, WHAT? DID THE PROFES-SOR ALMOST DIE JUST NOW?
HE JUST VANISHED AND APPEARED WAY TO THE SIDE...
PLONK
FWUH!
I COULDN'T, MIRAI...

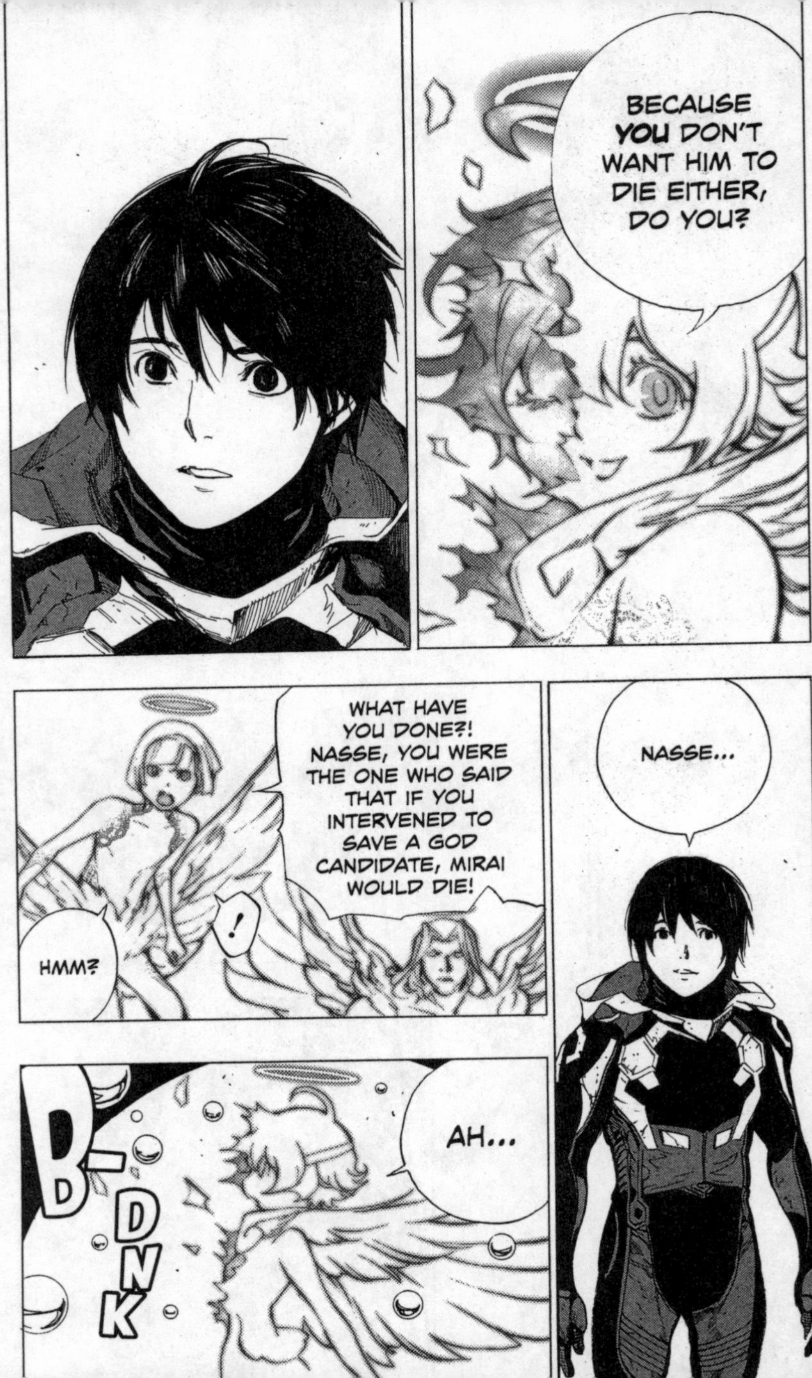
BECAUSE YOU DON'T WANT HIM TO DIE EITHER, DO YOU?
NASSE...
WHAT HAVE YOU DONE?! NASSE, YOU WERE THE ONE WHO SAID THAT IF YOU INTERVENED TO SAVE A GOD CANDIDATE, MIRAI WOULD DIE!
!
HMM?
AH...
B-DNK

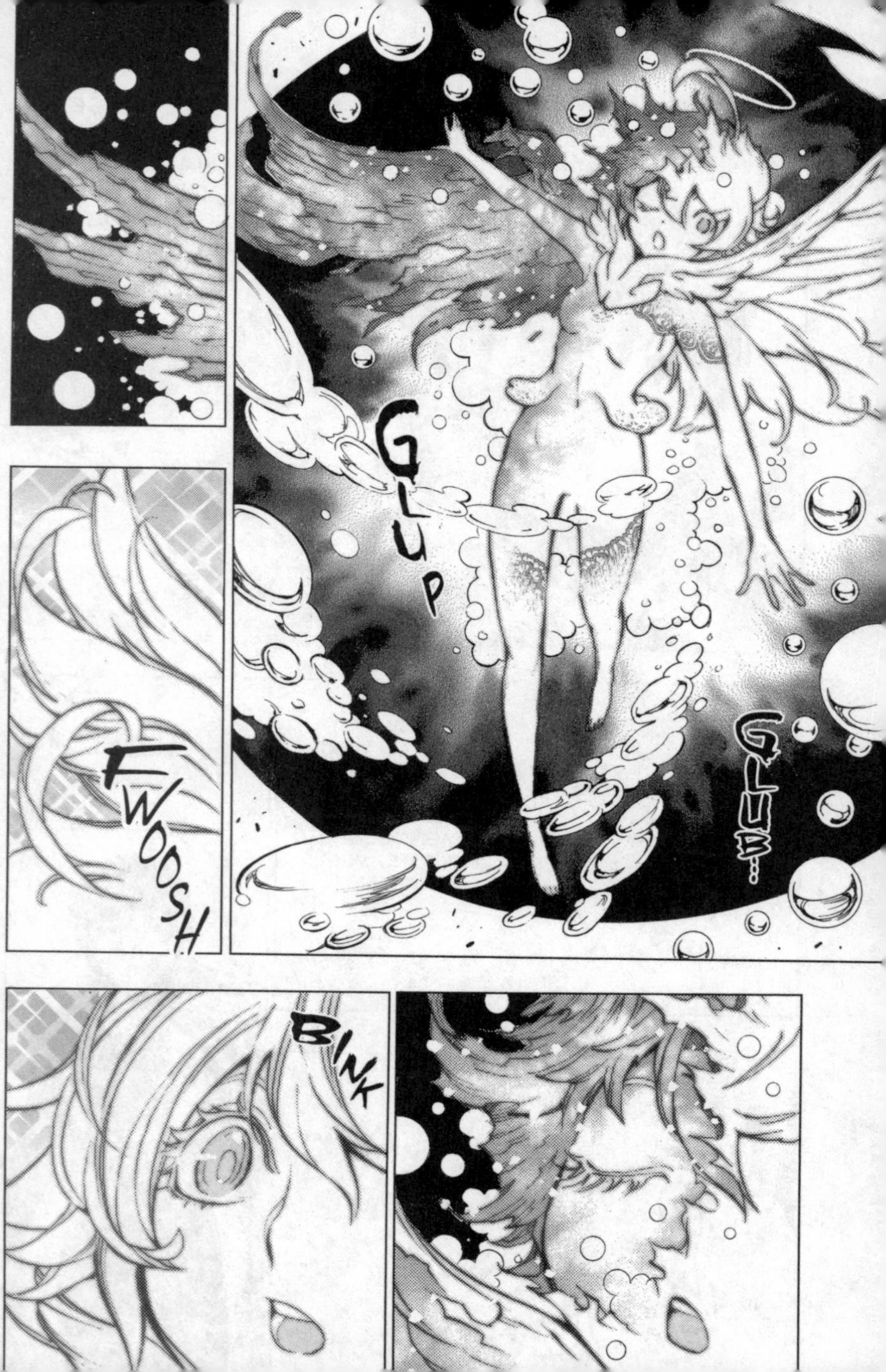
GLUB...
GLUP
FWOOSH
BINK

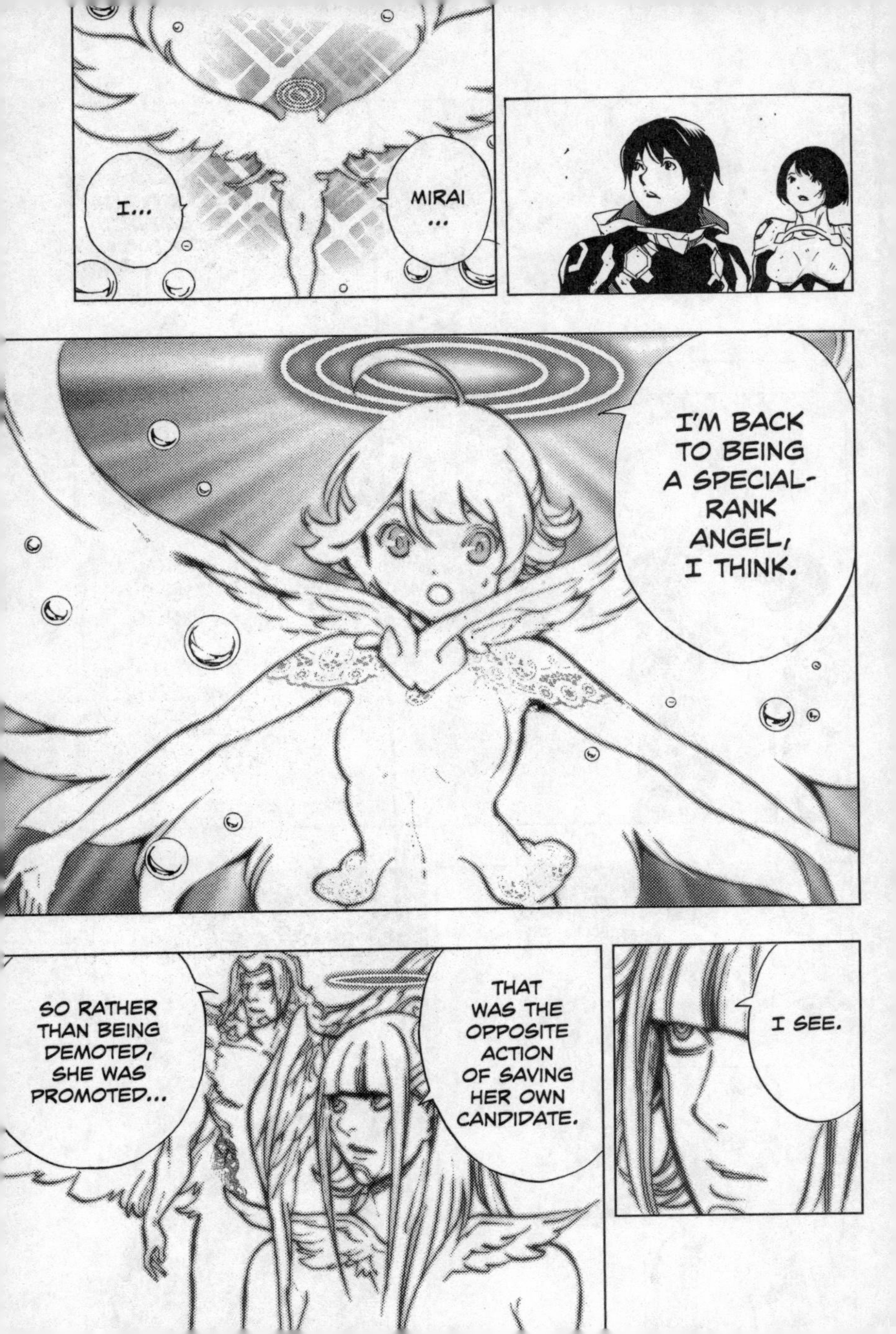
MIRAI ...
I...
I'M BACK TO BEING A SPECIAL-RANK ANGEL, I THINK.
I SEE.
THAT WAS THE OPPOSITE ACTION OF SAVING HER OWN CANDIDATE.
SO RATHER THAN BEING DEMOTED, SHE WAS PROMOTED...

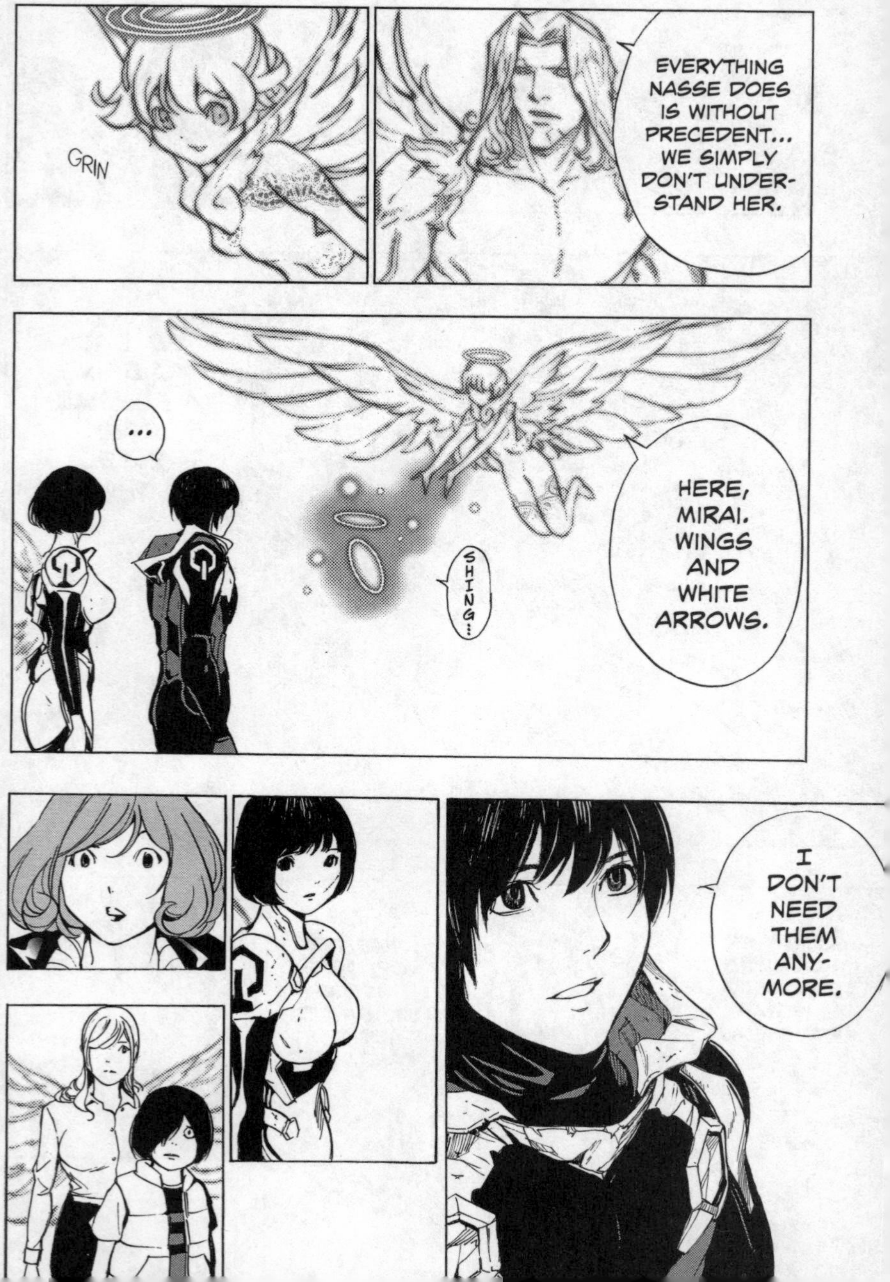
EVERYTHING NASSE DOES IS WITHOUT PRECEDENT... WE SIMPLY DON'T UNDER-STAND HER.
GRIN
HERE, MIRAI. WINGS AND WHITE ARROWS.
SHING...
...
I DON'T NEED THEM ANY-MORE.

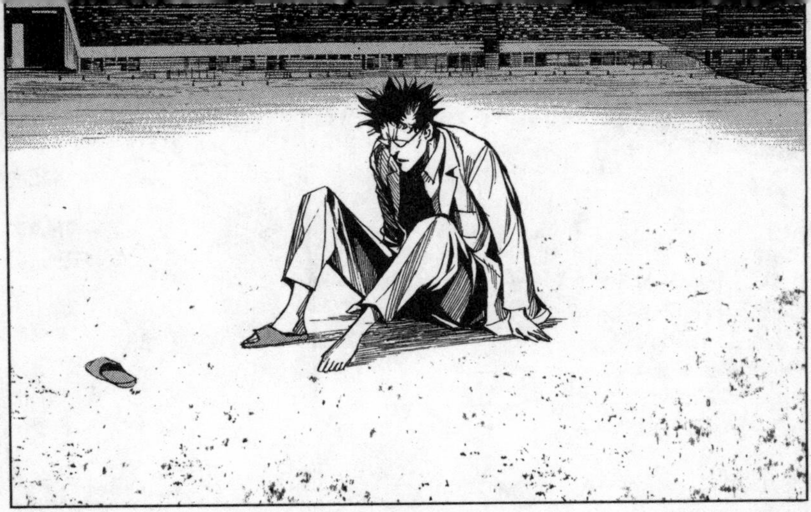
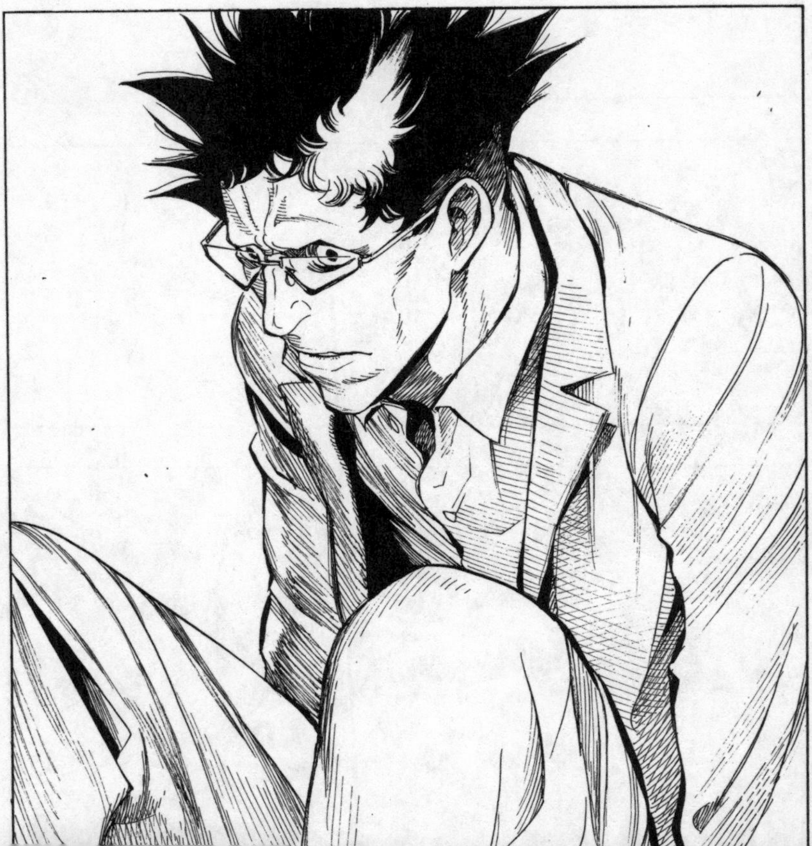

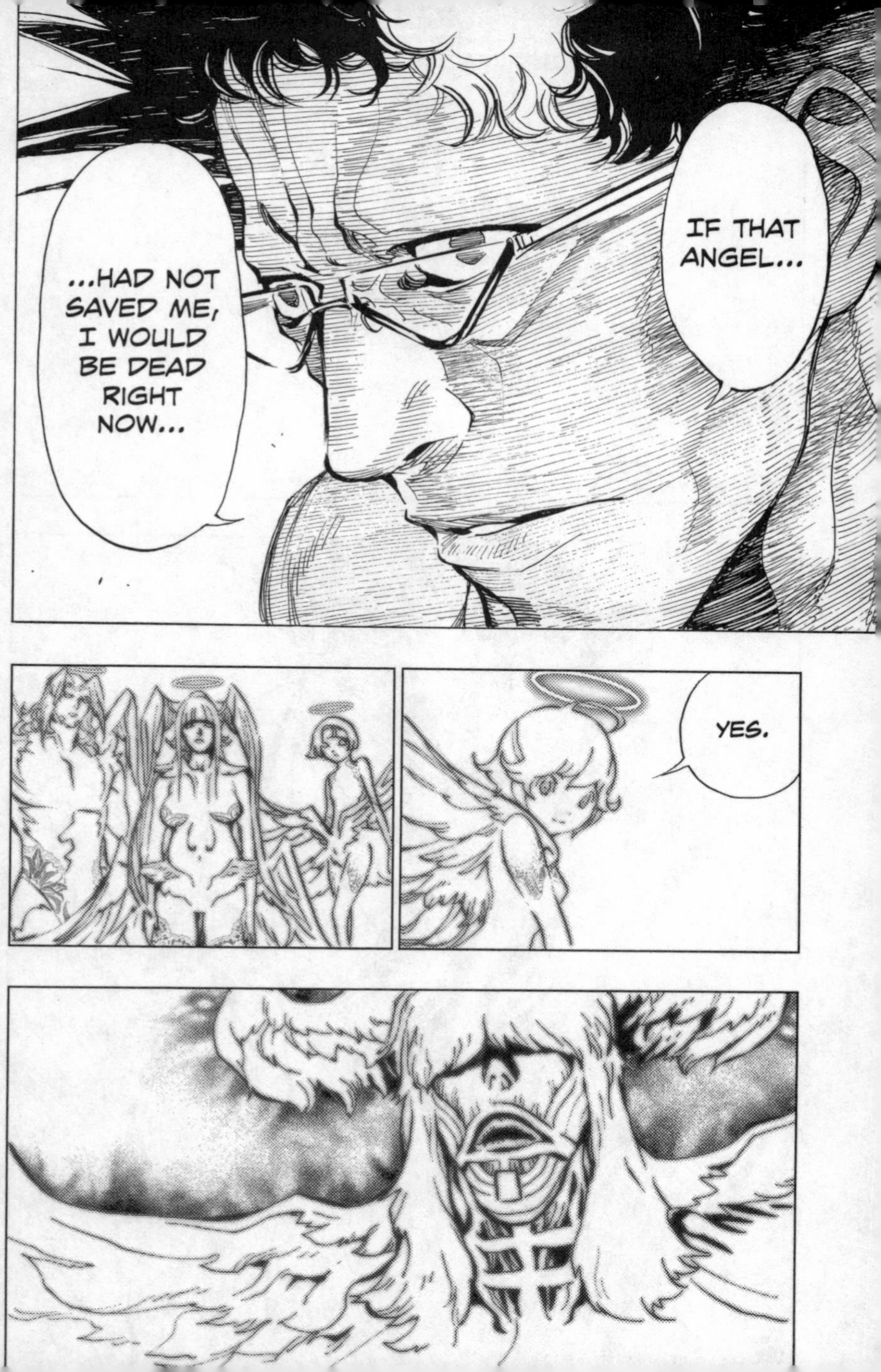
IF THAT ANGEL...
...HAD NOT SAVED ME, I WOULD BE DEAD RIGHT NOW...
YES.

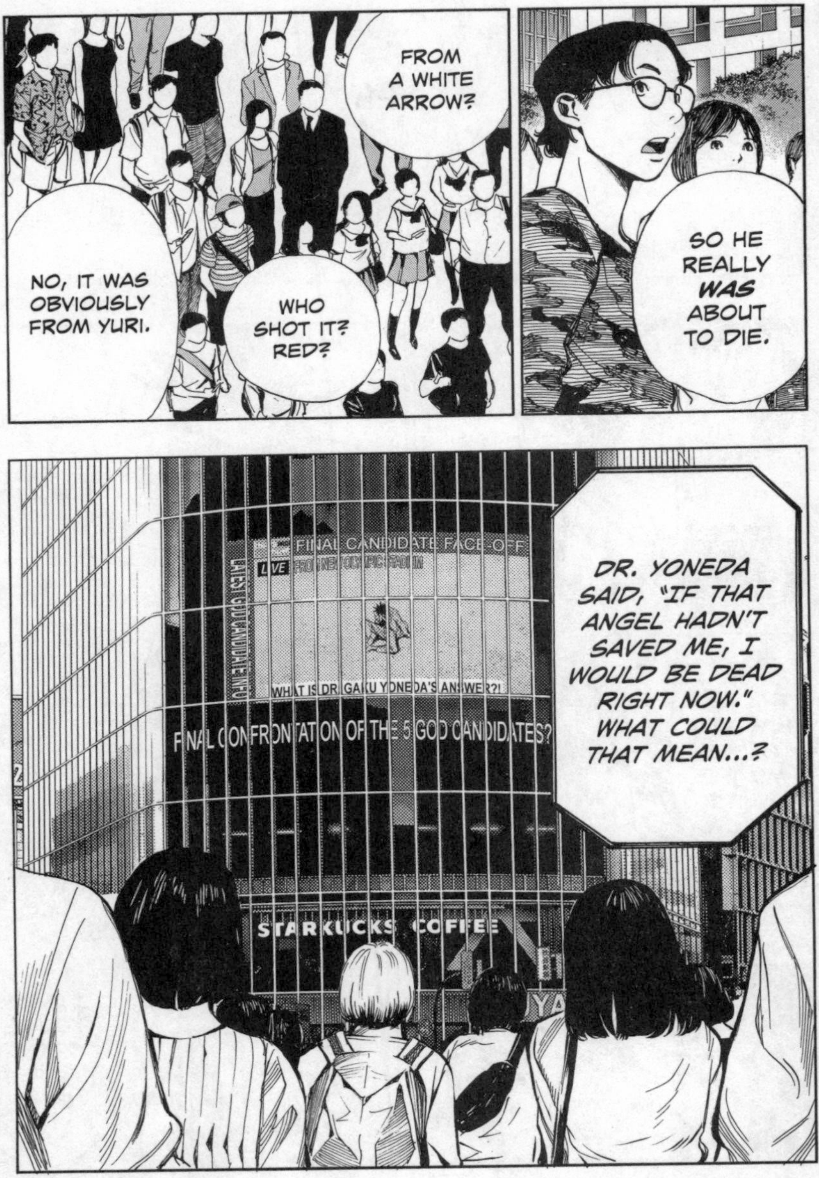
SO HE REALLY *WAS* ABOUT TO DIE.
FROM A WHITE ARROW?
WHO SHOT IT? RED?
NO, IT WAS OBVIOUSLY FROM YURI.
DR. YONEDA SAID, "IF THAT ANGEL HADN'T SAVED ME, I WOULD BE DEAD RIGHT NOW." WHAT COULD THAT MEAN...?
FINAL CANDIDATE FACE-OFF
LIVE
WHAT IS DR. GAKU YONEDA'S ANSWER?!
FINAL CONFRONTATION OF THE 5 GOD CANDIDATES?
STARKUCKS COFFEE

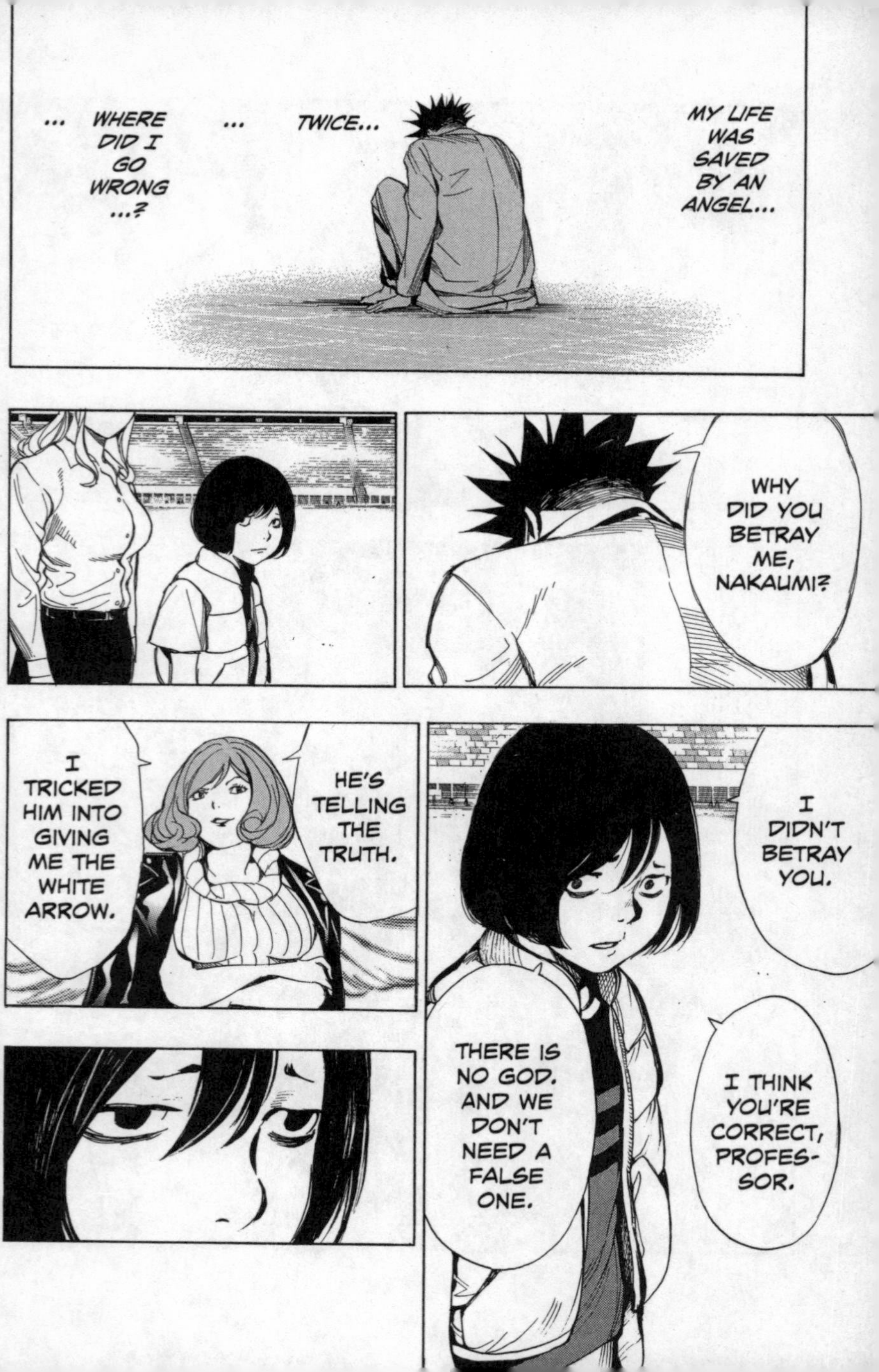
MY LIFE WAS SAVED BY AN ANGEL...
TWICE...
...
... WHERE DID I GO WRONG ...?
WHY DID YOU BETRAY ME, NAKAUMI?
I DIDN'T BETRAY YOU.
I THINK YOU'RE CORRECT, PROFES-SOR.
THERE IS NO GOD. AND WE DON'T NEED A FALSE ONE.
HE'S TELLING THE TRUTH.
I TRICKED HIM INTO GIVING ME THE WHITE ARROW.

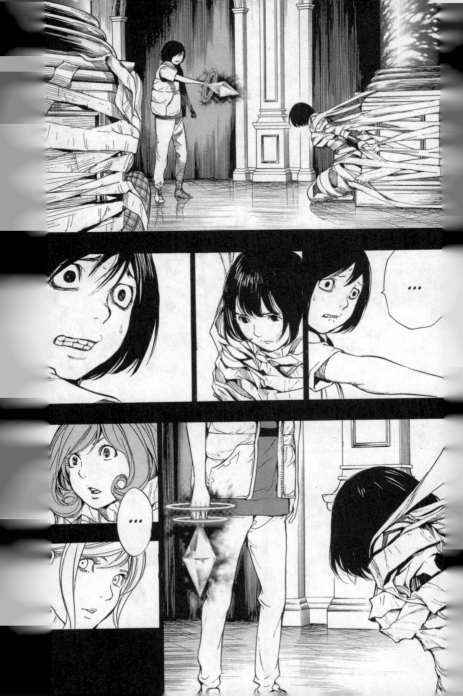

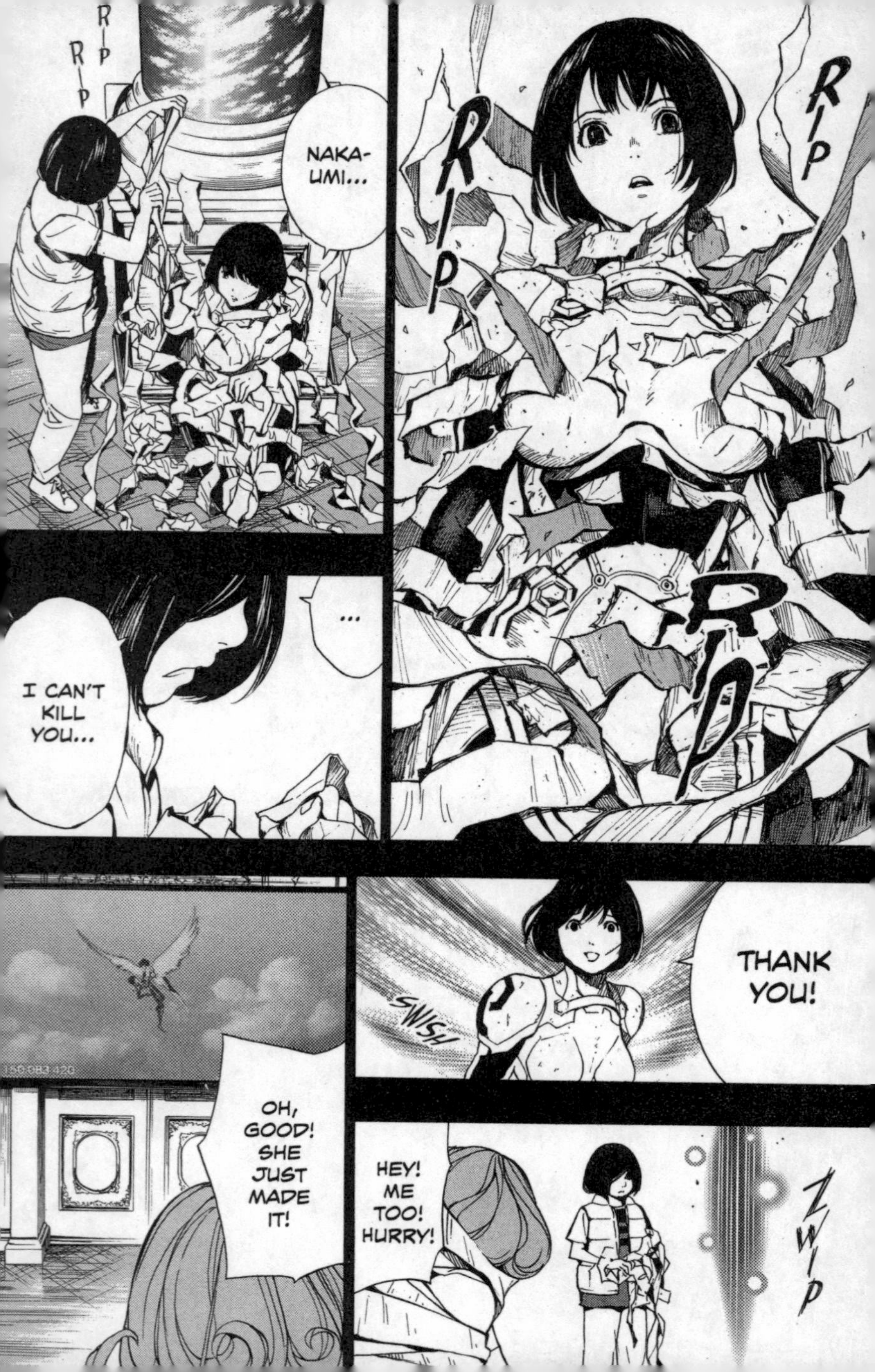
RIP
RIP
RIP
RIP
RIP
NAKA-UMI...
...
I CAN'T KILL YOU...
THANK YOU!
SWISH
ZWIP
HEY! ME TOO! HURRY!
150,083,420
OH, GOOD! SHE JUST MADE IT!

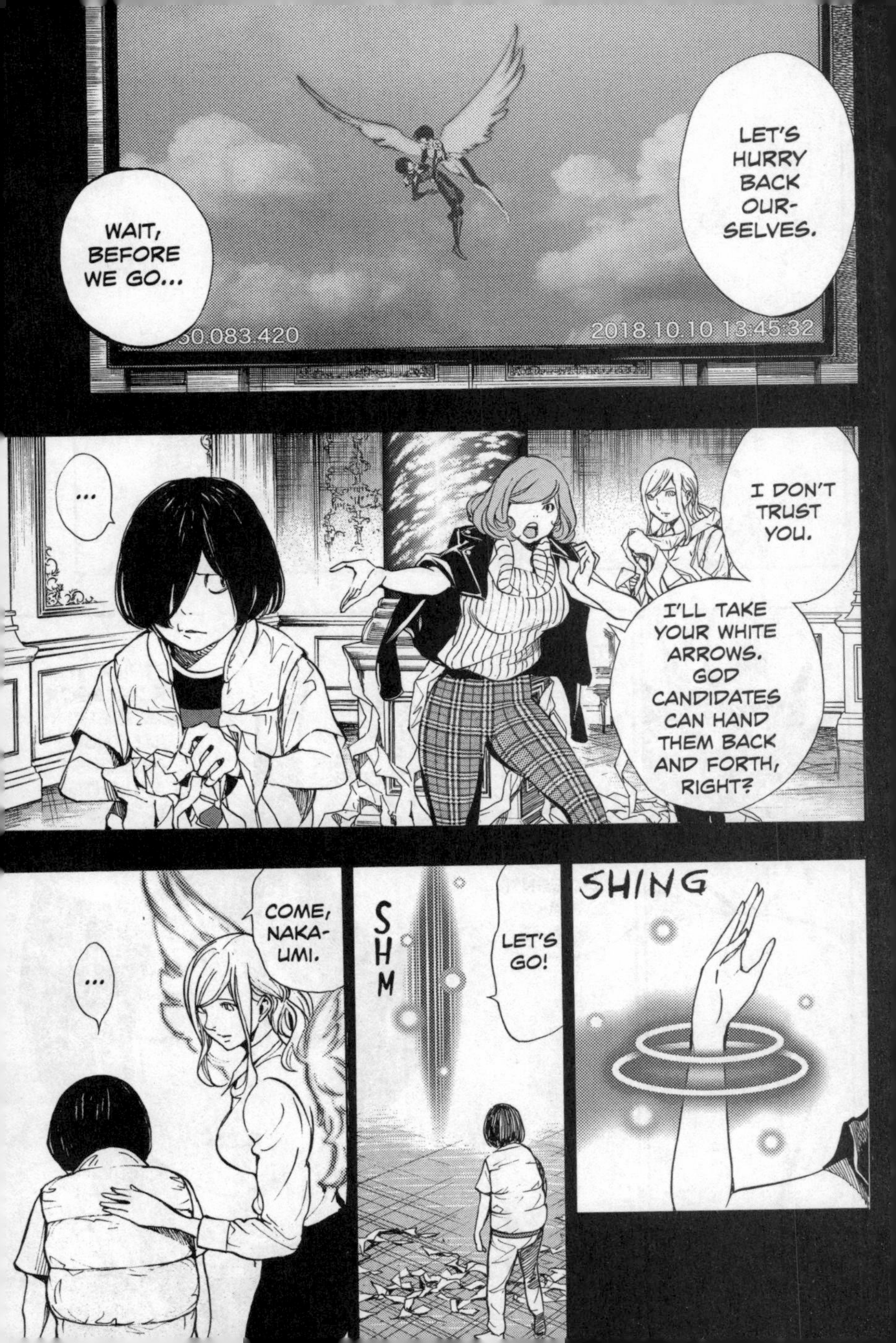
LET'S HURRY BACK OUR-SELVES.
WAIT, BEFORE WE GO...
2018.10.10 13:45:32
I DON'T TRUST YOU.
I'LL TAKE YOUR WHITE ARROWS. GOD CANDIDATES CAN HAND THEM BACK AND FORTH, RIGHT?
...
SHING
LET'S GO!
SHM
COME, NAKA-UMI.
...

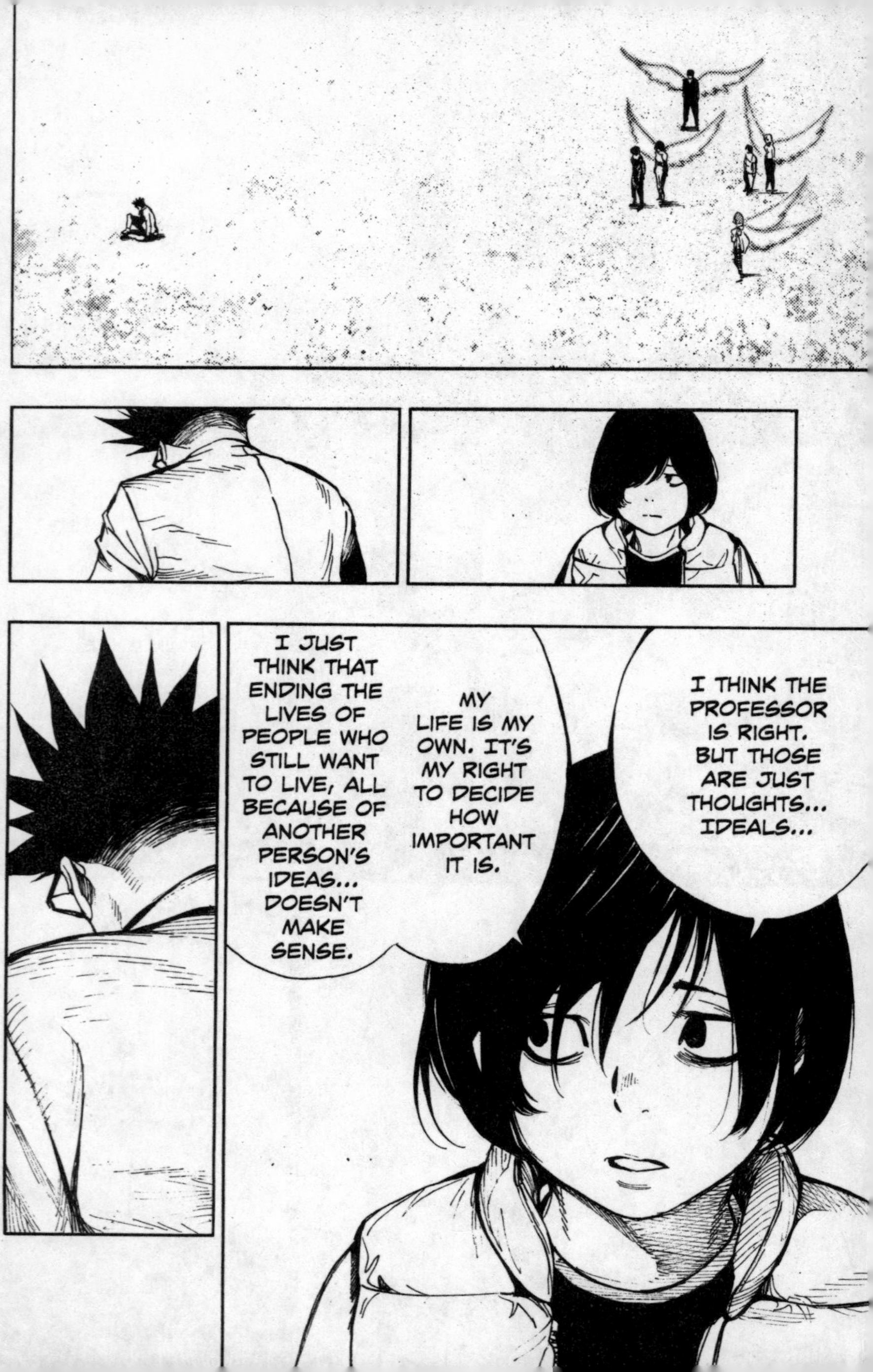
I THINK THE PROFESSOR IS RIGHT. BUT THOSE ARE JUST THOUGHTS... IDEALS...
MY LIFE IS MY OWN. IT'S MY RIGHT TO DECIDE HOW IMPORTANT IT IS.
I JUST THINK THAT ENDING THE LIVES OF PEOPLE WHO STILL WANT TO LIVE, ALL BECAUSE OF ANOTHER PERSON'S IDEAS... DOESN'T MAKE SENSE.

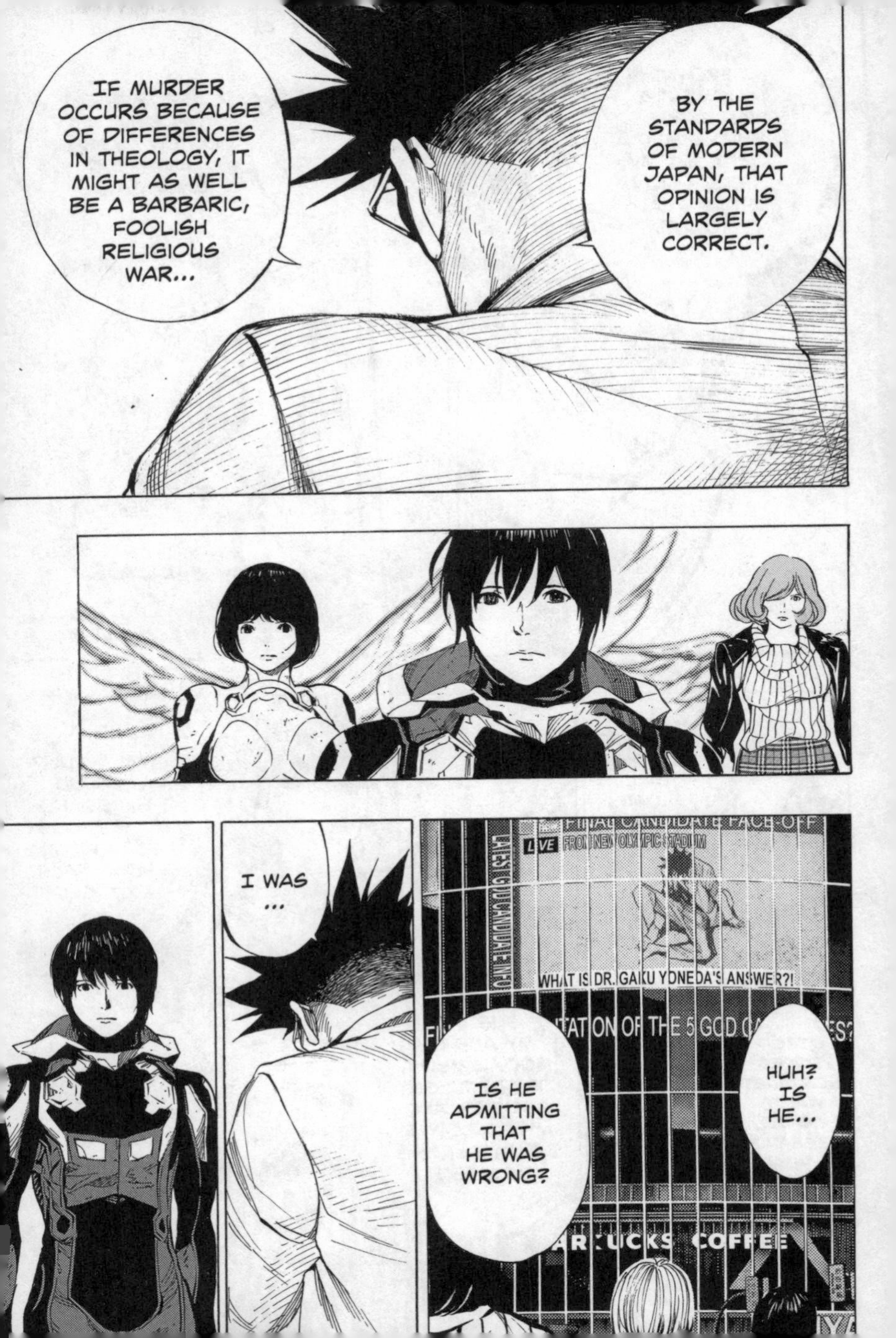
BY THE STANDARDS OF MODERN JAPAN, THAT OPINION IS LARGELY CORRECT.
IF MURDER OCCURS BECAUSE OF DIFFERENCES IN THEOLOGY, IT MIGHT AS WELL BE A BARBARIC, FOOLISH RELIGIOUS WAR...
FINAL CANDIDATE FACE-OFF
LIVE FROM NEW OLYMPIC STADIUM
WHAT IS DR. GAKU YONEDA'S ANSWER?!
HUH? IS HE...
IS HE ADMITTING THAT HE WAS WRONG?
I WAS ...

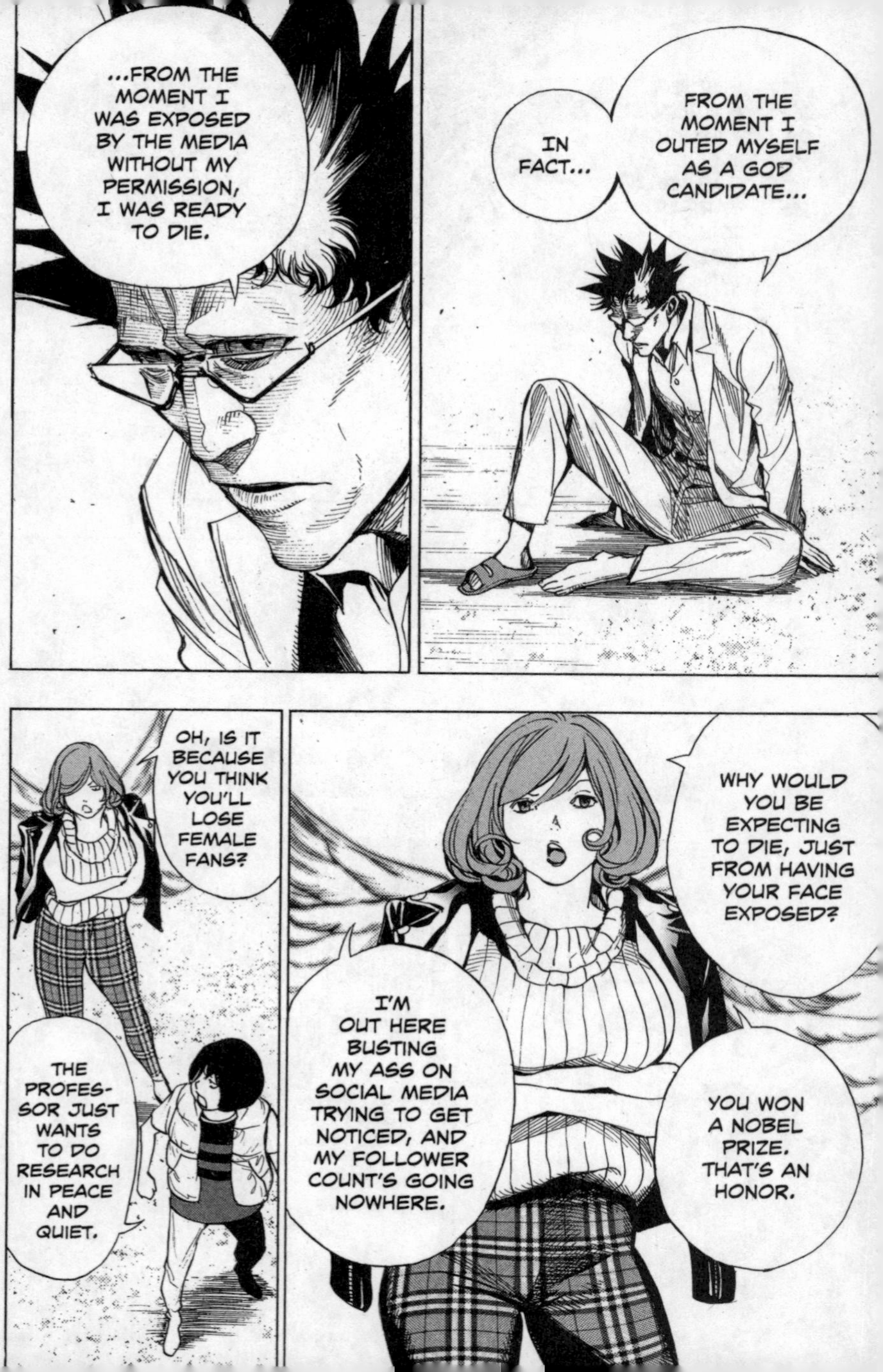
FROM THE MOMENT I OUTED MYSELF AS A GOD CANDIDATE...
IN FACT...
...FROM THE MOMENT I WAS EXPOSED BY THE MEDIA WITHOUT MY PERMISSION, I WAS READY TO DIE.
WHY WOULD YOU BE EXPECTING TO DIE, JUST FROM HAVING YOUR FACE EXPOSED?
YOU WON A NOBEL PRIZE. THAT'S AN HONOR.
I'M OUT HERE BUSTING MY ASS ON SOCIAL MEDIA TRYING TO GET NOTICED, AND MY FOLLOWER COUNT'S GOING NOWHERE.
OH, IS IT BECAUSE YOU THINK YOU'LL LOSE FEMALE FANS?
THE PROFES-SOR JUST WANTS TO DO RESEARCH IN PEACE AND QUIET.

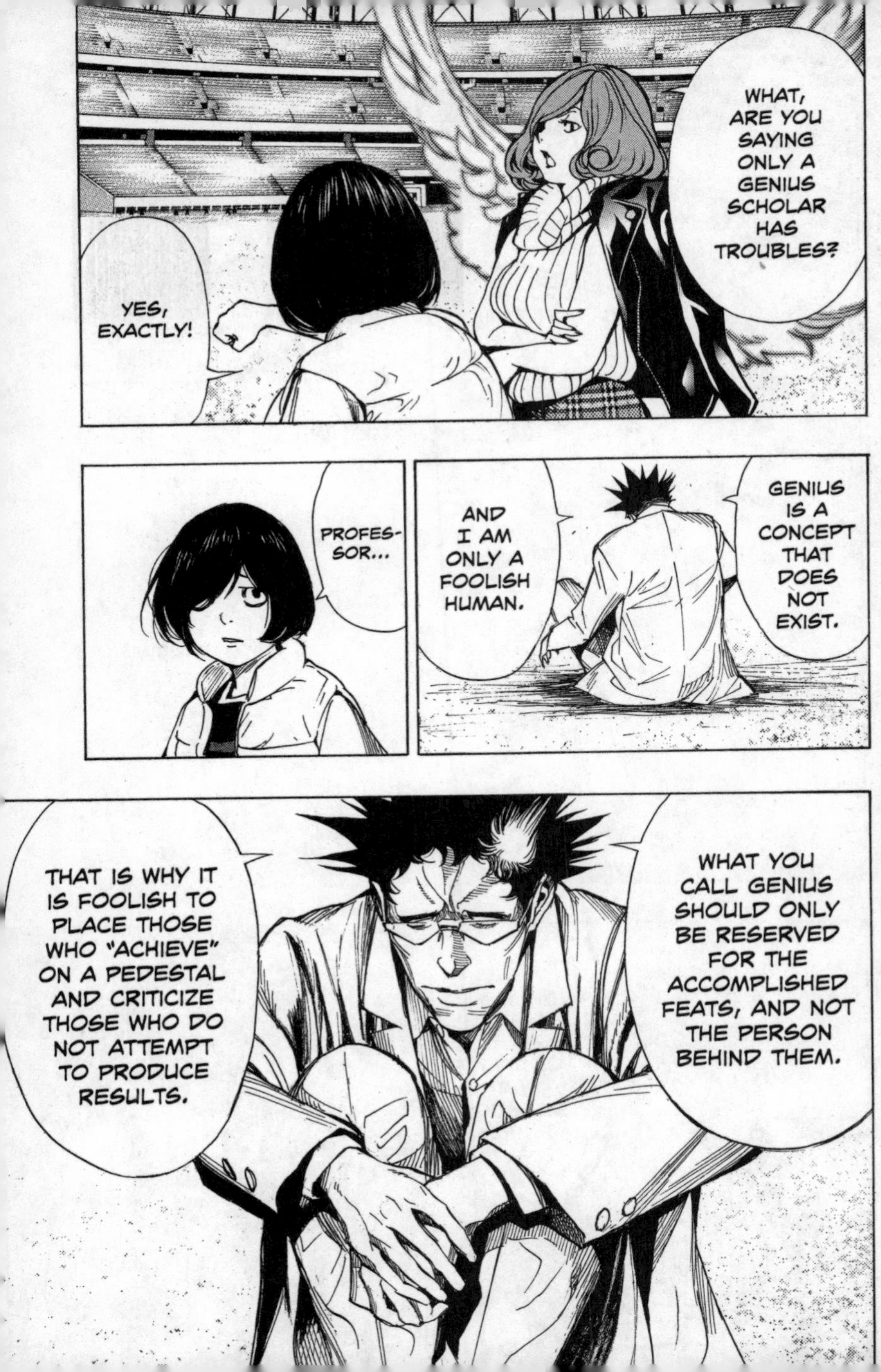
WHAT, ARE YOU SAYING ONLY A GENIUS SCHOLAR HAS TROUBLES?
YES, EXACTLY!
GENIUS IS A CONCEPT THAT DOES NOT EXIST.
AND I AM ONLY A FOOLISH HUMAN.
PROFES-SOR...
WHAT YOU CALL GENIUS SHOULD ONLY BE RESERVED FOR THE ACCOMPLISHED FEATS, AND NOT THE PERSON BEHIND THEM.
THAT IS WHY IT IS FOOLISH TO PLACE THOSE WHO "ACHIEVE" ON A PEDESTAL AND CRITICIZE THOSE WHO DO NOT ATTEMPT TO PRODUCE RESULTS.

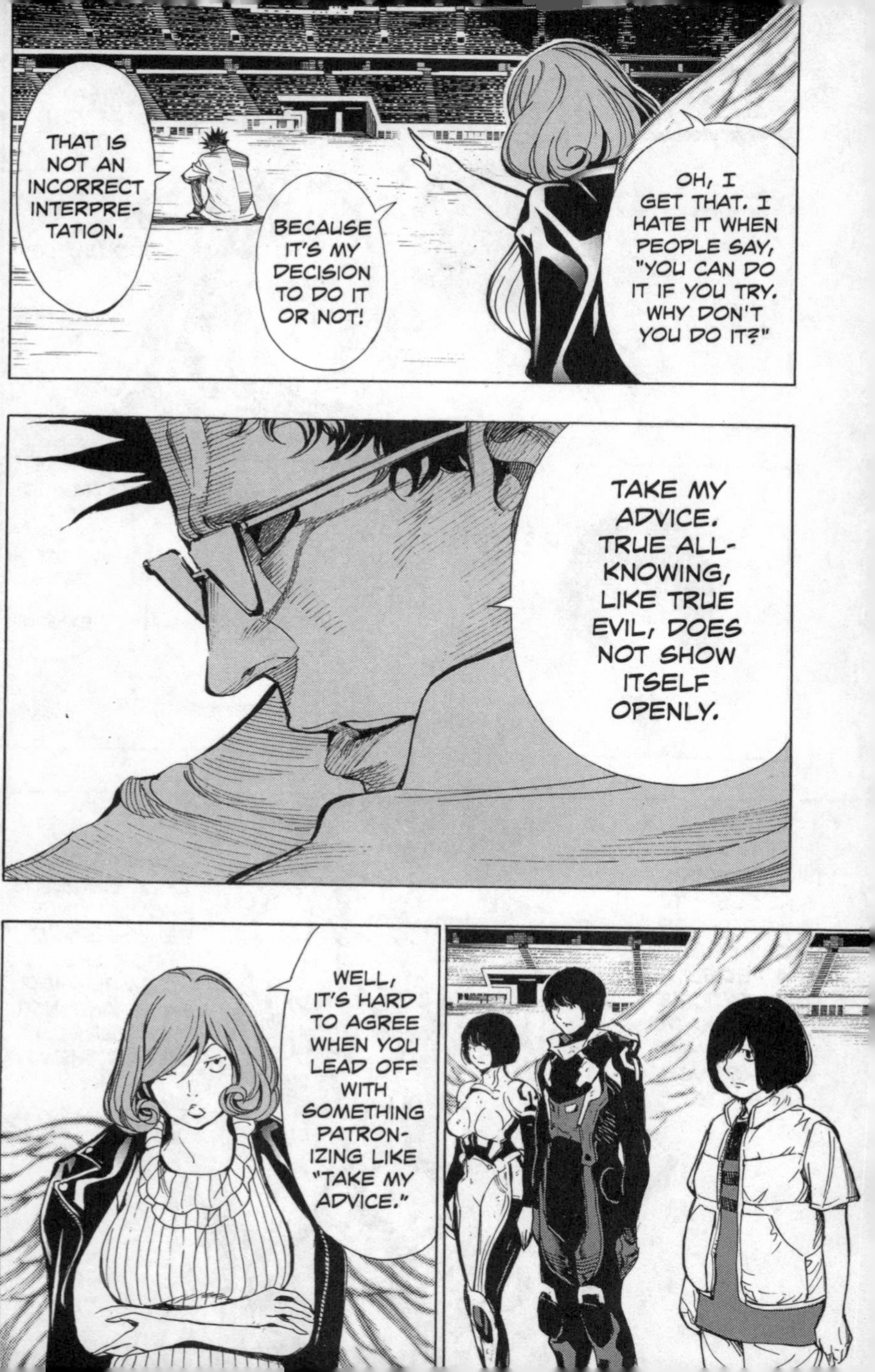
OH, I GET THAT. I HATE IT WHEN PEOPLE SAY, "YOU CAN DO IT IF YOU TRY. WHY DON'T YOU DO IT?"
BECAUSE IT'S MY DECISION TO DO IT OR NOT!
THAT IS NOT AN INCORRECT INTERPRE-TATION.
TAKE MY ADVICE. TRUE ALL-KNOWING, LIKE TRUE EVIL, DOES NOT SHOW ITSELF OPENLY.
WELL, IT'S HARD TO AGREE WHEN YOU LEAD OFF WITH SOMETHING PATRON-IZING LIKE "TAKE MY ADVICE."

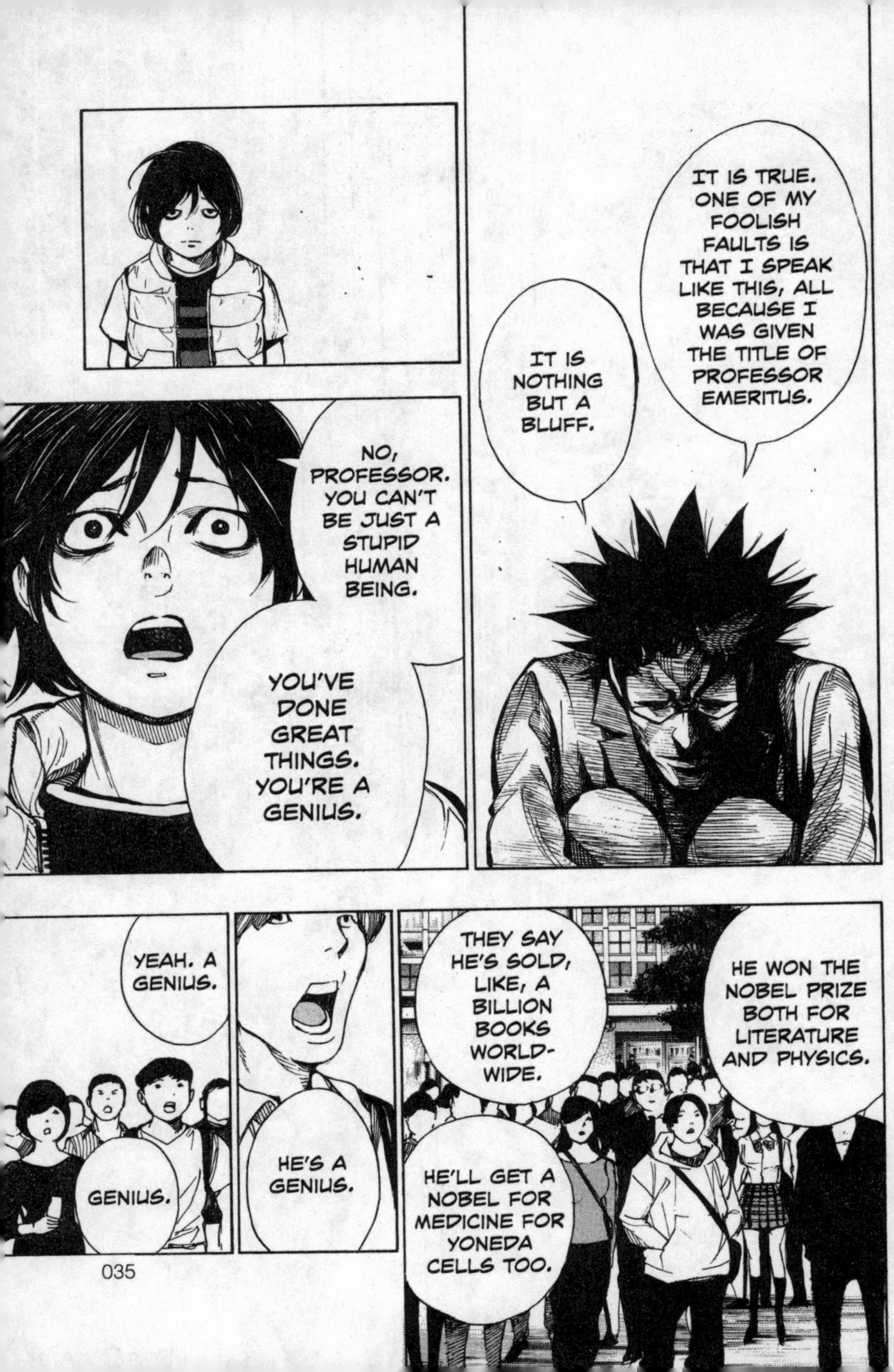
IT IS TRUE. ONE OF MY FOOLISH FAULTS IS THAT I SPEAK LIKE THIS, ALL BECAUSE I WAS GIVEN THE TITLE OF PROFESSOR EMERITUS.
IT IS NOTHING BUT A BLUFF.
NO, PROFESSOR. YOU CAN'T BE JUST A STUPID HUMAN BEING.
YOU'VE DONE GREAT THINGS. YOU'RE A GENIUS.
HE WON THE NOBEL PRIZE BOTH FOR LITERATURE AND PHYSICS.
THEY SAY HE'S SOLD, LIKE, A BILLION BOOKS WORLD-WIDE.
HE'LL GET A NOBEL FOR MEDICINE FOR YONEDA CELLS TOO.
HE'S A GENIUS.
YEAH. A GENIUS.
GENIUS.

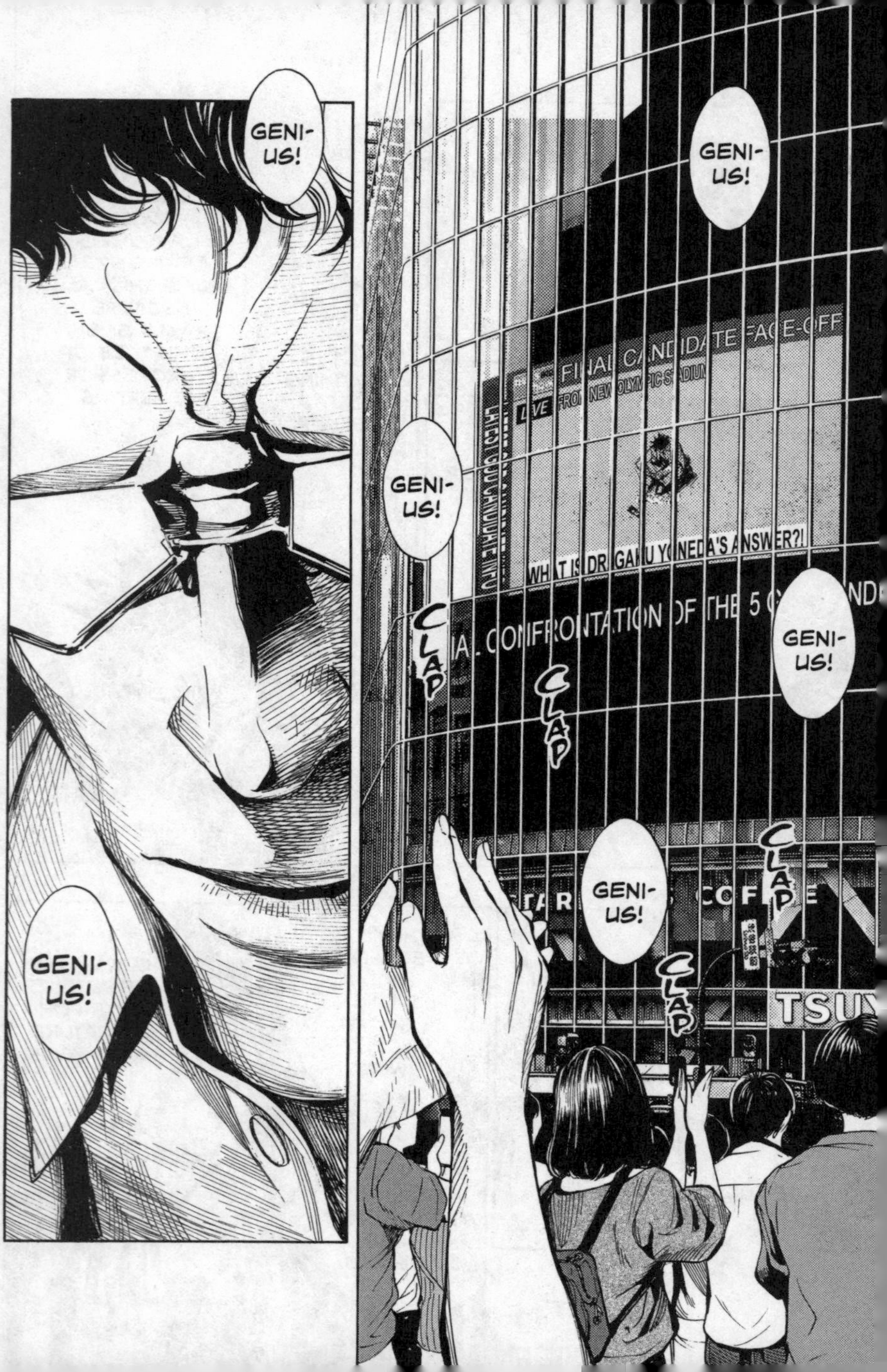

GENI-US!
FINAL CANDIDATE FACE-OFF
LIVE FROM NEW OLYMPIC STADIUM
WHAT IS DR. GAKU YONEDA'S ANSWER?!
GENI-US!
GENI-US!
CLAP
CLAP
CLAP
GENI-US!
CLAP
GENI-US!
GENI-US!

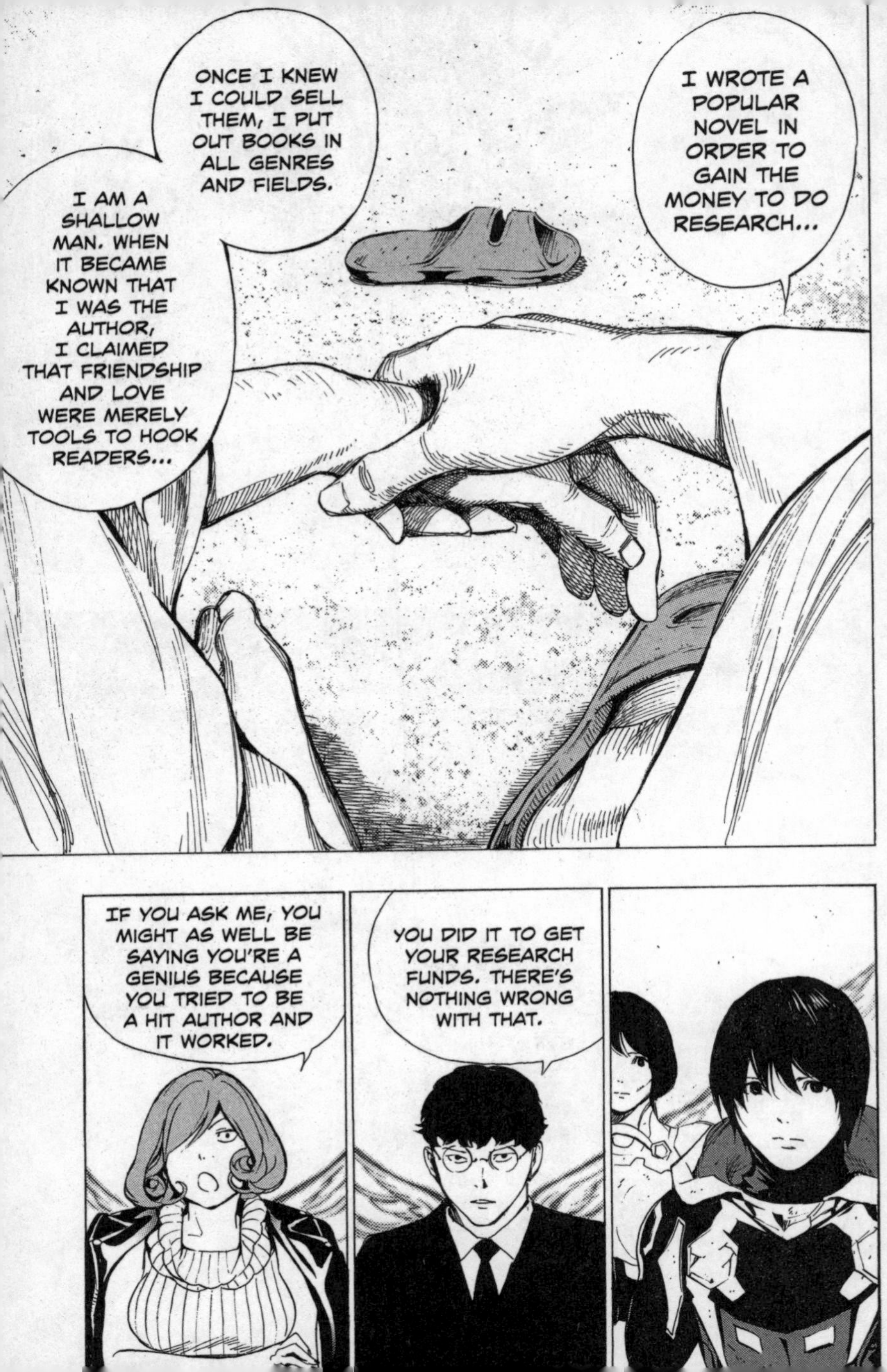
I WROTE A POPULAR NOVEL IN ORDER TO GAIN THE MONEY TO DO RESEARCH...
ONCE I KNEW I COULD SELL THEM, I PUT OUT BOOKS IN ALL GENRES AND FIELDS.
I AM A SHALLOW MAN. WHEN IT BECAME KNOWN THAT I WAS THE AUTHOR, I CLAIMED THAT FRIENDSHIP AND LOVE WERE MERELY TOOLS TO HOOK READERS...
YOU DID IT TO GET YOUR RESEARCH FUNDS. THERE'S NOTHING WRONG WITH THAT.
IF YOU ASK ME, YOU MIGHT AS WELL BE SAYING YOU'RE A GENIUS BECAUSE YOU TRIED TO BE A HIT AUTHOR AND IT WORKED.

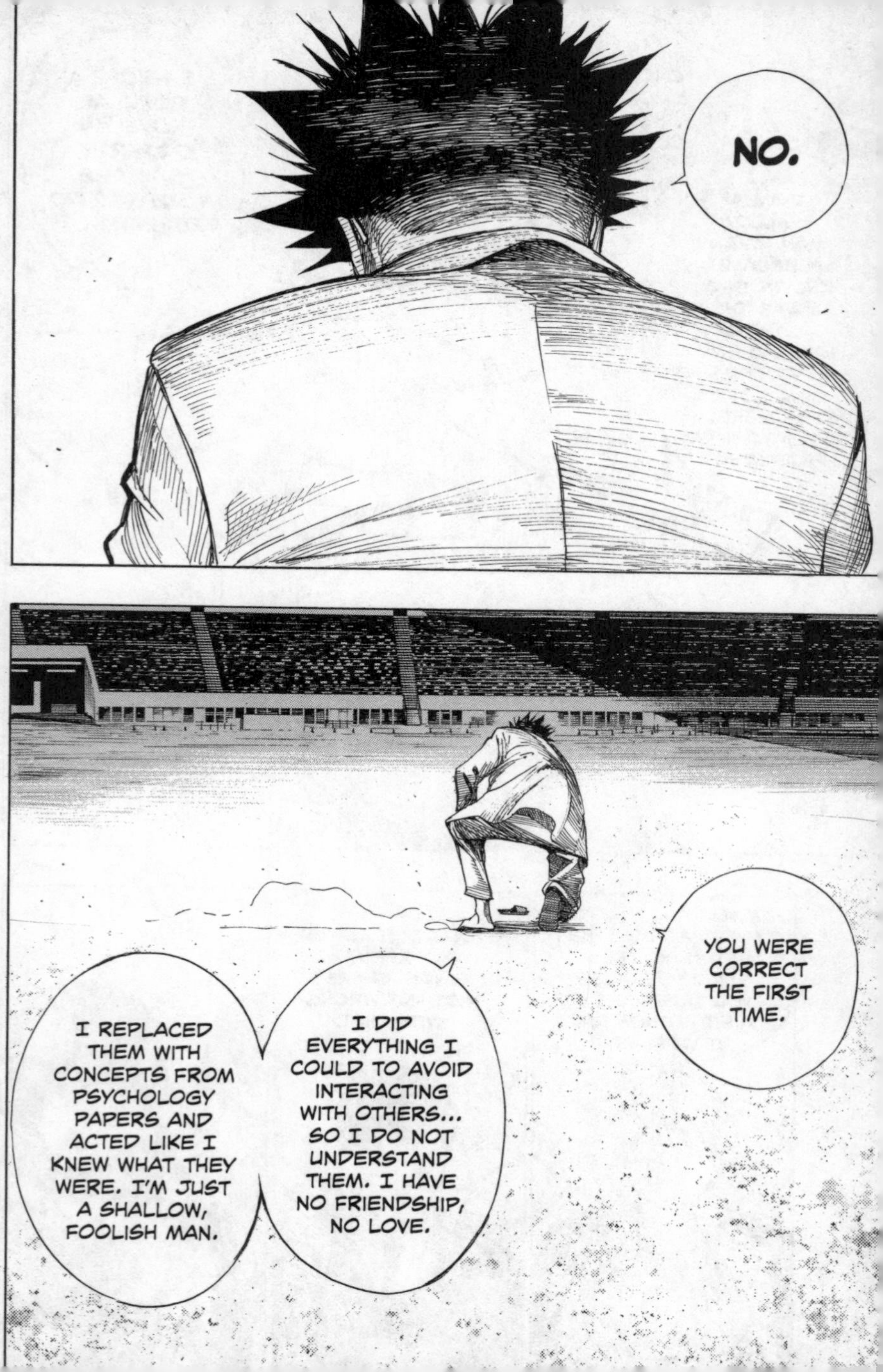
NO.
YOU WERE CORRECT THE FIRST TIME.
I DID EVERYTHING I COULD TO AVOID INTERACTING WITH OTHERS... SO I DO NOT UNDERSTAND THEM. I HAVE NO FRIENDSHIP, NO LOVE.
I REPLACED THEM WITH CONCEPTS FROM PSYCHOLOGY PAPERS AND ACTED LIKE I KNEW WHAT THEY WERE. I'M JUST A SHALLOW, FOOLISH MAN.

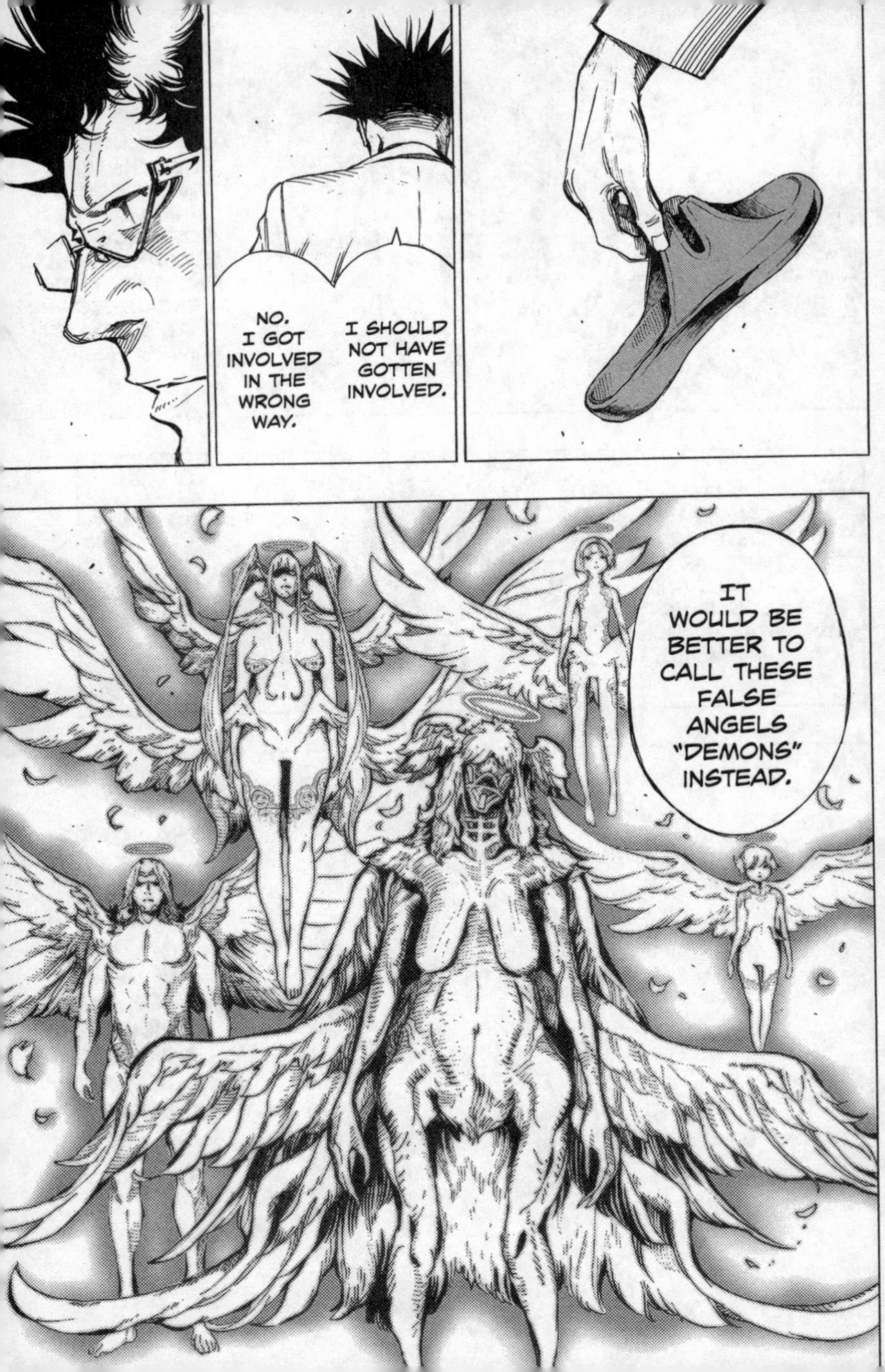
I SHOULD NOT HAVE GOTTEN INVOLVED.
NO. I GOT INVOLVED IN THE WRONG WAY.
IT WOULD BE BETTER TO CALL THESE FALSE ANGELS "DEMONS" INSTEAD.

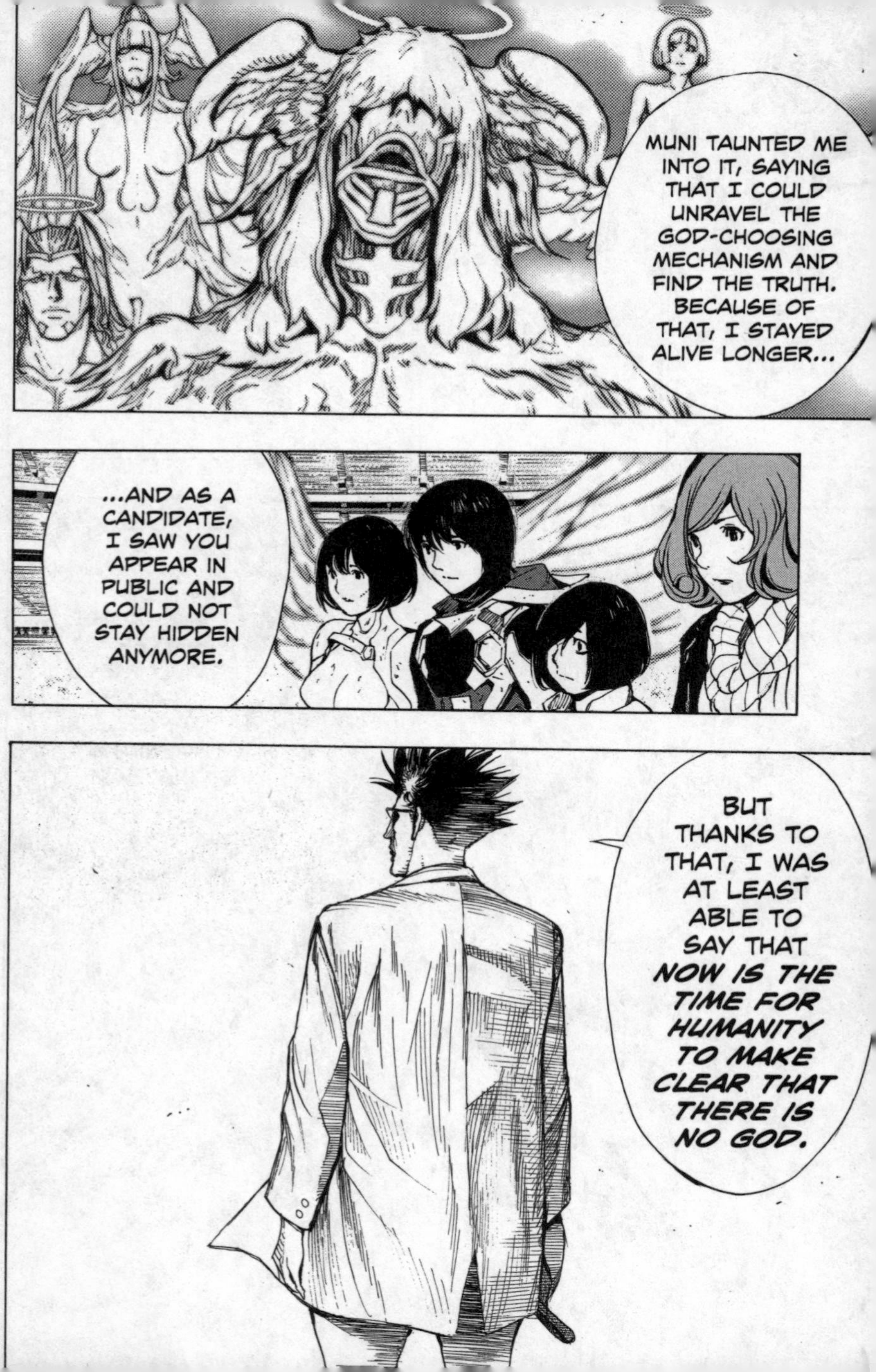
MUNI TAUNTED ME INTO IT, SAYING THAT I COULD UNRAVEL THE GOD-CHOOSING MECHANISM AND FIND THE TRUTH. BECAUSE OF THAT, I STAYED ALIVE LONGER...
...AND AS A CANDIDATE, I SAW YOU APPEAR IN PUBLIC AND COULD NOT STAY HIDDEN ANYMORE.
BUT THANKS TO THAT, I WAS AT LEAST ABLE TO SAY THAT *NOW IS THE TIME FOR HUMANITY TO MAKE CLEAR THAT THERE IS NO GOD.*

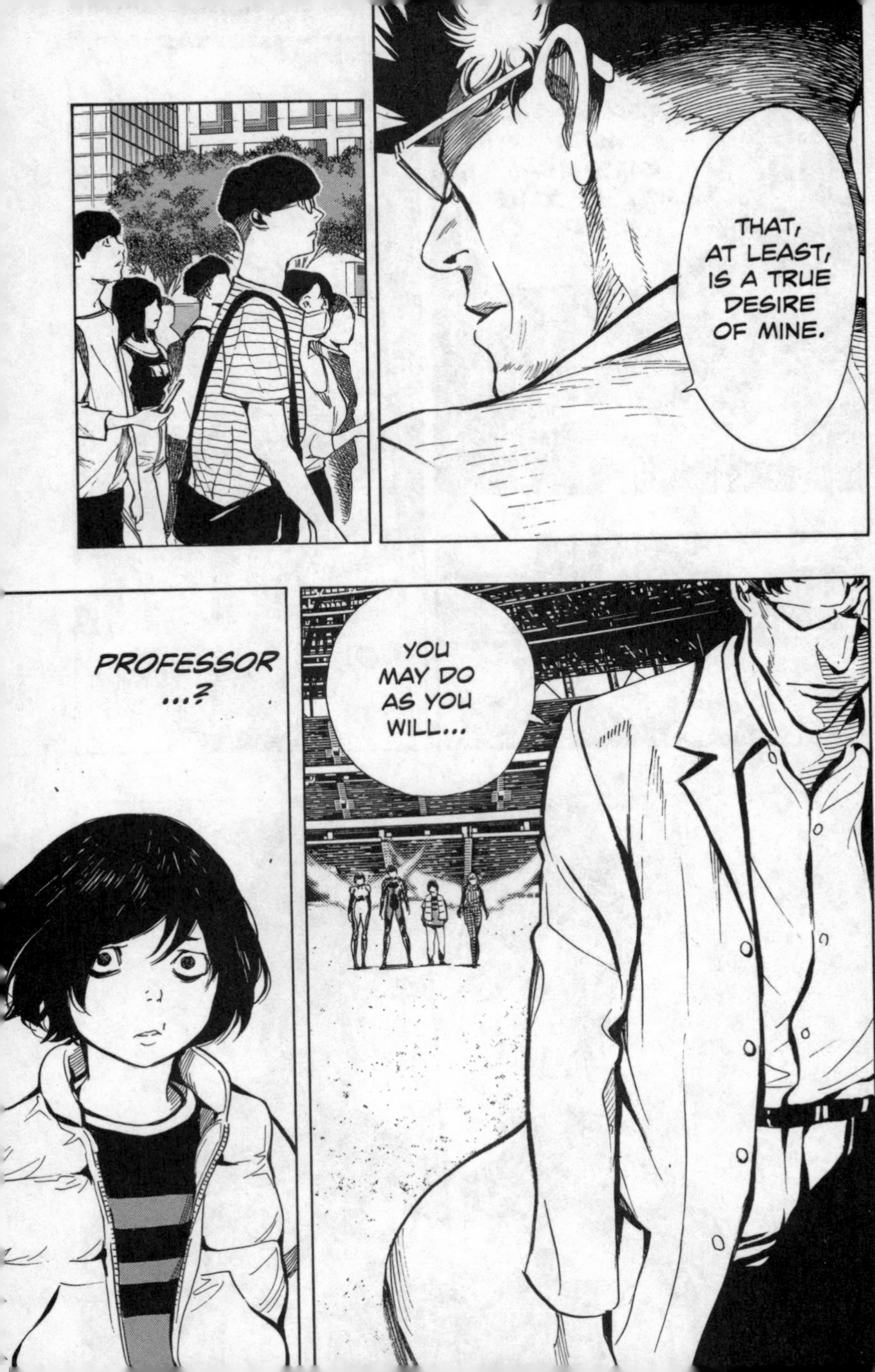
THAT, AT LEAST, IS A TRUE DESIRE OF MINE.
YOU MAY DO AS YOU WILL...
PROFESSOR ...?

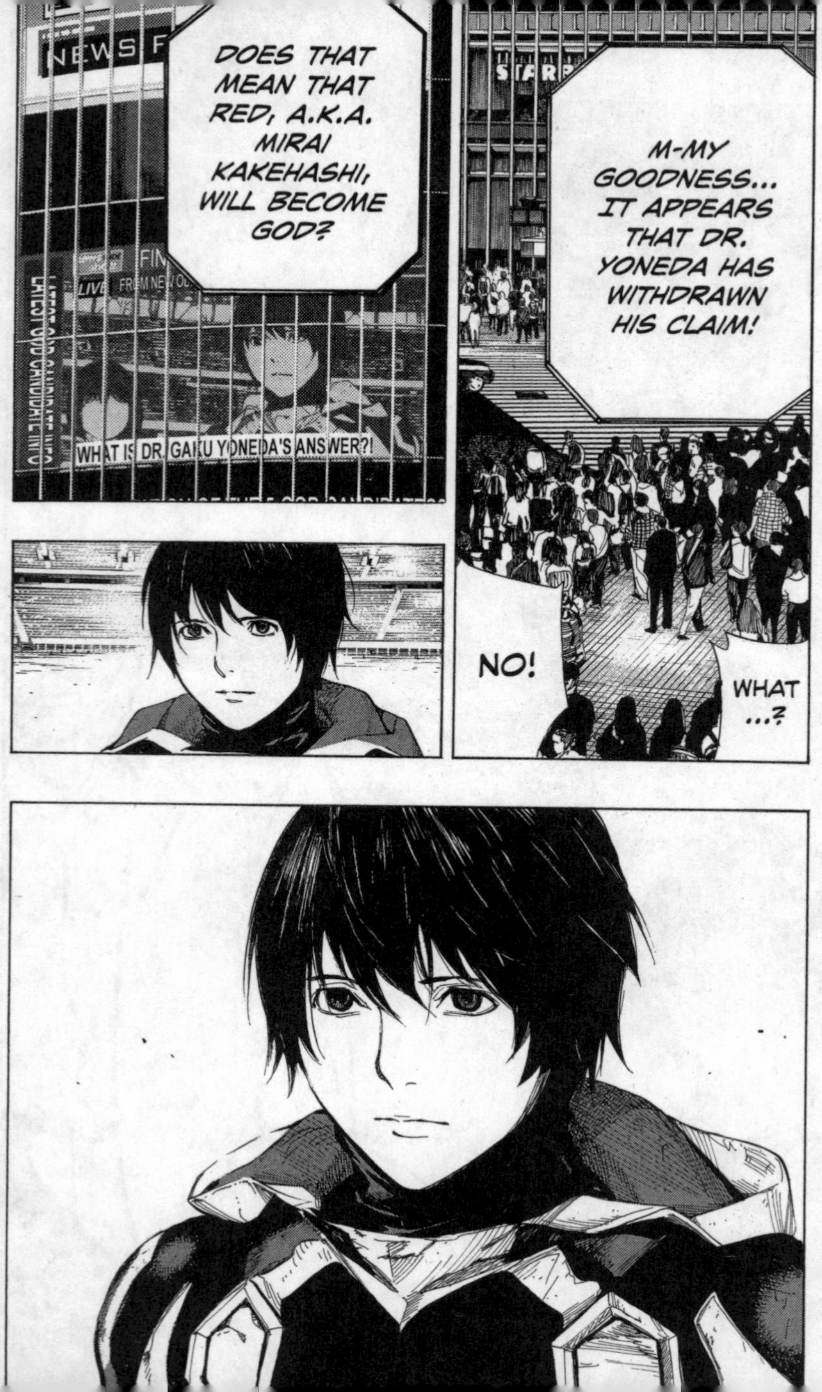
M-MY GOODNESS... IT APPEARS THAT DR. YONEDA HAS WITHDRAWN HIS CLAIM!
WHAT ...?
NO!
DOES THAT MEAN THAT RED, A.K.A. MIRAI KAKEHASHI, WILL BECOME GOD?
LIVE
WHAT IS DR. GAKU YONEDA'S ANSWER?!

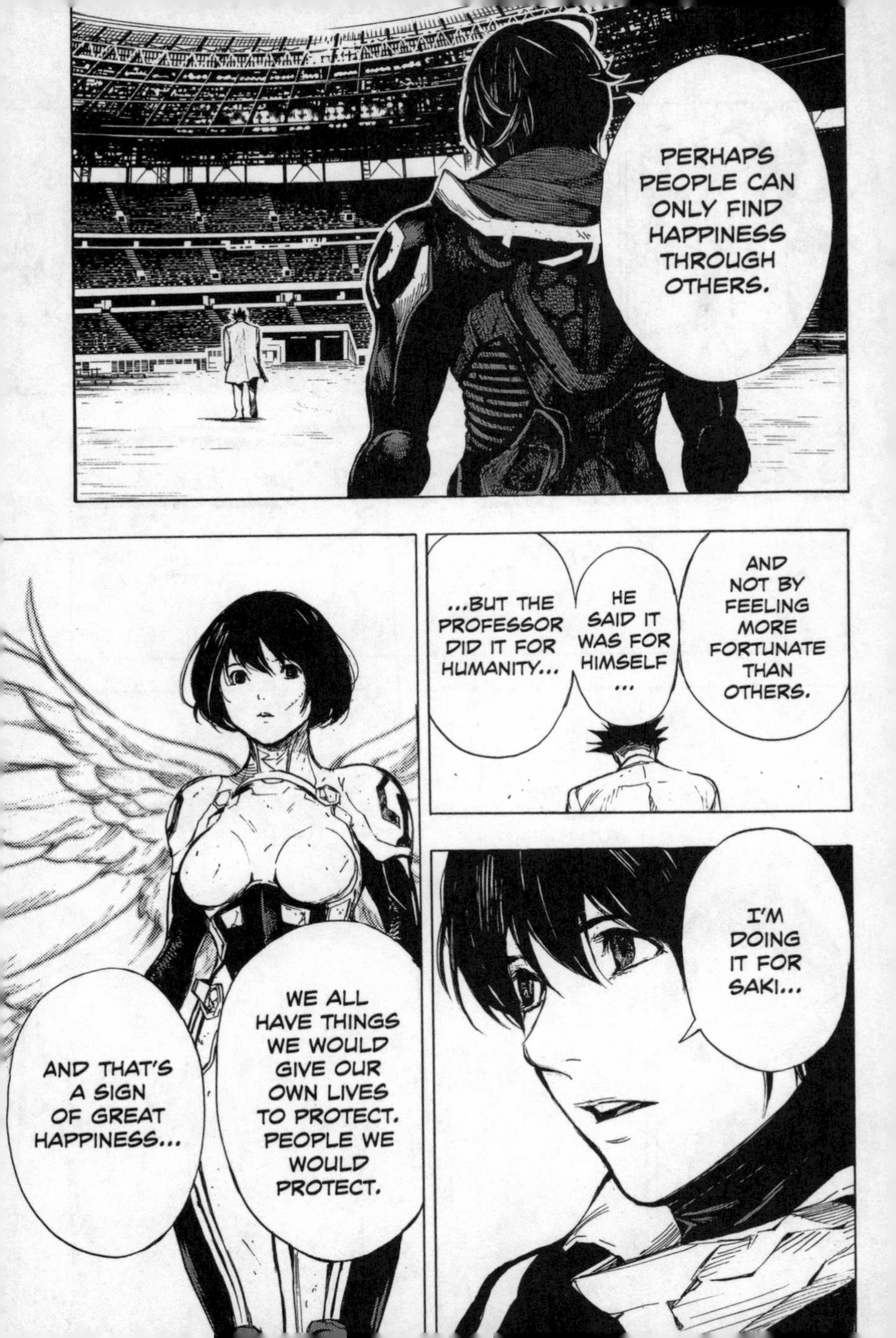
PERHAPS PEOPLE CAN ONLY FIND HAPPINESS THROUGH OTHERS.
AND NOT BY FEELING MORE FORTUNATE THAN OTHERS.
HE SAID IT WAS FOR HIMSELF ...
...BUT THE PROFESSOR DID IT FOR HUMANITY...
I'M DOING IT FOR SAKI...
WE ALL HAVE THINGS WE WOULD GIVE OUR OWN LIVES TO PROTECT. PEOPLE WE WOULD PROTECT.
AND THAT'S A SIGN OF GREAT HAPPINESS...

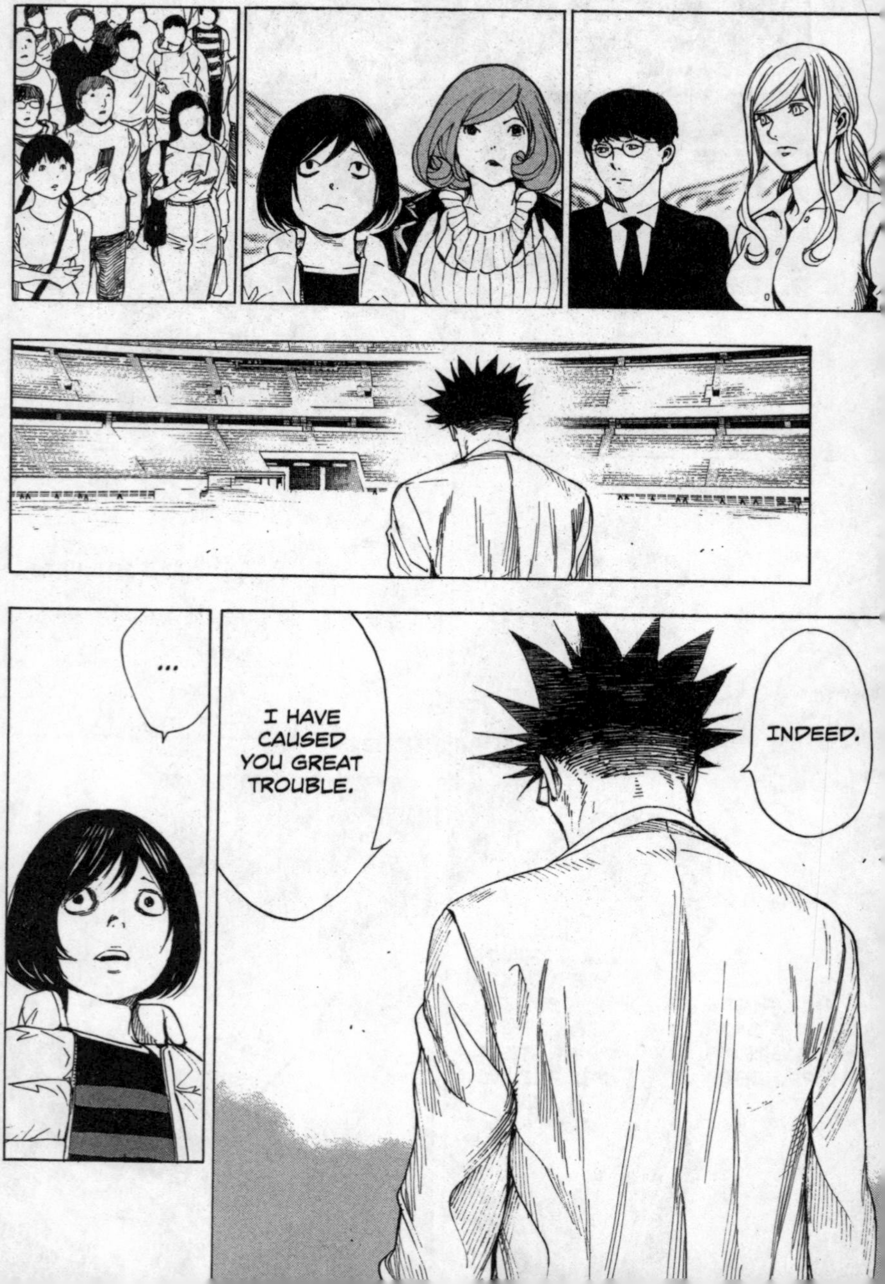
INDEED.
I HAVE CAUSED YOU GREAT TROUBLE.
...

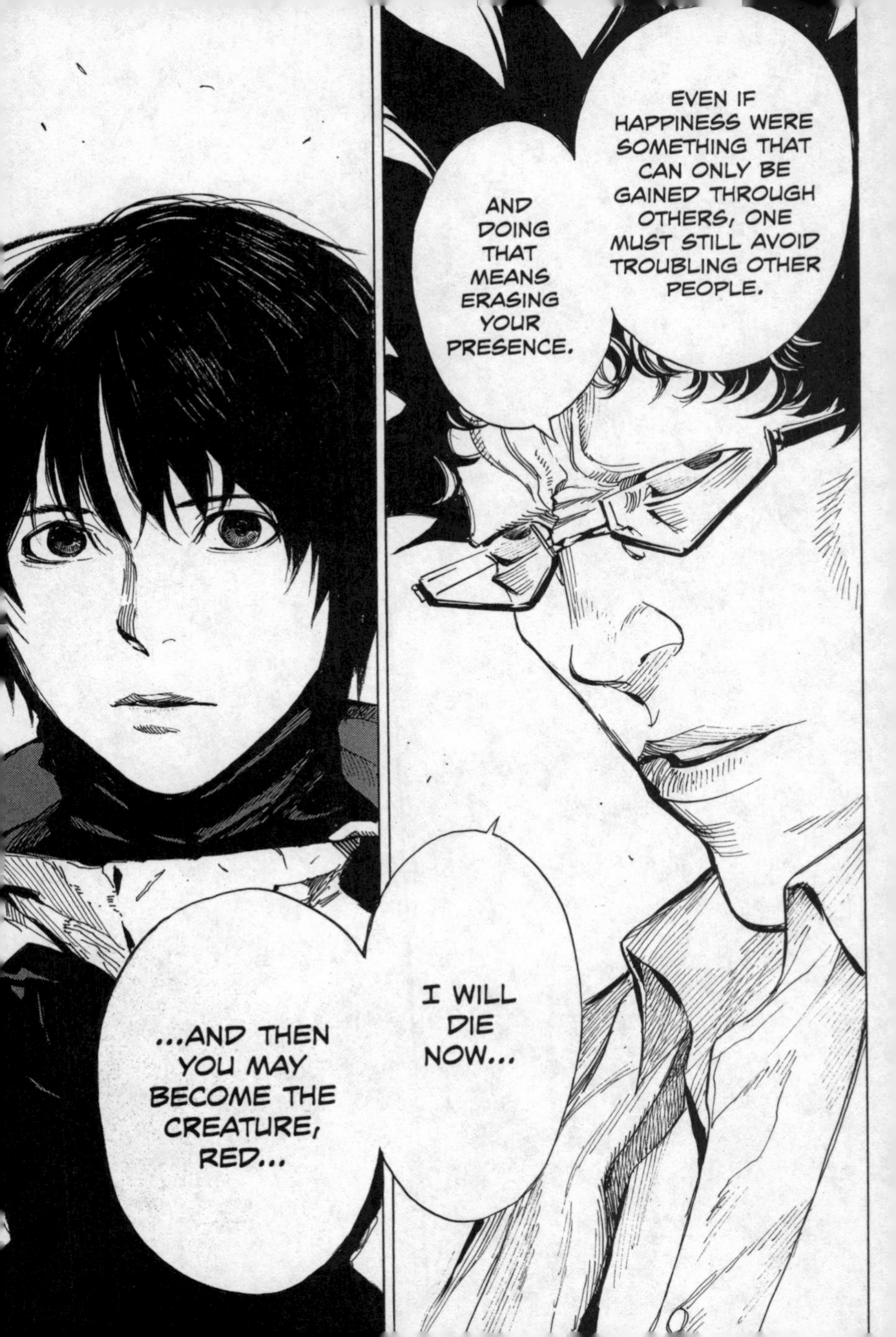
EVEN IF HAPPINESS WERE SOMETHING THAT CAN ONLY BE GAINED THROUGH OTHERS, ONE MUST STILL AVOID TROUBLING OTHER PEOPLE.
AND DOING THAT MEANS ERASING YOUR PRESENCE.
I WILL DIE NOW...
...AND THEN YOU MAY BECOME THE CREATURE, RED...

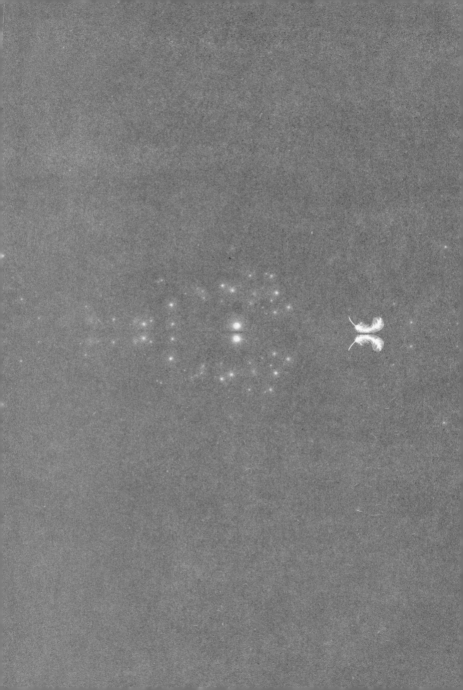

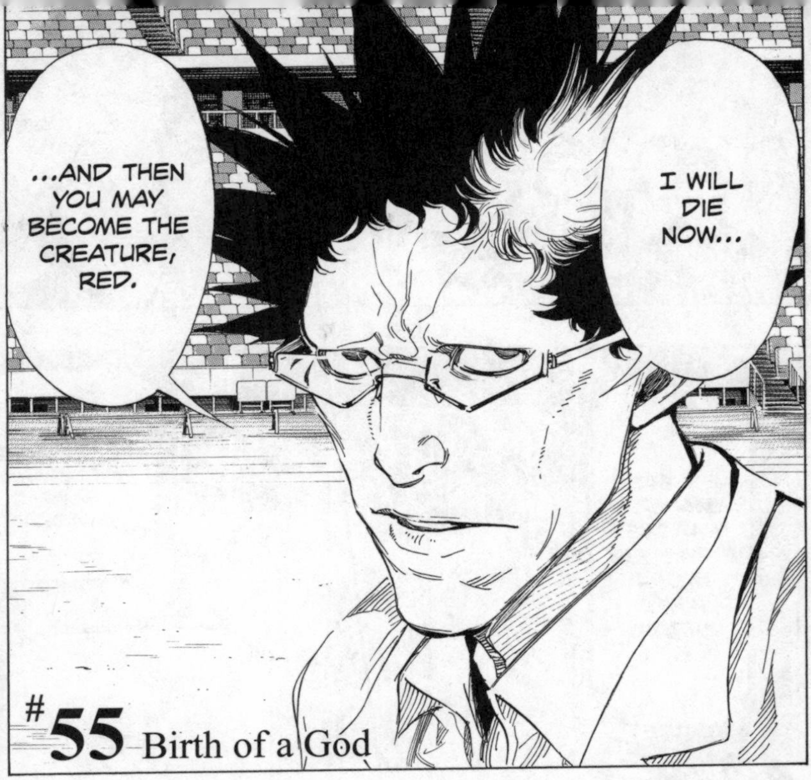
I WILL DIE NOW...
...AND THEN YOU MAY BECOME THE CREATURE, RED.

#55 Birth of a God

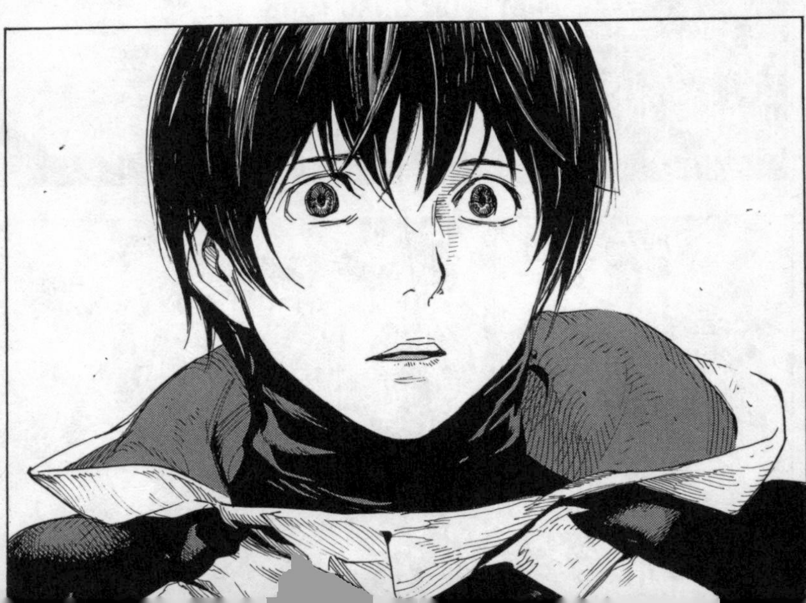

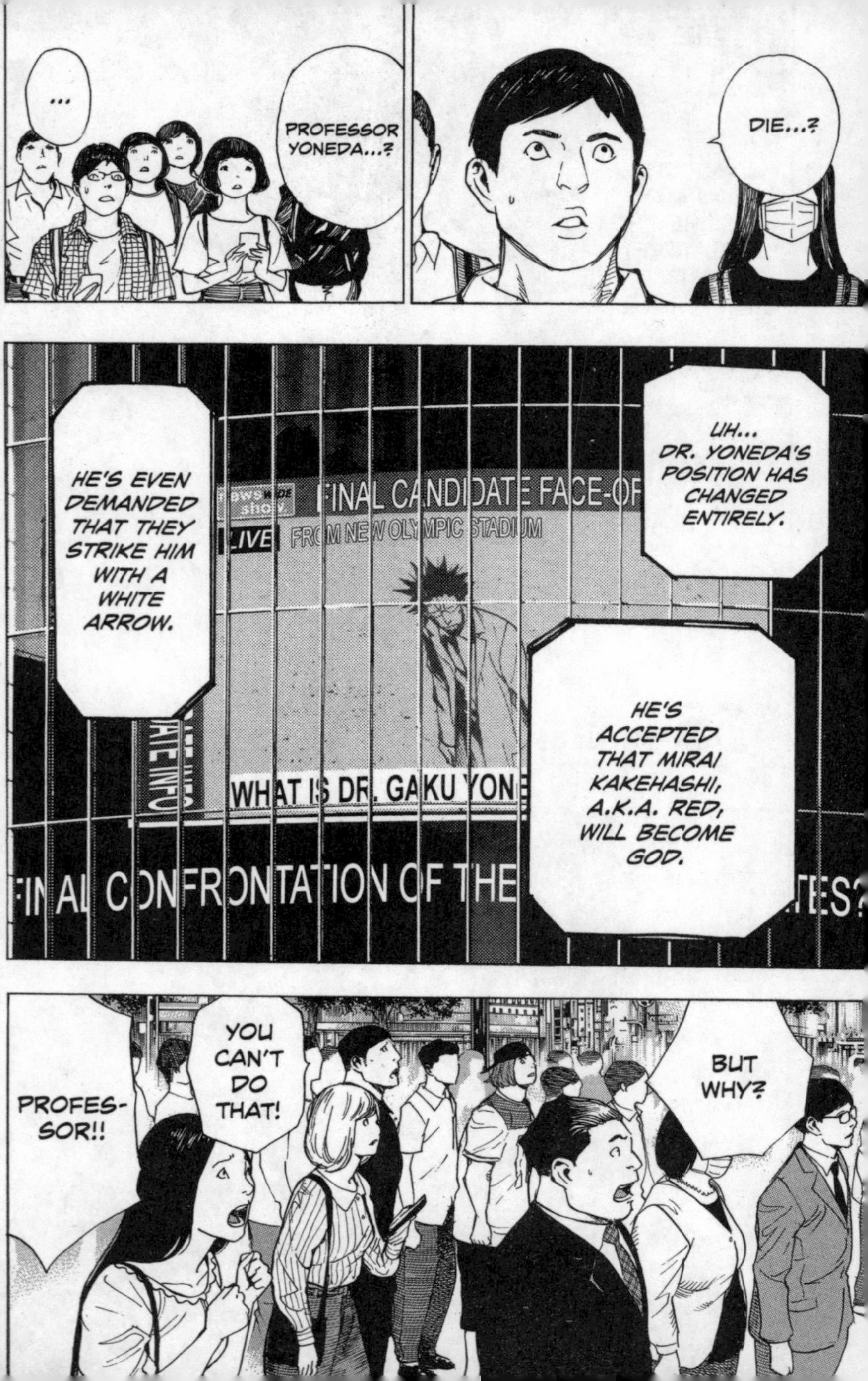
DIE...?
PROFESSOR YONEDA...?
...
UH... DR. YONEDA'S POSITION HAS CHANGED ENTIRELY.
HE'S ACCEPTED THAT MIRAI KAKEHASHI, A.K.A. RED, WILL BECOME GOD.
HE'S EVEN DEMANDED THAT THEY STRIKE HIM WITH A WHITE ARROW.
FINAL CANDIDATE FACE-OF
LIVE
FROM NEW OLYMPIC STADIUM
WHAT IS DR. GAKU YONE
FINAL CONFRONTATION OF THE
BUT WHY?
YOU CAN'T DO THAT!
PROFES-SOR!!

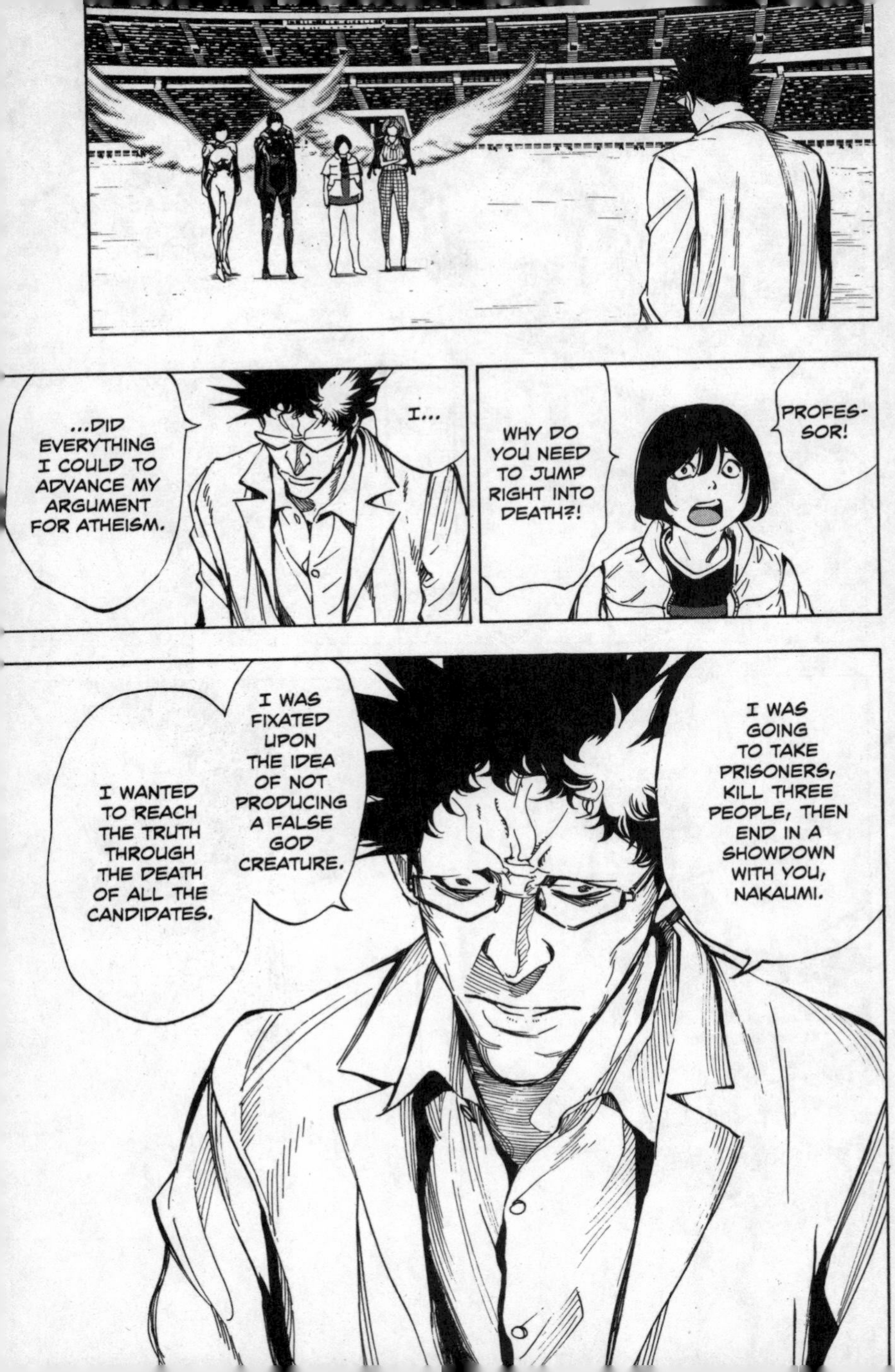
PROFES-SOR!
WHY DO YOU NEED TO JUMP RIGHT INTO DEATH?!
I...
...DID EVERYTHING I COULD TO ADVANCE MY ARGUMENT FOR ATHEISM.
I WAS GOING TO TAKE PRISONERS, KILL THREE PEOPLE, THEN END IN A SHOWDOWN WITH YOU, NAKAUMI.
I WAS FIXATED UPON THE IDEA OF NOT PRODUCING A FALSE GOD CREATURE.
I WANTED TO REACH THE TRUTH THROUGH THE DEATH OF ALL THE CANDIDATES.

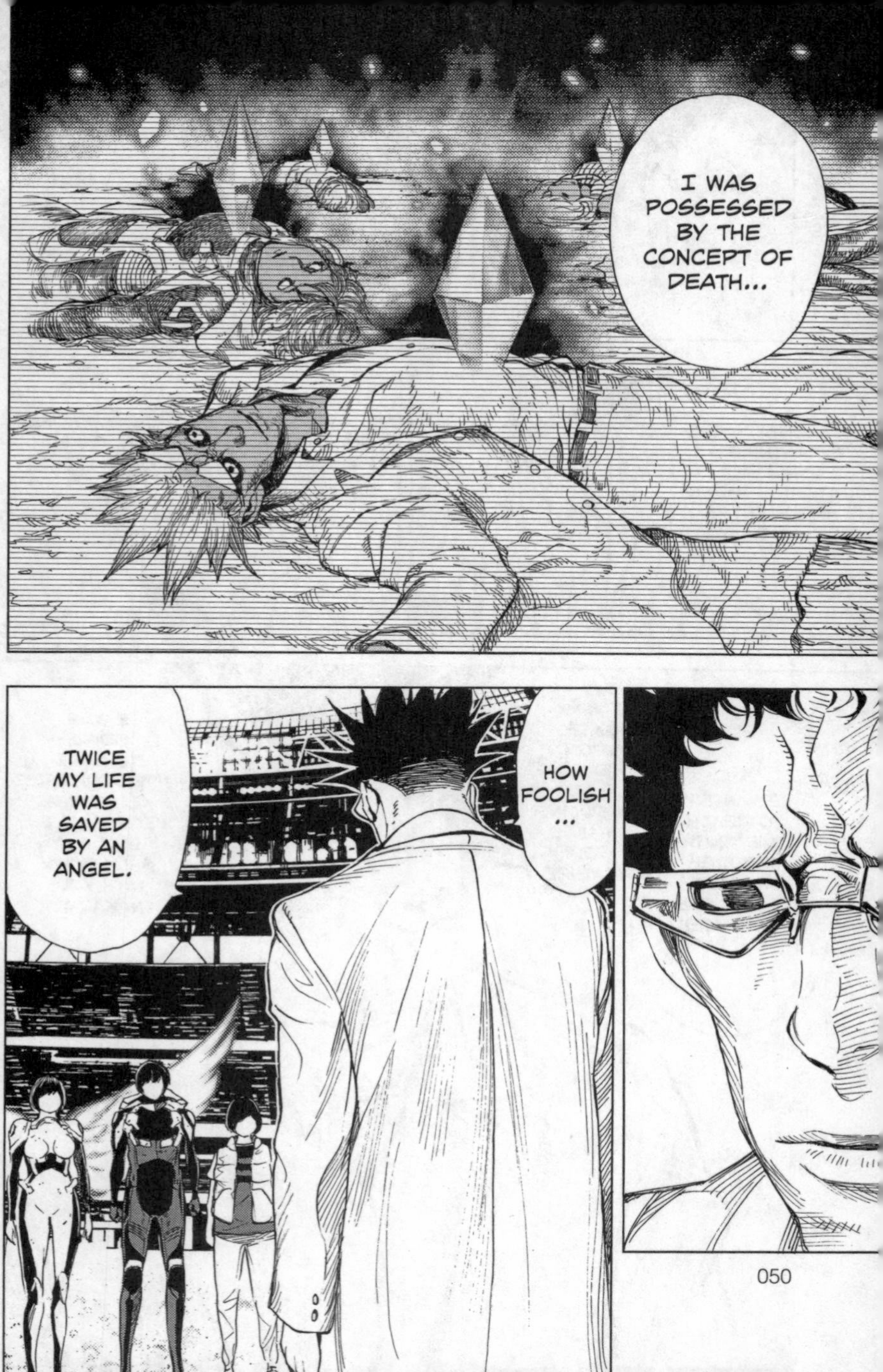
I WAS POSSESSED BY THE CONCEPT OF DEATH...
HOW FOOLISH...
TWICE MY LIFE WAS SAVED BY AN ANGEL.

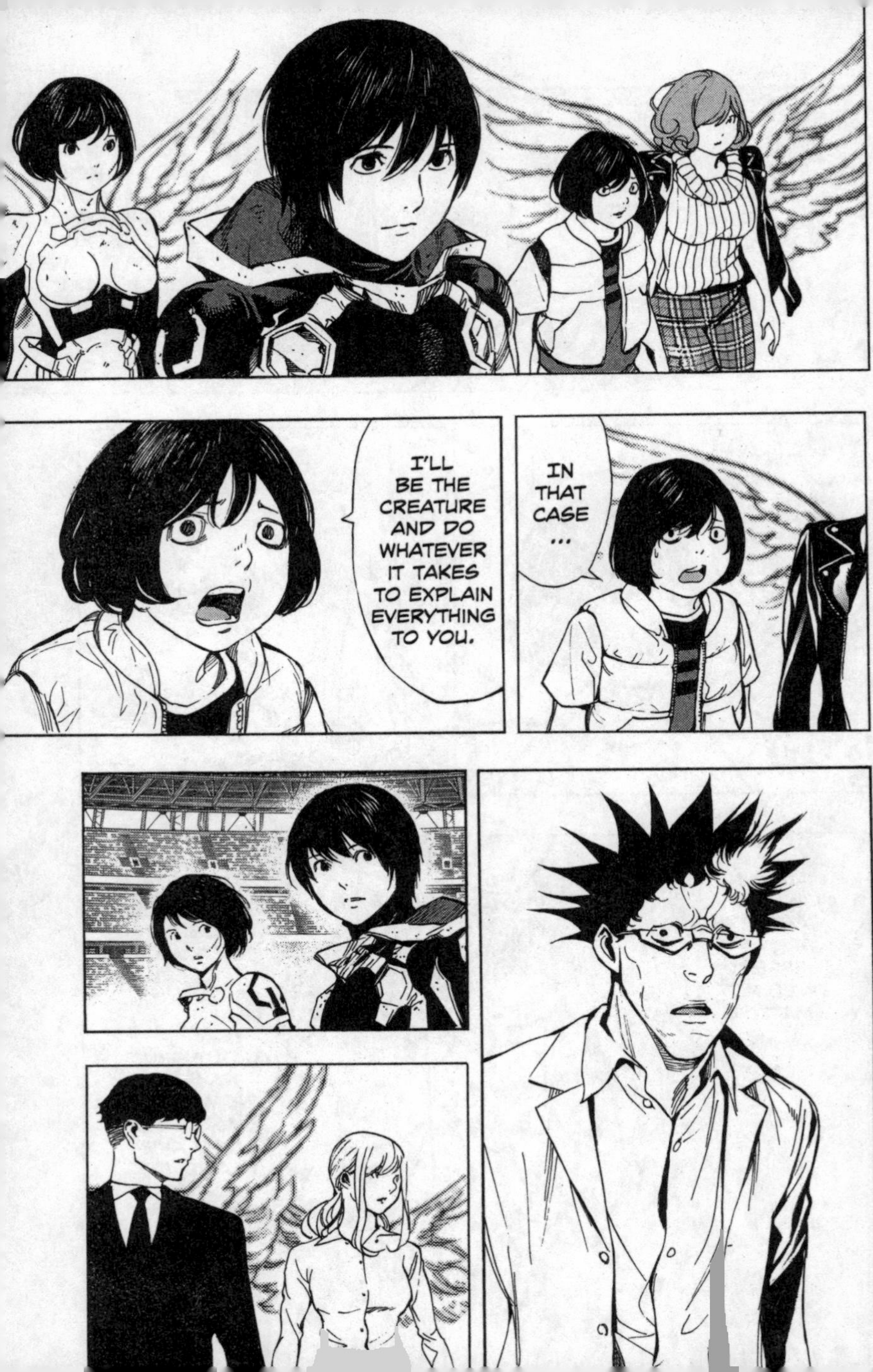
IN THAT CASE ...
I'LL BE THE CREATURE AND DO WHATEVER IT TAKES TO EXPLAIN EVERYTHING TO YOU.

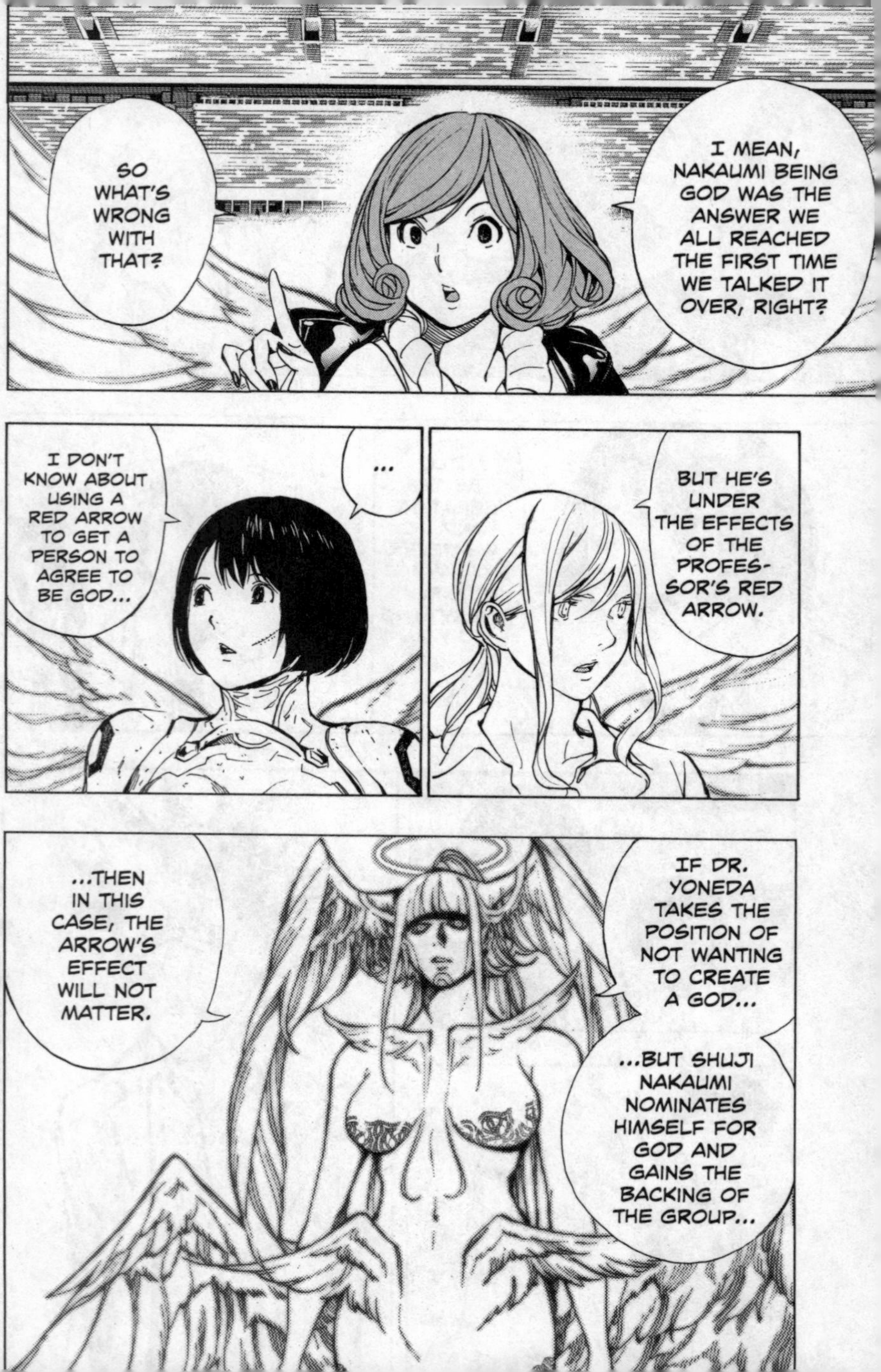

I MEAN, NAKAUMI BEING GOD WAS THE ANSWER WE ALL REACHED THE FIRST TIME WE TALKED IT OVER, RIGHT?
SO WHAT'S WRONG WITH THAT?
BUT HE'S UNDER THE EFFECTS OF THE PROFES-SOR'S RED ARROW.
...
I DON'T KNOW ABOUT USING A RED ARROW TO GET A PERSON TO AGREE TO BE GOD...
IF DR. YONEDA TAKES THE POSITION OF NOT WANTING TO CREATE A GOD...
...BUT SHUJI NAKAUMI NOMINATES HIMSELF FOR GOD AND GAINS THE BACKING OF THE GROUP...
...THEN IN THIS CASE, THE ARROW'S EFFECT WILL NOT MATTER.

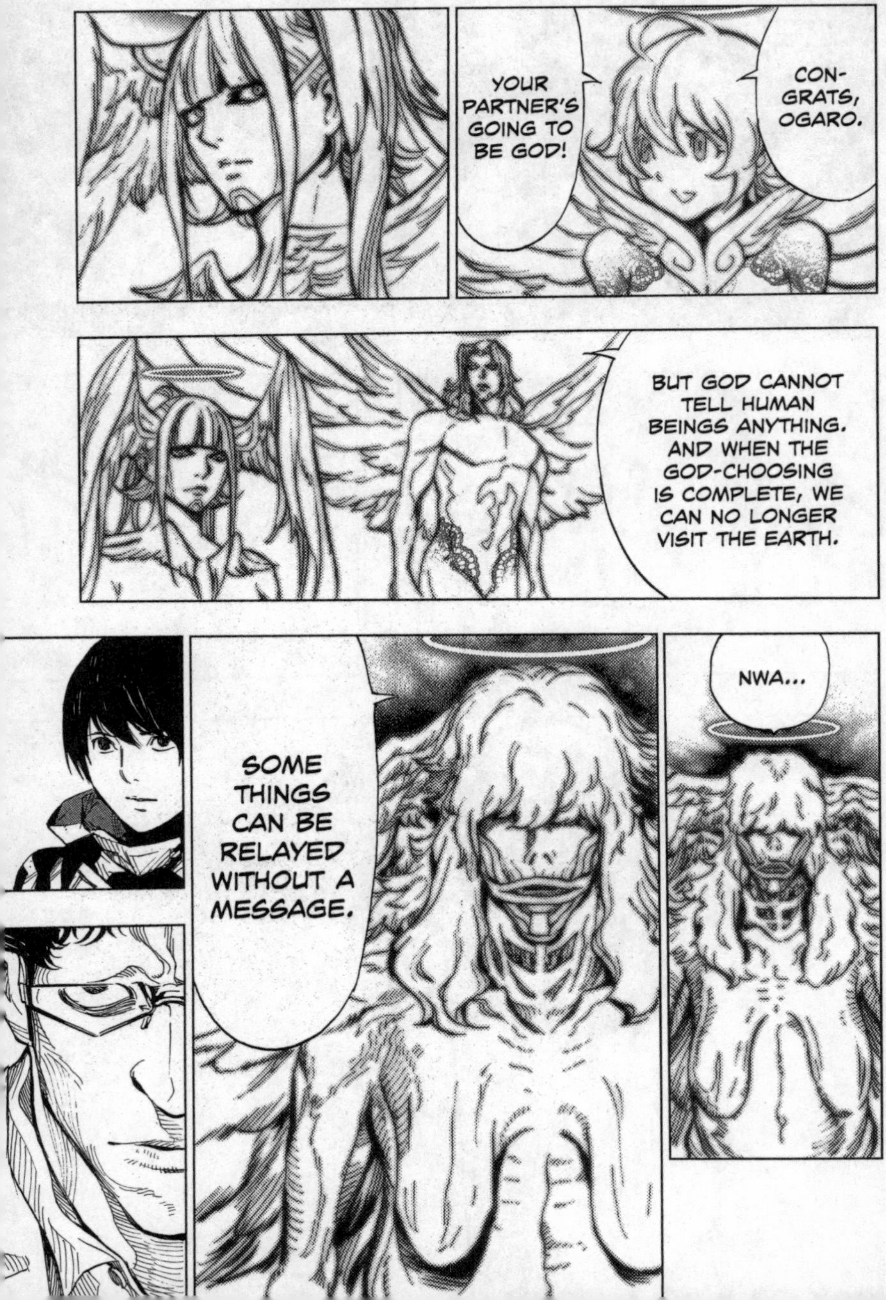
CON-GRATS, OGARO.
YOUR PARTNER'S GOING TO BE GOD!
BUT GOD CANNOT TELL HUMAN BEINGS ANYTHING. AND WHEN THE GOD-CHOOSING IS COMPLETE, WE CAN NO LONGER VISIT THE EARTH.
NWA...
SOME THINGS CAN BE RELAYED WITHOUT A MESSAGE.

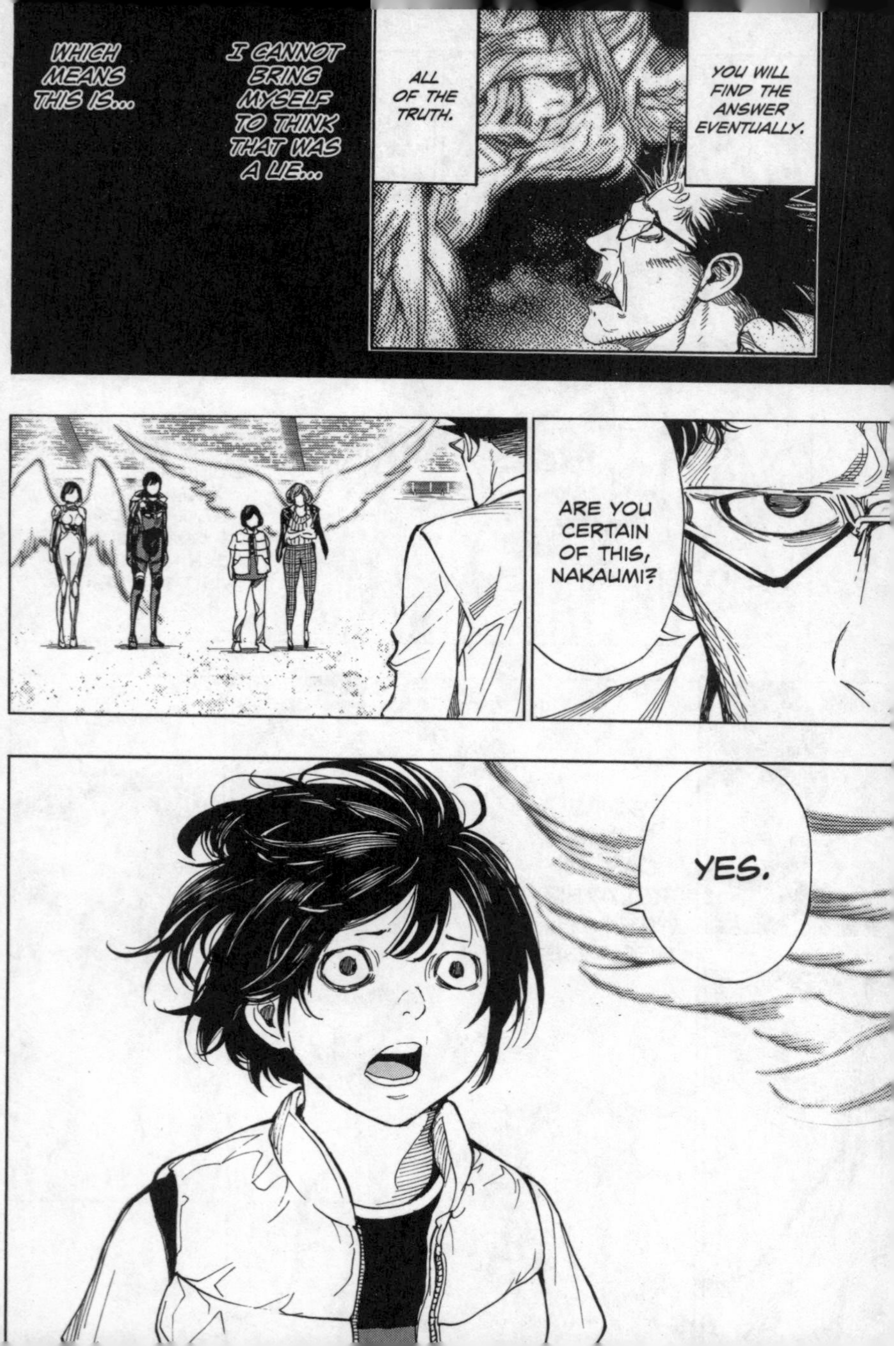
YOU WILL FIND THE ANSWER EVENTUALLY.
ALL OF THE TRUTH.
I CANNOT BRING MYSELF TO THINK THAT WAS A LIE...
WHICH MEANS THIS IS...
ARE YOU CERTAIN OF THIS, NAKAUMI?
YES.

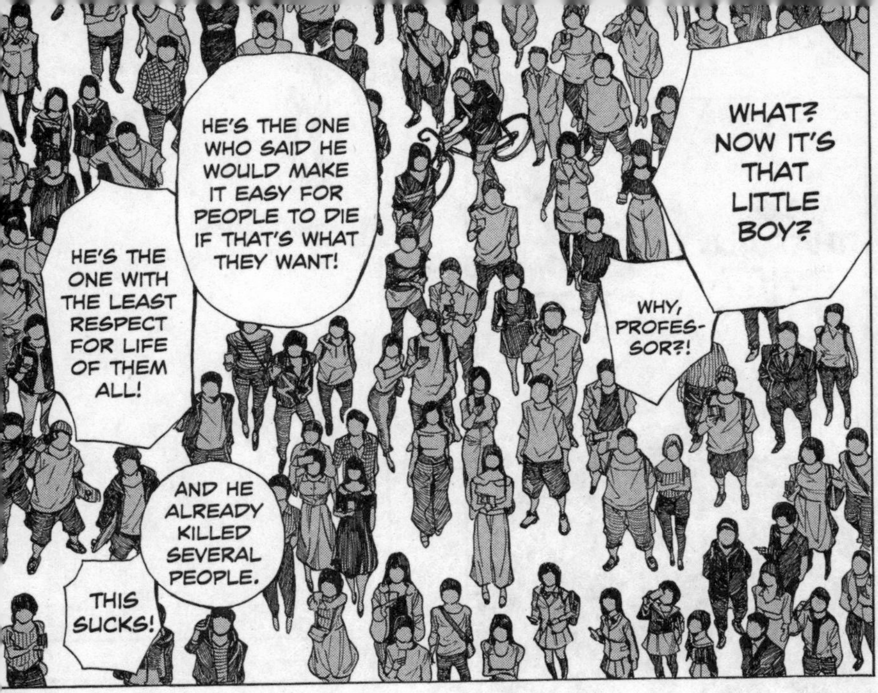
WHAT? NOW IT'S THAT LITTLE BOY?
WHY, PROFES-SOR?!
HE'S THE ONE WHO SAID HE WOULD MAKE IT EASY FOR PEOPLE TO DIE IF THAT'S WHAT THEY WANT!
HE'S THE ONE WITH THE LEAST RESPECT FOR LIFE OF THEM ALL!
AND HE ALREADY KILLED SEVERAL PEOPLE.
THIS SUCKS!

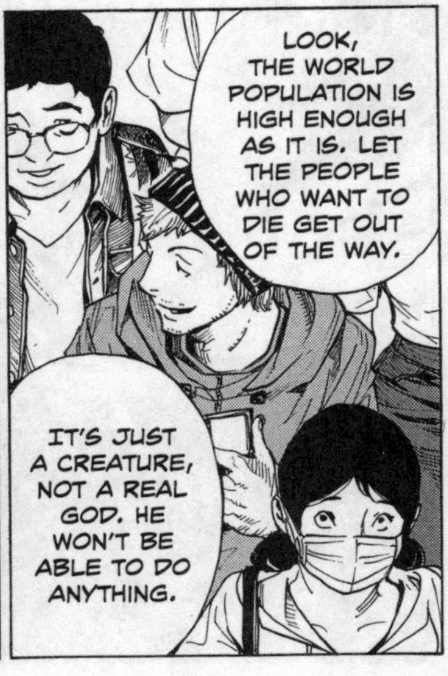
LOOK, THE WORLD POPULATION IS HIGH ENOUGH AS IT IS. LET THE PEOPLE WHO WANT TO DIE GET OUT OF THE WAY.
IT'S JUST A CREATURE, NOT A REAL GOD. HE WON'T BE ABLE TO DO ANYTHING.

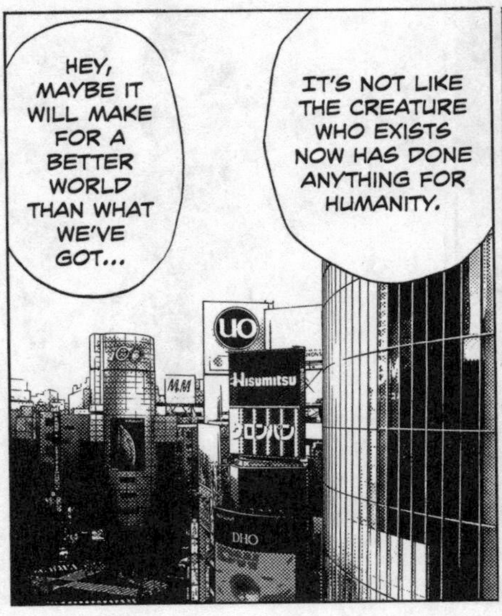
IT'S NOT LIKE THE CREATURE WHO EXISTS NOW HAS DONE ANYTHING FOR HUMANITY.
HEY, MAYBE IT WILL MAKE FOR A BETTER WORLD THAN WHAT WE'VE GOT...
UO
Hisumitsu

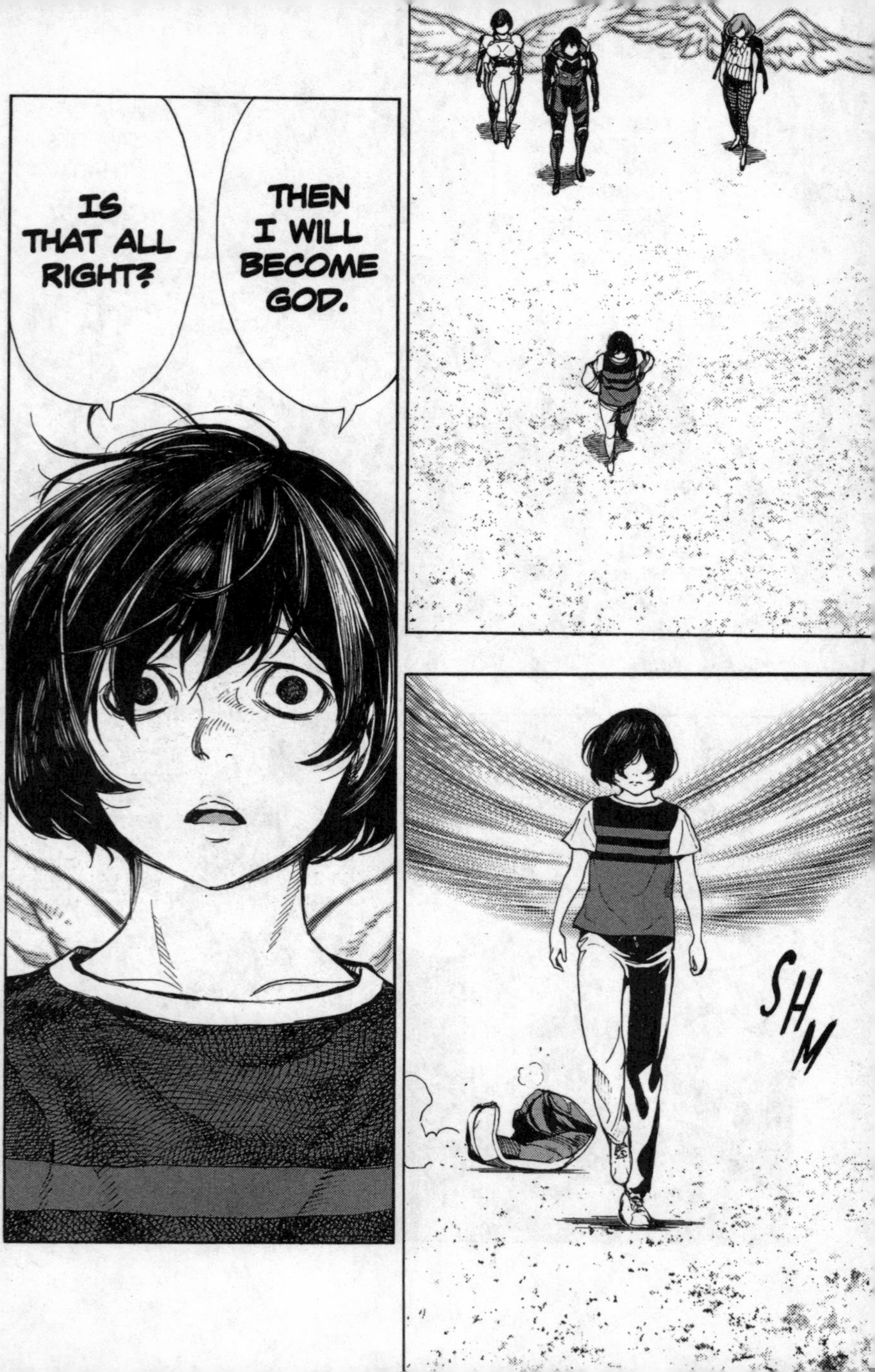
SHM
THEN I WILL BECOME GOD.
IS THAT ALL RIGHT?

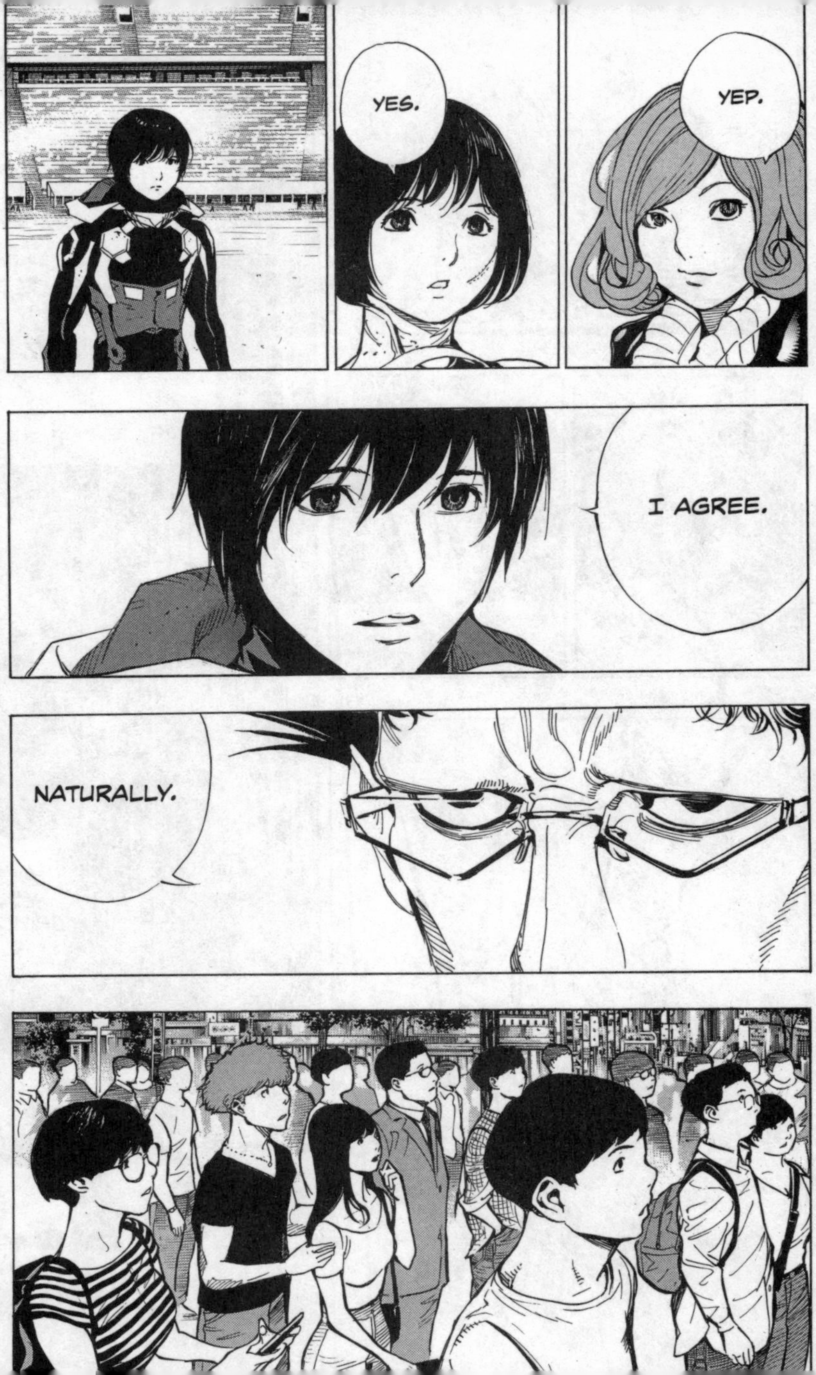
YEP.
YES.
I AGREE.
NATURALLY.

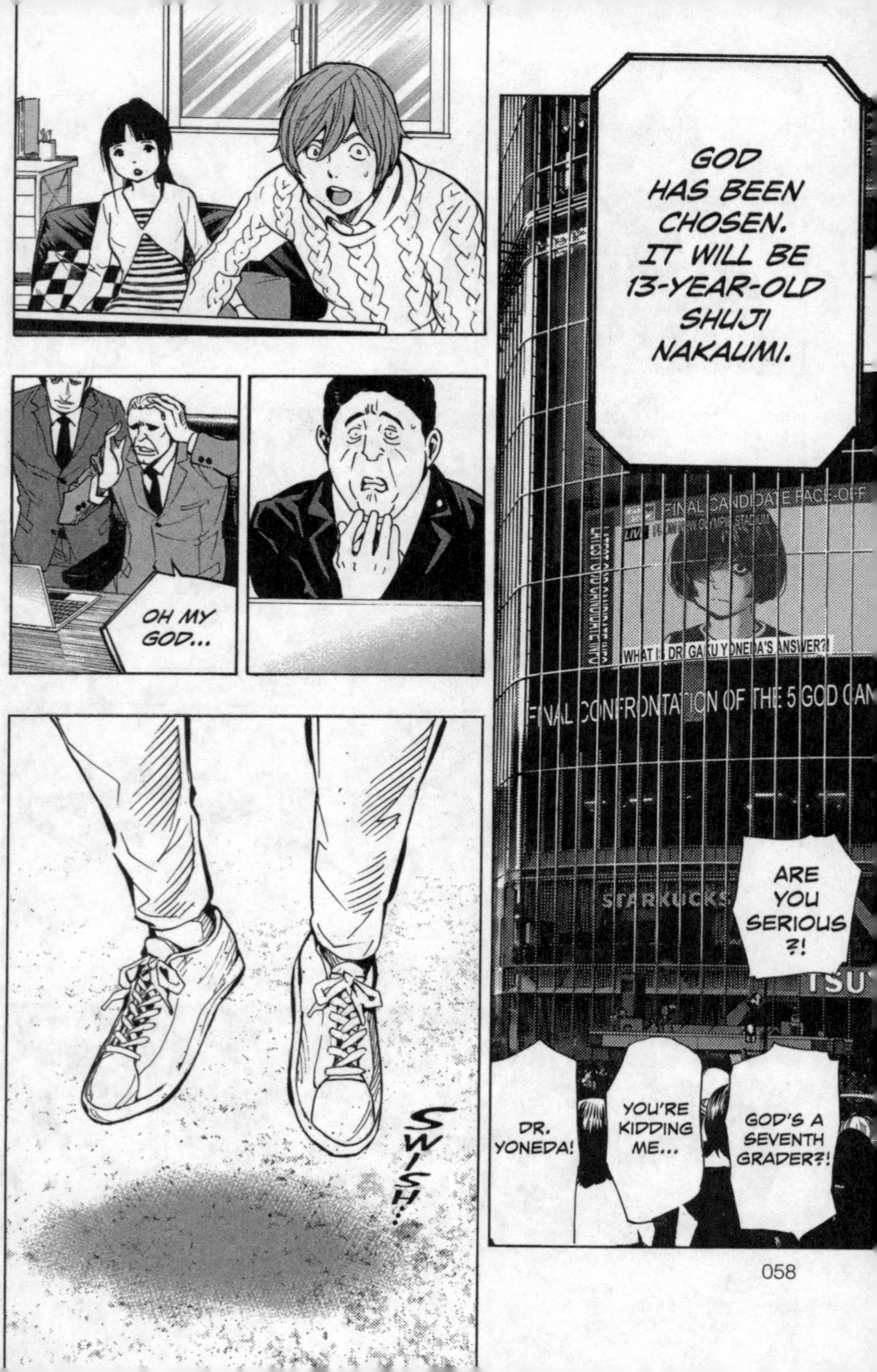
GOD HAS BEEN CHOSEN. IT WILL BE 13-YEAR-OLD SHUJI NAKAUMI.
FINAL CANDIDATE FACE-OFF
WHAT IS DR. GAKU YONEDA'S ANSWER?!
STARKUCKS
ARE YOU SERIOUS?!
GOD'S A SEVENTH GRADER?!
YOU'RE KIDDING ME...
DR. YONEDA!
OH MY GOD...
SWISH!!

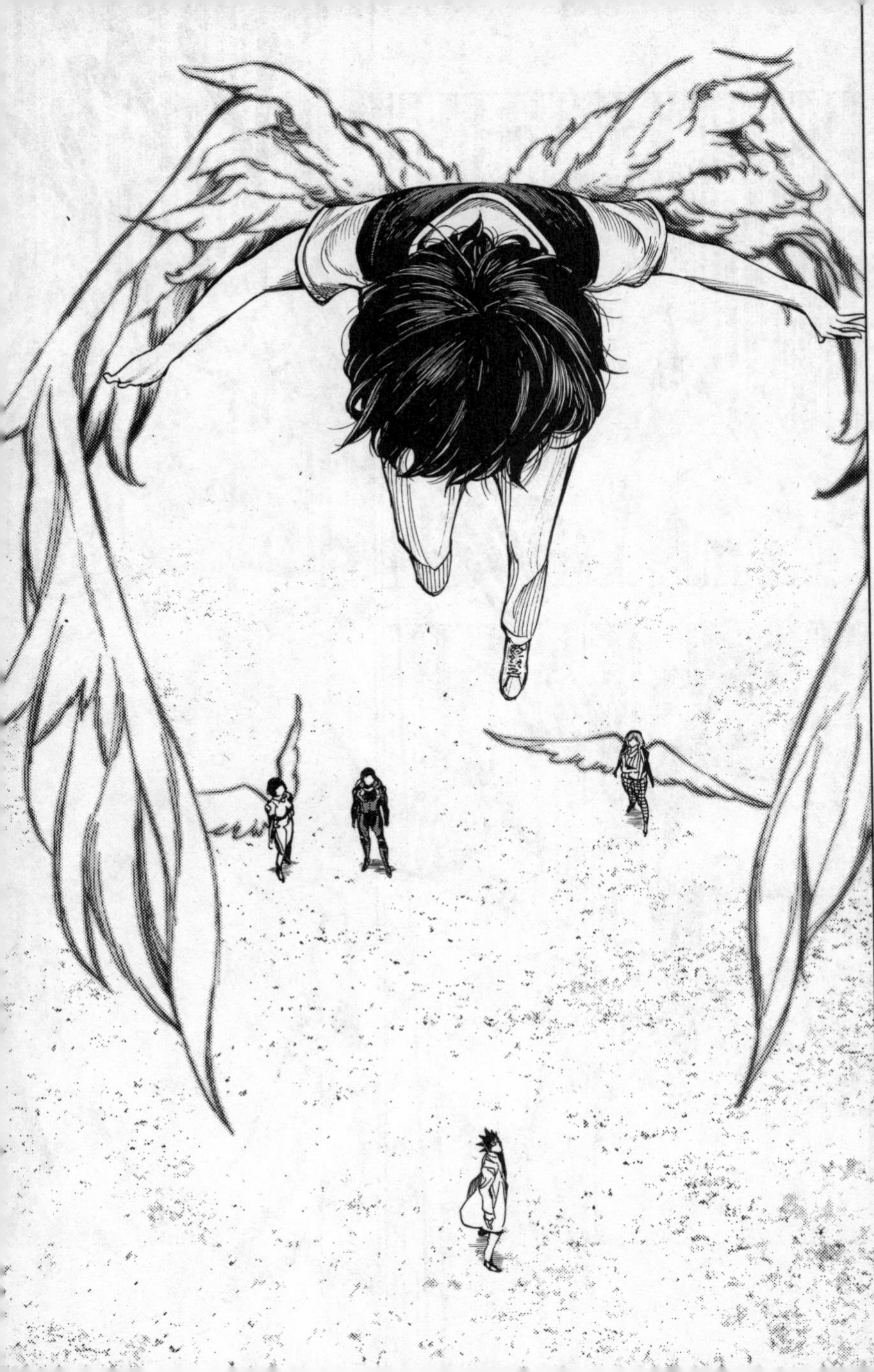

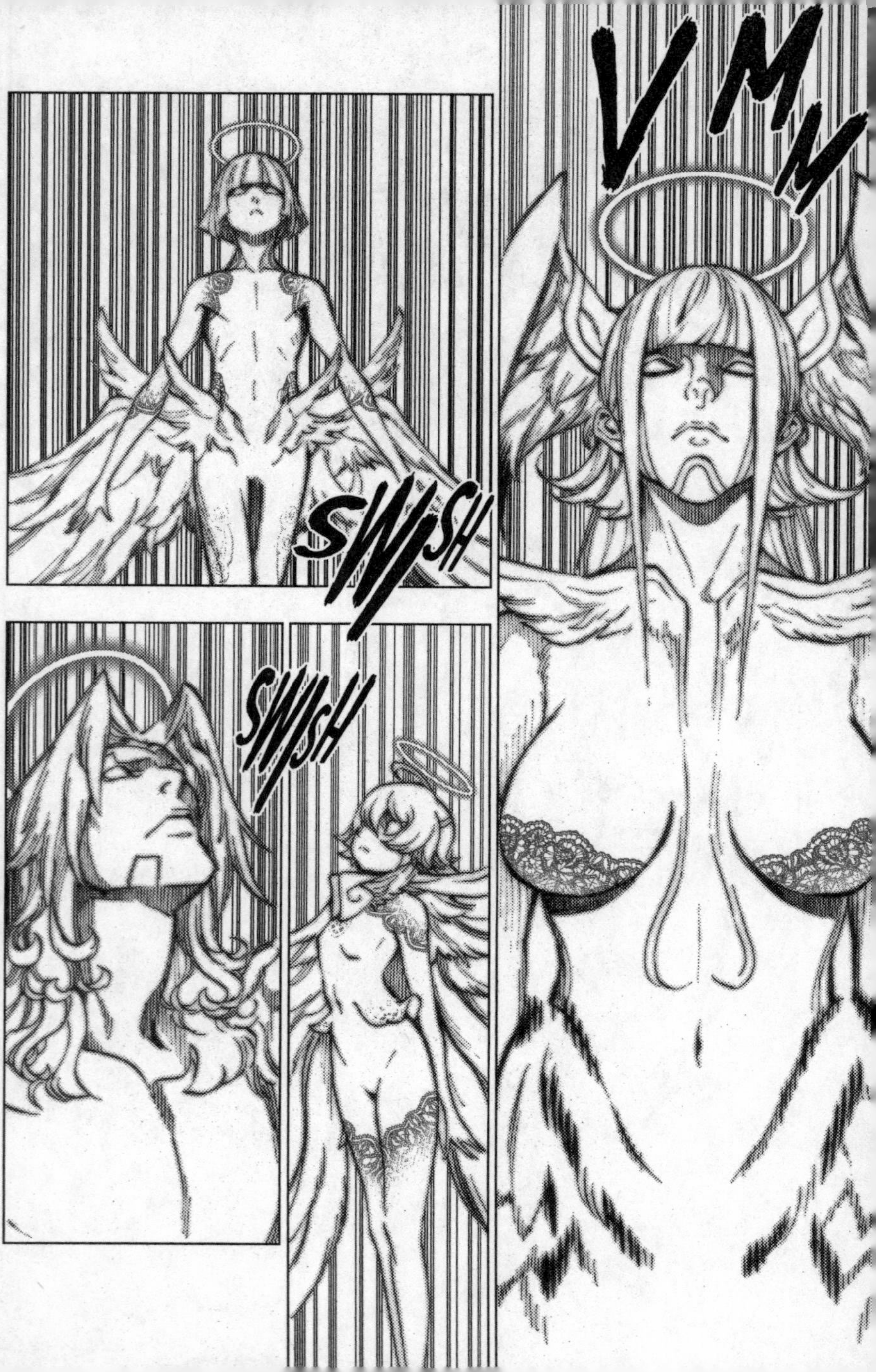
VMM
SWISH
SWISH

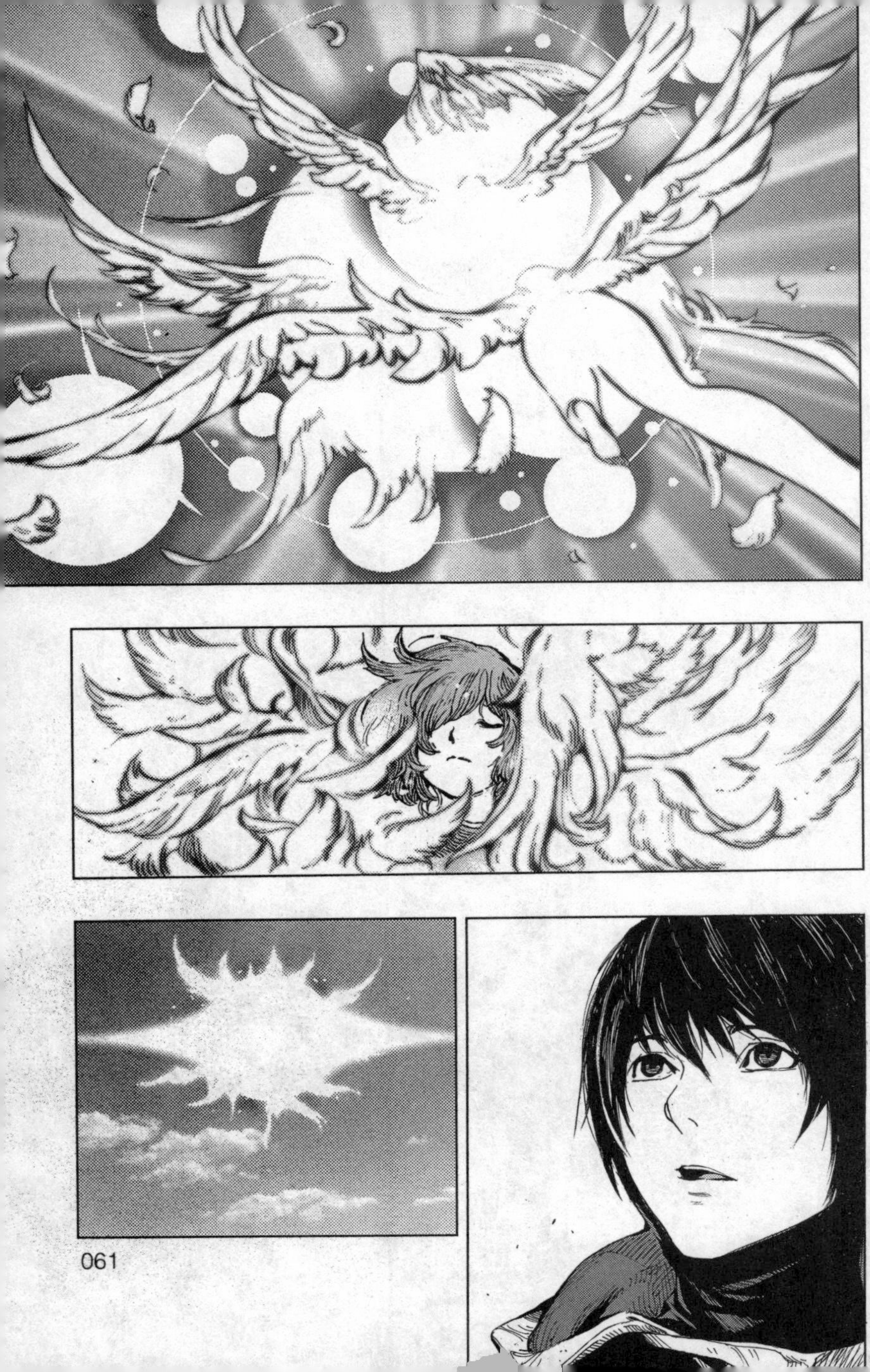

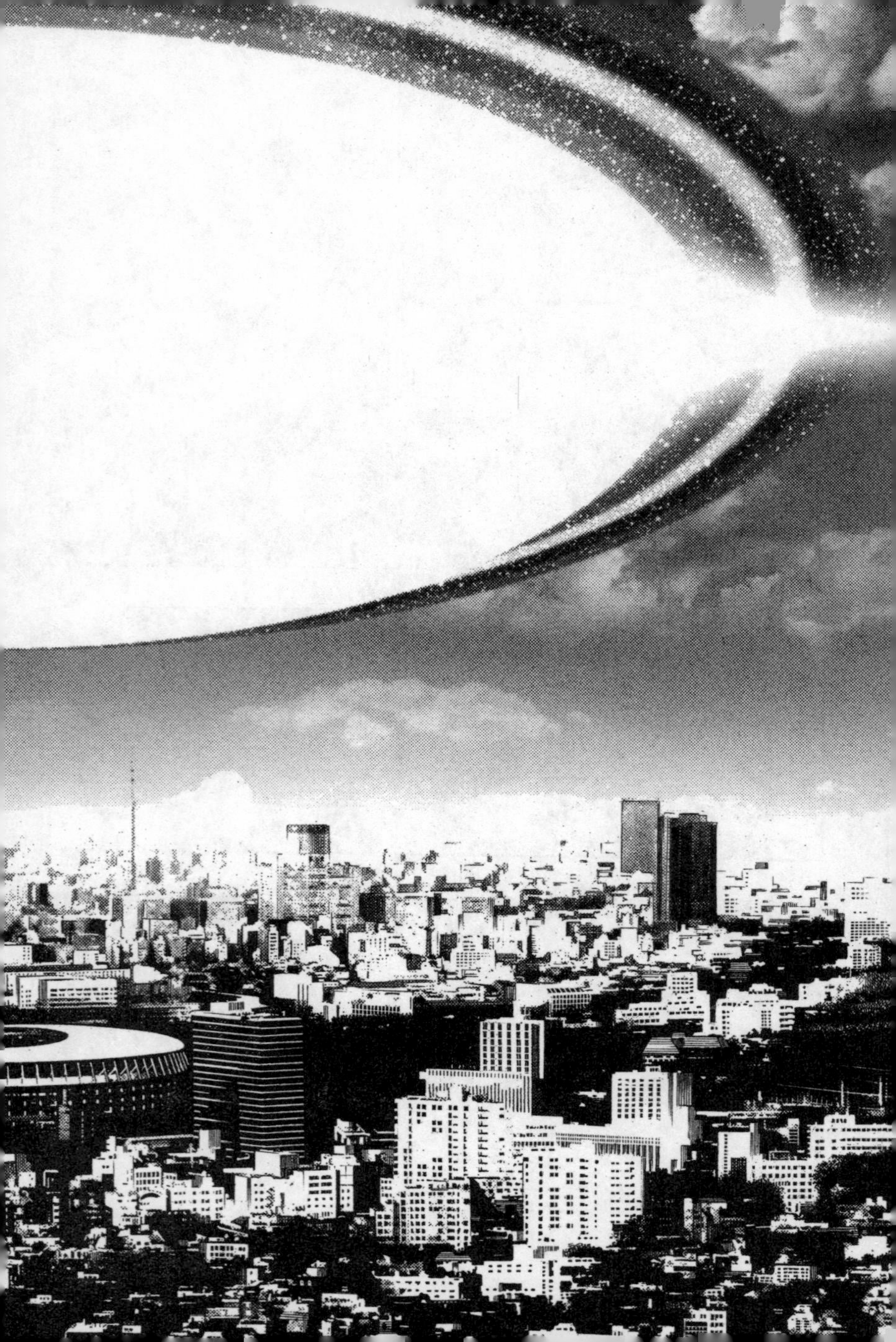

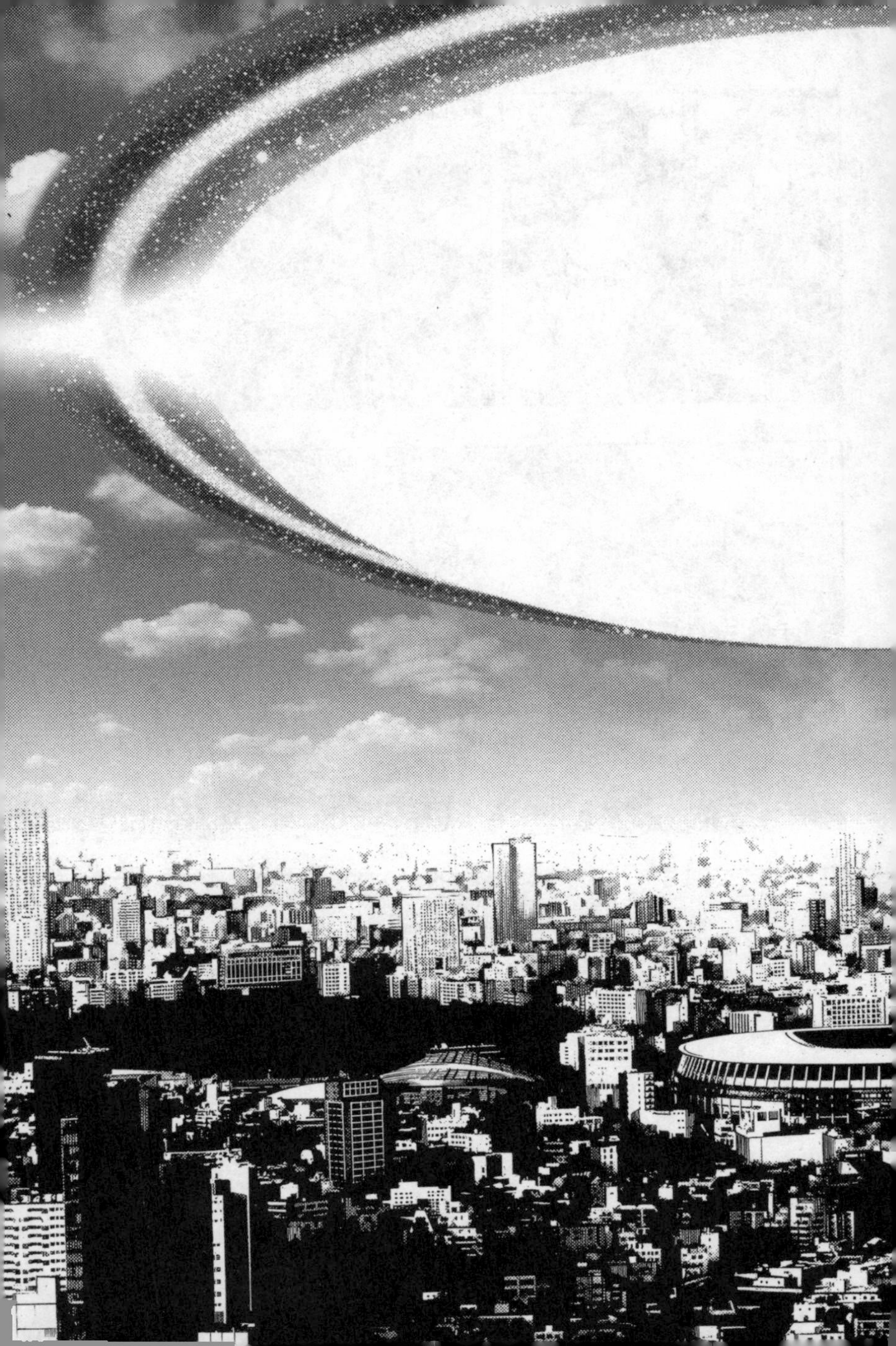

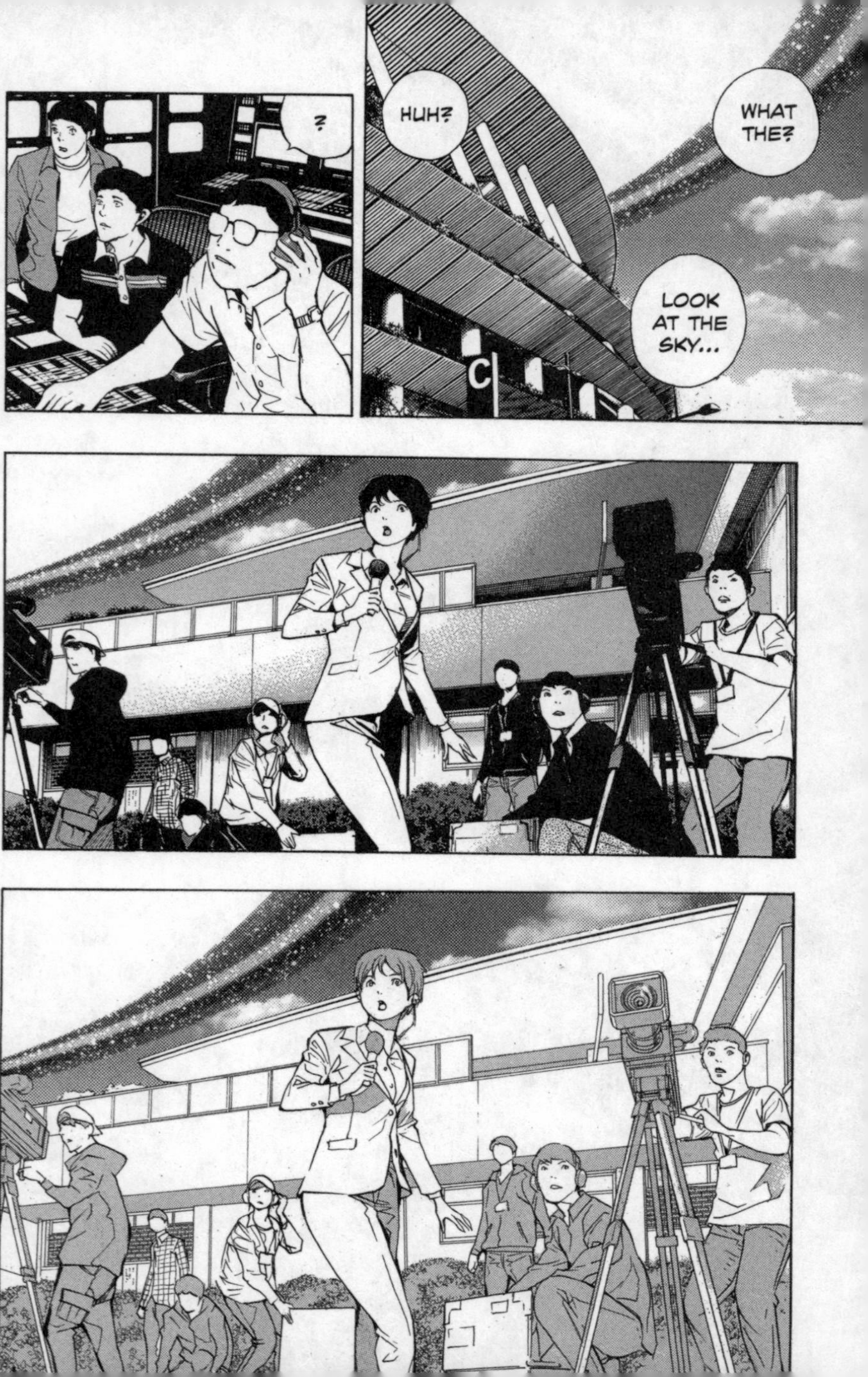
WHAT THE?
HUH?
LOOK AT THE SKY...
?

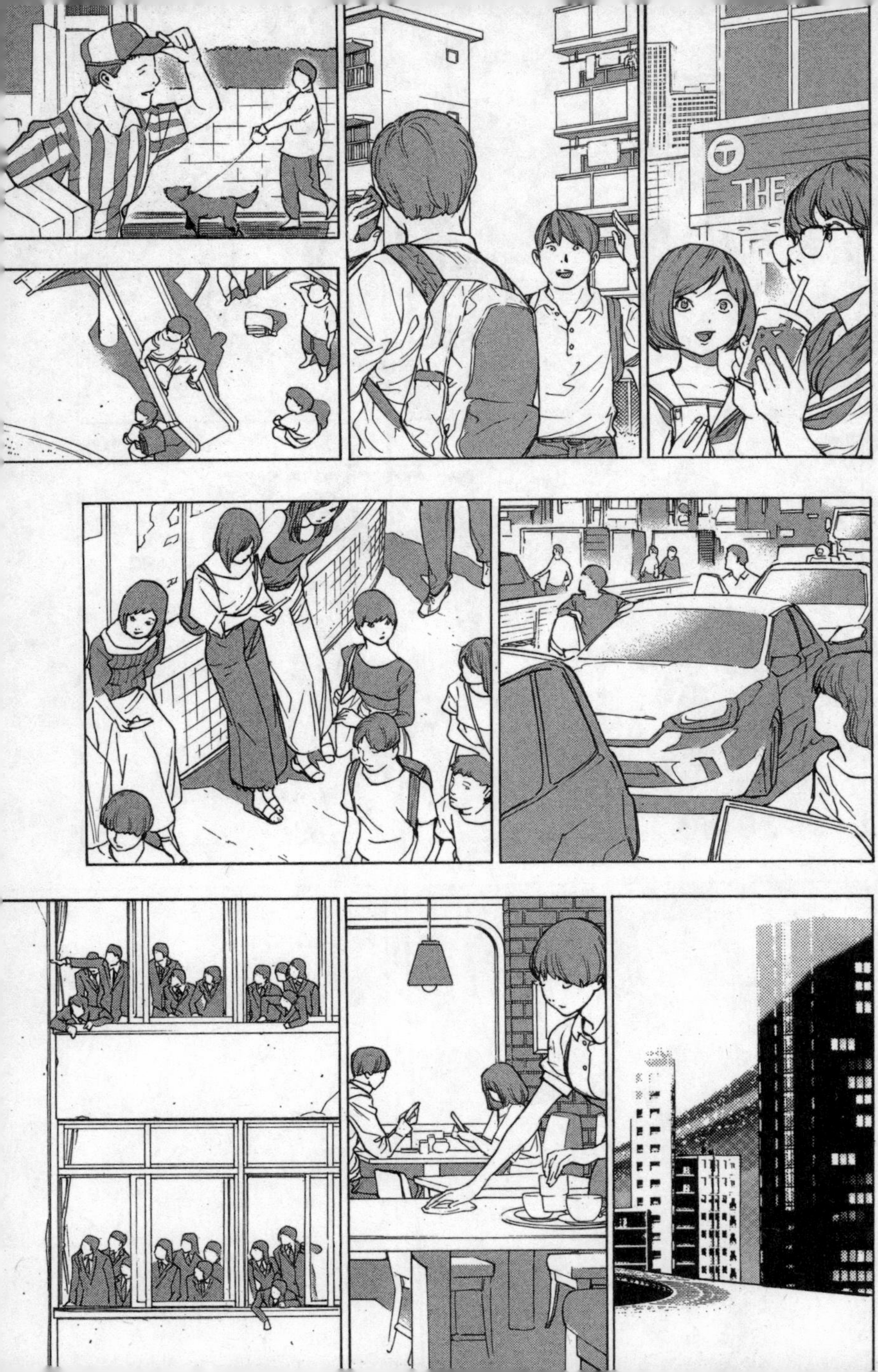
THE

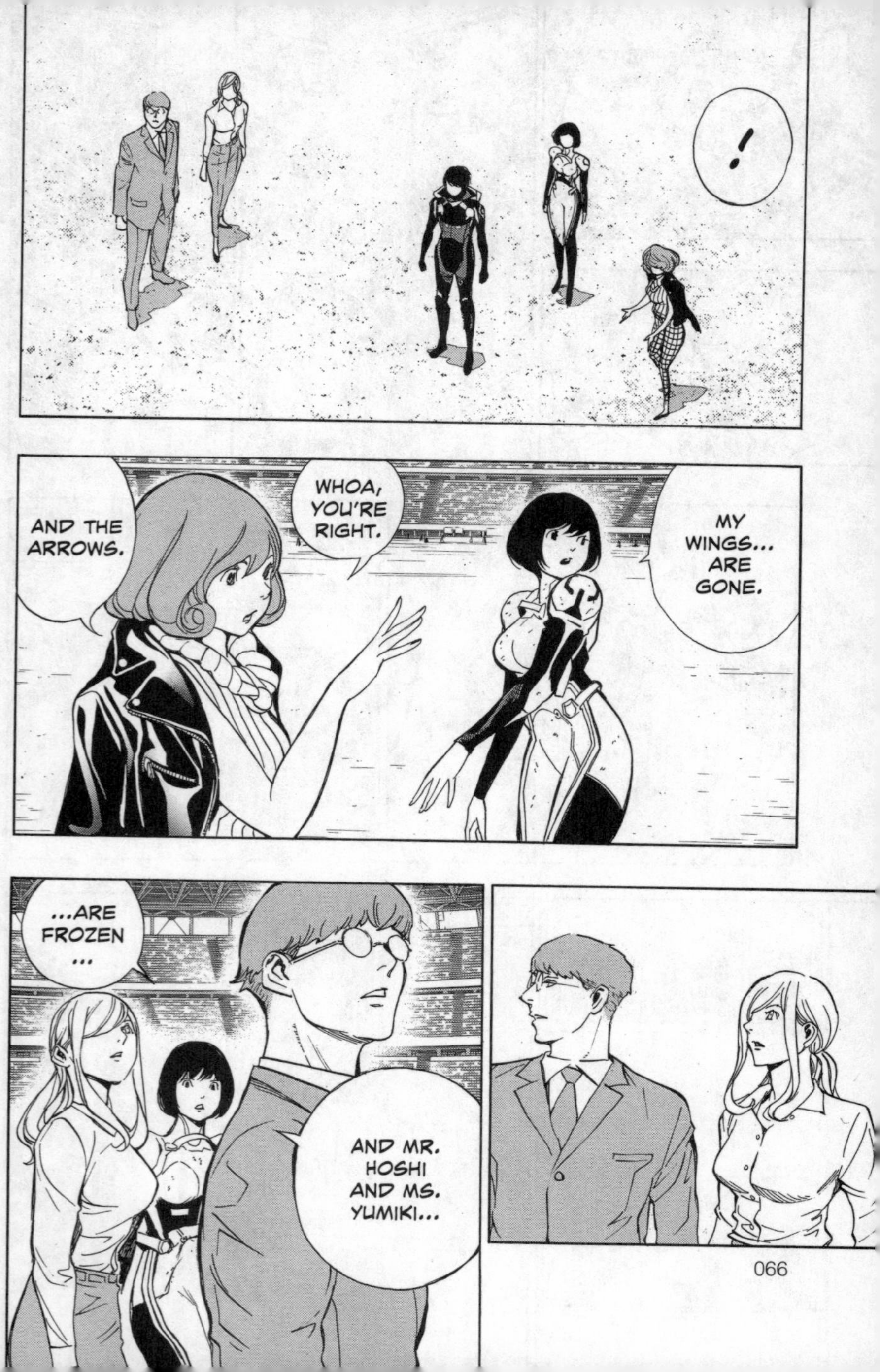
!
MY WINGS... ARE GONE.
WHOA, YOU'RE RIGHT.
AND THE ARROWS.
AND MR. HOSHI AND MS. YUMIKI...
...ARE FROZEN ...

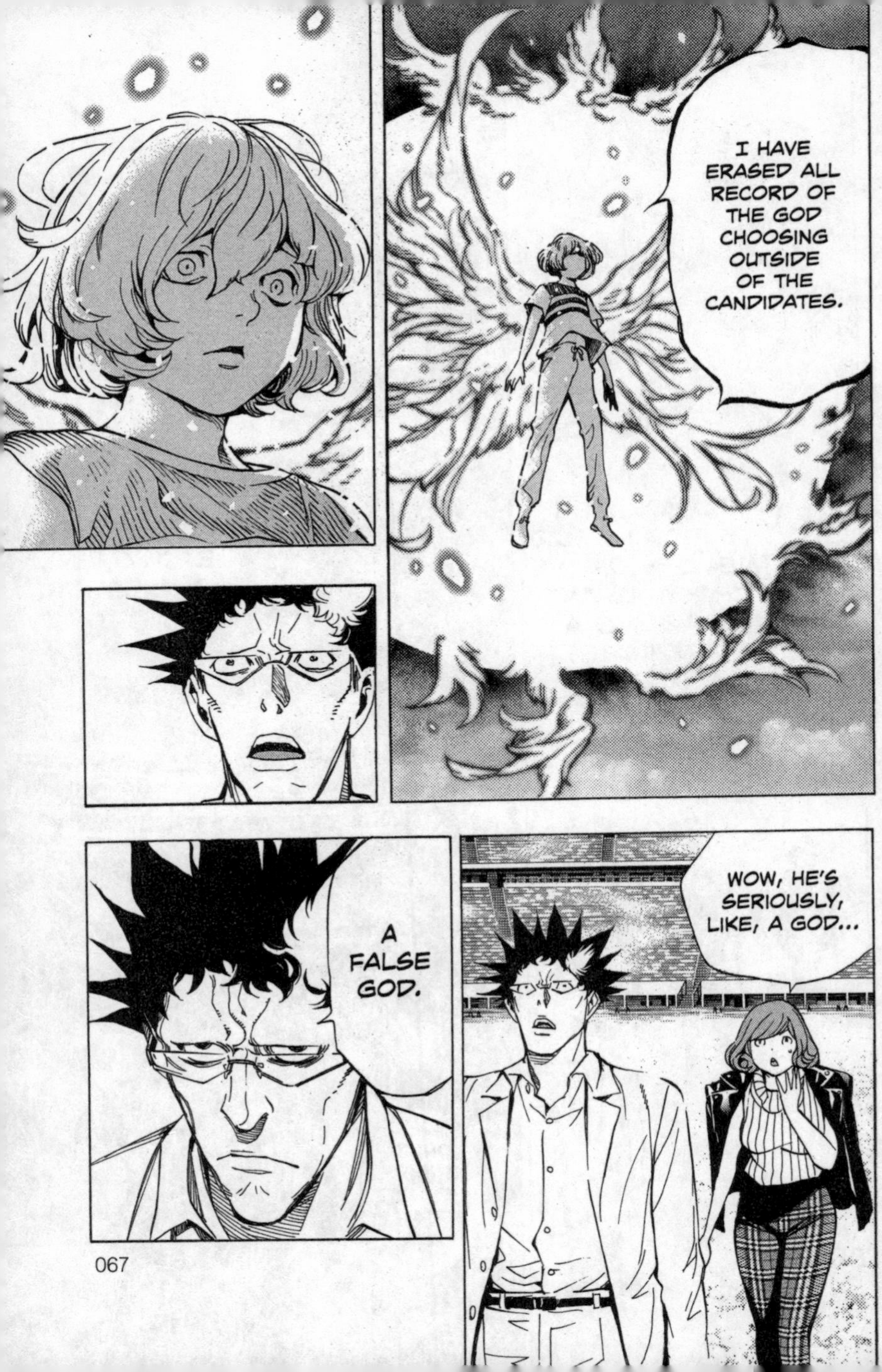
I HAVE ERASED ALL RECORD OF THE GOD CHOOSING OUTSIDE OF THE CANDIDATES.
WOW, HE'S SERIOUSLY, LIKE, A GOD...
A FALSE GOD.

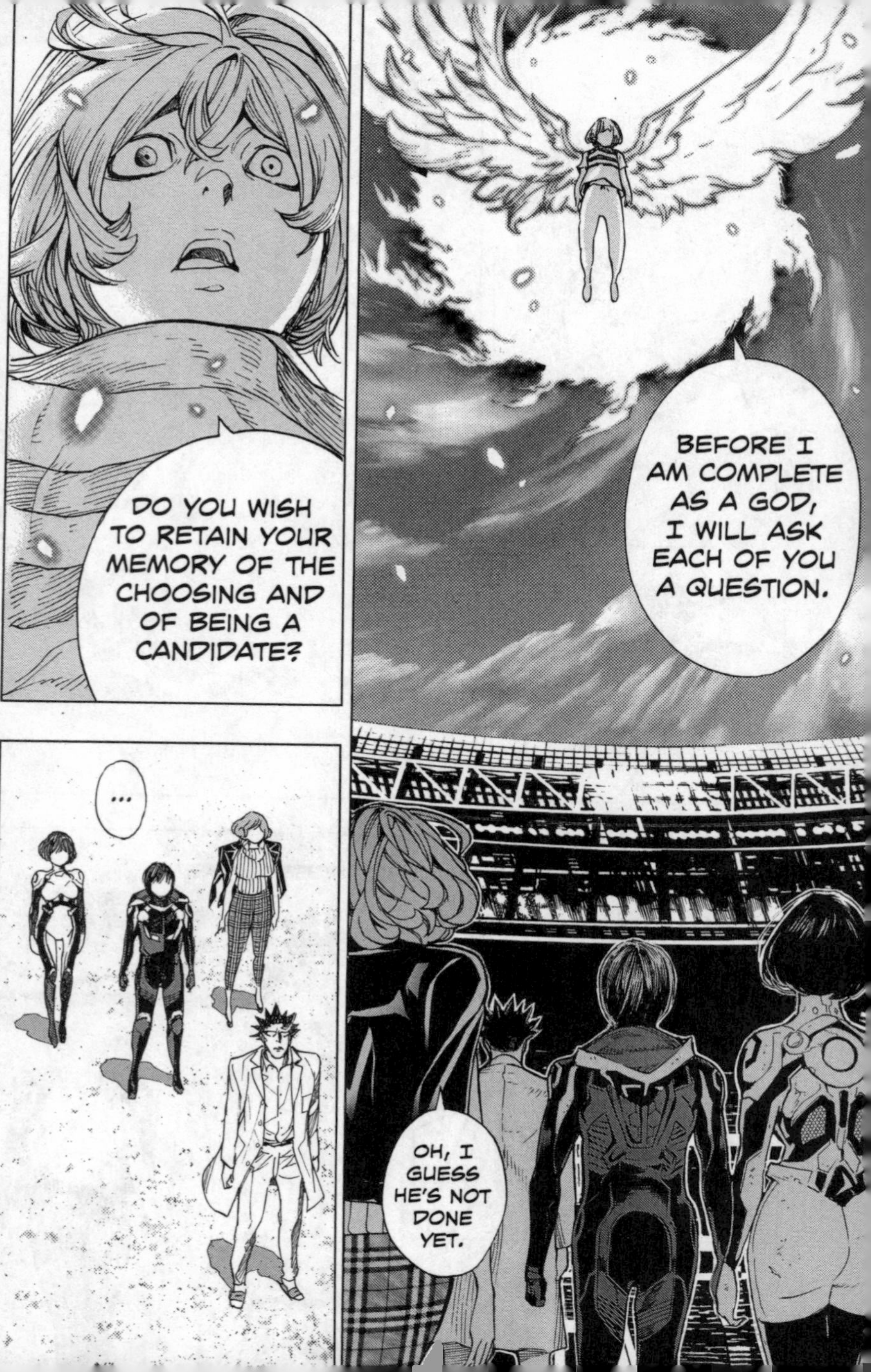
BEFORE I AM COMPLETE AS A GOD, I WILL ASK EACH OF YOU A QUESTION.
DO YOU WISH TO RETAIN YOUR MEMORY OF THE CHOOSING AND OF BEING A CANDIDATE?
OH, I GUESS HE'S NOT DONE YET.
...

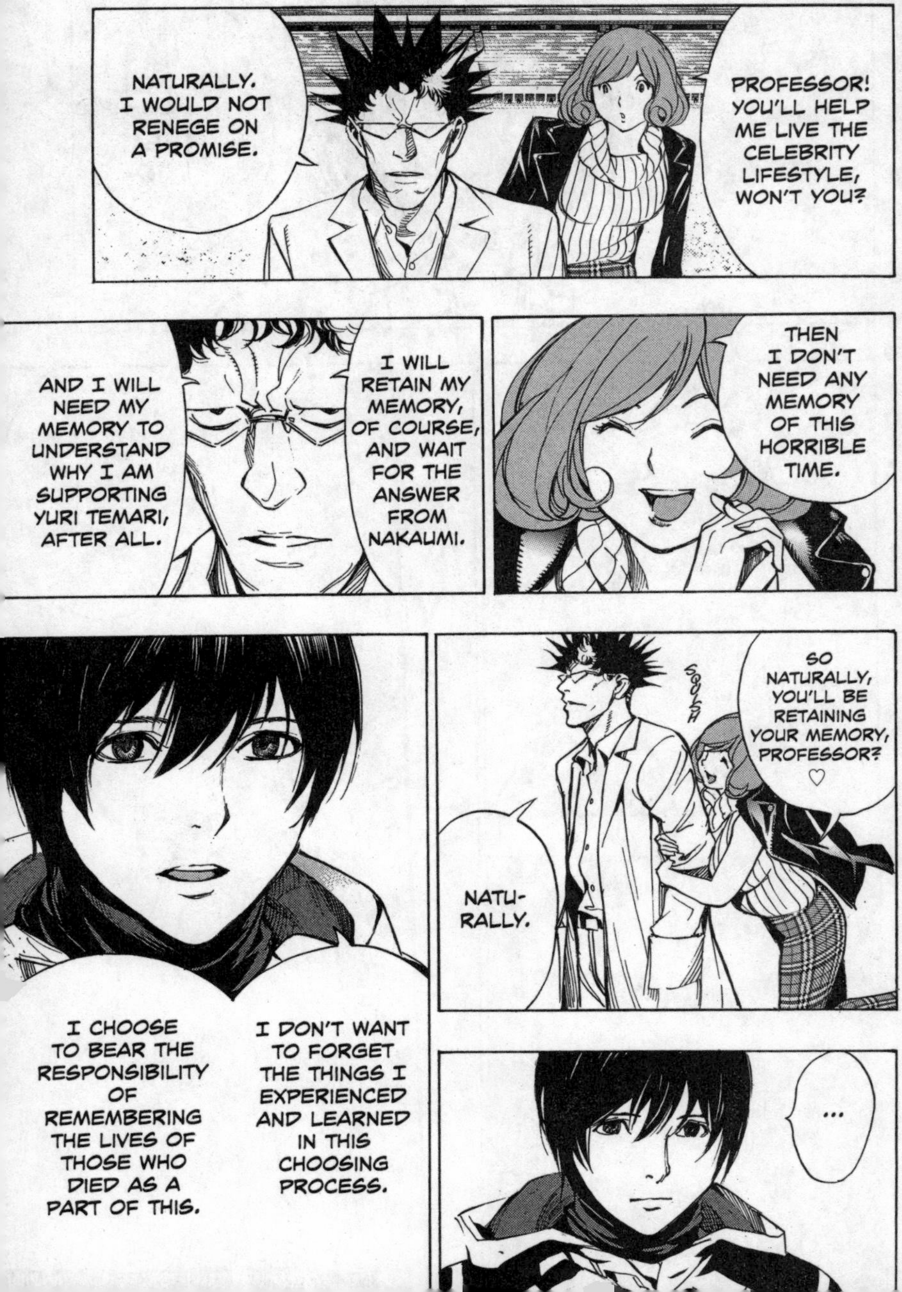
PROFESSOR! YOU'LL HELP ME LIVE THE CELEBRITY LIFESTYLE, WON'T YOU?
NATURALLY. I WOULD NOT RENEGE ON A PROMISE.
THEN I DON'T NEED ANY MEMORY OF THIS HORRIBLE TIME.
I WILL RETAIN MY MEMORY, OF COURSE, AND WAIT FOR THE ANSWER FROM NAKAUMI.
AND I WILL NEED MY MEMORY TO UNDERSTAND WHY I AM SUPPORTING YURI TEMARI, AFTER ALL.
SO NATURALLY, YOU'LL BE RETAINING YOUR MEMORY, PROFESSOR? ♡
SQUISH
NATU-RALLY.
...
I DON'T WANT TO FORGET THE THINGS I EXPERIENCED AND LEARNED IN THIS CHOOSING PROCESS.
I CHOOSE TO BEAR THE RESPONSIBILITY OF REMEMBERING THE LIVES OF THOSE WHO DIED AS A PART OF THIS.

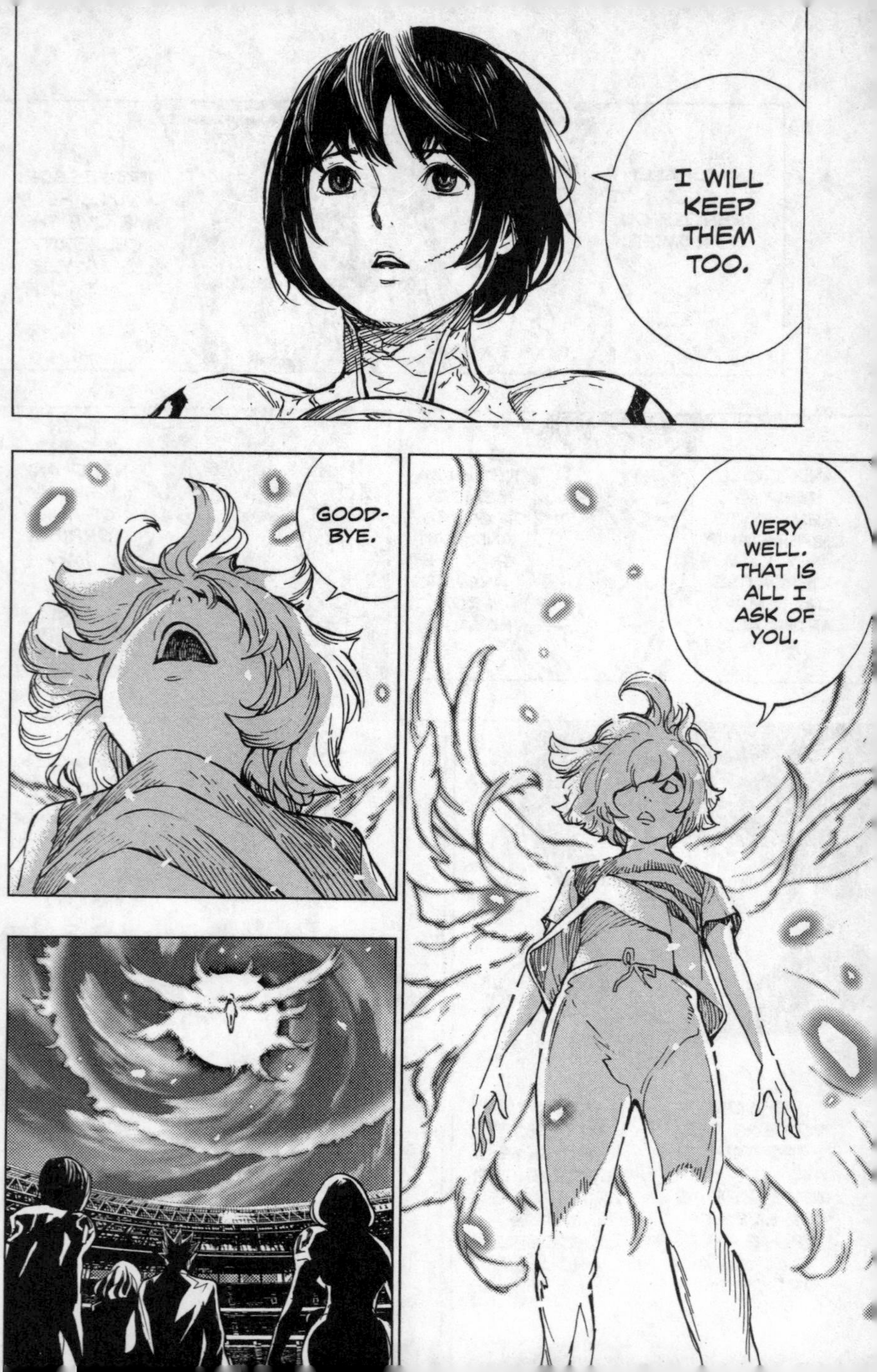
I WILL KEEP THEM TOO.
VERY WELL. THAT IS ALL I ASK OF YOU.
GOOD-BYE.

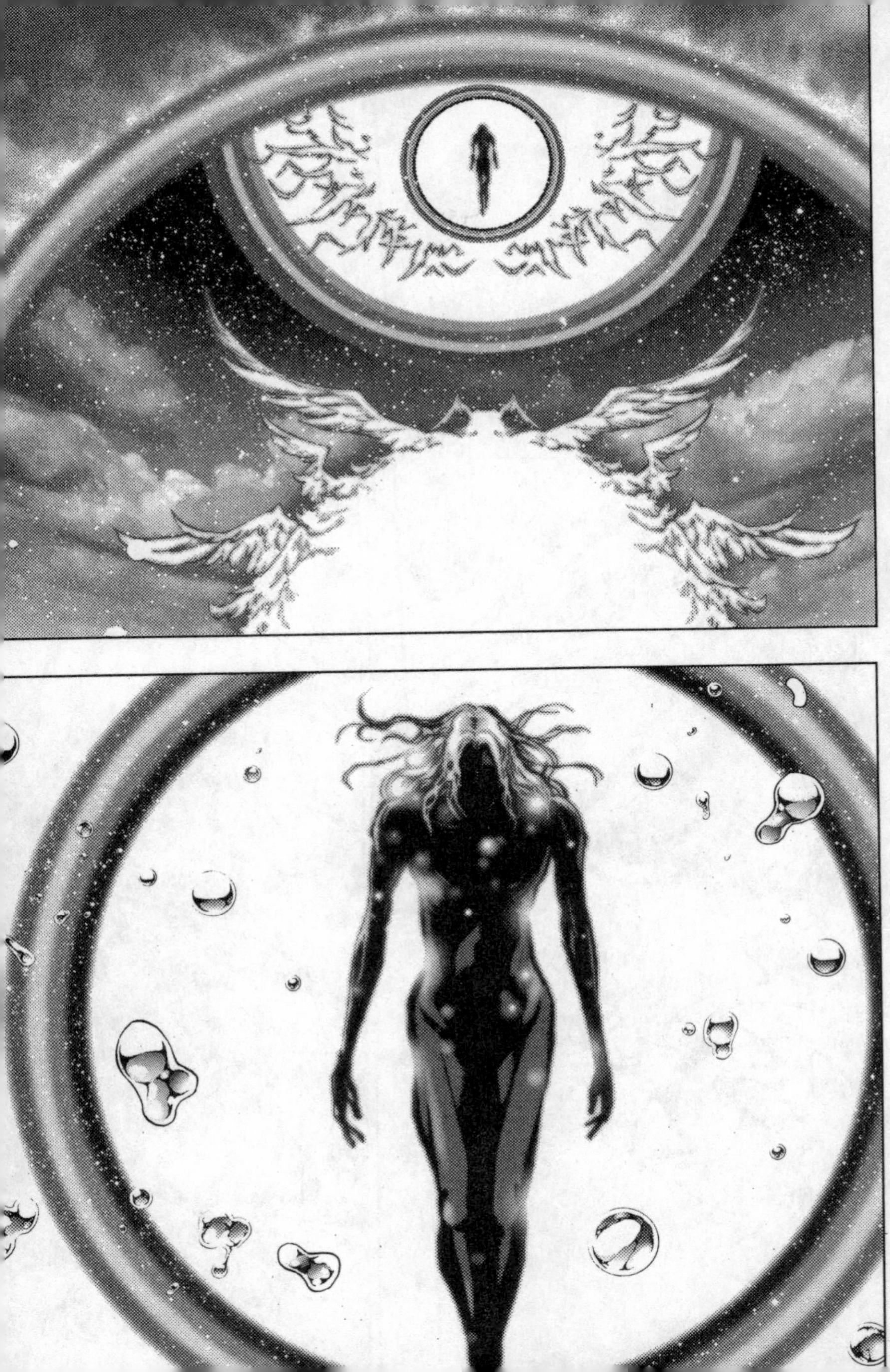

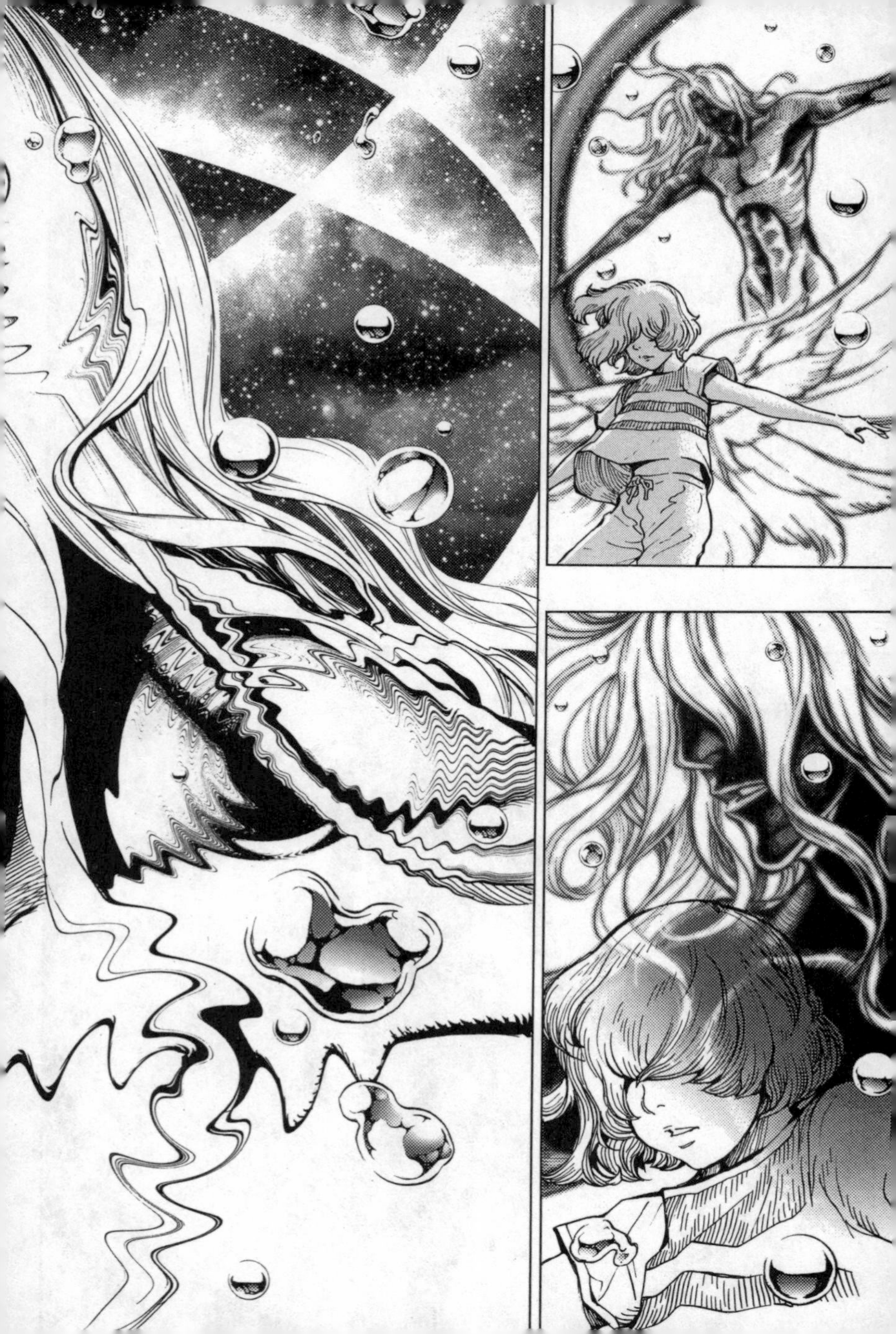

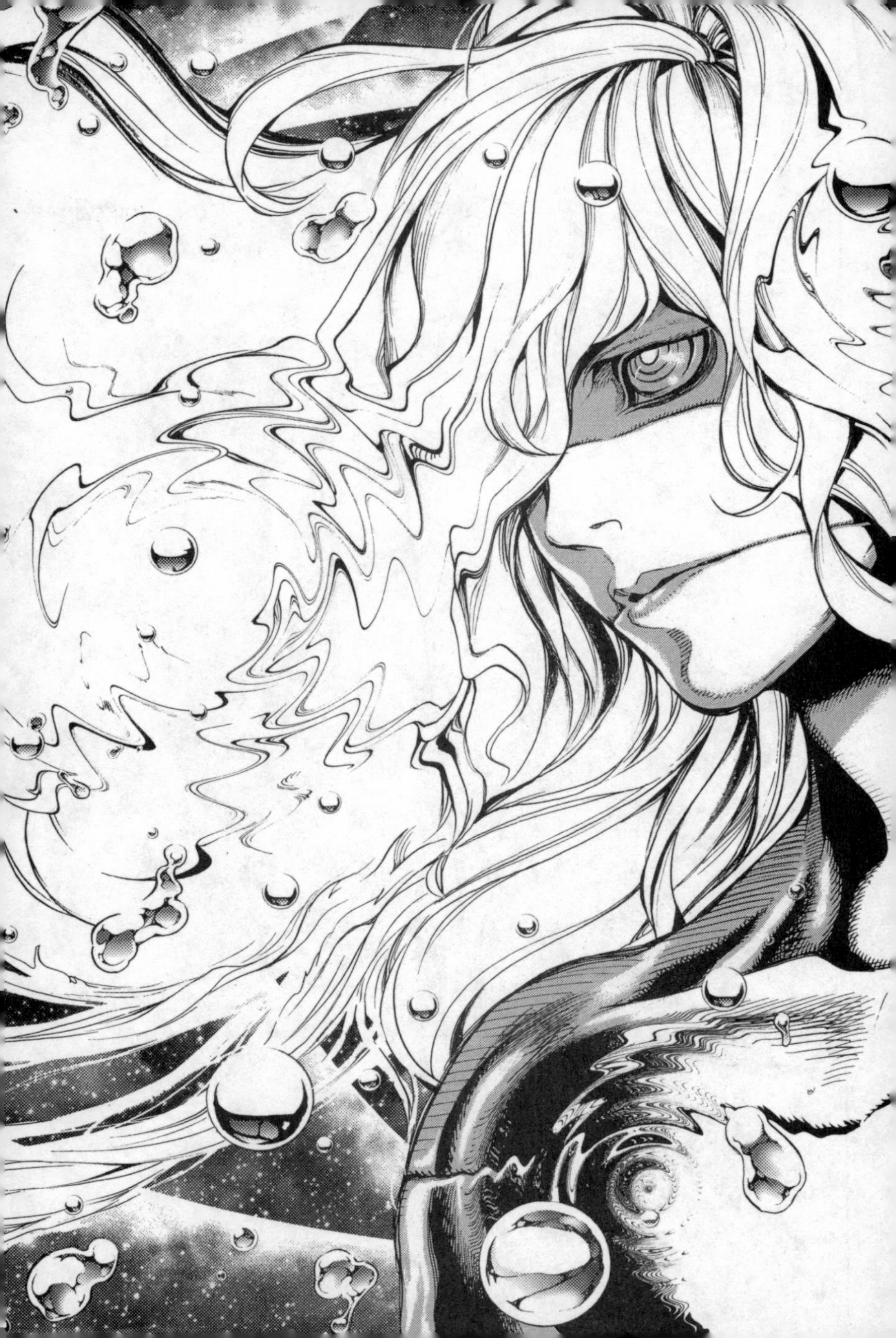

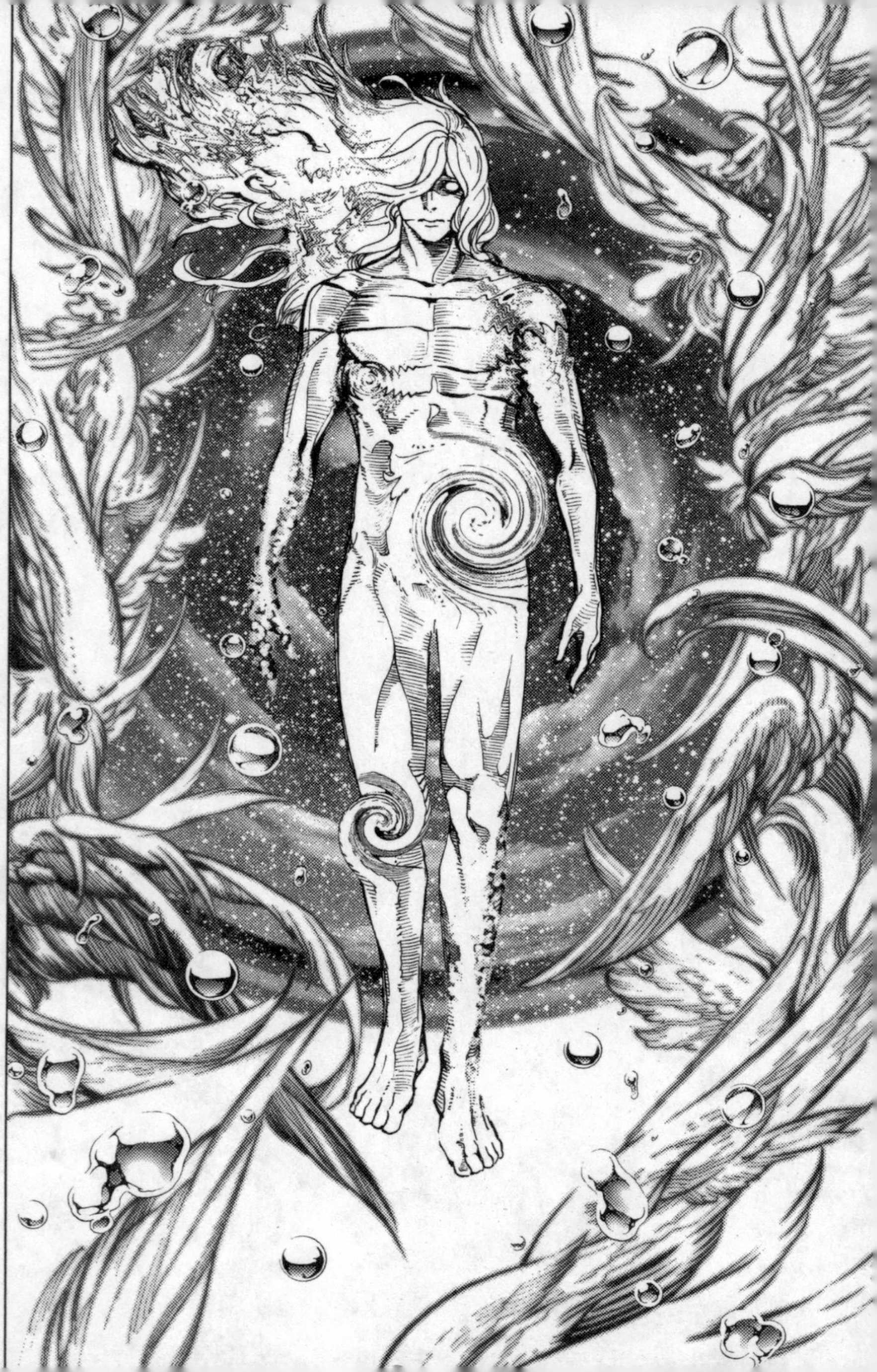

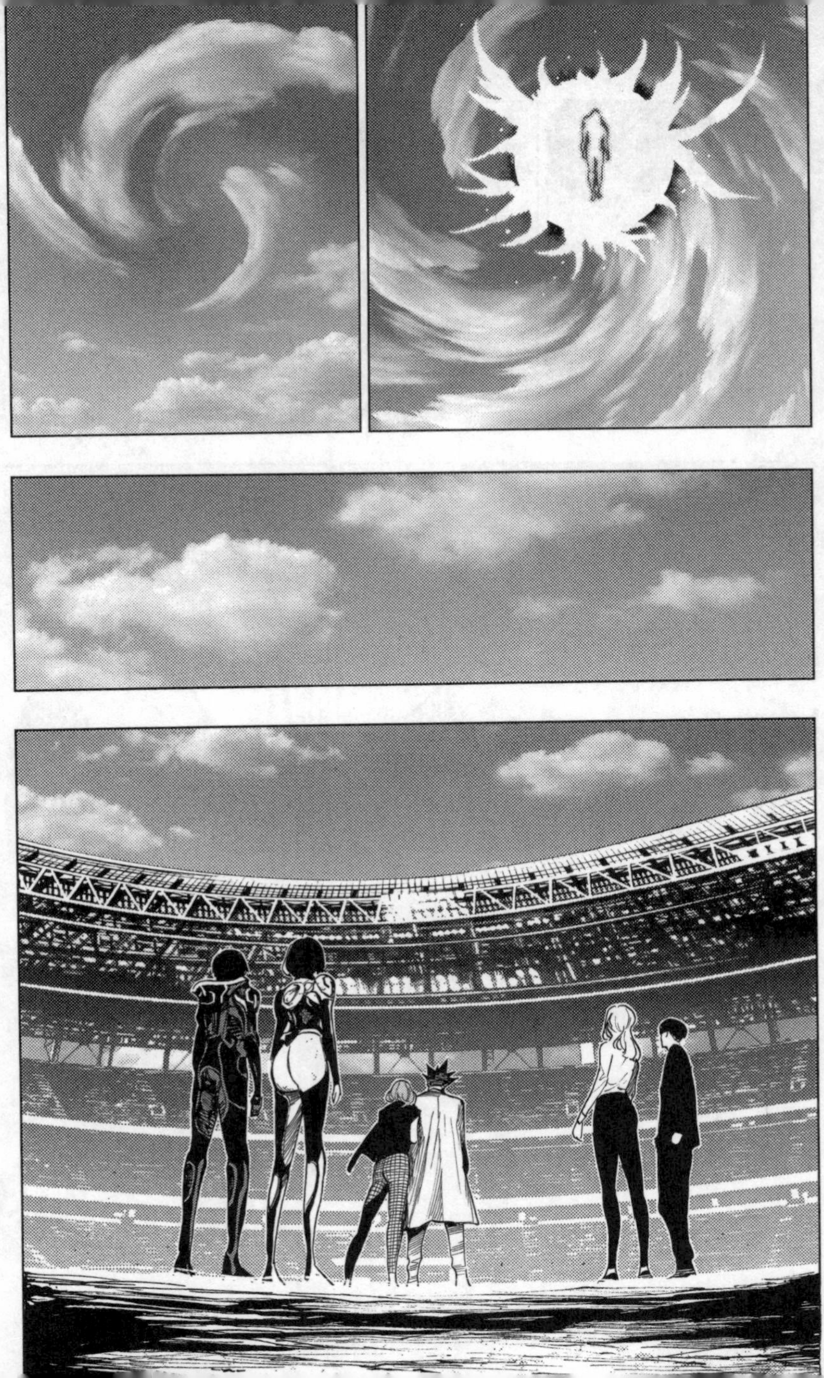

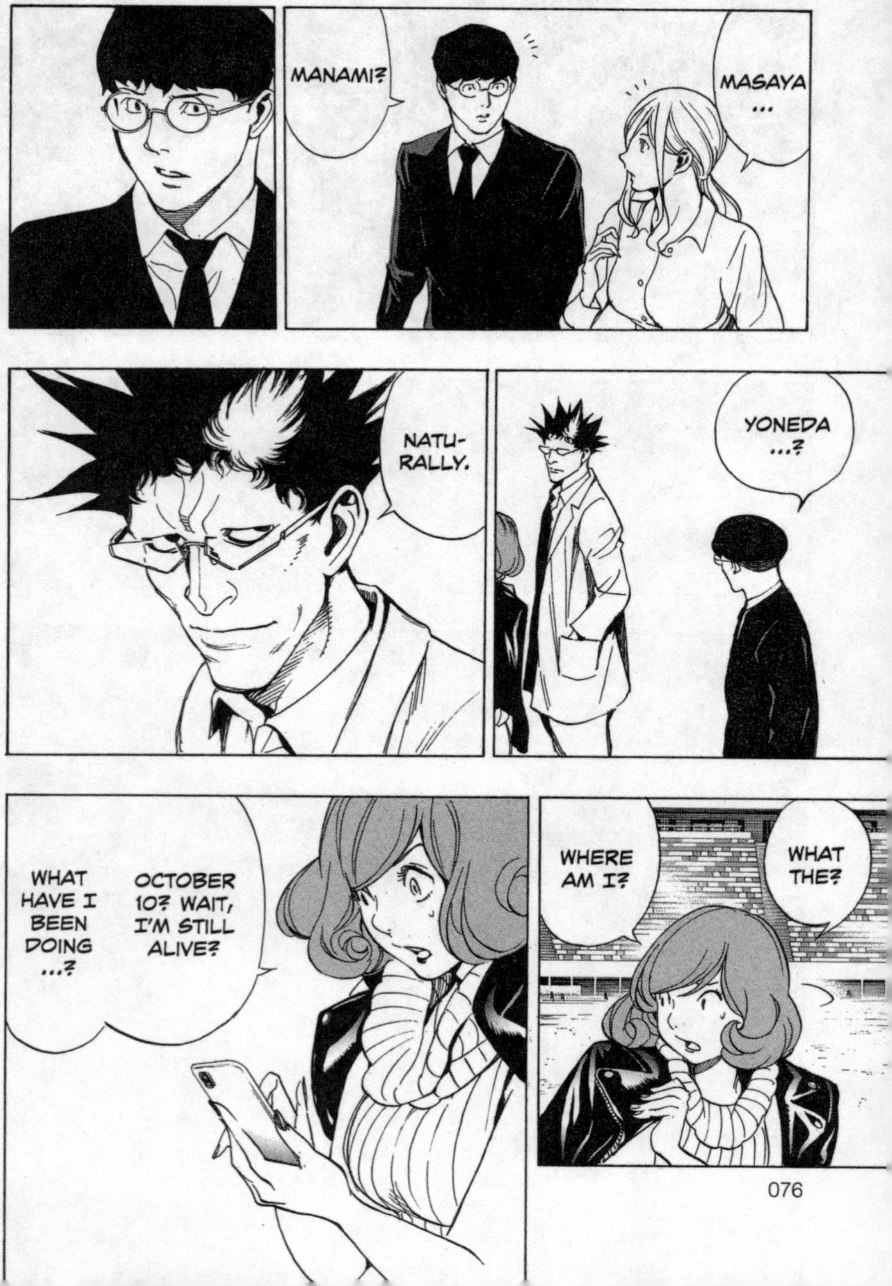
MASAYA ...
MANAMI?
YONEDA ...?
NATU-RALLY.
WHAT THE?
WHERE AM I?
OCTOBER 10? WAIT, I'M STILL ALIVE?
WHAT HAVE I BEEN DOING ...?

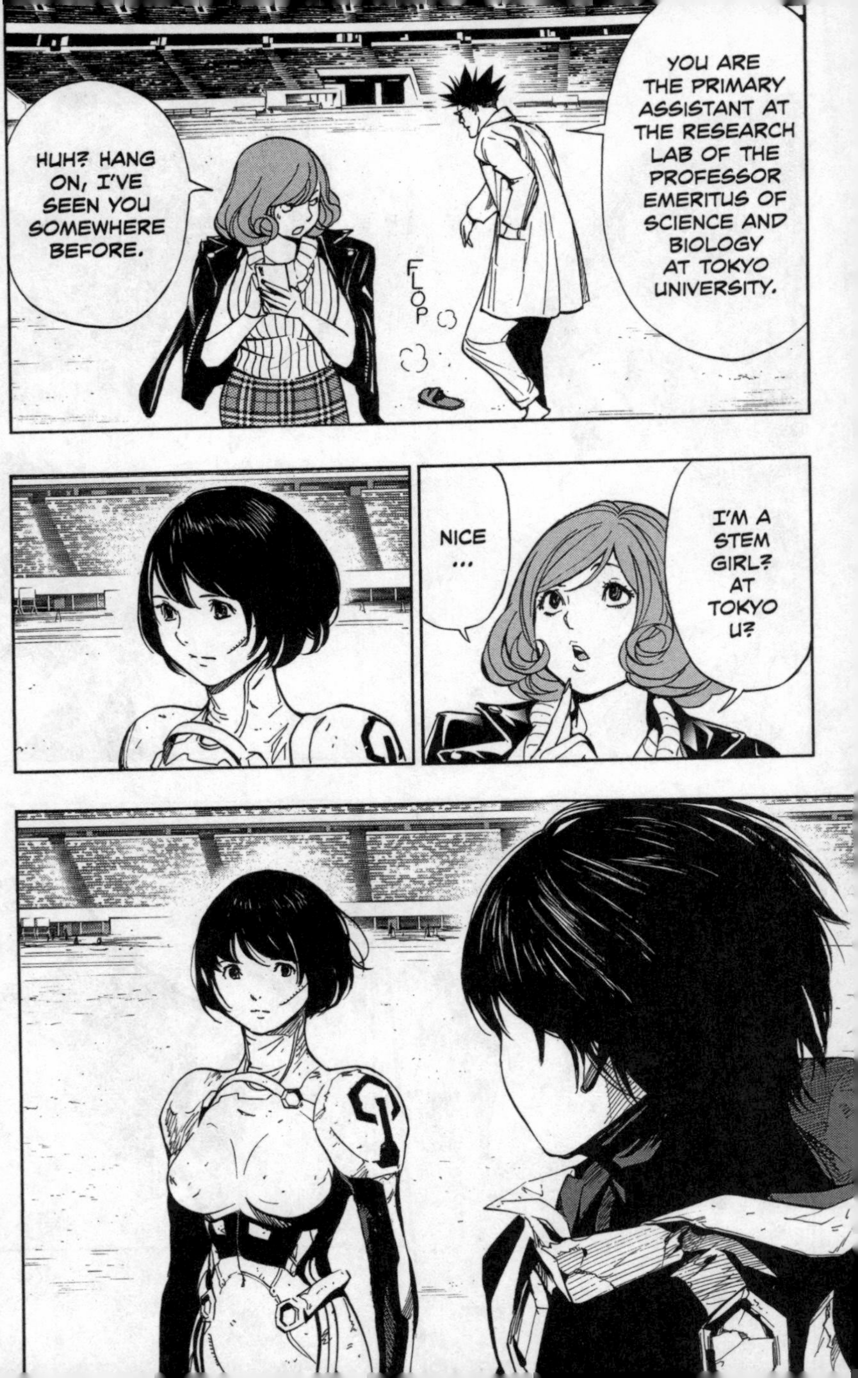
YOU ARE THE PRIMARY ASSISTANT AT THE RESEARCH LAB OF THE PROFESSOR EMERITUS OF SCIENCE AND BIOLOGY AT TOKYO UNIVERSITY.
HUH? HANG ON, I'VE SEEN YOU SOMEWHERE BEFORE.
FLOP
I'M A STEM GIRL? AT TOKYO U?
NICE ...

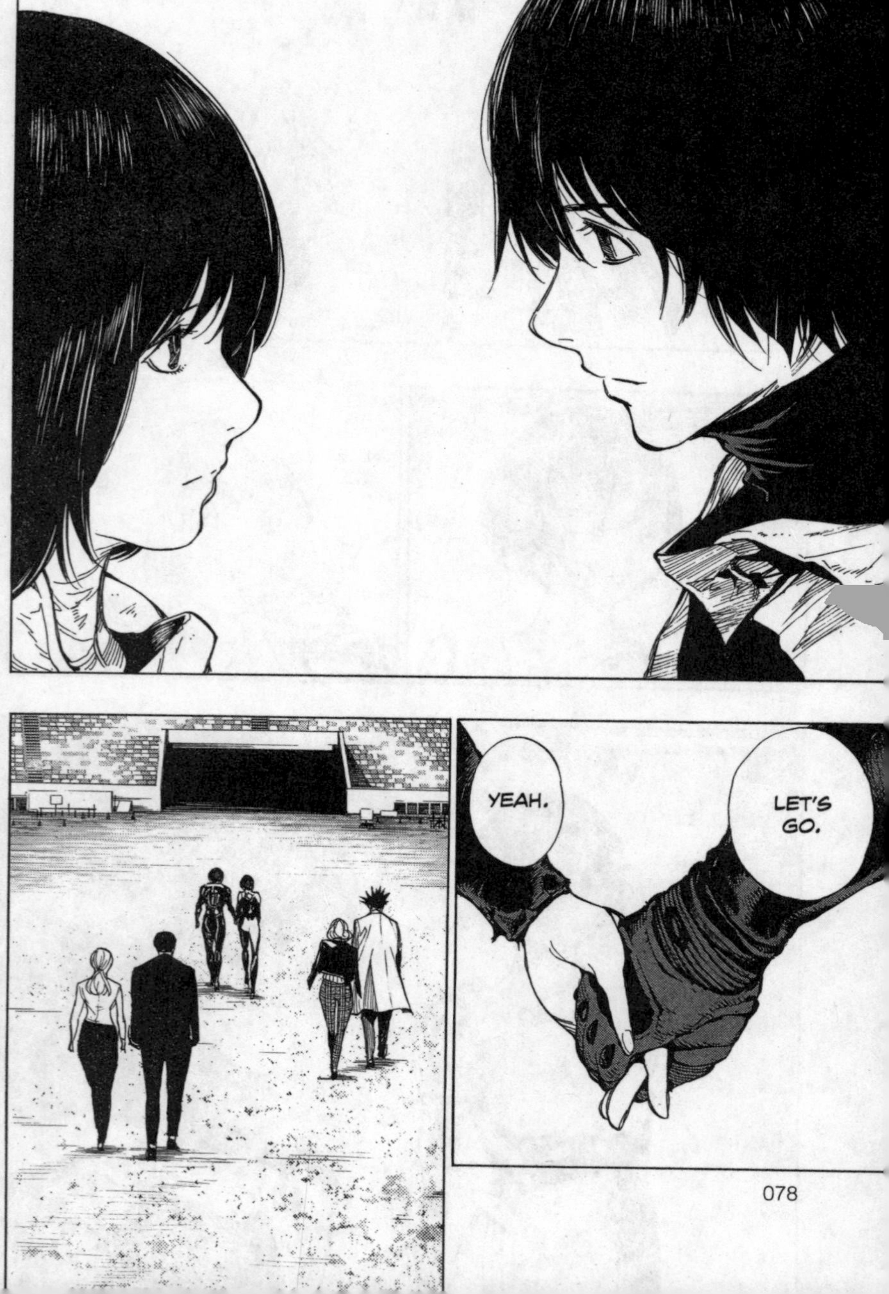
LET'S GO.
YEAH.

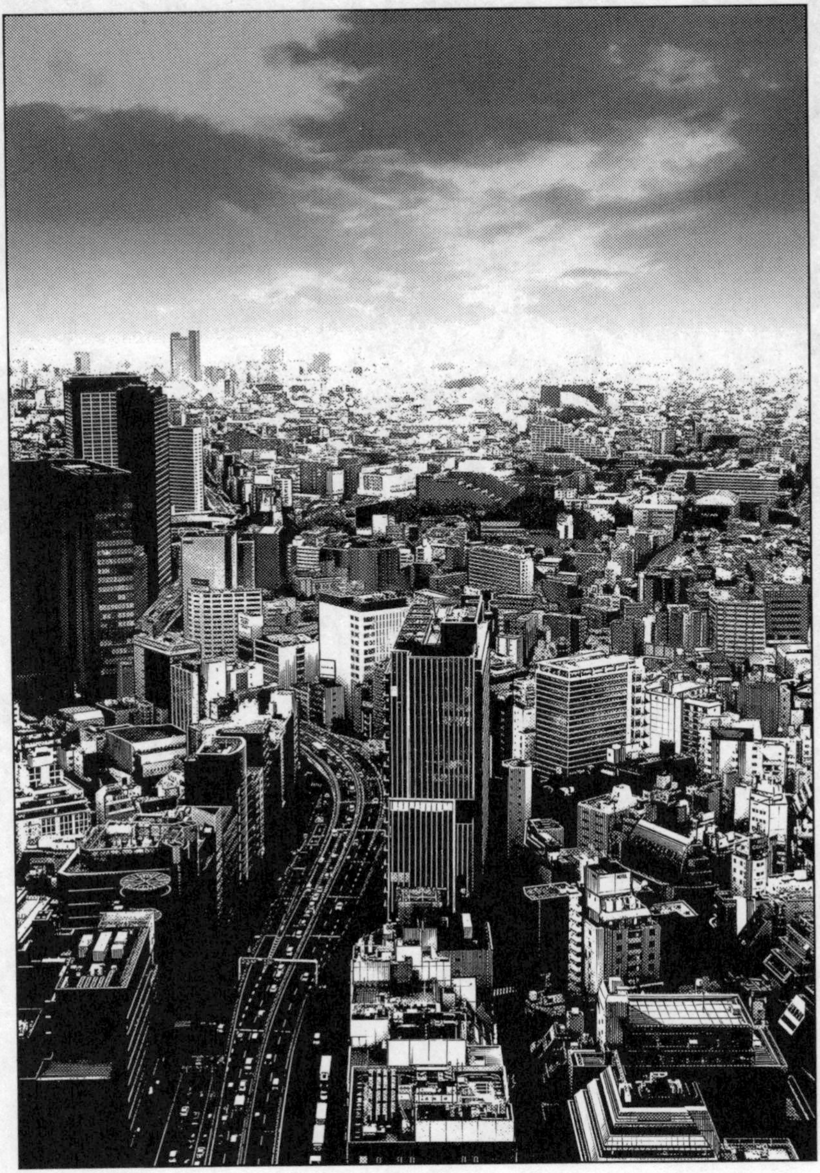

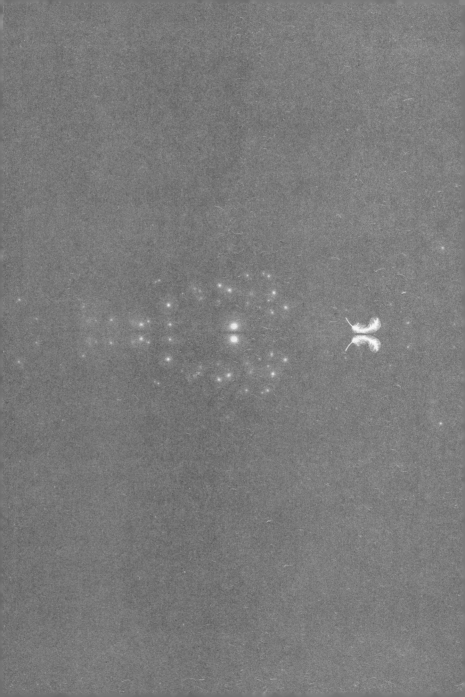

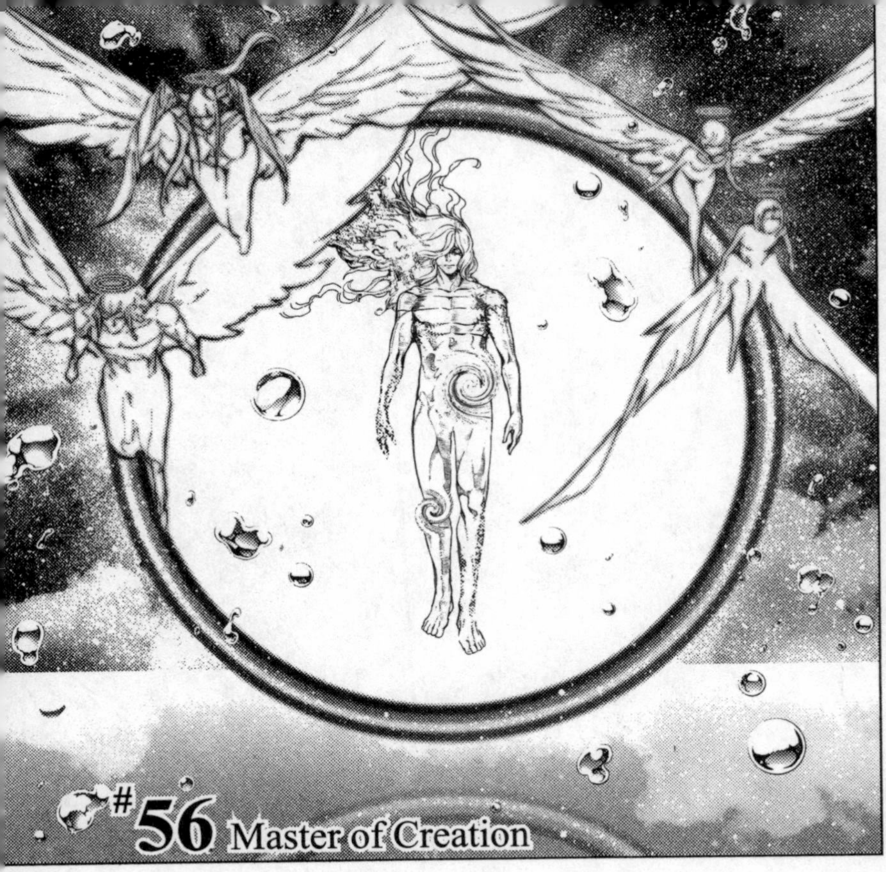
#56 Master of Creation
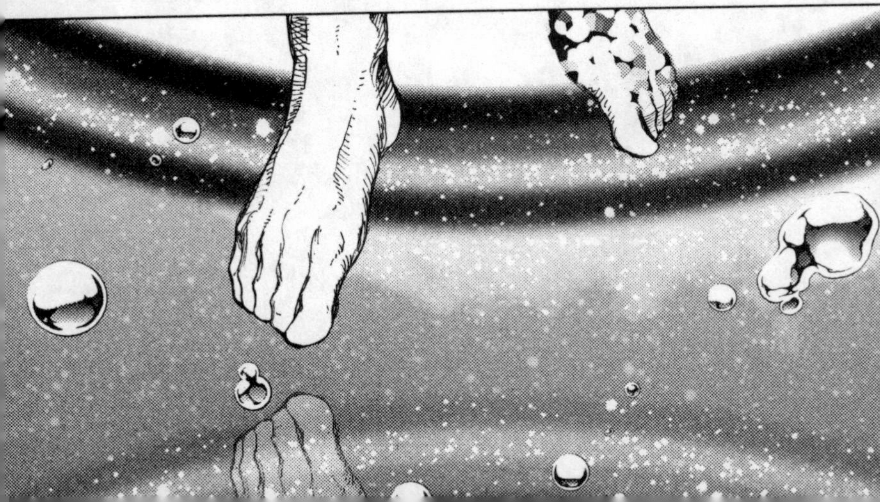

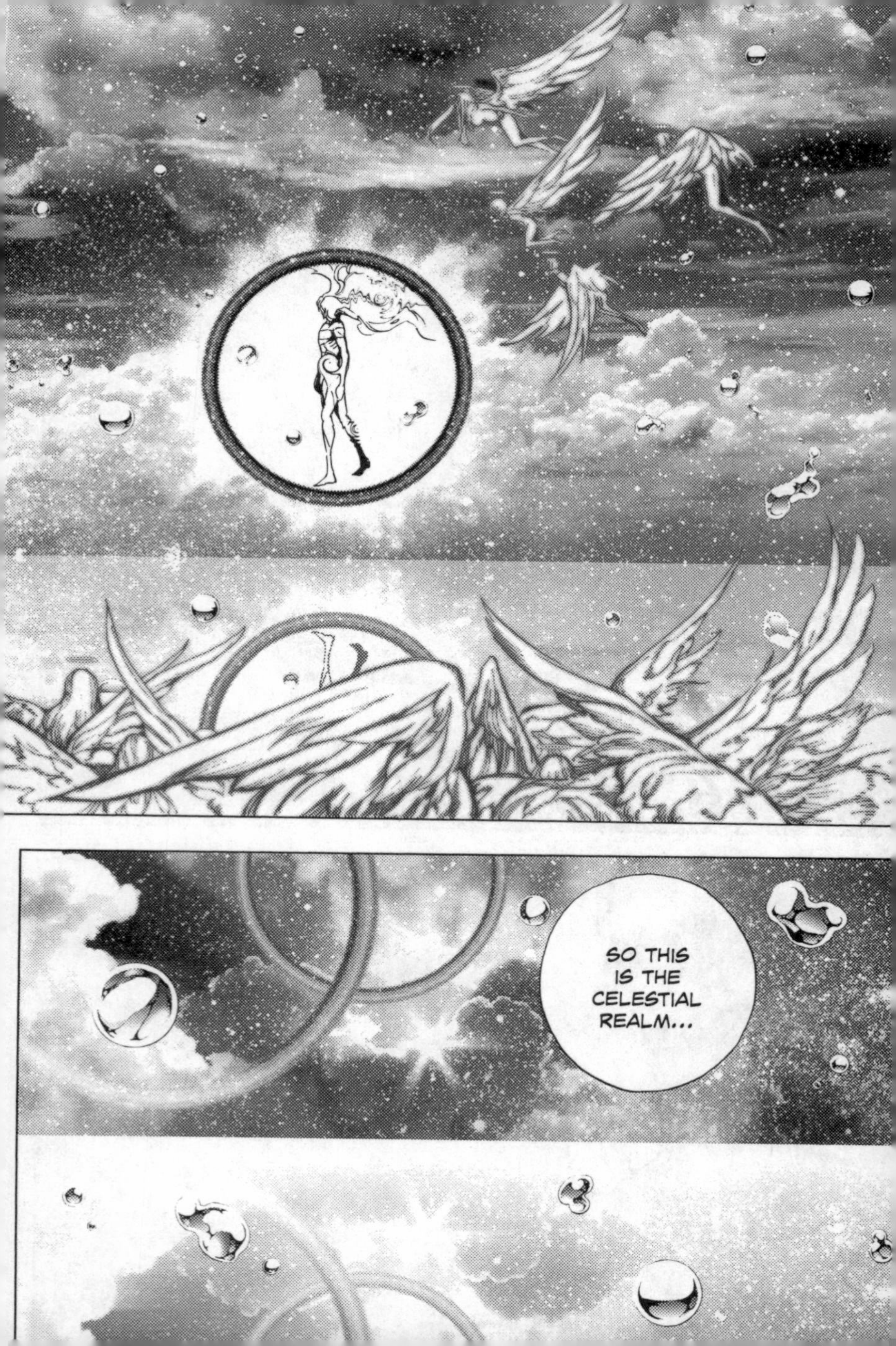
SO THIS IS THE CELESTIAL REALM...

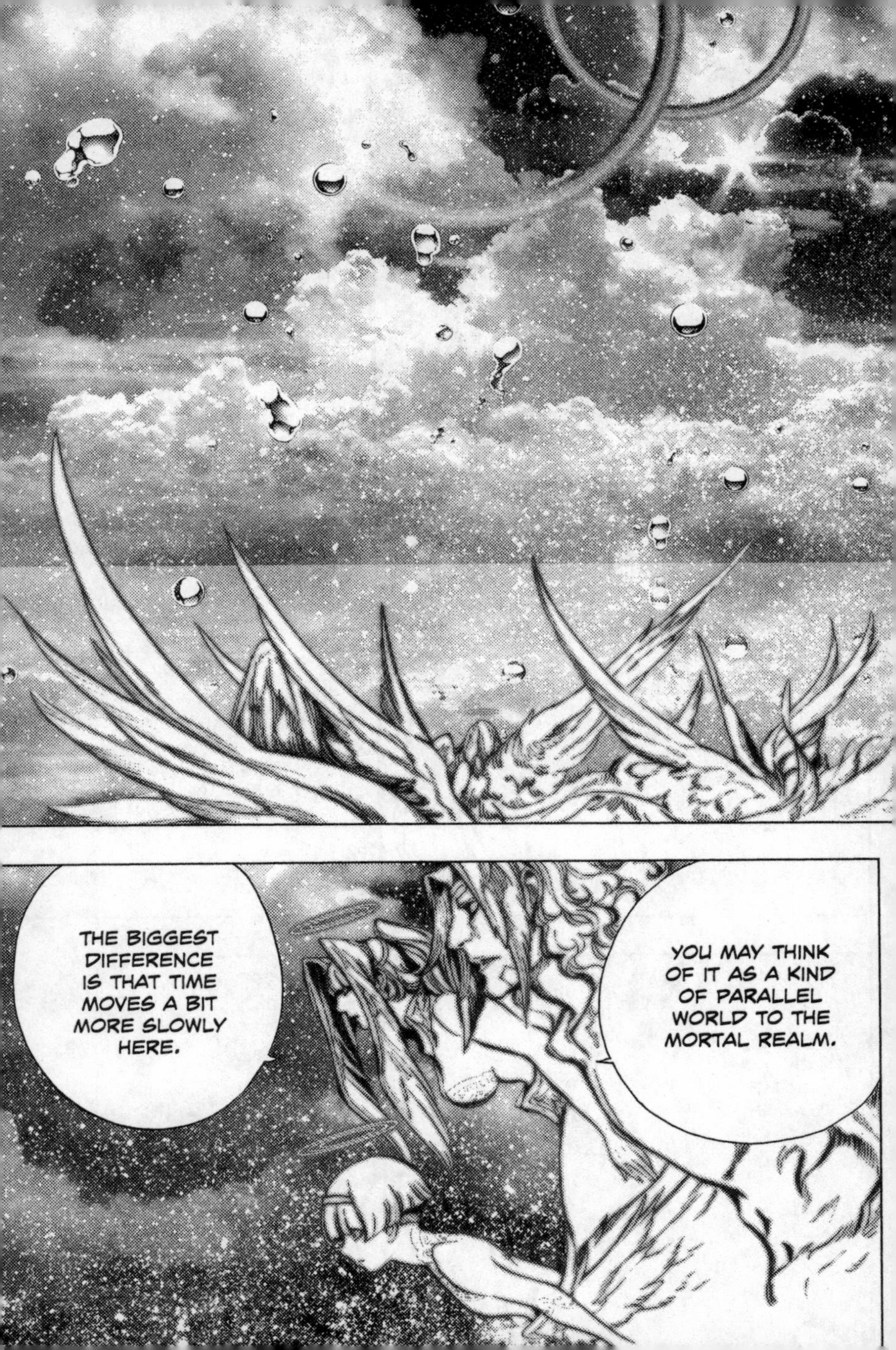
YOU MAY THINK OF IT AS A KIND OF PARALLEL WORLD TO THE MORTAL REALM.
THE BIGGEST DIFFERENCE IS THAT TIME MOVES A BIT MORE SLOWLY HERE.

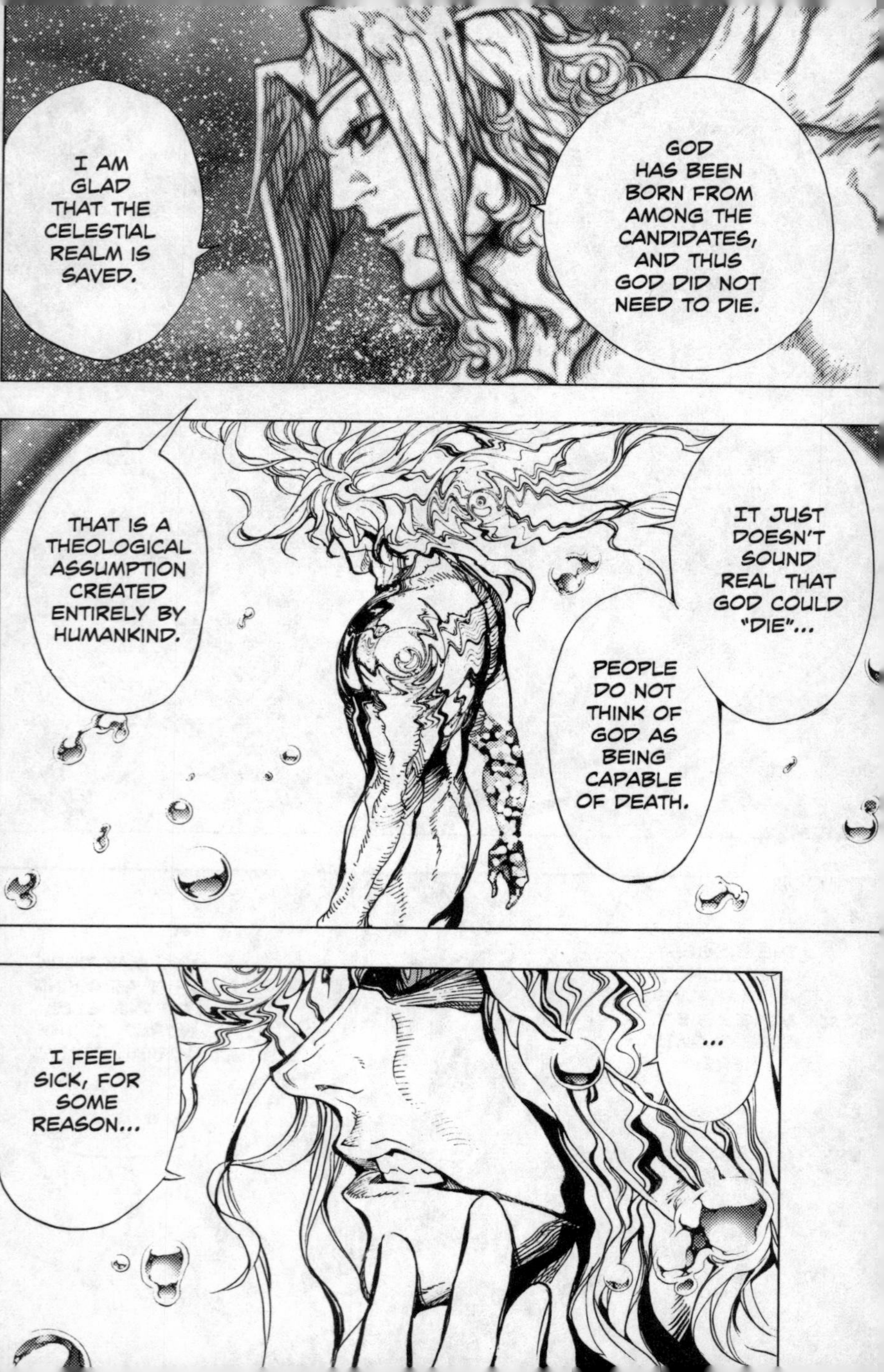
GOD HAS BEEN BORN FROM AMONG THE CANDIDATES, AND THUS GOD DID NOT NEED TO DIE.
I AM GLAD THAT THE CELESTIAL REALM IS SAVED.
IT JUST DOESN'T SOUND REAL THAT GOD COULD "DIE"...
PEOPLE DO NOT THINK OF GOD AS BEING CAPABLE OF DEATH.
THAT IS A THEOLOGICAL ASSUMPTION CREATED ENTIRELY BY HUMANKIND.
...
I FEEL SICK, FOR SOME REASON...

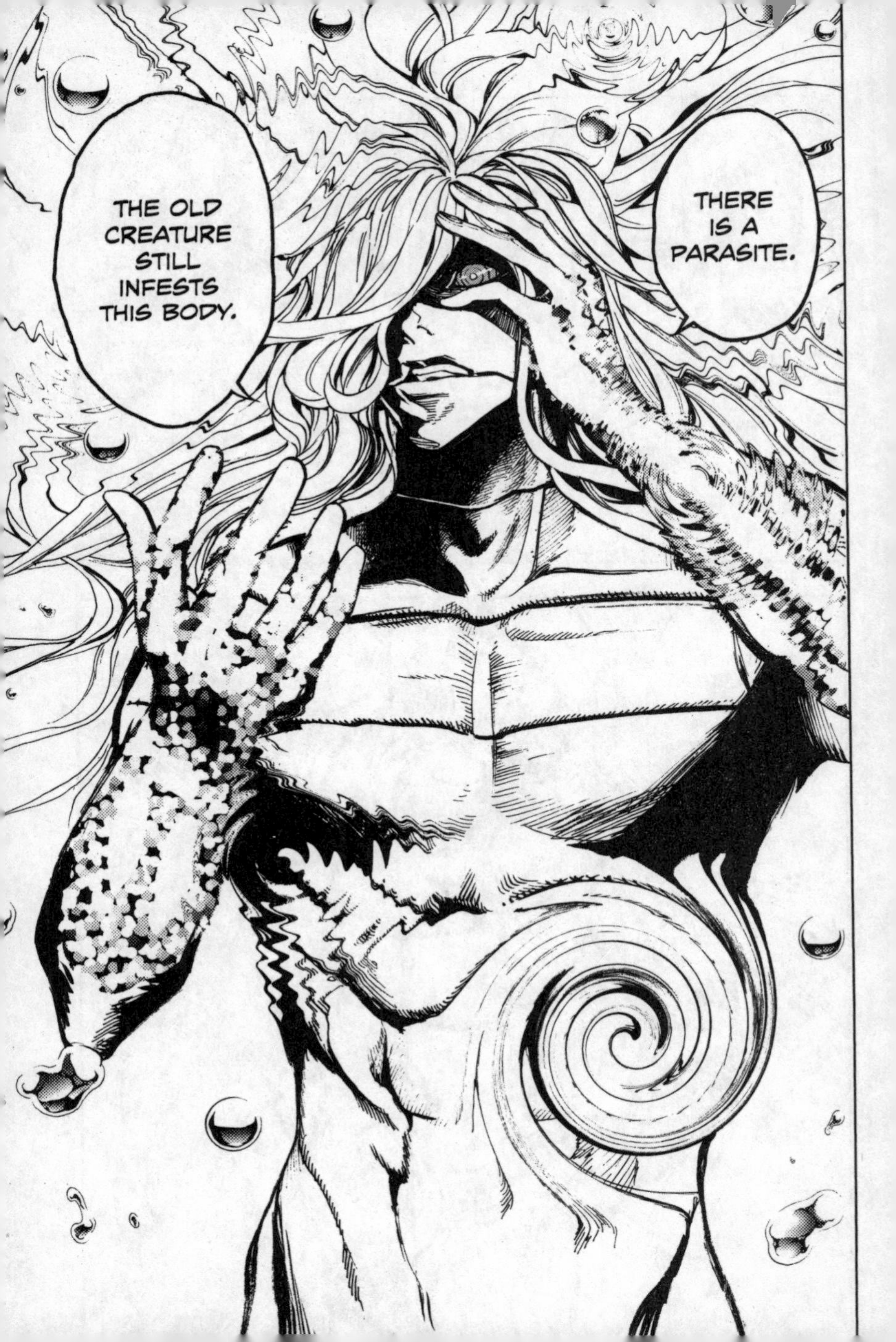
THERE IS A PARASITE.
THE OLD CREATURE STILL INFESTS THIS BODY.

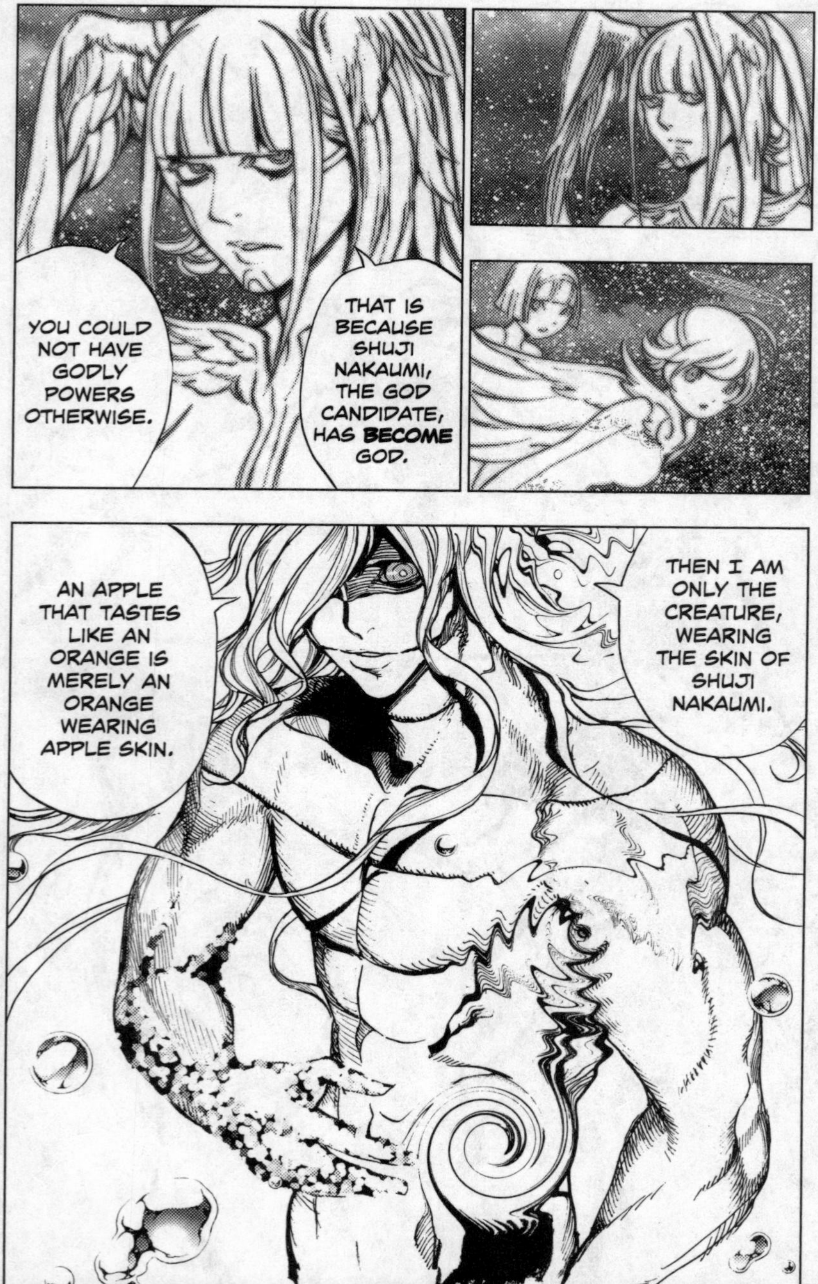
THAT IS BECAUSE SHUJI NAKAUMI, THE GOD CANDIDATE, HAS **BECOME** GOD.
YOU COULD NOT HAVE GODLY POWERS OTHERWISE.
THEN I AM ONLY THE CREATURE, WEARING THE SKIN OF SHUJI NAKAUMI.
AN APPLE THAT TASTES LIKE AN ORANGE IS MERELY AN ORANGE WEARING APPLE SKIN.

YOU DEFINITELY **SOUND** LIKE GOD NOW, NAKAUMI.

IT'S GOD! NOT "NAKAUMI"!

THE CREATURE'S MIND STILL EXISTS INSIDE MY HEAD...

WILL IT INVADE MY BODY AND CONSCIOUSNESS?

THAT IS NOT THE CASE. THERE MIGHT BE TWO MINDS NOW, BUT THE MIND THAT WAS ONCE SHUJI NAKAUMI WILL CONTROL THE PREVIOUS GOD UNTIL YOU FUSE IN THE END.

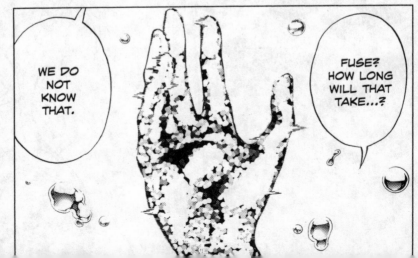

FUSE? HOW LONG WILL THAT TAKE...?

WE DO NOT KNOW THAT.

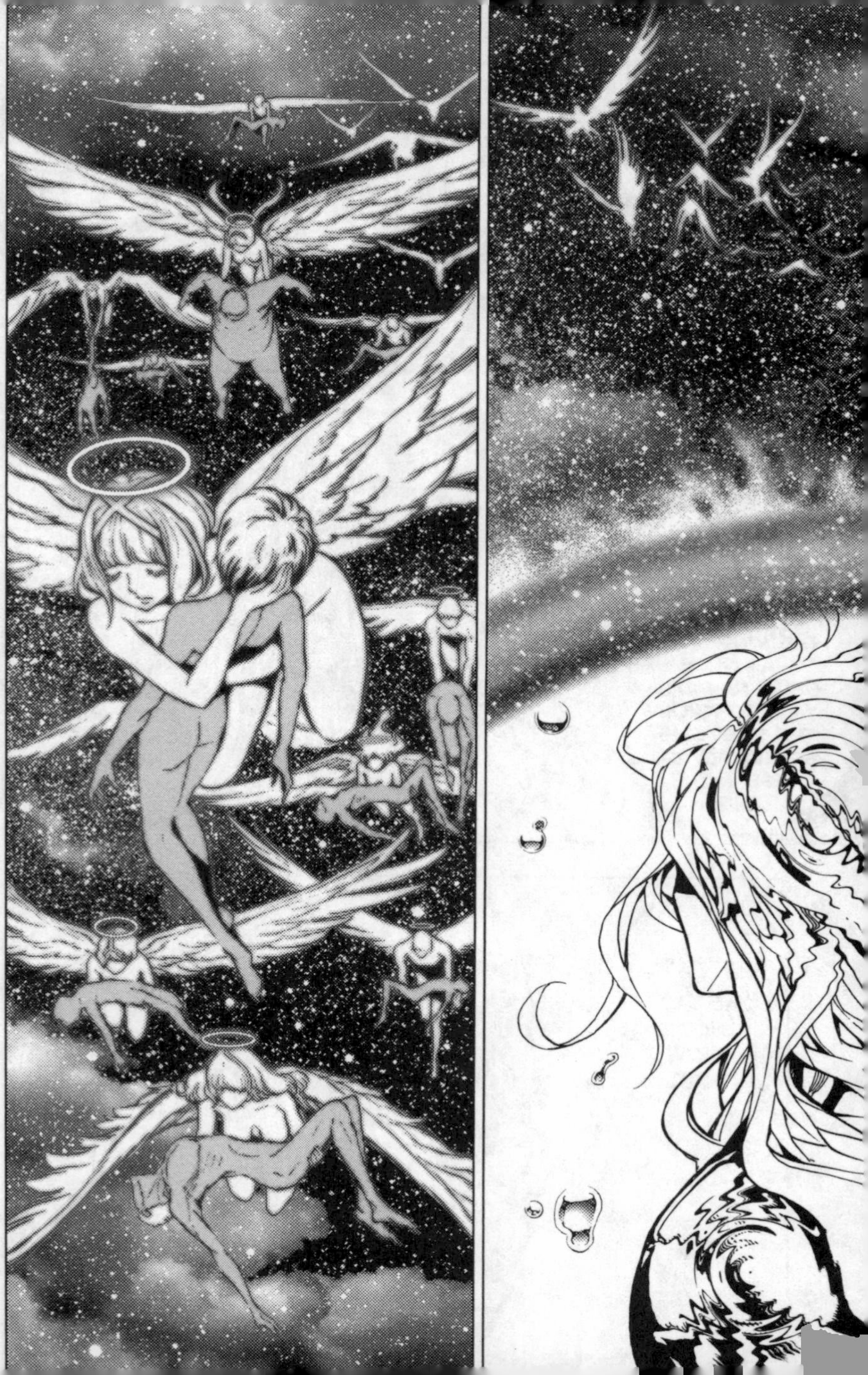

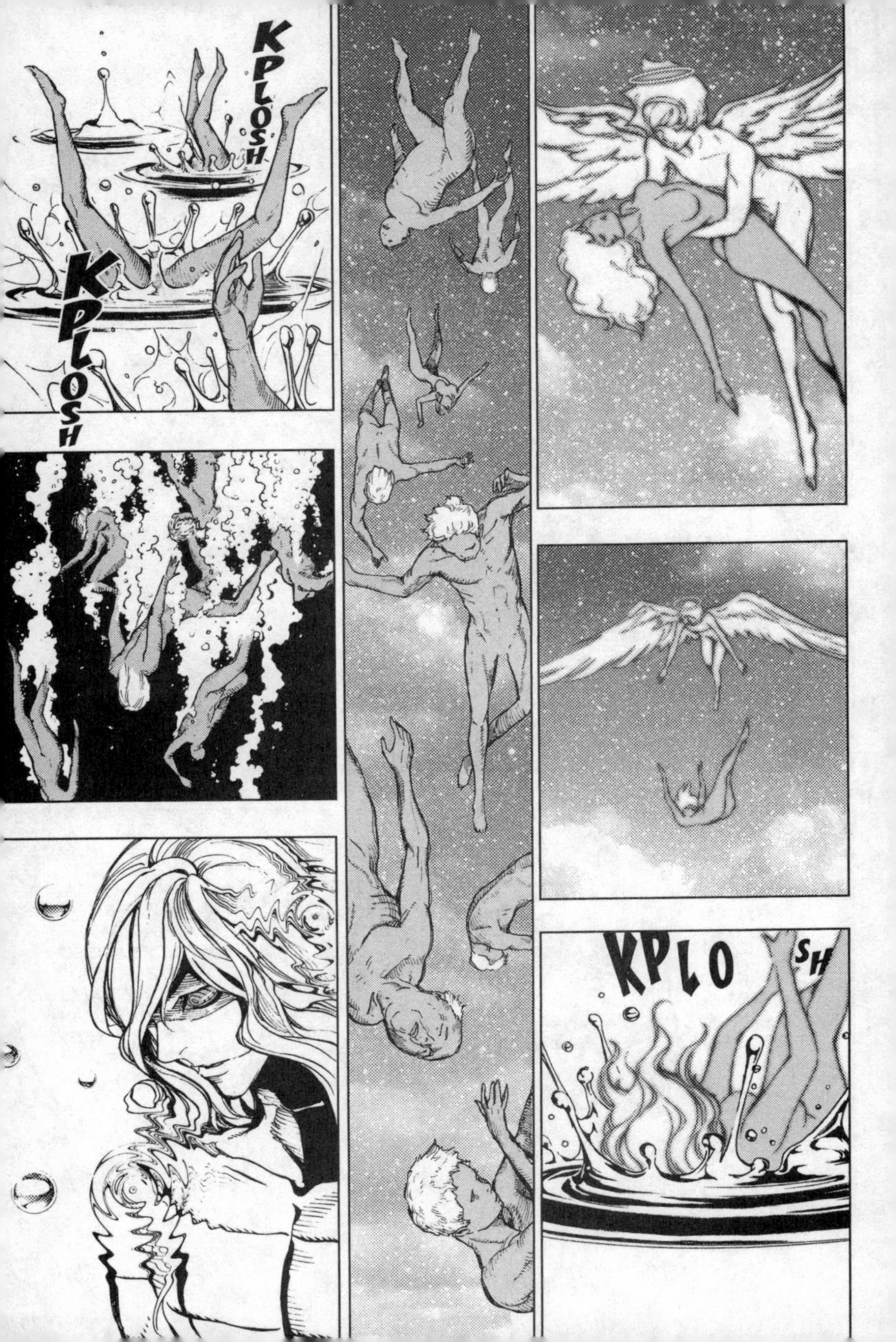
KPLOSH
KPLOSH
KPLOSH

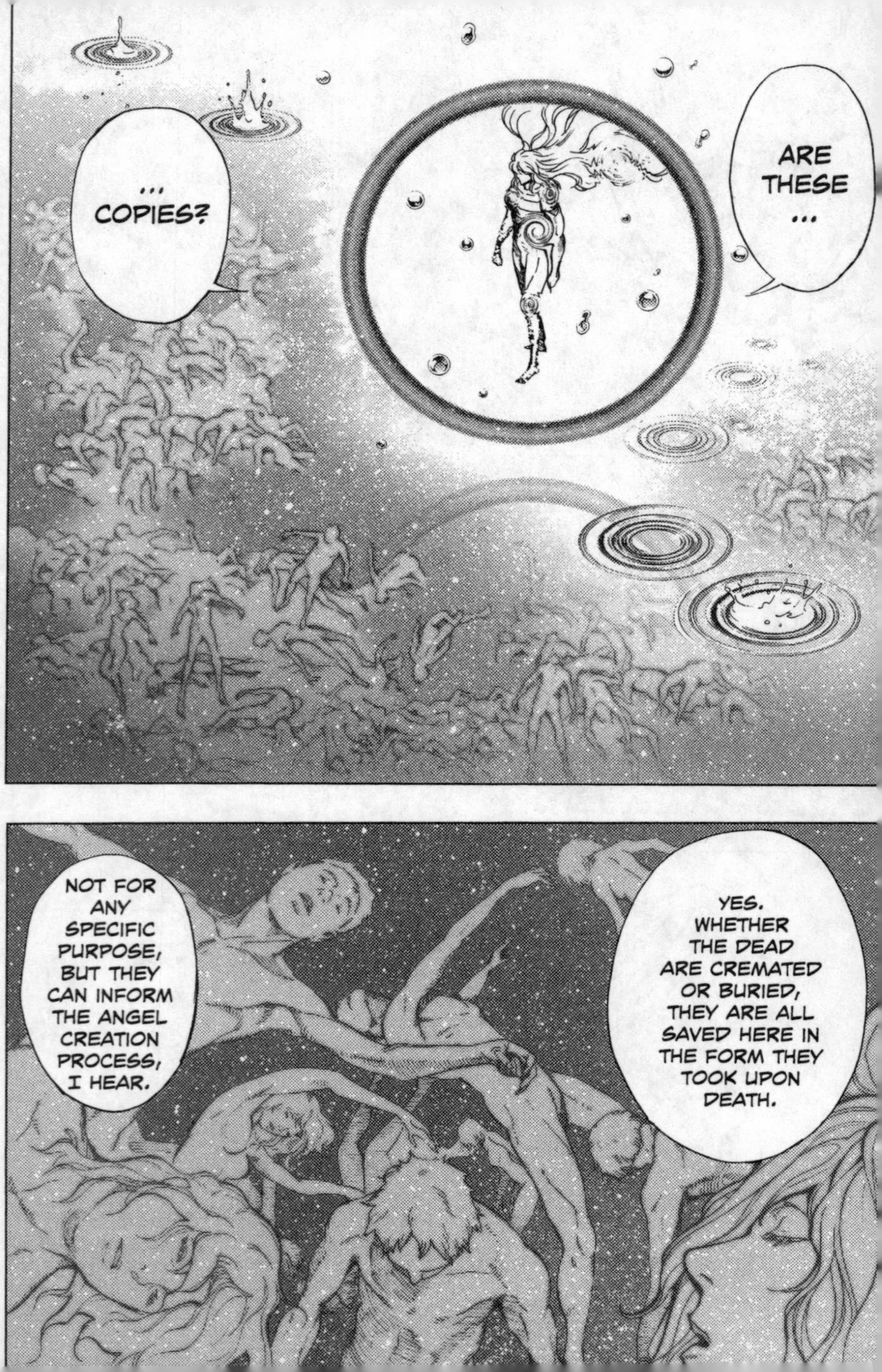
ARE THESE ...
... COPIES?
YES. WHETHER THE DEAD ARE CREMATED OR BURIED, THEY ARE ALL SAVED HERE IN THE FORM THEY TOOK UPON DEATH.
NOT FOR ANY SPECIFIC PURPOSE, BUT THEY CAN INFORM THE ANGEL CREATION PROCESS, I HEAR.

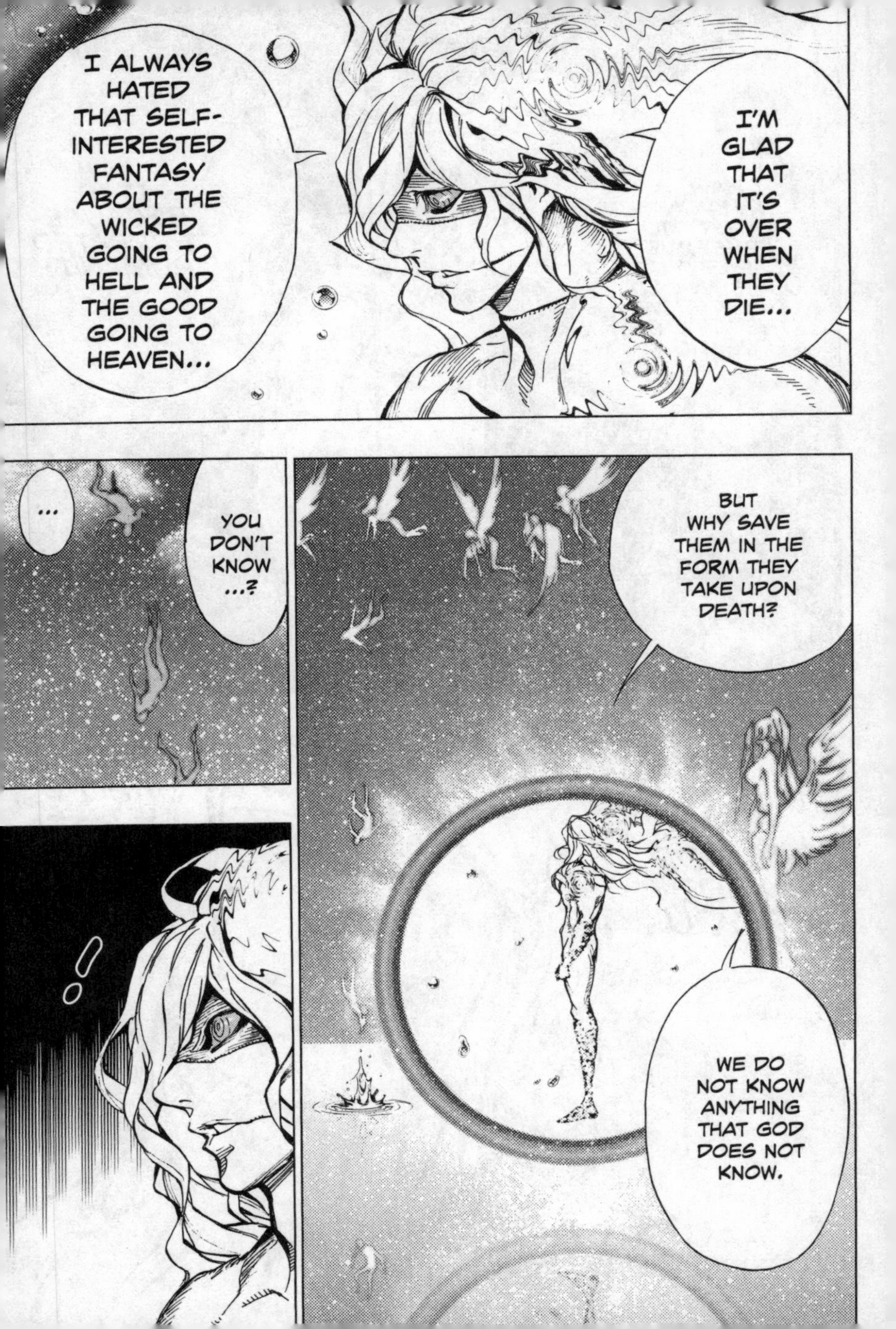
I'M GLAD THAT IT'S OVER WHEN THEY DIE...
I ALWAYS HATED THAT SELF-INTERESTED FANTASY ABOUT THE WICKED GOING TO HELL AND THE GOOD GOING TO HEAVEN...
BUT WHY SAVE THEM IN THE FORM THEY TAKE UPON DEATH?
WE DO NOT KNOW ANYTHING THAT GOD DOES NOT KNOW.
YOU DON'T KNOW ...?
...
!!

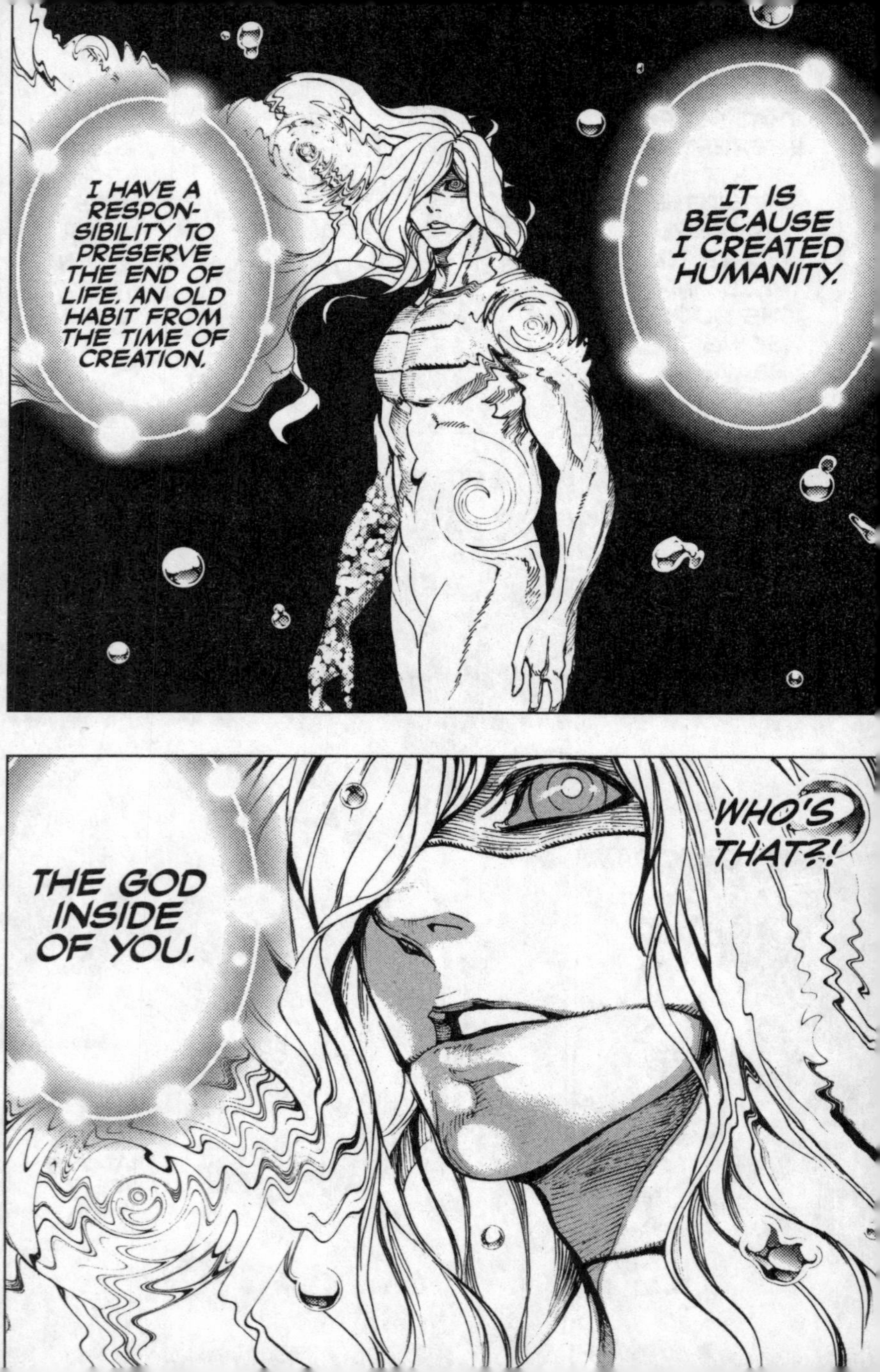
IT IS BECAUSE I CREATED HUMANITY.
I HAVE A RESPON-SIBILITY TO PRESERVE THE END OF LIFE. AN OLD HABIT FROM THE TIME OF CREATION.
WHO'S THAT?!
THE GOD INSIDE OF YOU.

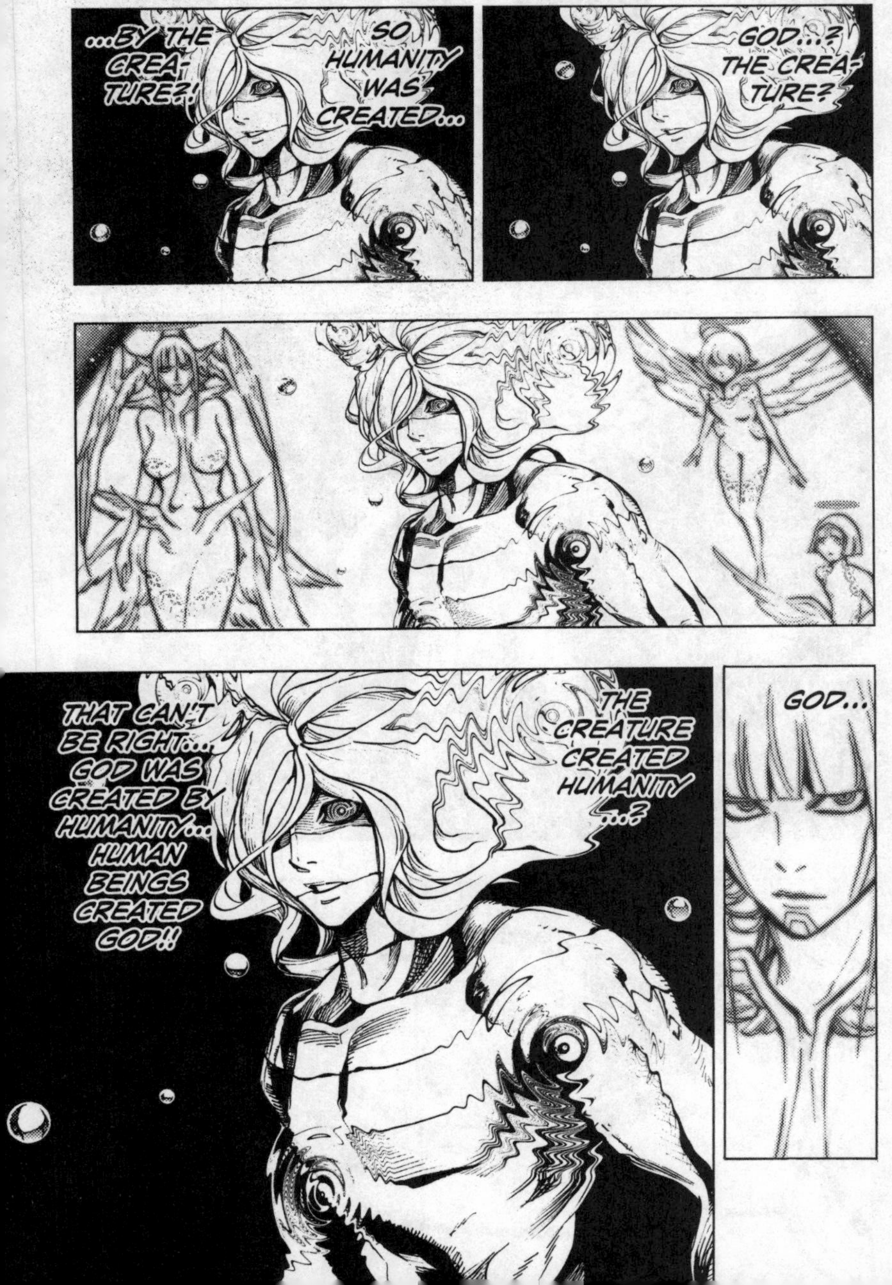
GOD...? THE CREA-TURE?
SO HUMANITY WAS CREATED...
...BY THE CREA-TURE?!
GOD...
THE CREATURE CREATED HUMANITY ...?
THAT CAN'T BE RIGHT... GOD WAS CREATED BY HUMANITY... HUMAN BEINGS CREATED GOD!!

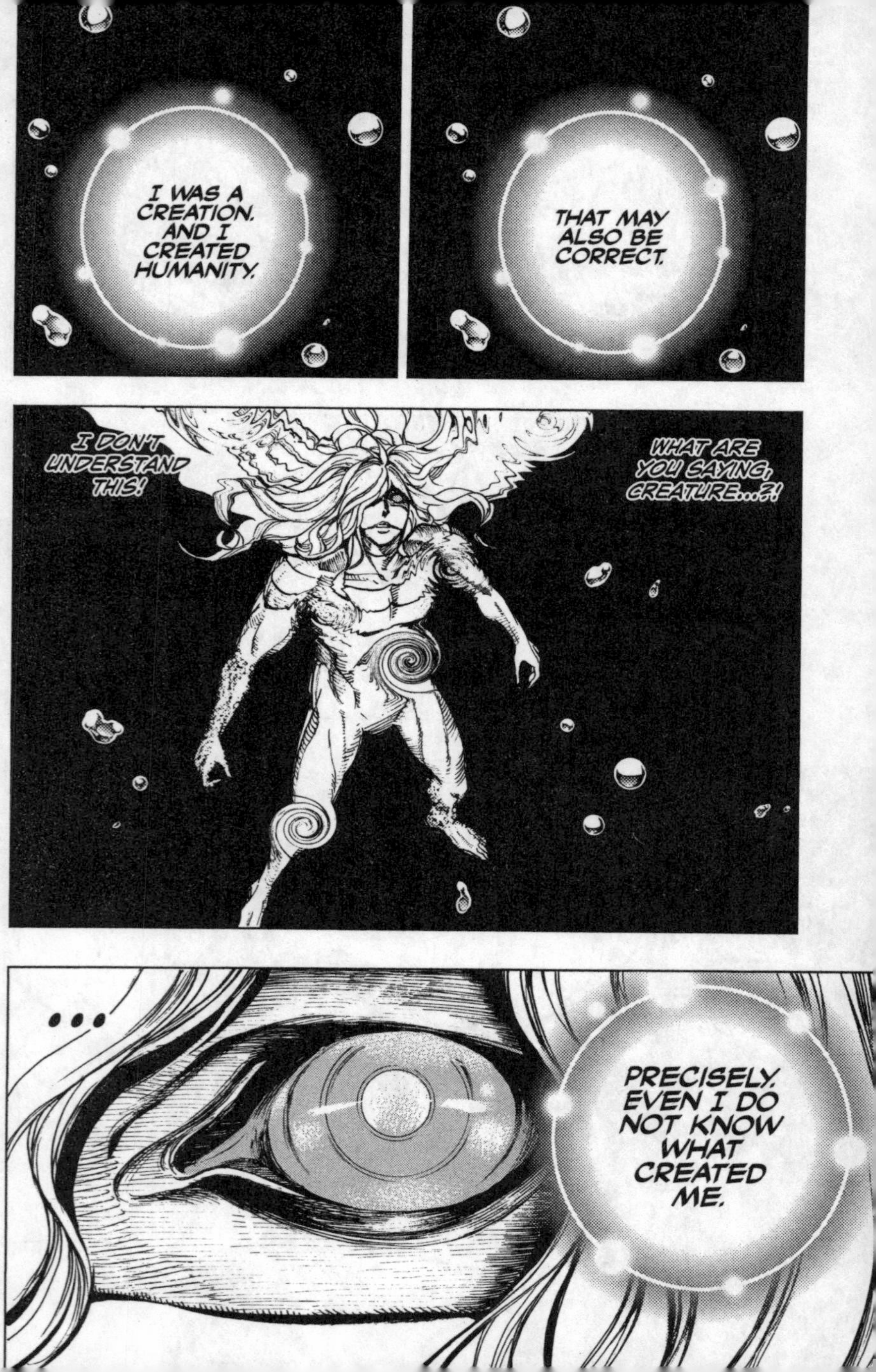
THAT MAY ALSO BE CORRECT.
I WAS A CREATION. AND I CREATED HUMANITY.
WHAT ARE YOU SAYING, CREATURE...?!
I DON'T UNDERSTAND THIS!
PRECISELY. EVEN I DO NOT KNOW WHAT CREATED ME.
...

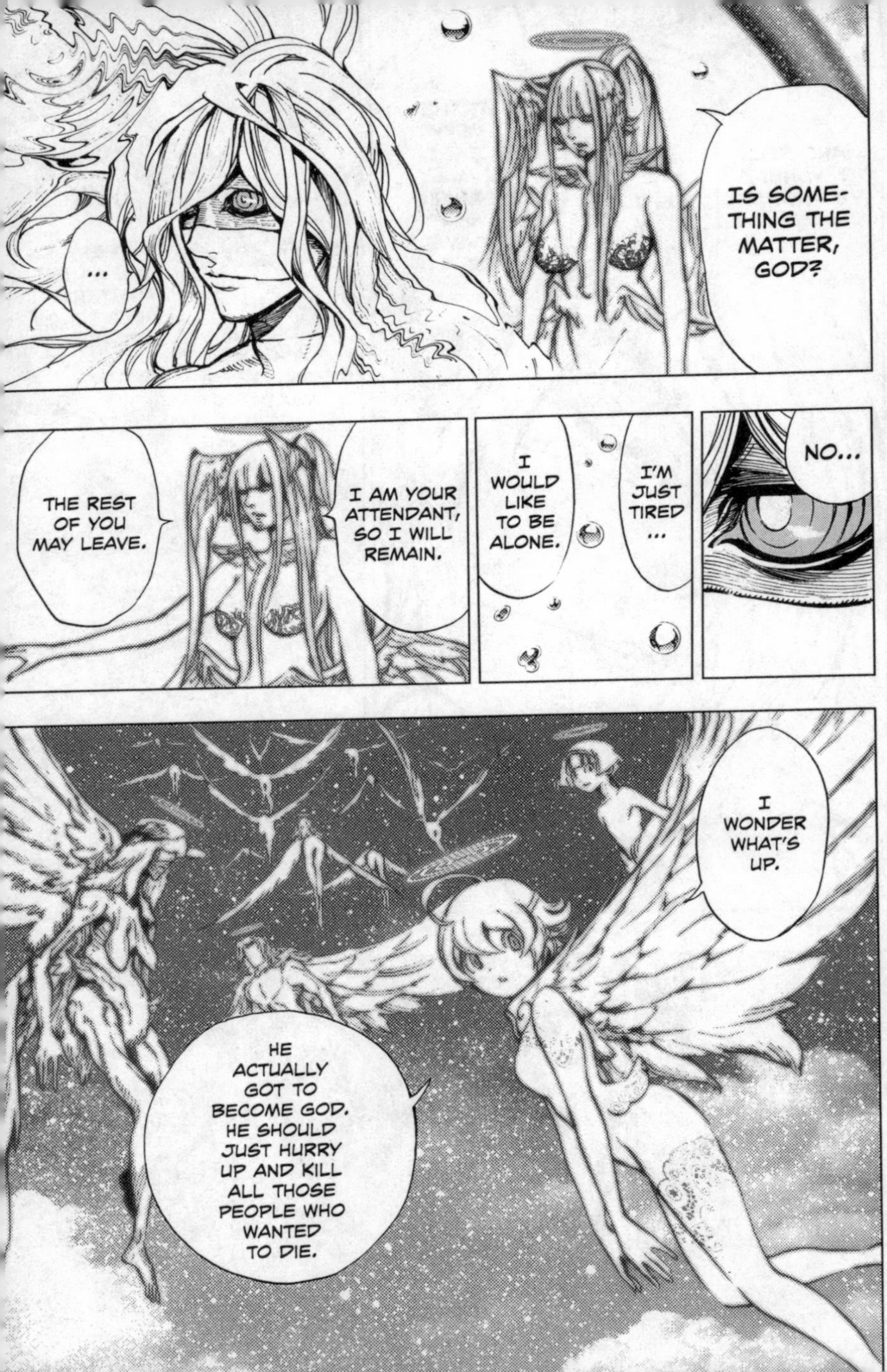
IS SOMETHING THE MATTER, GOD?
...
NO...
I'M JUST TIRED ...
I WOULD LIKE TO BE ALONE.
I AM YOUR ATTENDANT, SO I WILL REMAIN.
THE REST OF YOU MAY LEAVE.
I WONDER WHAT'S UP.
HE ACTUALLY GOT TO BECOME GOD. HE SHOULD JUST HURRY UP AND KILL ALL THOSE PEOPLE WHO WANTED TO DIE.

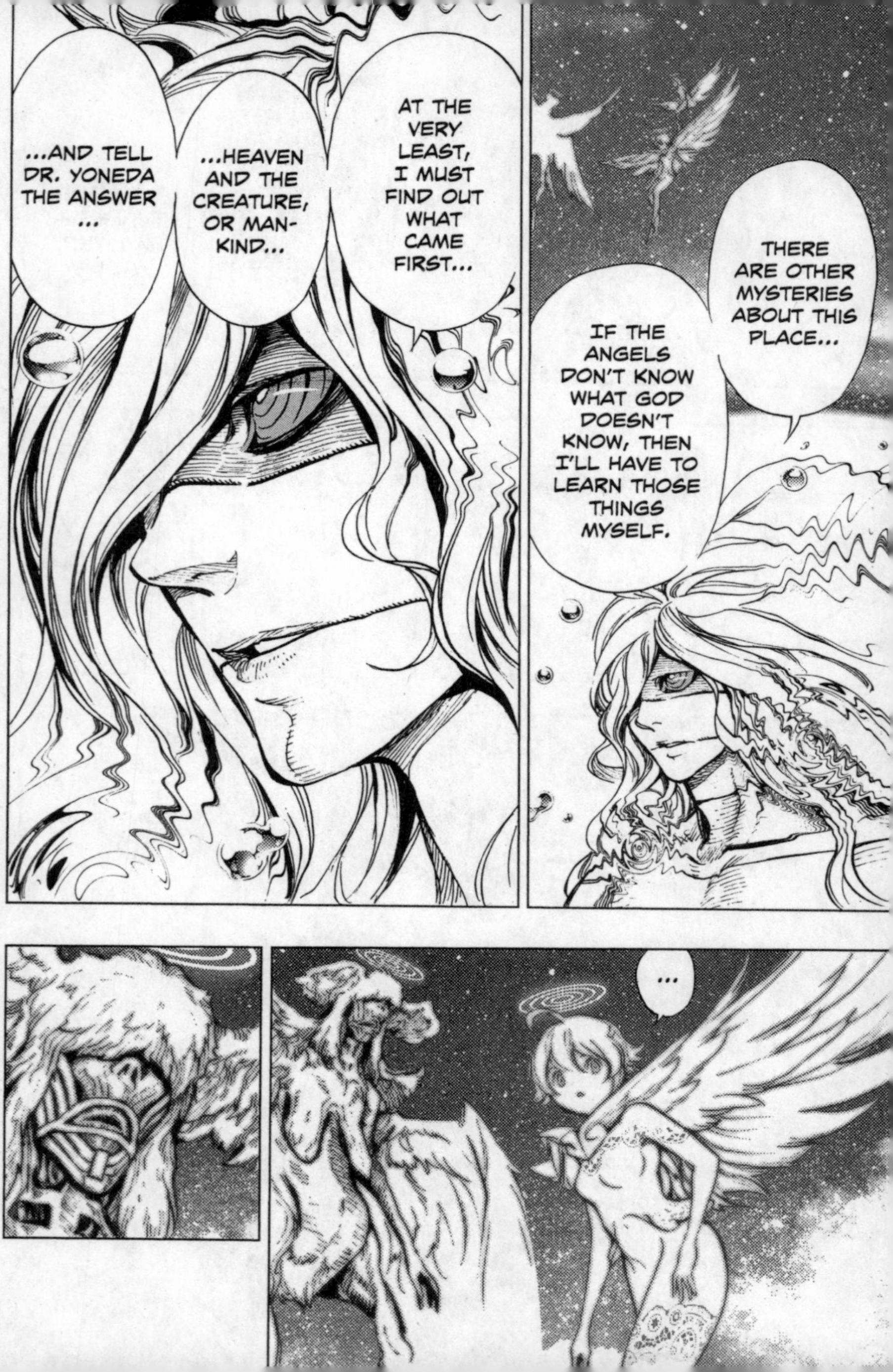
THERE ARE OTHER MYSTERIES ABOUT THIS PLACE...
IF THE ANGELS DON'T KNOW WHAT GOD DOESN'T KNOW, THEN I'LL HAVE TO LEARN THOSE THINGS MYSELF.
AT THE VERY LEAST, I MUST FIND OUT WHAT CAME FIRST...
...HEAVEN AND THE CREATURE, OR MAN-KIND...
...AND TELL DR. YONEDA THE ANSWER ...
...

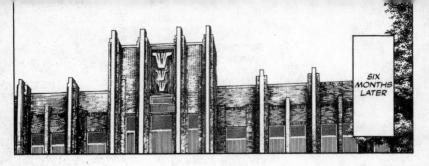

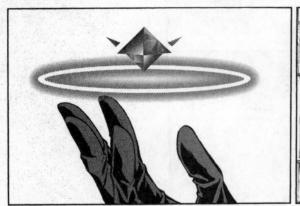

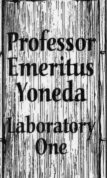

Professor
Emeritus
Yoneda

Laboratory
One

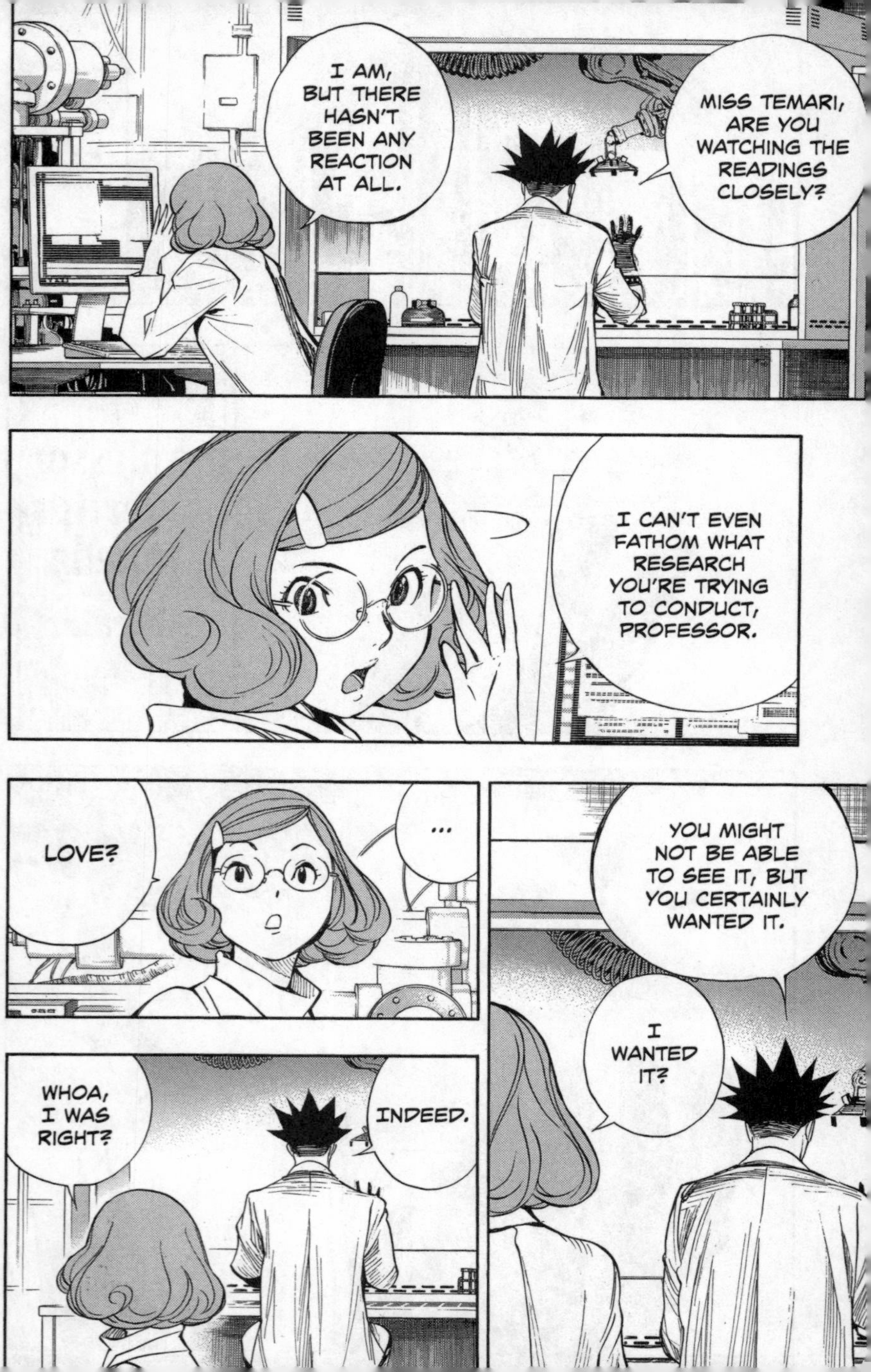
MISS TEMARI, ARE YOU WATCHING THE READINGS CLOSELY?
I AM, BUT THERE HASN'T BEEN ANY REACTION AT ALL.
I CAN'T EVEN FATHOM WHAT RESEARCH YOU'RE TRYING TO CONDUCT, PROFESSOR.
YOU MIGHT NOT BE ABLE TO SEE IT, BUT YOU CERTAINLY WANTED IT.
I WANTED IT?
...
LOVE?
INDEED.
WHOA, I WAS RIGHT?

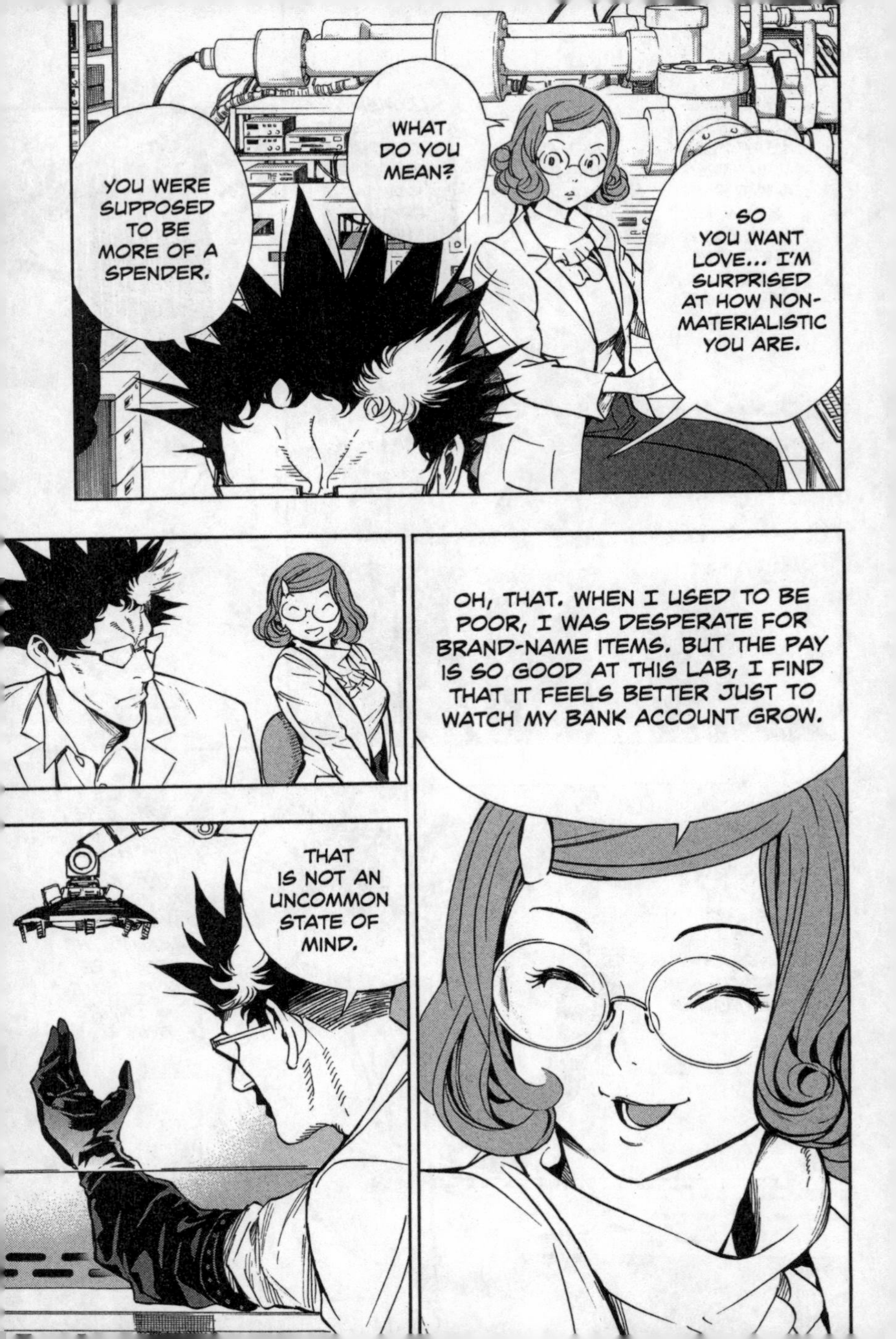
SO YOU WANT LOVE... I'M SURPRISED AT HOW NON-MATERIALISTIC YOU ARE.
WHAT DO YOU MEAN?
YOU WERE SUPPOSED TO BE MORE OF A SPENDER.
OH, THAT. WHEN I USED TO BE POOR, I WAS DESPERATE FOR BRAND-NAME ITEMS. BUT THE PAY IS SO GOOD AT THIS LAB, I FIND THAT IT FEELS BETTER JUST TO WATCH MY BANK ACCOUNT GROW.
THAT IS NOT AN UNCOMMON STATE OF MIND.

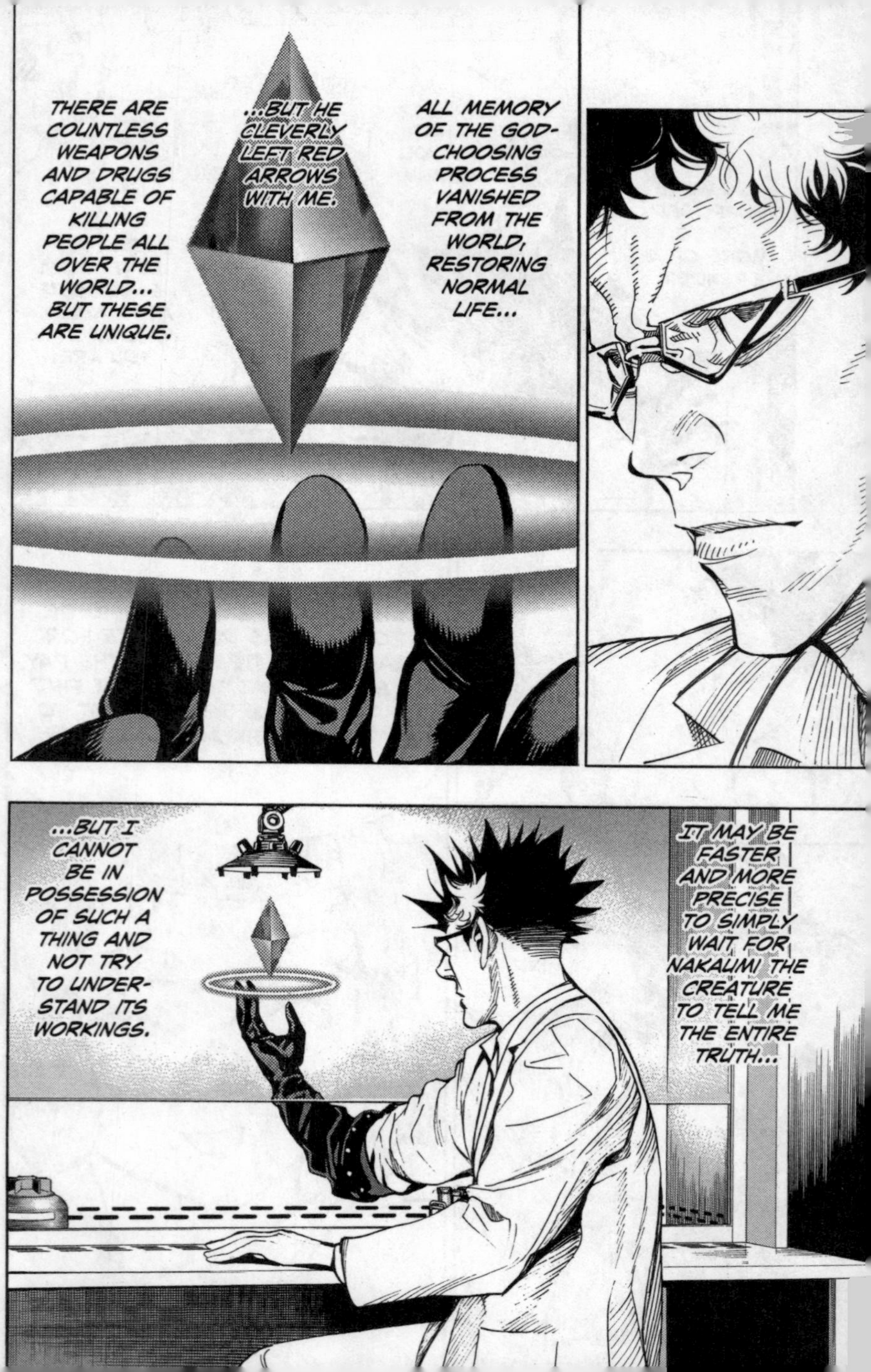
ALL MEMORY OF THE GOD-CHOOSING PROCESS VANISHED FROM THE WORLD, RESTORING NORMAL LIFE...
...BUT HE CLEVERLY LEFT RED ARROWS WITH ME.
THERE ARE COUNTLESS WEAPONS AND DRUGS CAPABLE OF KILLING PEOPLE ALL OVER THE WORLD... BUT THESE ARE UNIQUE.
IT MAY BE FASTER AND MORE PRECISE TO SIMPLY WAIT FOR NAKAUMI THE CREATURE TO TELL ME THE ENTIRE TRUTH...
...BUT I CANNOT BE IN POSSESSION OF SUCH A THING AND NOT TRY TO UNDER-STAND ITS WORKINGS.

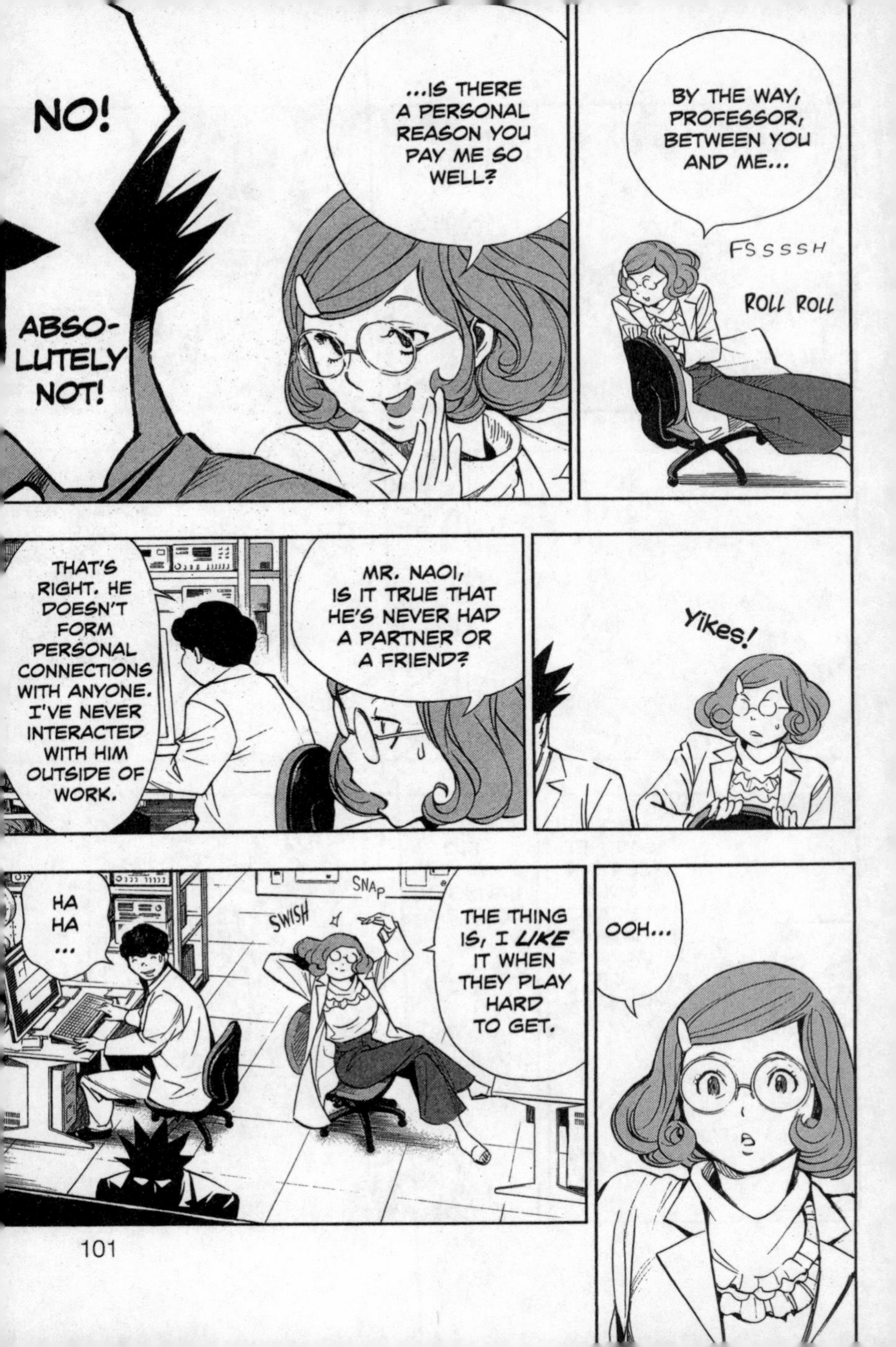
BY THE WAY, PROFESSOR, BETWEEN YOU AND ME...
FSSSSH
ROLL ROLL
...IS THERE A PERSONAL REASON YOU PAY ME SO WELL?
NO!
ABSO-LUTELY NOT!
Yikes!
MR. NAOI, IS IT TRUE THAT HE'S NEVER HAD A PARTNER OR A FRIEND?
THAT'S RIGHT. HE DOESN'T FORM PERSONAL CONNECTIONS WITH ANYONE. I'VE NEVER INTERACTED WITH HIM OUTSIDE OF WORK.
OOH...
SNAP
SWISH
THE THING IS, I LIKE IT WHEN THEY PLAY HARD TO GET.
HA HA ...

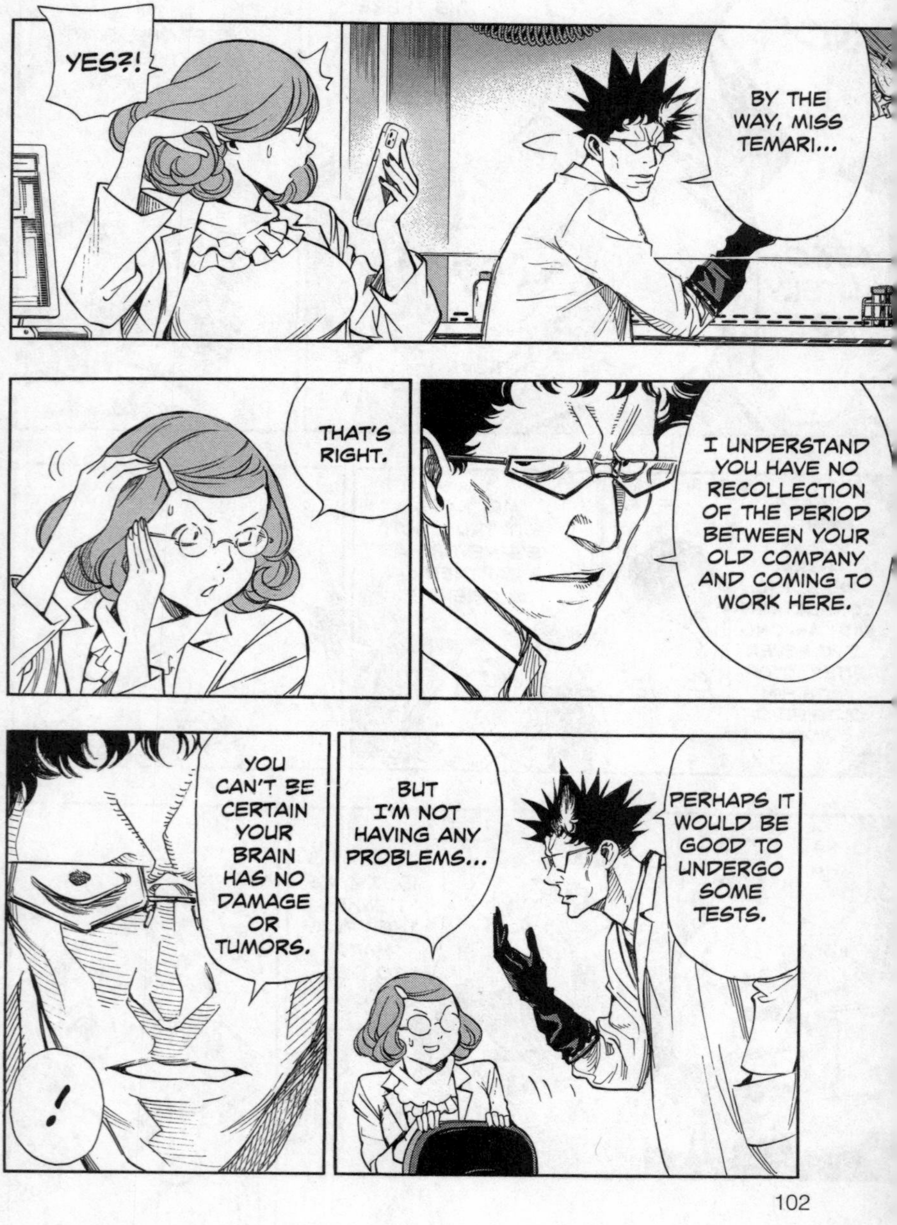
BY THE WAY, MISS TEMARI...
YES?!
I UNDERSTAND YOU HAVE NO RECOLLECTION OF THE PERIOD BETWEEN YOUR OLD COMPANY AND COMING TO WORK HERE.
THAT'S RIGHT.
PERHAPS IT WOULD BE GOOD TO UNDERGO SOME TESTS.
BUT I'M NOT HAVING ANY PROBLEMS...
YOU CAN'T BE CERTAIN YOUR BRAIN HAS NO DAMAGE OR TUMORS.
!

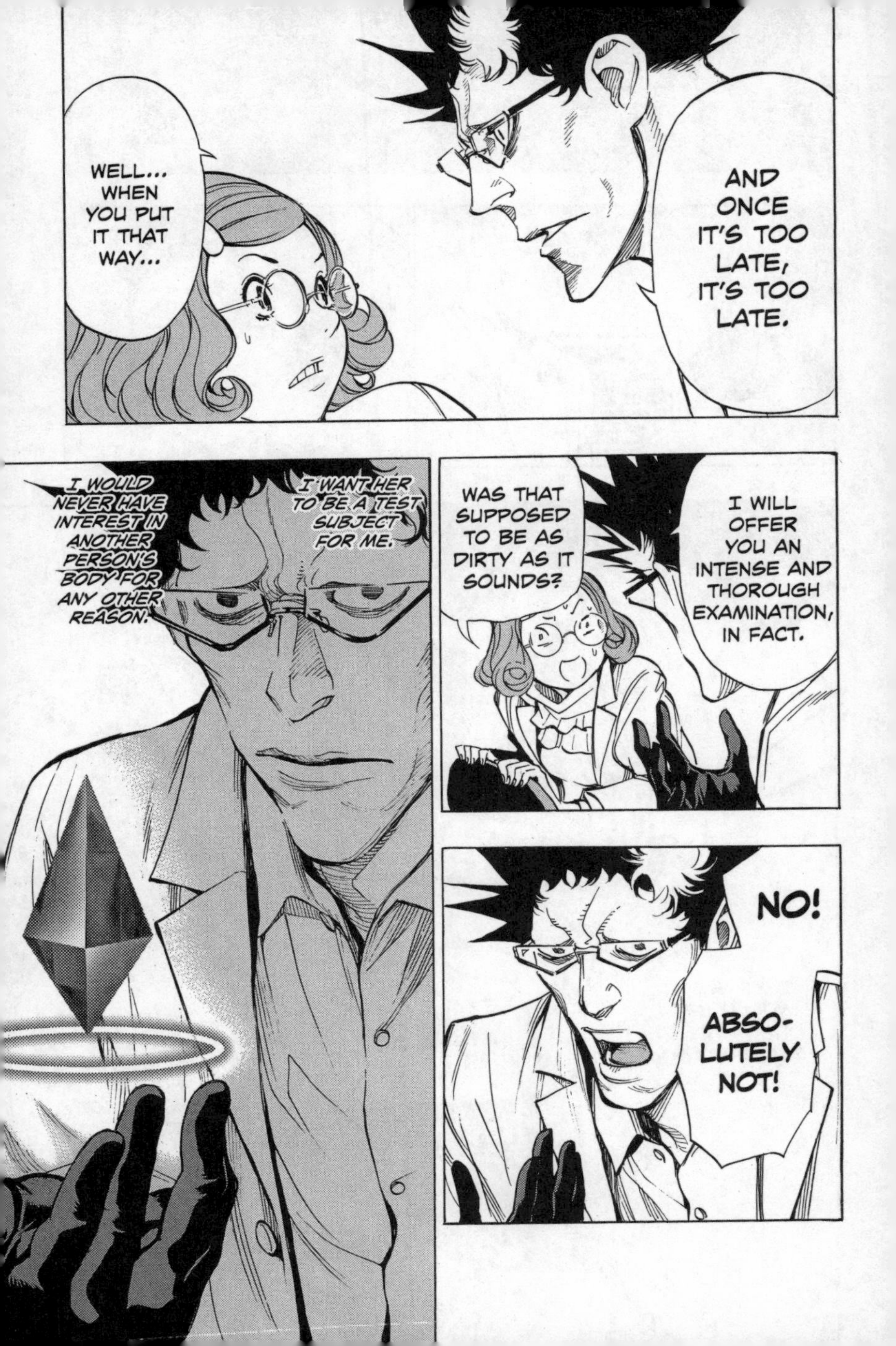
AND ONCE IT'S TOO LATE, IT'S TOO LATE.
WELL... WHEN YOU PUT IT THAT WAY...
I WILL OFFER YOU AN INTENSE AND THOROUGH EXAMINATION, IN FACT.
WAS THAT SUPPOSED TO BE AS DIRTY AS IT SOUNDS?
NO!
ABSO-LUTELY NOT!
I WANT HER TO BE A TEST SUBJECT FOR ME.
I WOULD NEVER HAVE INTEREST IN ANOTHER PERSON'S BODY FOR ANY OTHER REASON.

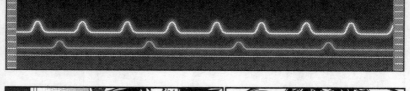

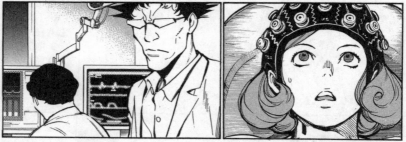

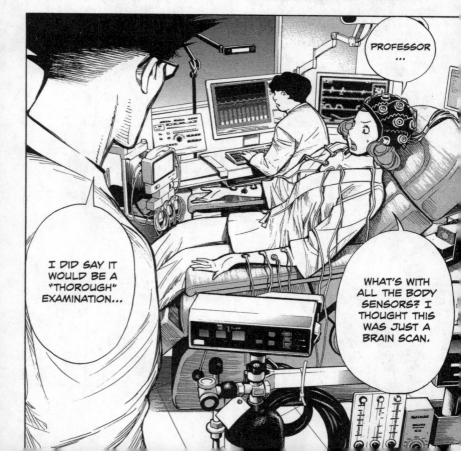

PROFESSOR ...
WHAT'S WITH ALL THE BODY SENSORS? I THOUGHT THIS WAS JUST A BRAIN SCAN.
I DID SAY IT WOULD BE A "THOROUGH" EXAMINATION...

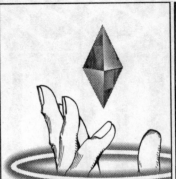

I'M ON IT.

NOW WE'LL BEGIN. START RECORDING SIGNALS, NAOI.

SHMM

?

HUH?

HER HEART RATE JUST SHOT UP...

LOOK AT THESE HORMONE LEVELS!

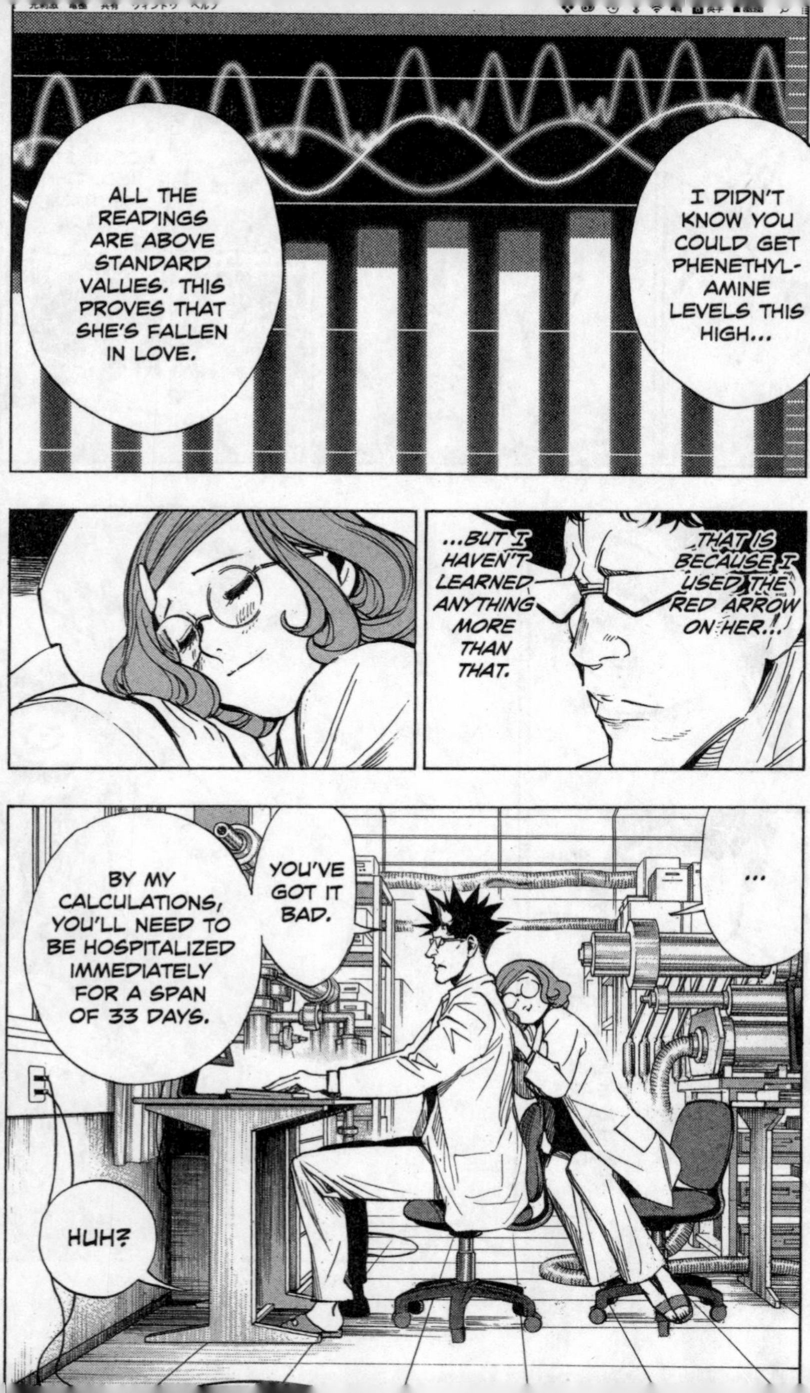
I DIDN'T KNOW YOU COULD GET PHENETHYL-AMINE LEVELS THIS HIGH...
ALL THE READINGS ARE ABOVE STANDARD VALUES. THIS PROVES THAT SHE'S FALLEN IN LOVE.
THAT IS BECAUSE I USED THE RED ARROW ON HER...
...BUT I HAVEN'T LEARNED ANYTHING MORE THAN THAT.
...
YOU'VE GOT IT BAD.
BY MY CALCULATIONS, YOU'LL NEED TO BE HOSPITALIZED IMMEDIATELY FOR A SPAN OF 33 DAYS.
HUH?

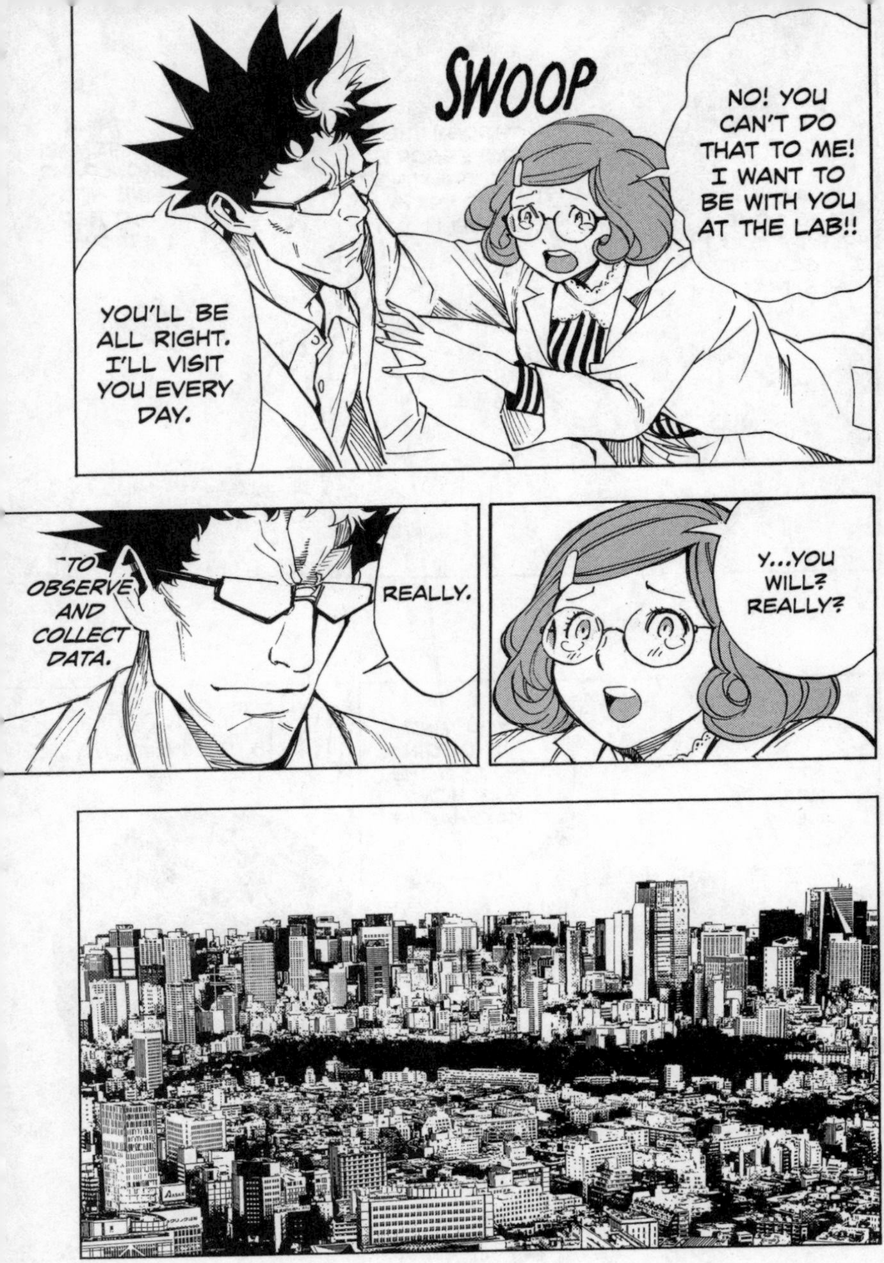
SWOOP
NO! YOU CAN'T DO THAT TO ME! I WANT TO BE WITH YOU AT THE LAB!!
YOU'LL BE ALL RIGHT. I'LL VISIT YOU EVERY DAY.
Y...YOU WILL? REALLY?
REALLY.
–TO OBSERVE AND COLLECT DATA.

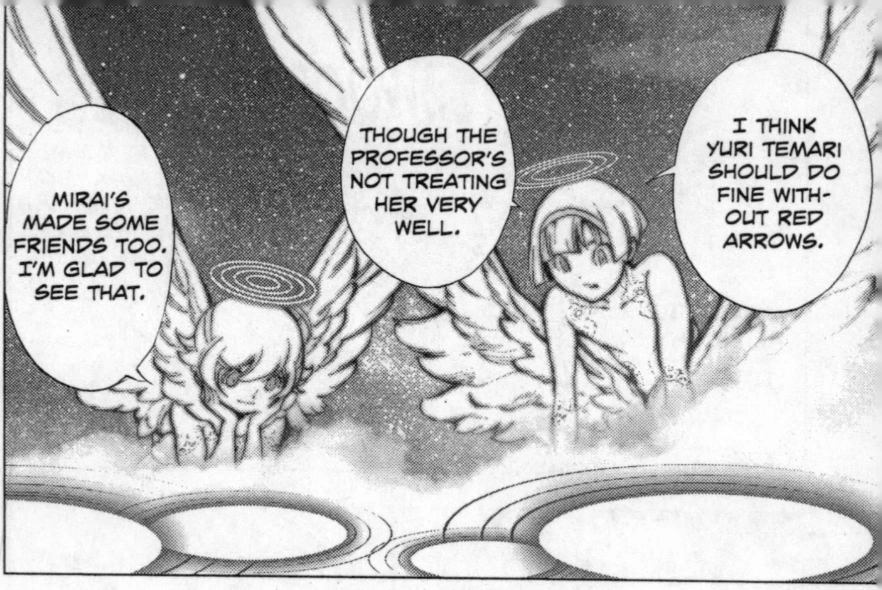
I THINK YURI TEMARI SHOULD DO FINE WITH-OUT RED ARROWS.
THOUGH THE PROFESSOR'S NOT TREATING HER VERY WELL.
MIRAI'S MADE SOME FRIENDS TOO. I'M GLAD TO SEE THAT.

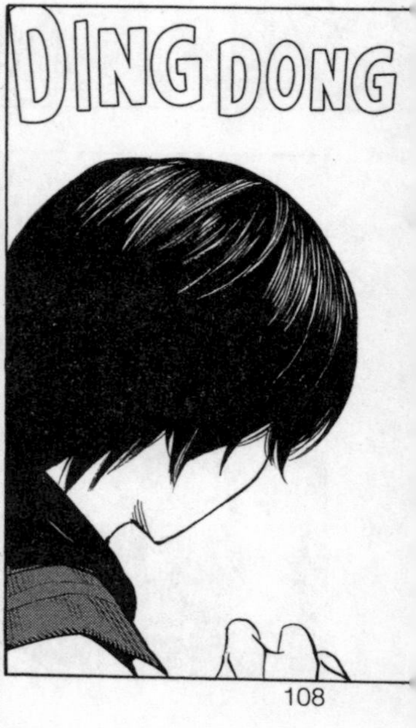
DING DONG

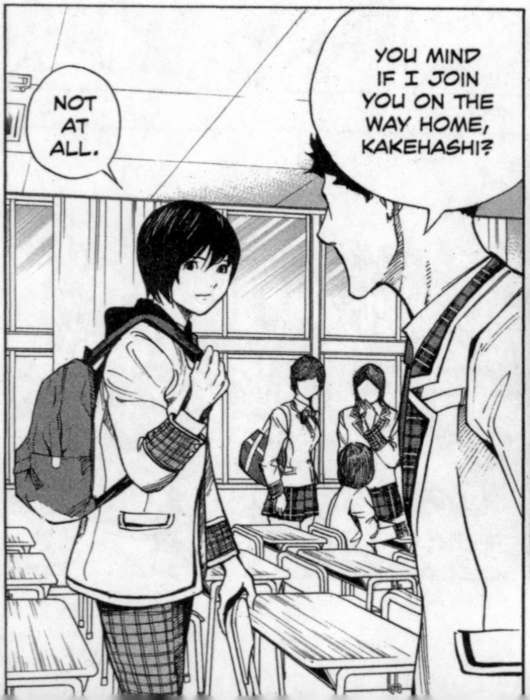
YOU MIND IF I JOIN YOU ON THE WAY HOME, KAKEHASHI?
NOT AT ALL.

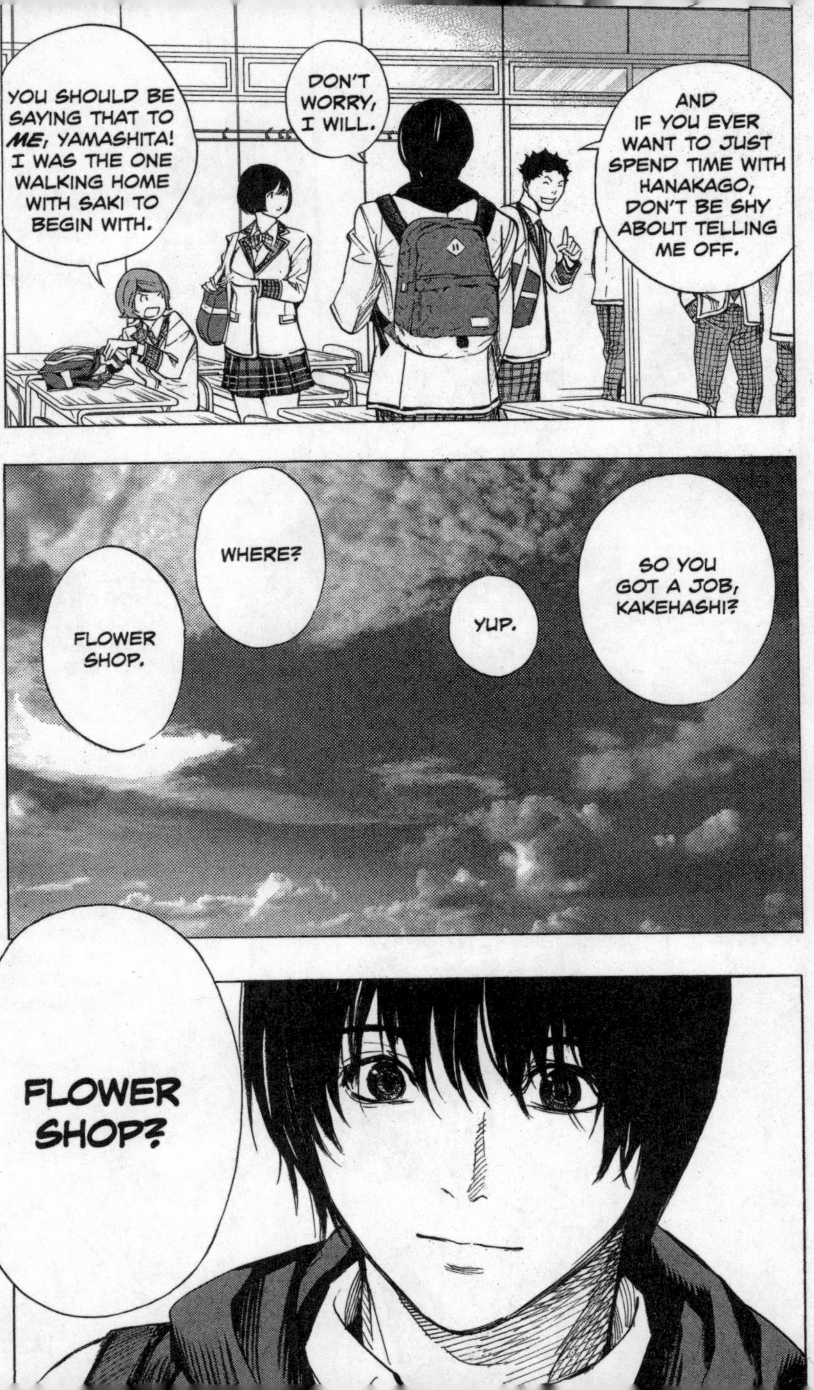
AND IF YOU EVER WANT TO JUST SPEND TIME WITH HANAKAGO, DON'T BE SHY ABOUT TELLING ME OFF.
DON'T WORRY, I WILL.
YOU SHOULD BE SAYING THAT TO *ME*, YAMASHITA! I WAS THE ONE WALKING HOME WITH SAKI TO BEGIN WITH.
SO YOU GOT A JOB, KAKEHASHI?
YUP.
WHERE?
FLOWER SHOP.
FLOWER SHOP?

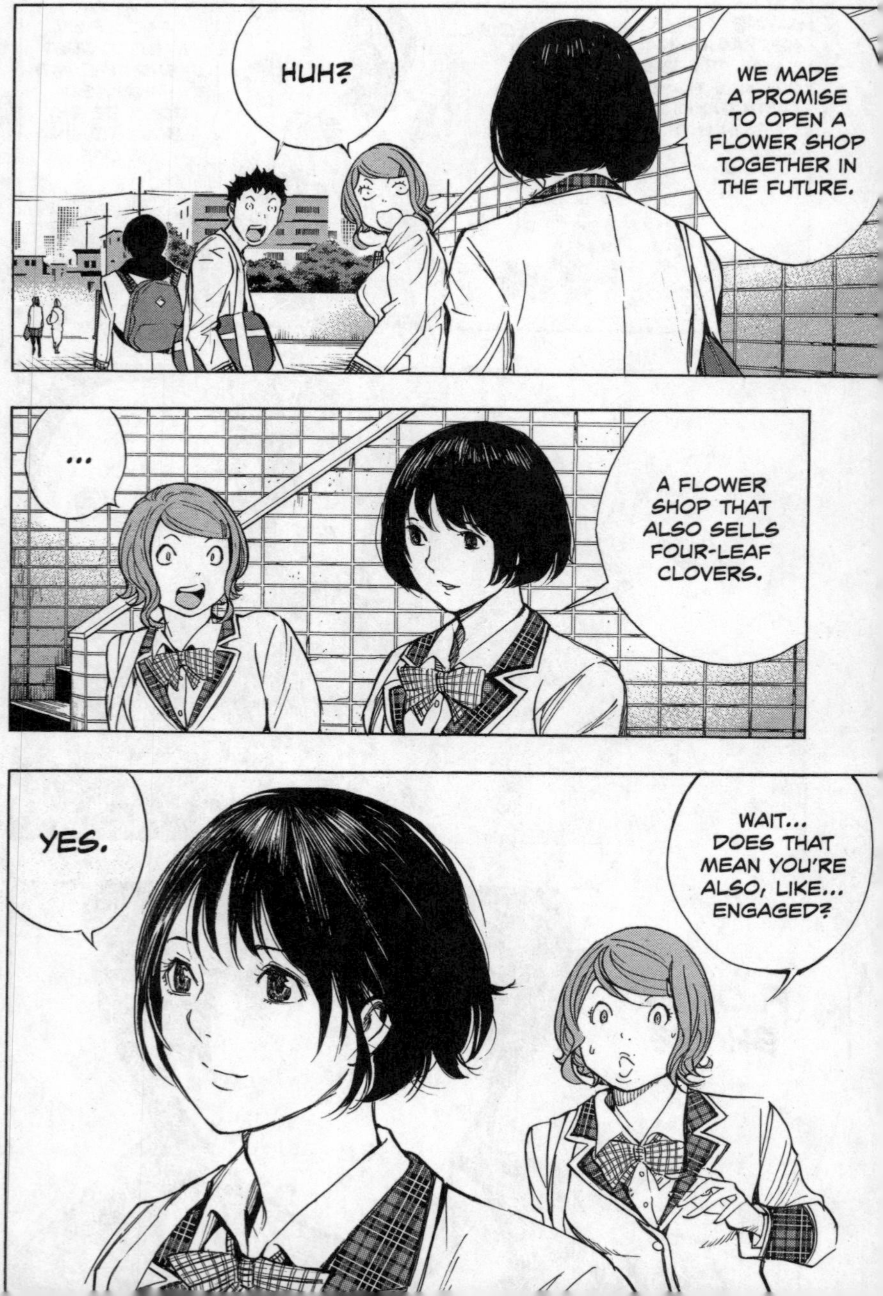
WE MADE A PROMISE TO OPEN A FLOWER SHOP TOGETHER IN THE FUTURE.
HUH?
A FLOWER SHOP THAT ALSO SELLS FOUR-LEAF CLOVERS.
...
WAIT... DOES THAT MEAN YOU'RE ALSO, LIKE... ENGAGED?
YES.

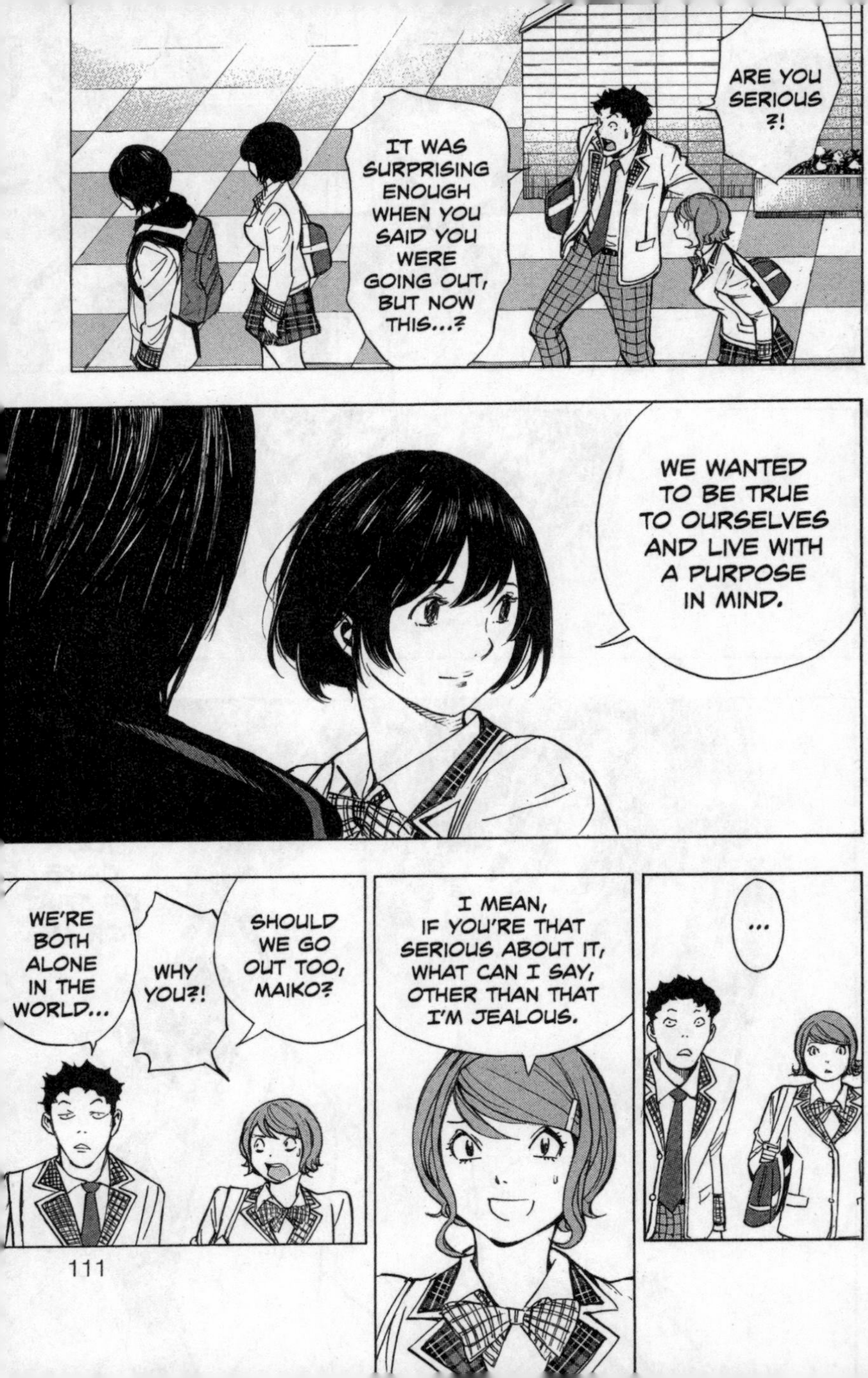
ARE YOU SERIOUS?!
IT WAS SURPRISING ENOUGH WHEN YOU SAID YOU WERE GOING OUT, BUT NOW THIS...?
WE WANTED TO BE TRUE TO OURSELVES AND LIVE WITH A PURPOSE IN MIND.
...
I MEAN, IF YOU'RE THAT SERIOUS ABOUT IT, WHAT CAN I SAY, OTHER THAN THAT I'M JEALOUS.
SHOULD WE GO OUT TOO, MAIKO?
WHY YOU?!
WE'RE BOTH ALONE IN THE WORLD...

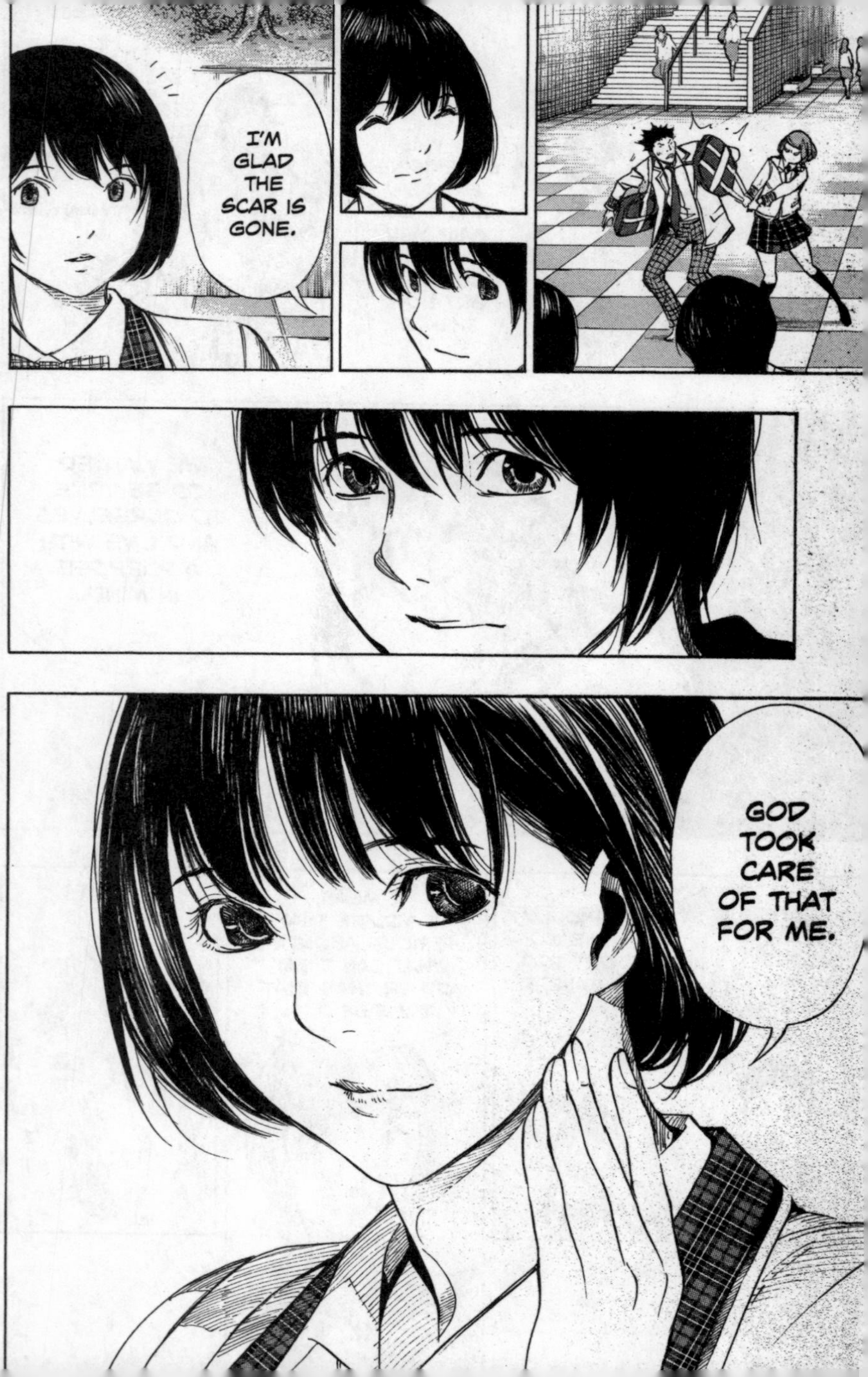
I'M GLAD THE SCAR IS GONE.
GOD TOOK CARE OF THAT FOR ME.

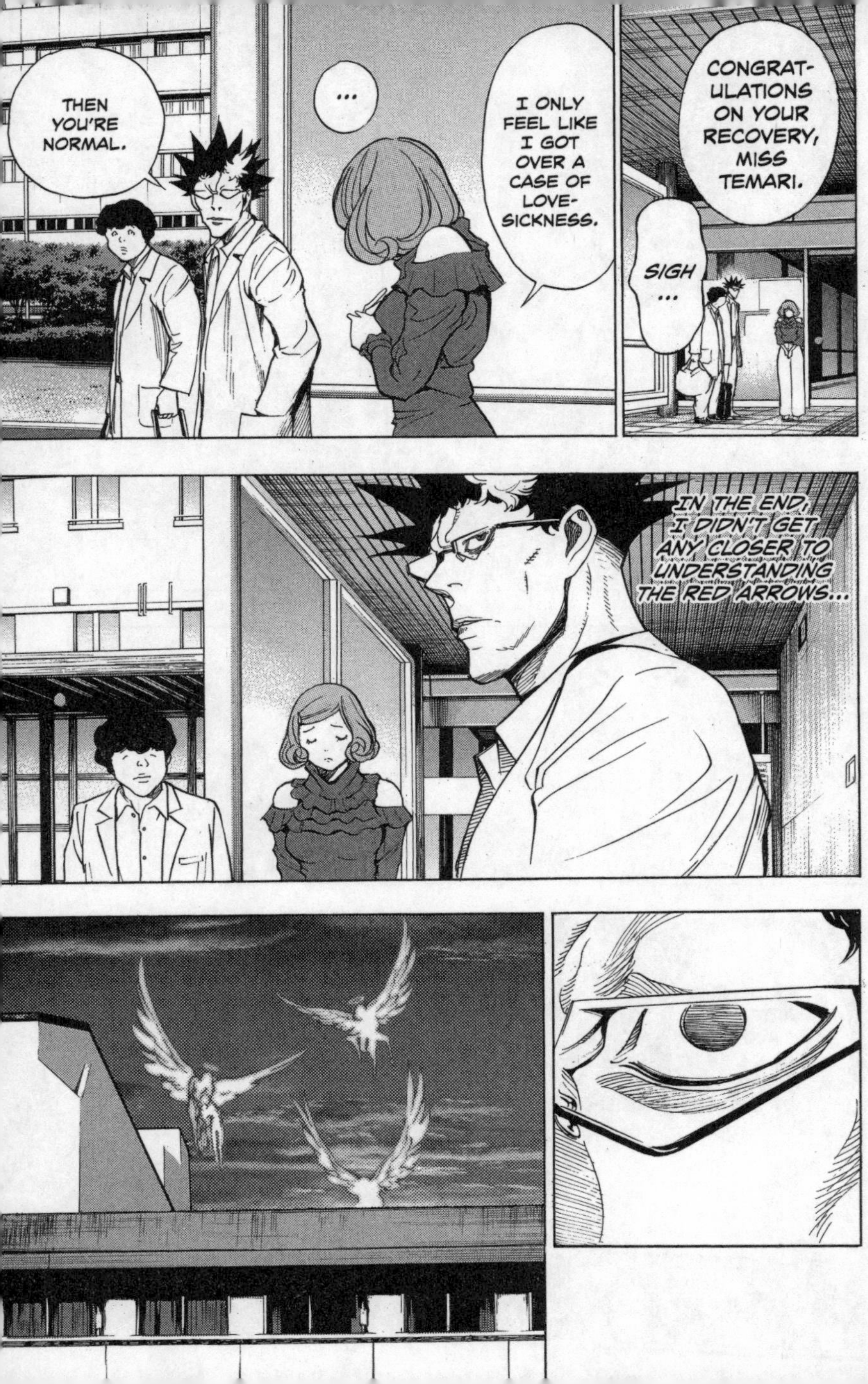
CONGRATULATIONS ON YOUR RECOVERY, MISS TEMARI.
SIGH...
I ONLY FEEL LIKE I GOT OVER A CASE OF LOVE-SICKNESS.
...
THEN YOU'RE NORMAL.
IN THE END, I DIDN'T GET ANY CLOSER TO UNDERSTANDING THE RED ARROWS...

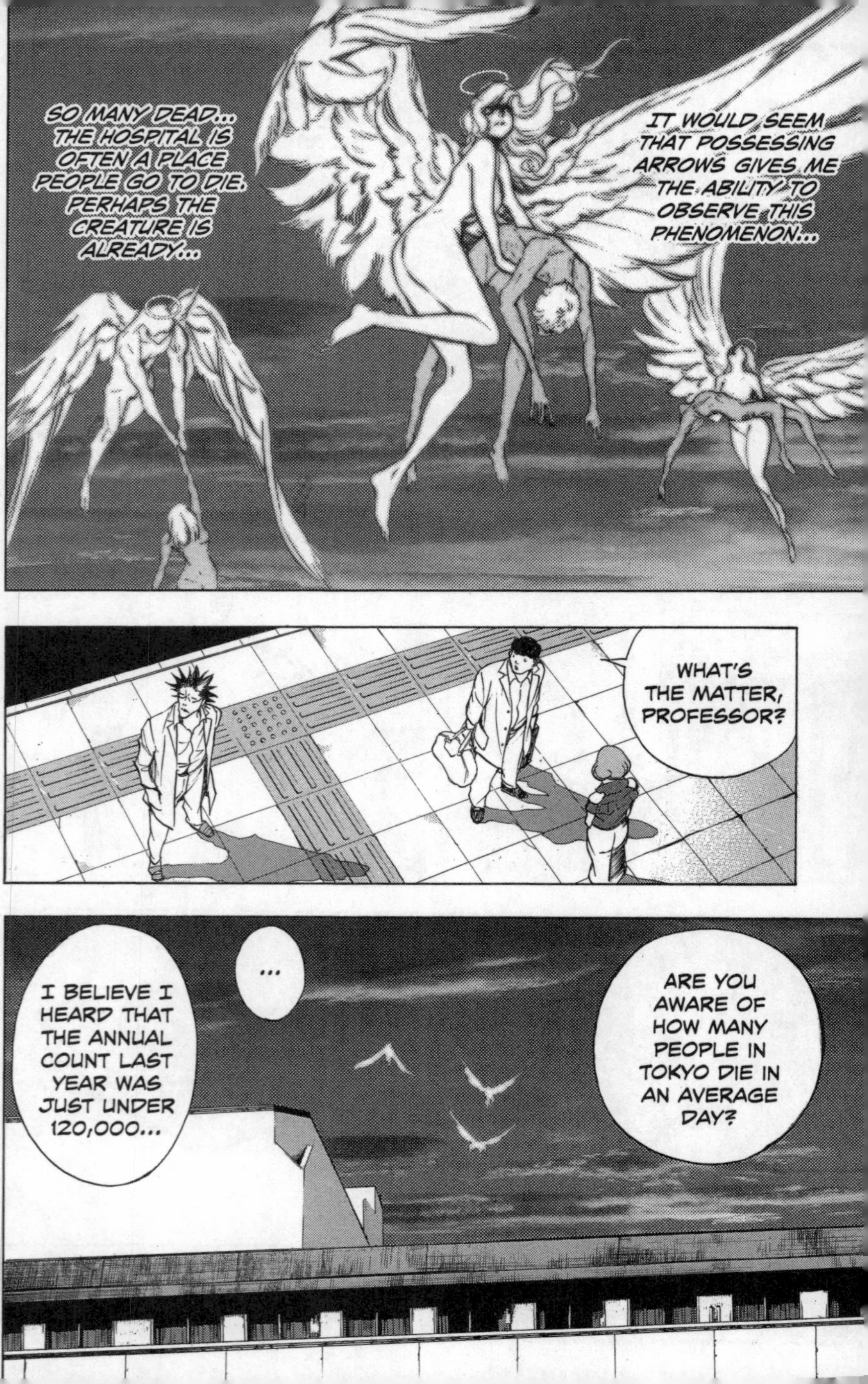
IT WOULD SEEM THAT POSSESSING ARROWS GIVES ME THE ABILITY TO OBSERVE THIS PHENOMENON...
SO MANY DEAD... THE HOSPITAL IS OFTEN A PLACE PEOPLE GO TO DIE. PERHAPS THE CREATURE IS ALREADY...
WHAT'S THE MATTER, PROFESSOR?
ARE YOU AWARE OF HOW MANY PEOPLE IN TOKYO DIE IN AN AVERAGE DAY?
...
I BELIEVE I HEARD THAT THE ANNUAL COUNT LAST YEAR WAS JUST UNDER 120,000...

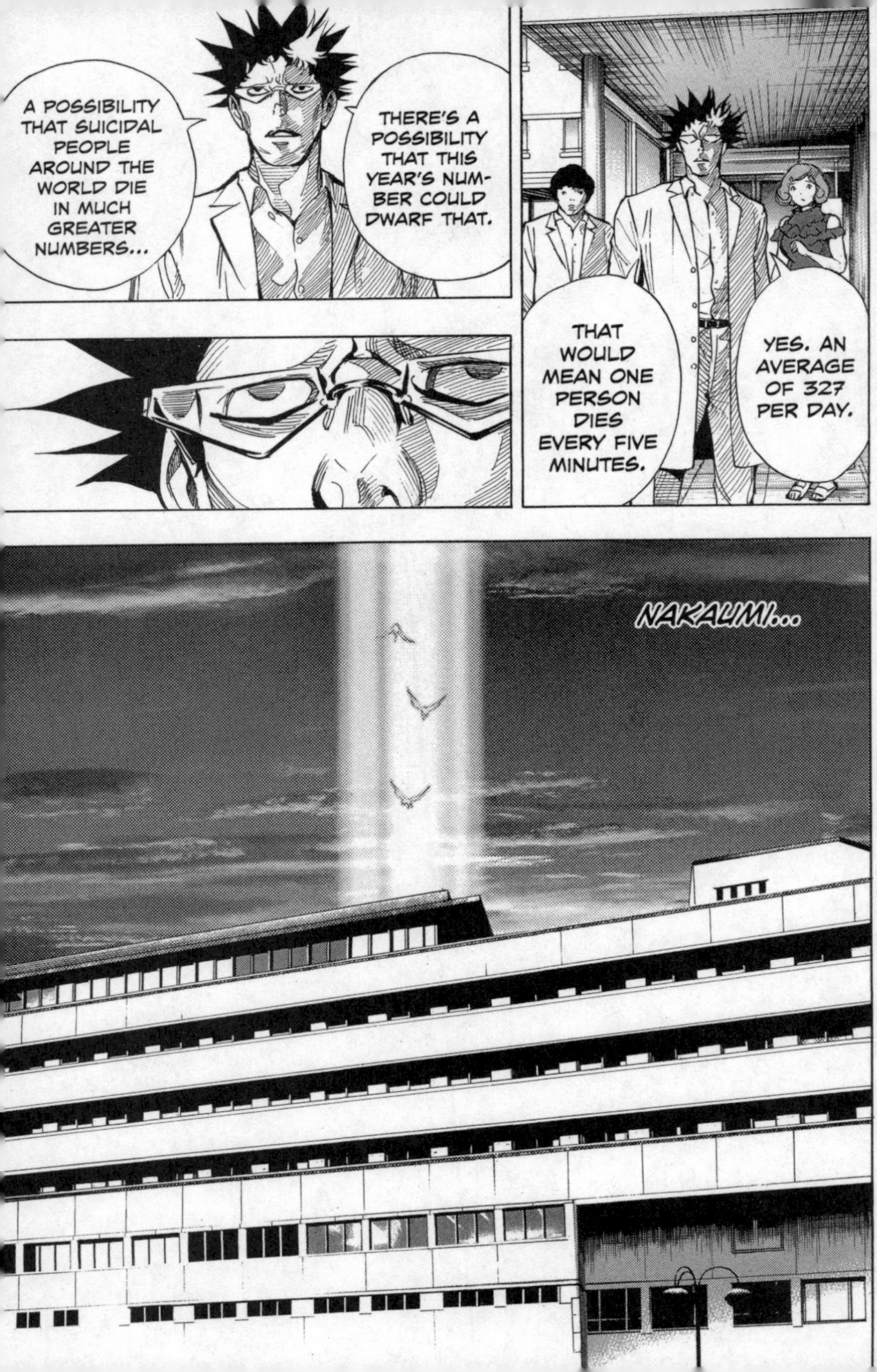
YES. AN AVERAGE OF 327 PER DAY.
THAT WOULD MEAN ONE PERSON DIES EVERY FIVE MINUTES.
THERE'S A POSSIBILITY THAT THIS YEAR'S NUMBER COULD DWARF THAT.
A POSSIBILITY THAT SUICIDAL PEOPLE AROUND THE WORLD DIE IN MUCH GREATER NUMBERS...
NAKAUMI...

#57 Each One's Happiness

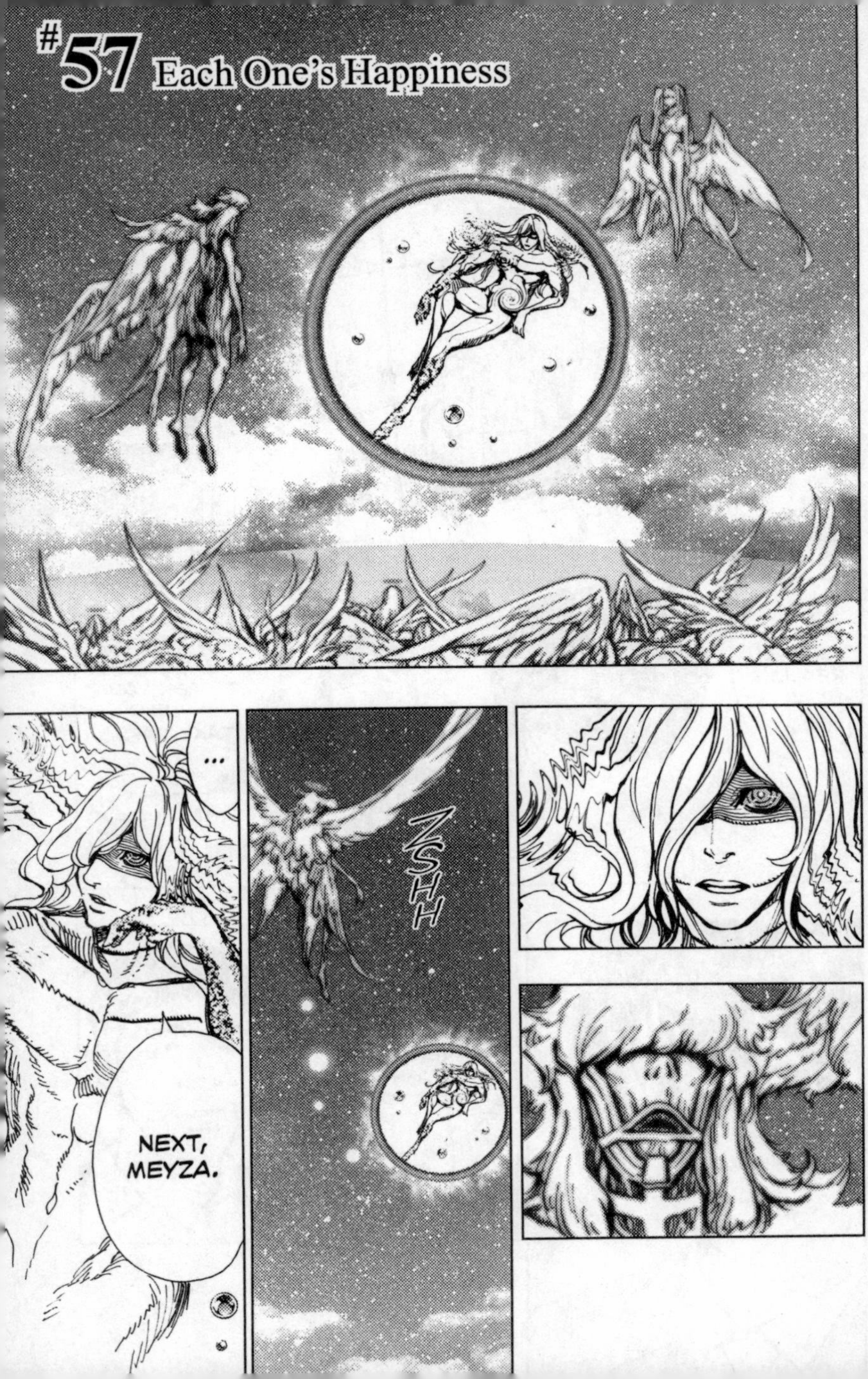
SHH
...
NEXT, MEYZA.

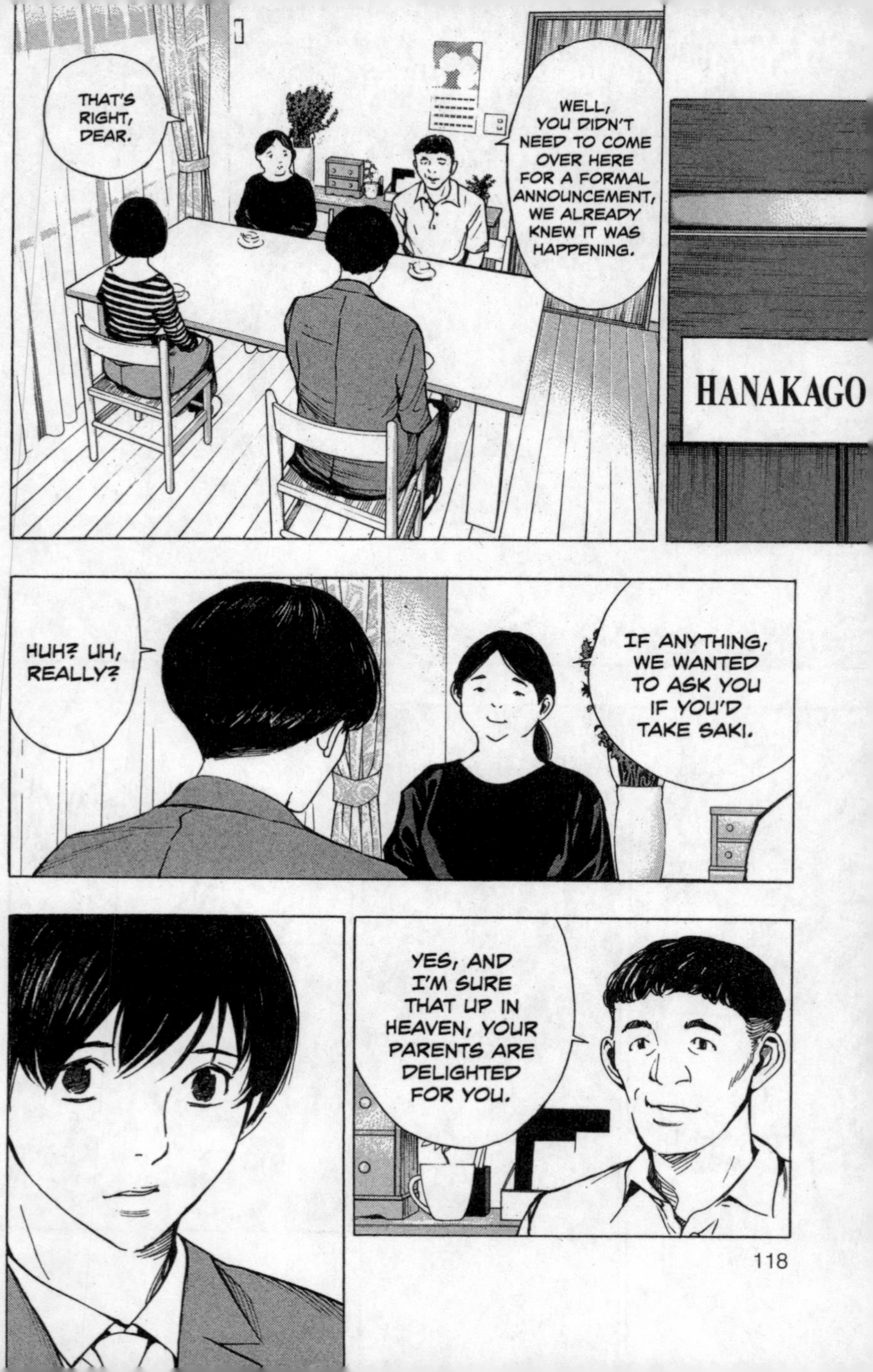
HANAKAGO
WELL, YOU DIDN'T NEED TO COME OVER HERE FOR A FORMAL ANNOUNCEMENT, WE ALREADY KNEW IT WAS HAPPENING.
THAT'S RIGHT, DEAR.
IF ANYTHING, WE WANTED TO ASK YOU IF YOU'D TAKE SAKI.
HUH? UH, REALLY?
YES, AND I'M SURE THAT UP IN HEAVEN, YOUR PARENTS ARE DELIGHTED FOR YOU.

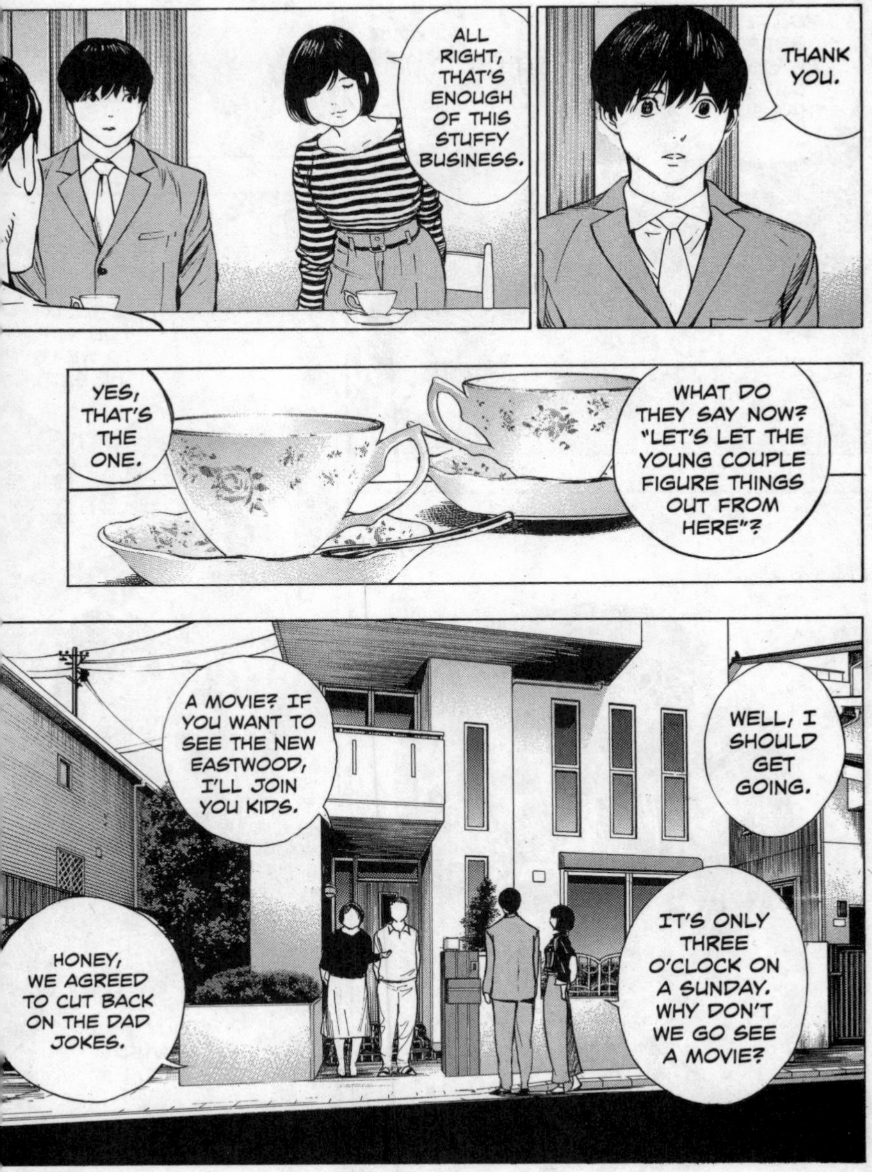
THANK YOU.
ALL RIGHT, THAT'S ENOUGH OF THIS STUFFY BUSINESS.
WHAT DO THEY SAY NOW? "LET'S LET THE YOUNG COUPLE FIGURE THINGS OUT FROM HERE"?
YES, THAT'S THE ONE.
WELL, I SHOULD GET GOING.
IT'S ONLY THREE O'CLOCK ON A SUNDAY. WHY DON'T WE GO SEE A MOVIE?
A MOVIE? IF YOU WANT TO SEE THE NEW EASTWOOD, I'LL JOIN YOU KIDS.
HONEY, WE AGREED TO CUT BACK ON THE DAD JOKES.

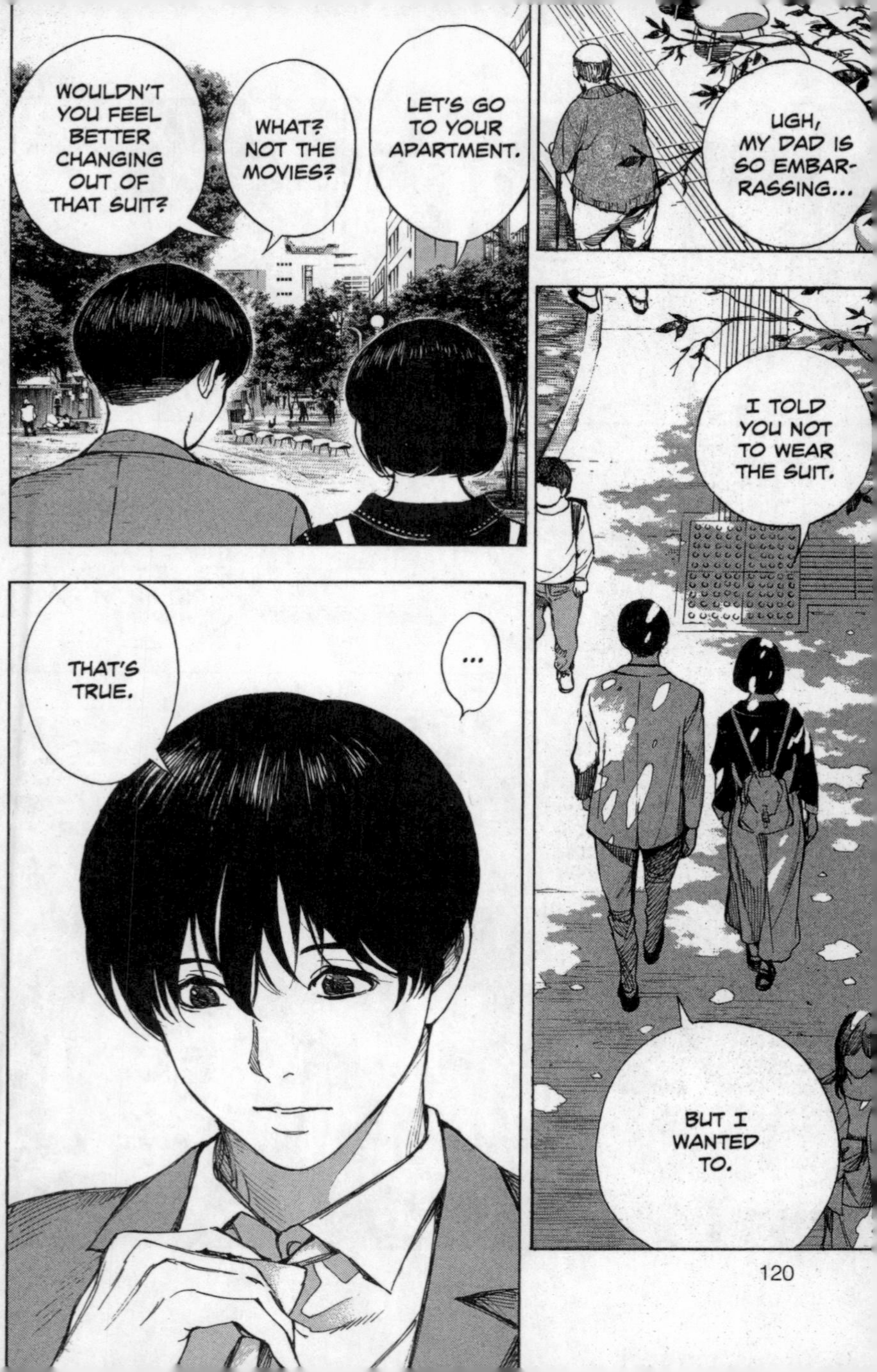
UGH, MY DAD IS SO EMBARRASSING...
LET'S GO TO YOUR APARTMENT.
WHAT? NOT THE MOVIES?
WOULDN'T YOU FEEL BETTER CHANGING OUT OF THAT SUIT?
I TOLD YOU NOT TO WEAR THE SUIT.
BUT I WANTED TO.
...
THAT'S TRUE.

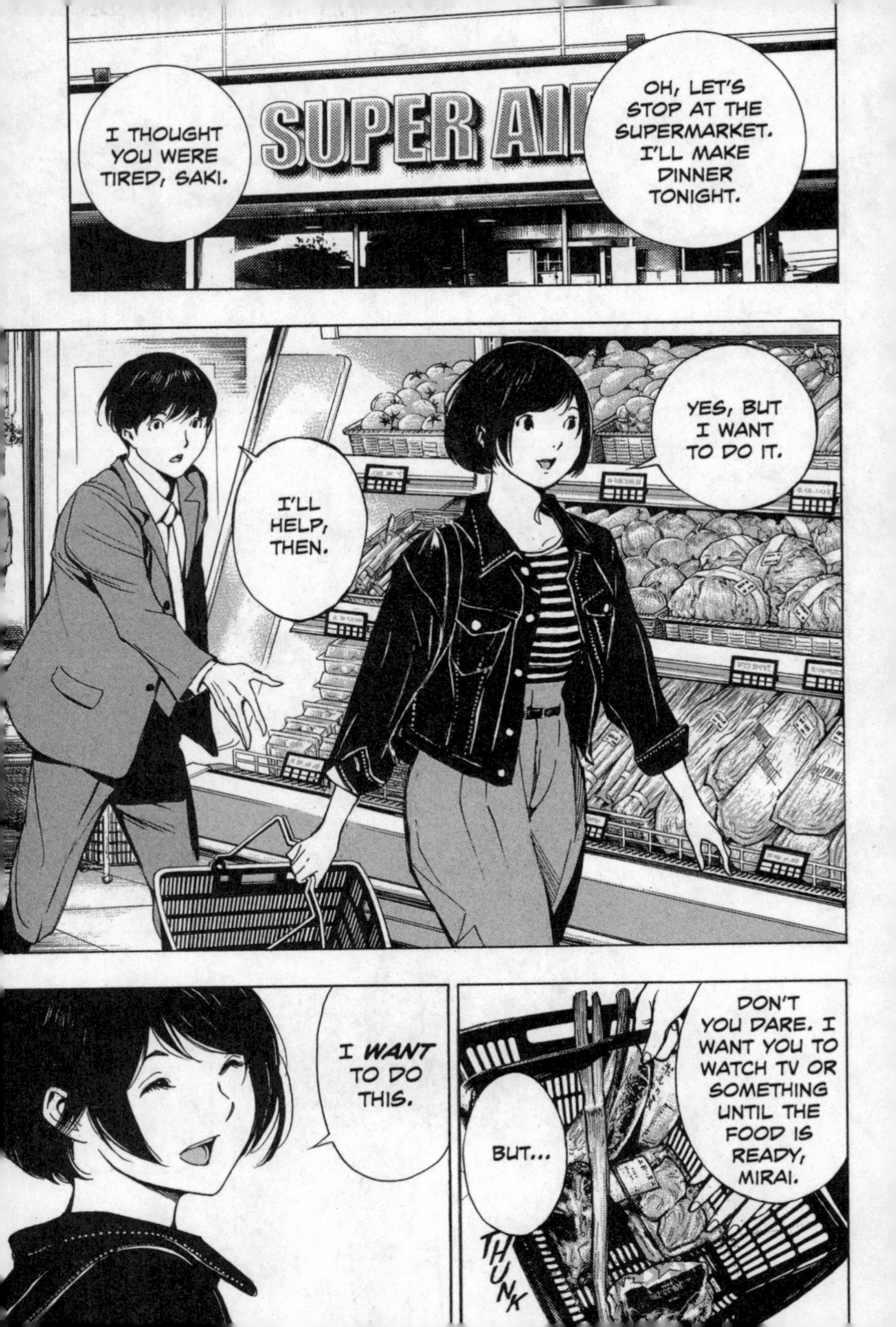
OH, LET'S STOP AT THE SUPERMARKET. I'LL MAKE DINNER TONIGHT.
I THOUGHT YOU WERE TIRED, SAKI.
YES, BUT I WANT TO DO IT.
I'LL HELP, THEN.
DON'T YOU DARE. I WANT YOU TO WATCH TV OR SOMETHING UNTIL THE FOOD IS READY, MIRAI.
BUT...
THUNK
I *WANT* TO DO THIS.

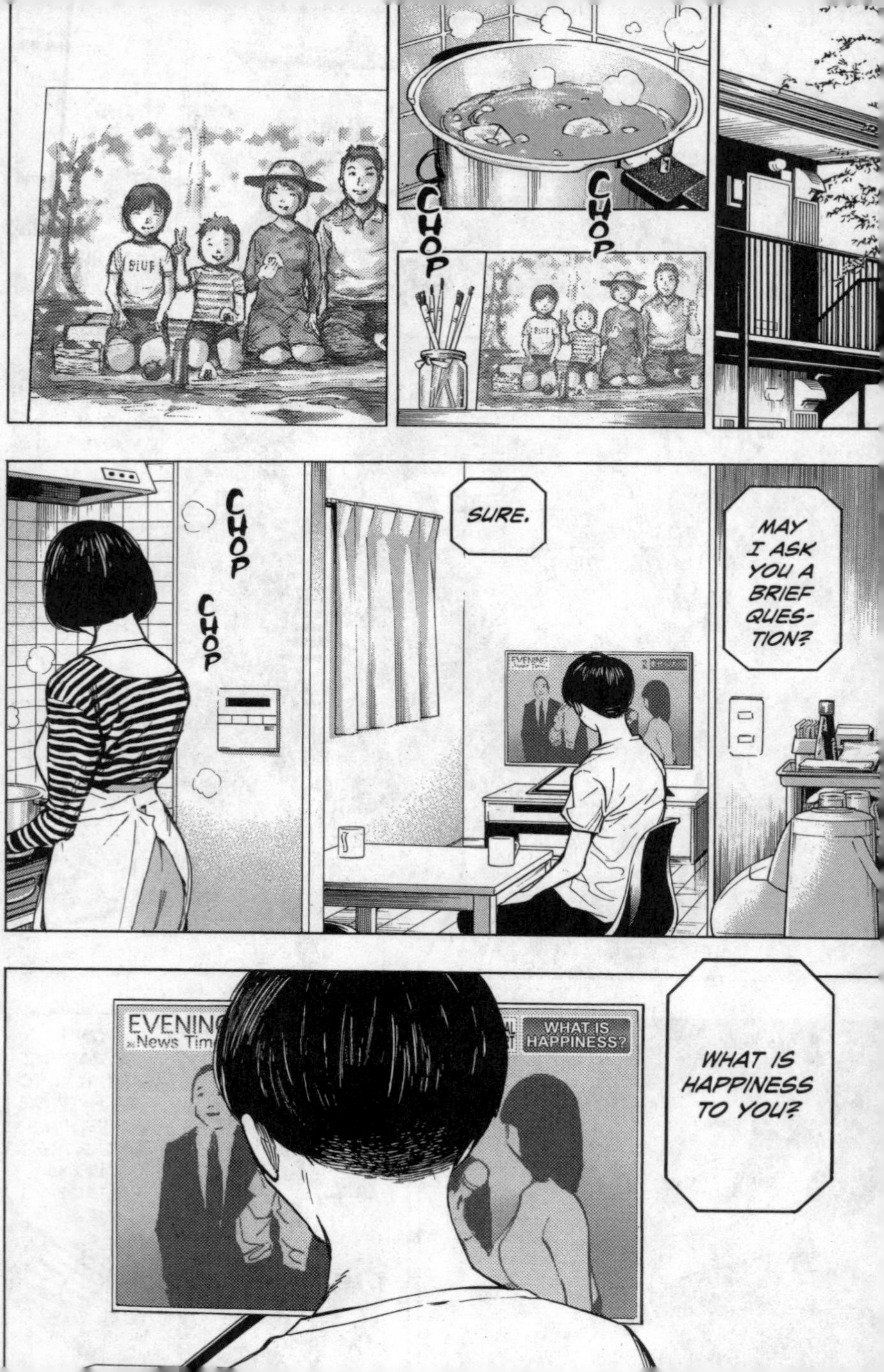
CHOP
CHOP
CHOP CHOP
MAY I ASK YOU A BRIEF QUES-TION?
SURE.
CHOP CHOP
WHAT IS HAPPINESS TO YOU?
WHAT IS HAPPINESS?
EVENING

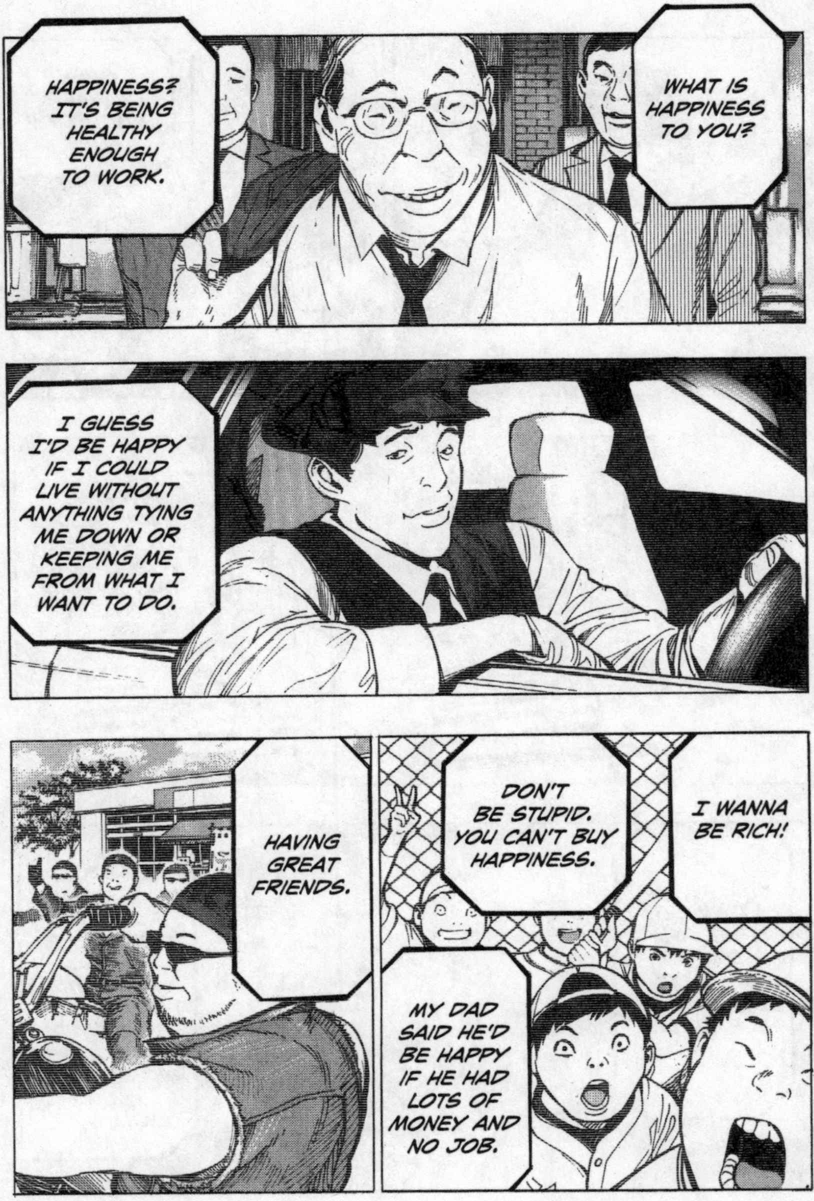
WHAT IS HAPPINESS TO YOU?
HAPPINESS? IT'S BEING HEALTHY ENOUGH TO WORK.
I GUESS I'D BE HAPPY IF I COULD LIVE WITHOUT ANYTHING TYING ME DOWN OR KEEPING ME FROM WHAT I WANT TO DO.
I WANNA BE RICH!
DON'T BE STUPID. YOU CAN'T BUY HAPPINESS.
MY DAD SAID HE'D BE HAPPY IF HE HAD LOTS OF MONEY AND NO JOB.
HAVING GREAT FRIENDS.

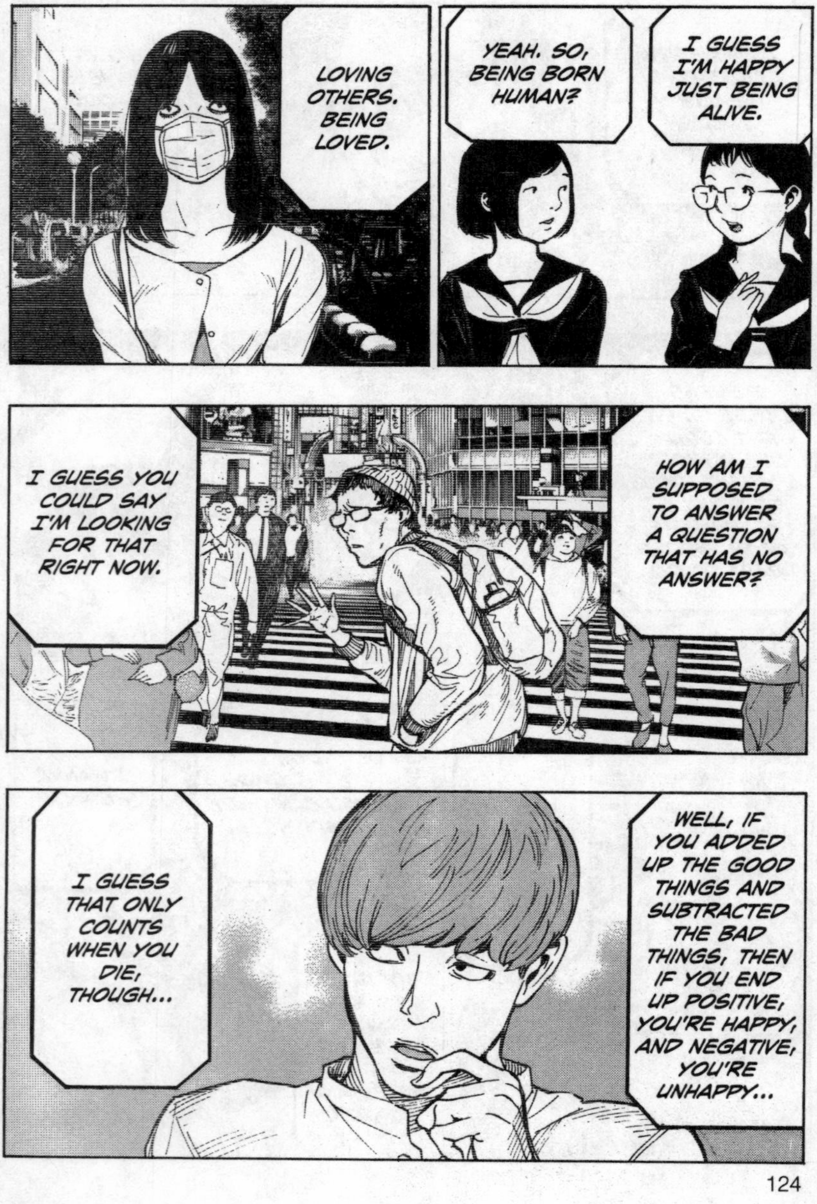
I GUESS I'M HAPPY JUST BEING ALIVE.
YEAH. SO, BEING BORN HUMAN?
LOVING OTHERS. BEING LOVED.
HOW AM I SUPPOSED TO ANSWER A QUESTION THAT HAS NO ANSWER?
I GUESS YOU COULD SAY I'M LOOKING FOR THAT RIGHT NOW.
WELL, IF YOU ADDED UP THE GOOD THINGS AND SUBTRACTED THE BAD THINGS, THEN IF YOU END UP POSITIVE, YOU'RE HAPPY, AND NEGATIVE, YOU'RE UNHAPPY...
I GUESS THAT ONLY COUNTS WHEN YOU DIE, THOUGH...

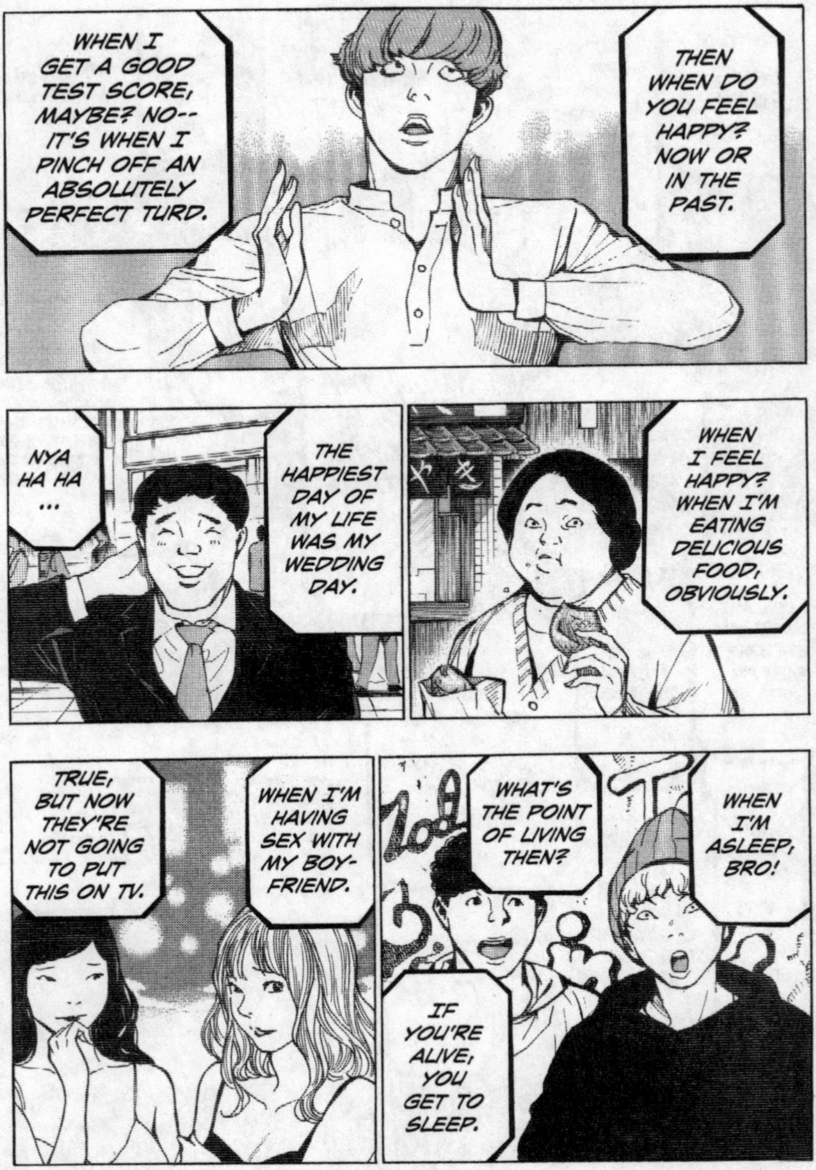
THEN WHEN DO YOU FEEL HAPPY? NOW OR IN THE PAST.
WHEN I GET A GOOD TEST SCORE, MAYBE? NO-- IT'S WHEN I PINCH OFF AN ABSOLUTELY PERFECT TURD.
WHEN I FEEL HAPPY? WHEN I'M EATING DELICIOUS FOOD, OBVIOUSLY.
THE HAPPIEST DAY OF MY LIFE WAS MY WEDDING DAY.
NYA HA HA ...
WHEN I'M ASLEEP, BRO!
WHAT'S THE POINT OF LIVING THEN?
IF YOU'RE ALIVE, YOU GET TO SLEEP.
WHEN I'M HAVING SEX WITH MY BOY-FRIEND.
TRUE, BUT NOW THEY'RE NOT GOING TO PUT THIS ON TV.

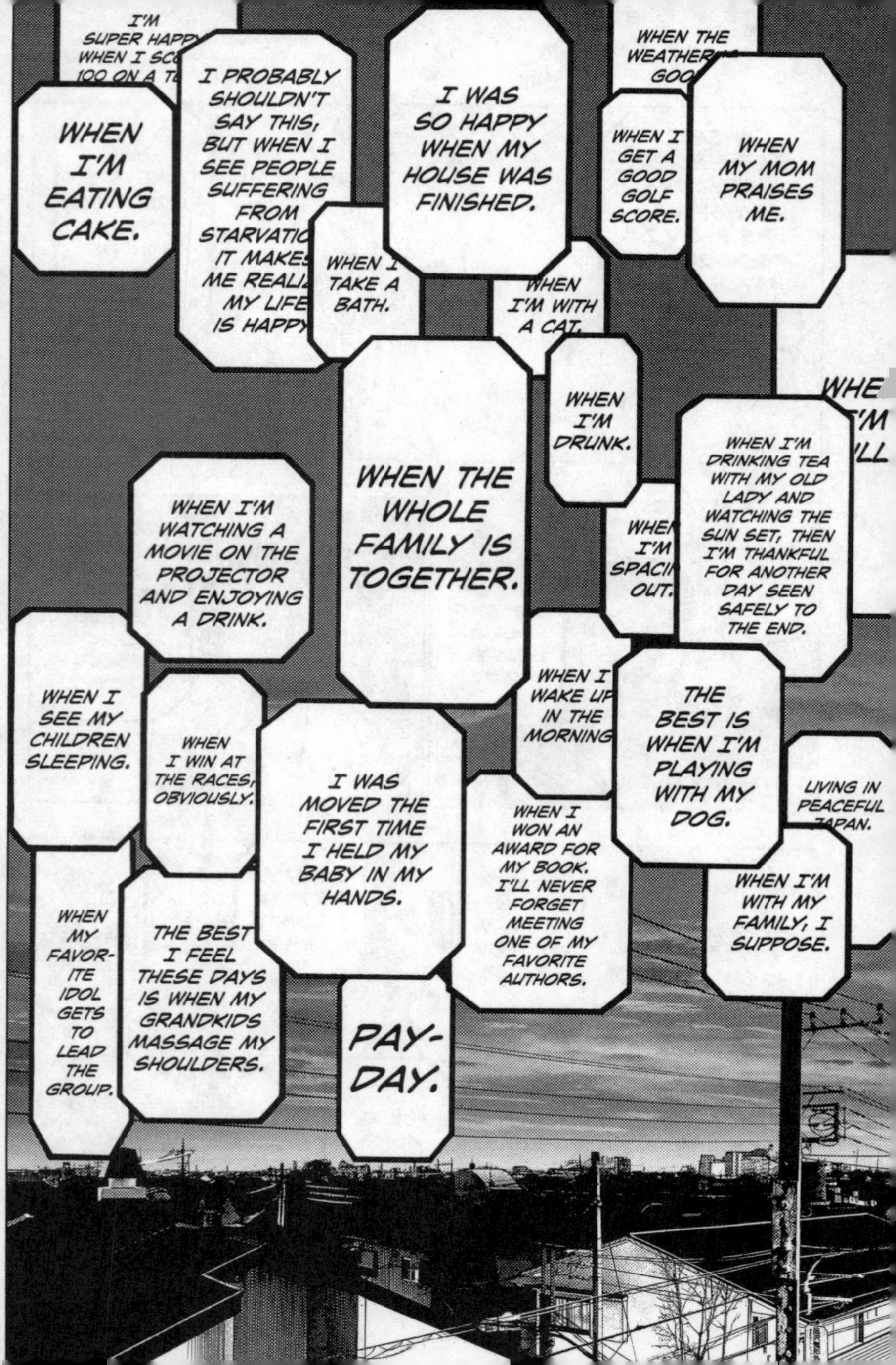

WHEN THE WEATHER
WHEN MY MOM PRAISES ME.
WHEN I GET A GOOD GOLF SCORE.
I WAS SO HAPPY WHEN MY HOUSE WAS FINISHED.
I'M SUPER WHEN I 100 ON A
I PROBABLY SHOULDN'T SAY THIS, BUT WHEN I SEE PEOPLE SUFFERING FROM IT ME MY IS
WHEN I'M EATING CAKE.
WHEN I'M WITH A CAT.
WHEN TAKE A BATH.
WHEN I'M DRUNK.
WHEN I'M DRINKING TEA WITH MY OLD LADY AND WATCHING THE SUN SET, THEN I'M THANKFUL FOR ANOTHER DAY SEEN SAFELY TO THE END.
I'M OUT.
WHEN THE WHOLE FAMILY IS TOGETHER.
WHEN I'M WATCHING A MOVIE ON THE PROJECTOR AND ENJOYING A DRINK.
LIVING IN PEACEFUL
THE BEST IS WHEN I'M PLAYING WITH MY DOG.
WHEN I WAKE IN THE
WHEN I SEE MY CHILDREN SLEEPING.
WHEN I WIN AT THE OBVIOUSLY.
WHEN I'M WITH MY FAMILY, I SUPPOSE.
WHEN I WON AN AWARD FOR MY BOOK. I'LL NEVER FORGET MEETING ONE OF MY FAVORITE AUTHORS.
I WAS MOVED THE FIRST TIME I HELD MY BABY IN MY HANDS.
PAY-DAY.
THE BEST I FEEL THESE DAYS IS WHEN MY GRANDKIDS MASSAGE MY SHOULDERS.
WHEN MY FAVOR-ITE IDOL GETS TO LEAD THE GROUP.

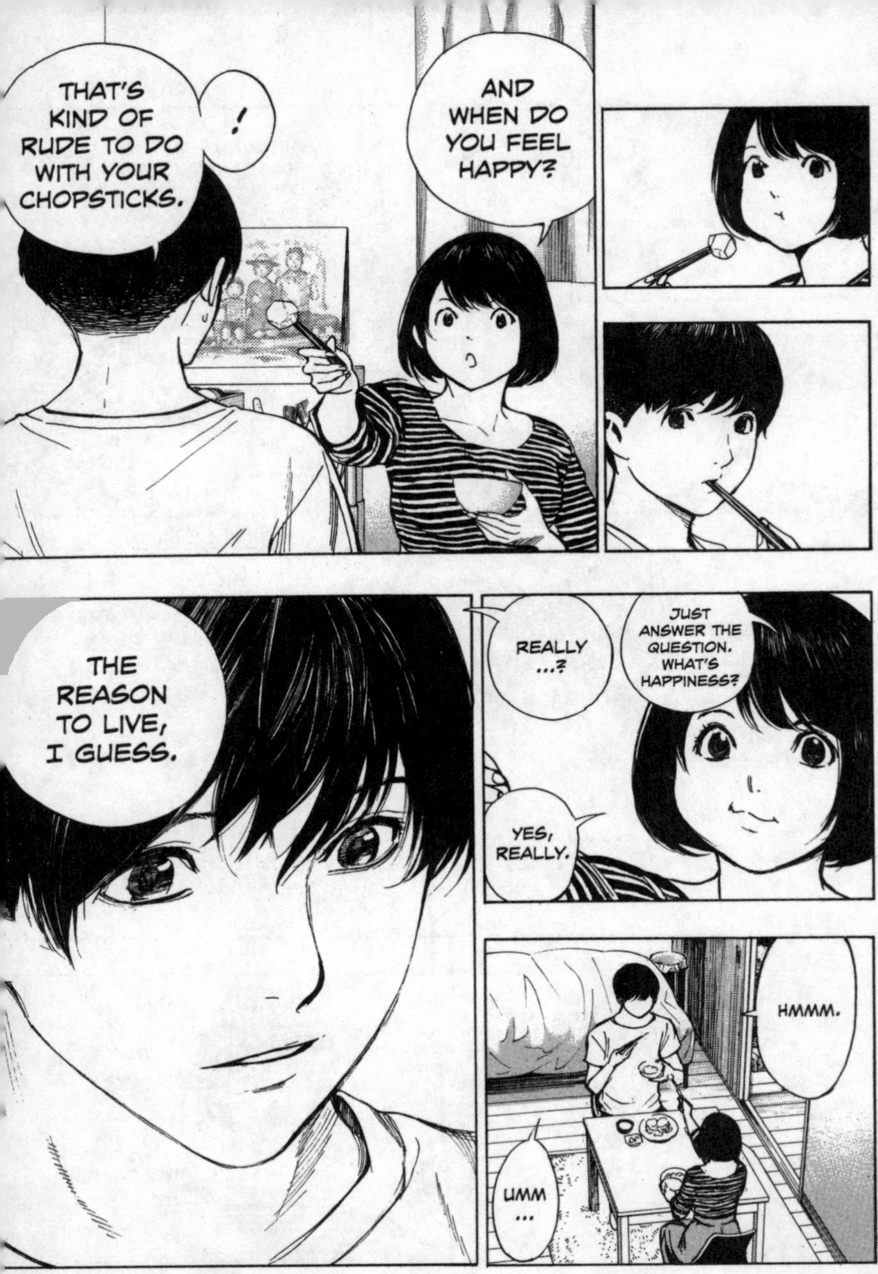
AND WHEN DO YOU FEEL HAPPY?
!
THAT'S KIND OF RUDE TO DO WITH YOUR CHOPSTICKS.
JUST ANSWER THE QUESTION. WHAT'S HAPPINESS?
REALLY ...?
YES, REALLY.
HMMM.
UMM ...
THE REASON TO LIVE, I GUESS.

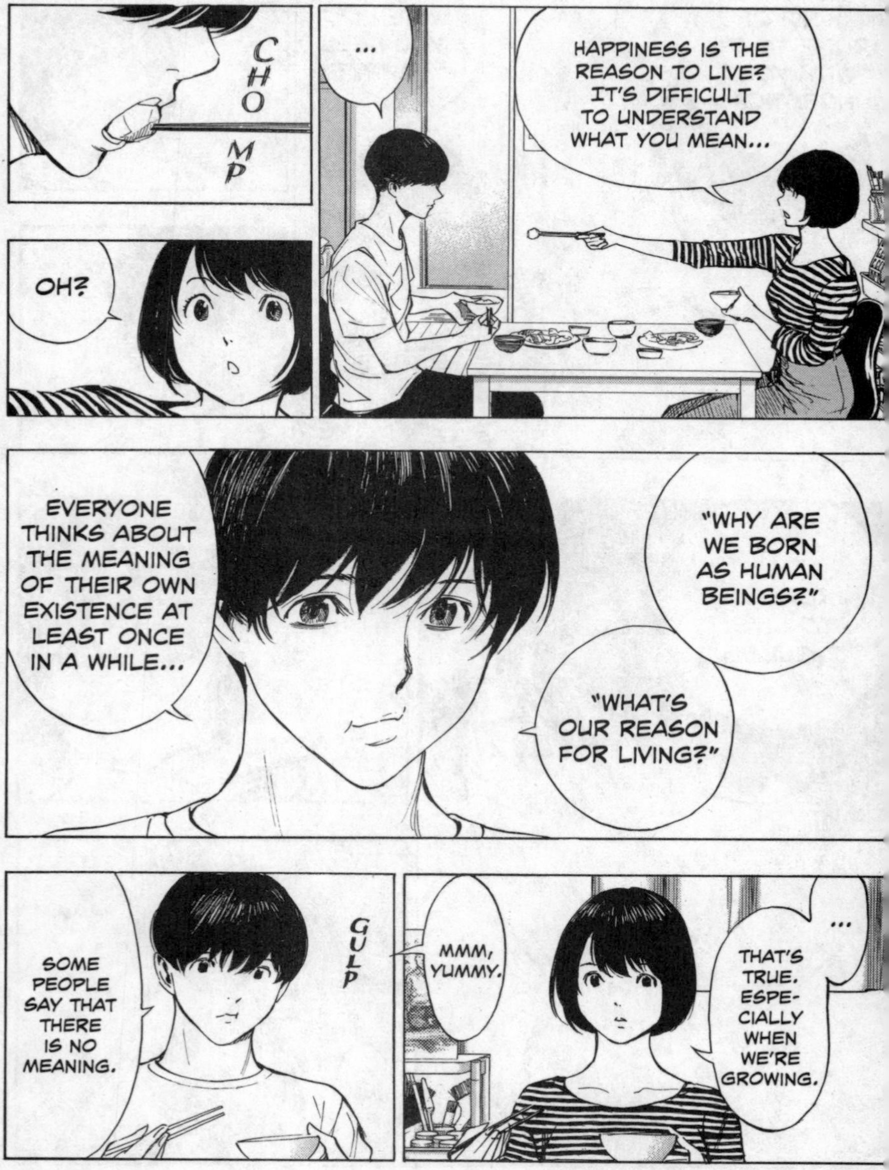
HAPPINESS IS THE REASON TO LIVE? IT'S DIFFICULT TO UNDERSTAND WHAT YOU MEAN...
...
CHOMP
OH?
"WHY ARE WE BORN AS HUMAN BEINGS?"
"WHAT'S OUR REASON FOR LIVING?"
EVERYONE THINKS ABOUT THE MEANING OF THEIR OWN EXISTENCE AT LEAST ONCE IN A WHILE...
...
THAT'S TRUE. ESPE-CIALLY WHEN WE'RE GROWING.
MMM, YUMMY.
GULP
SOME PEOPLE SAY THAT THERE IS NO MEANING.

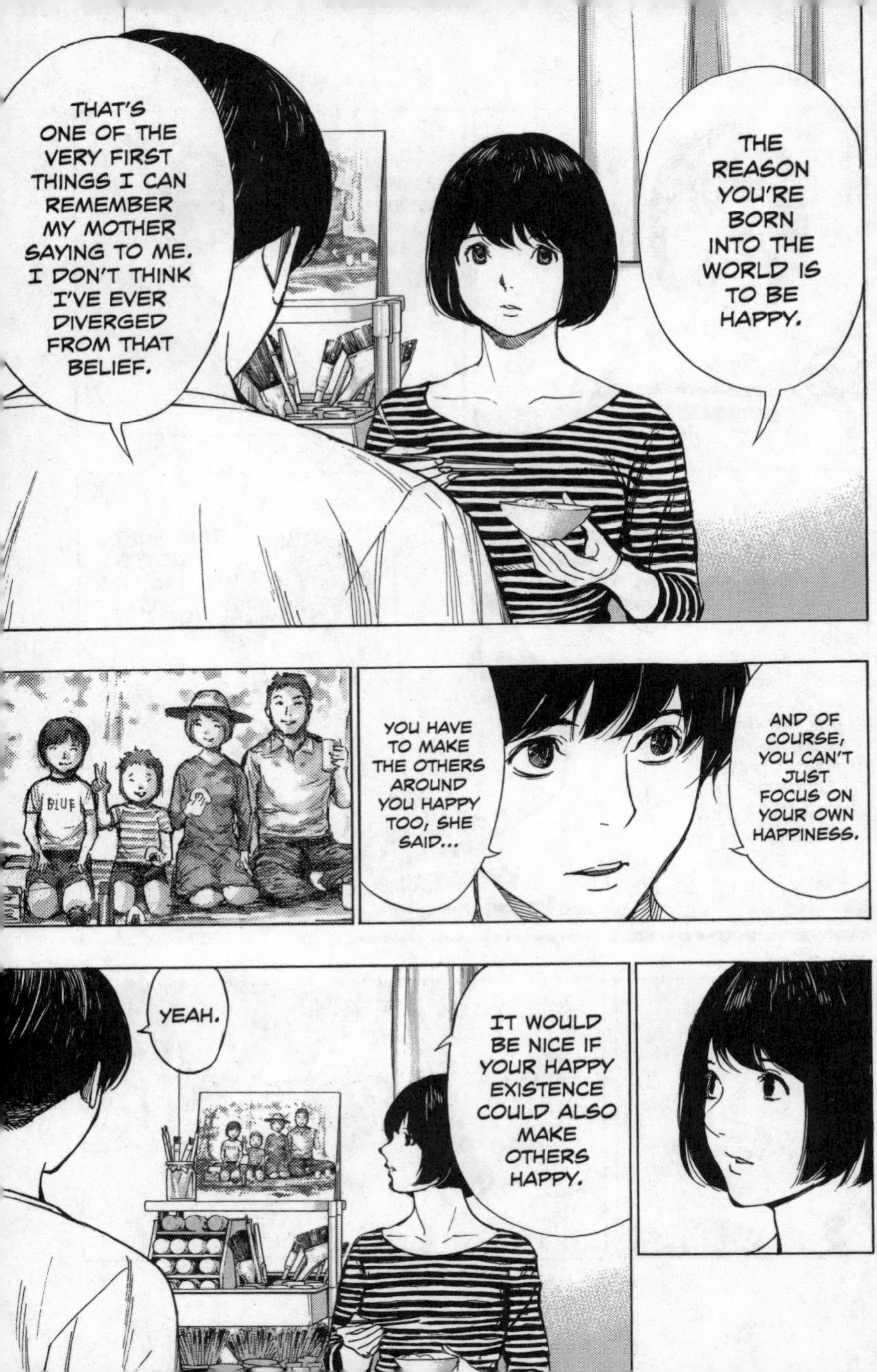
THE REASON YOU'RE BORN INTO THE WORLD IS TO BE HAPPY.
THAT'S ONE OF THE VERY FIRST THINGS I CAN REMEMBER MY MOTHER SAYING TO ME. I DON'T THINK I'VE EVER DIVERGED FROM THAT BELIEF.
AND OF COURSE, YOU CAN'T JUST FOCUS ON YOUR OWN HAPPINESS.
YOU HAVE TO MAKE THE OTHERS AROUND YOU HAPPY TOO, SHE SAID...
BLUE
IT WOULD BE NICE IF YOUR HAPPY EXISTENCE COULD ALSO MAKE OTHERS HAPPY.
YEAH.

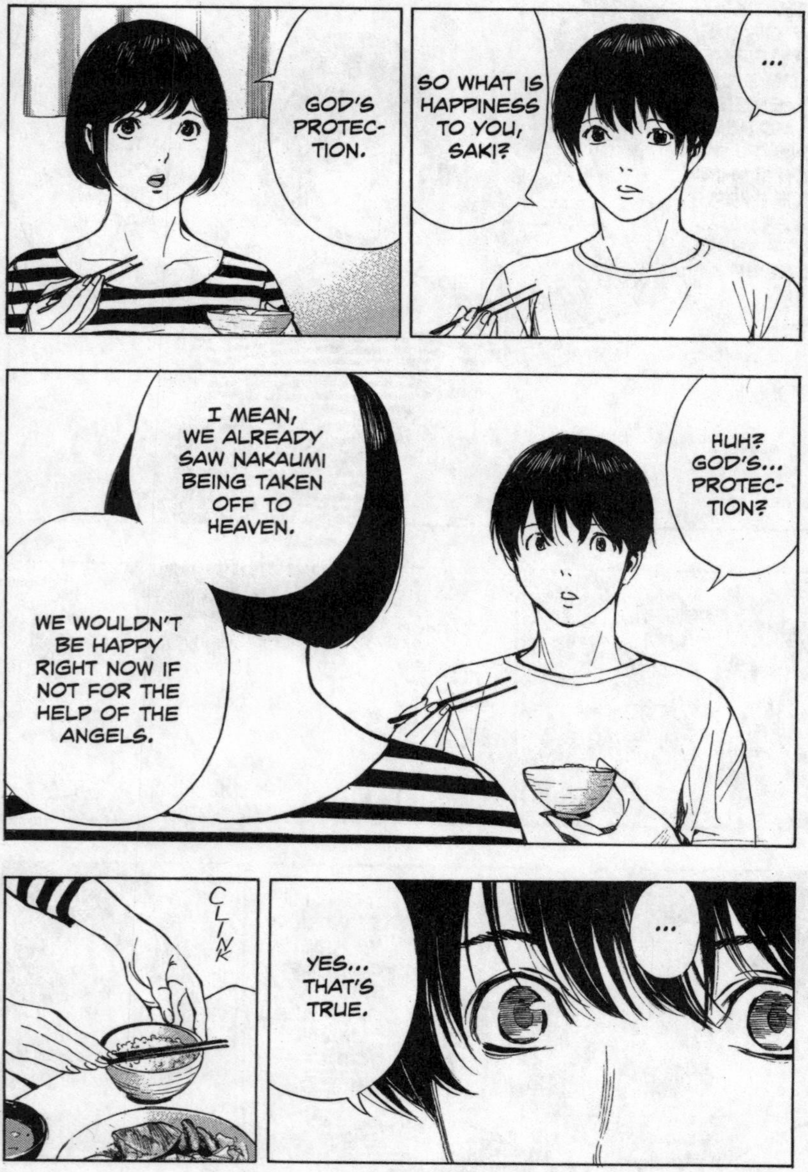
...
SO WHAT IS HAPPINESS TO YOU, SAKI?
GOD'S PROTECTION.
HUH? GOD'S... PROTECTION?
I MEAN, WE ALREADY SAW NAKAUMI BEING TAKEN OFF TO HEAVEN.
WE WOULDN'T BE HAPPY RIGHT NOW IF NOT FOR THE HELP OF THE ANGELS.
...
YES... THAT'S TRUE.
CLINK

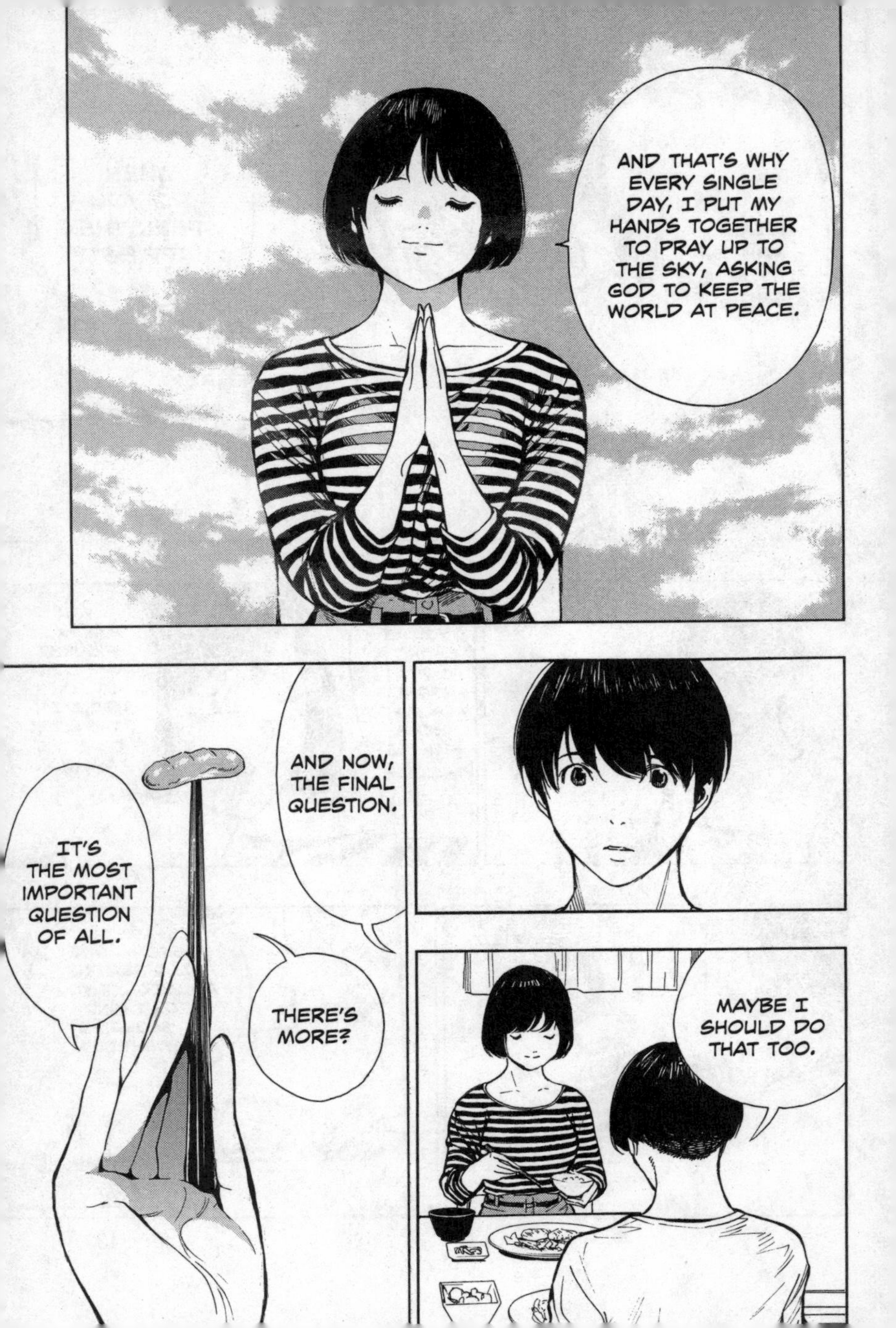
AND THAT'S WHY EVERY SINGLE DAY, I PUT MY HANDS TOGETHER TO PRAY UP TO THE SKY, ASKING GOD TO KEEP THE WORLD AT PEACE.
MAYBE I SHOULD DO THAT TOO.
AND NOW, THE FINAL QUESTION.
THERE'S MORE?
IT'S THE MOST IMPORTANT QUESTION OF ALL.

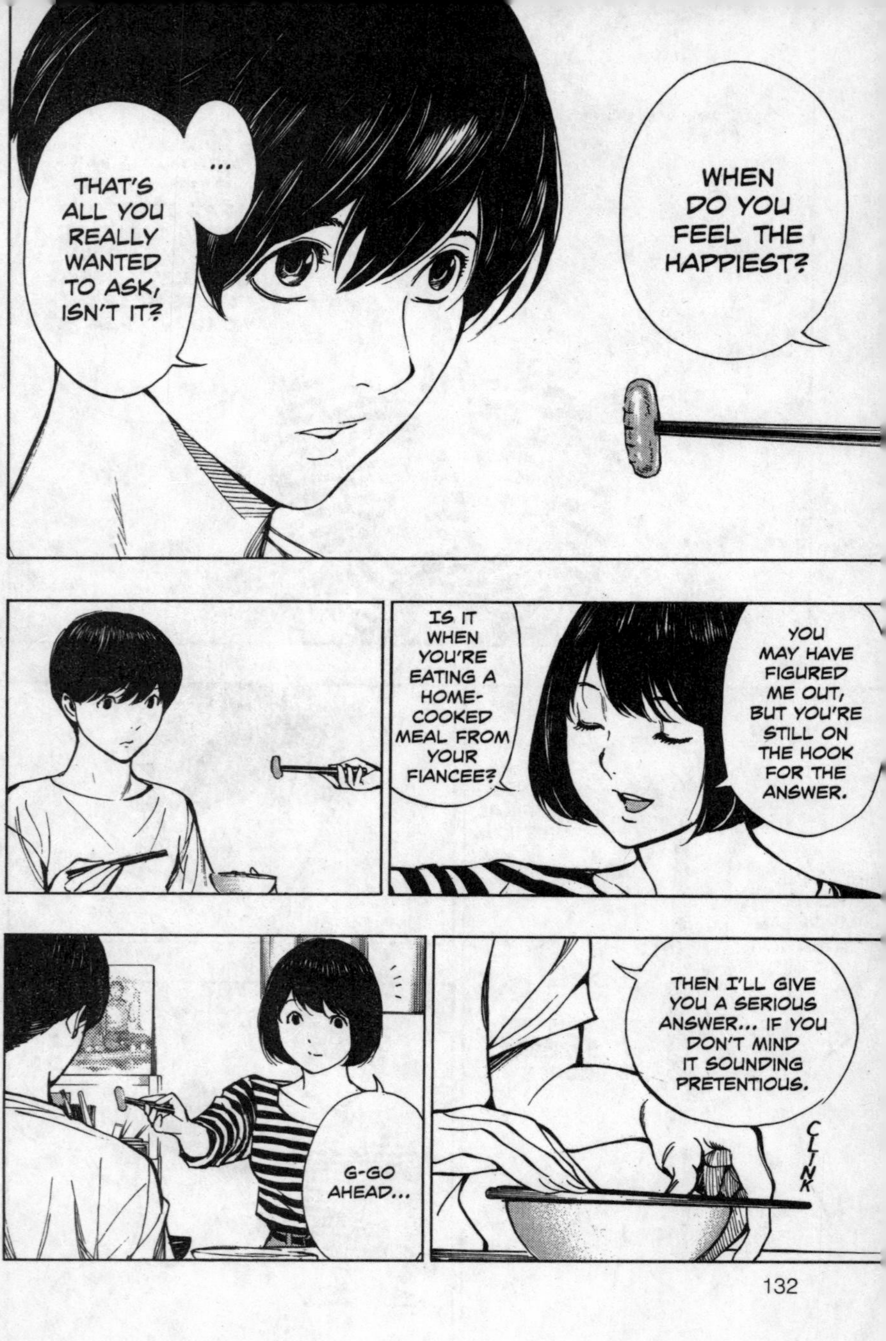
WHEN DO YOU FEEL THE HAPPIEST?
...
THAT'S ALL YOU REALLY WANTED TO ASK, ISN'T IT?
YOU MAY HAVE FIGURED ME OUT, BUT YOU'RE STILL ON THE HOOK FOR THE ANSWER.
IS IT WHEN YOU'RE EATING A HOME-COOKED MEAL FROM YOUR FIANCEE?
THEN I'LL GIVE YOU A SERIOUS ANSWER... IF YOU DON'T MIND IT SOUNDING PRETENTIOUS.
CLINK
G-GO AHEAD...

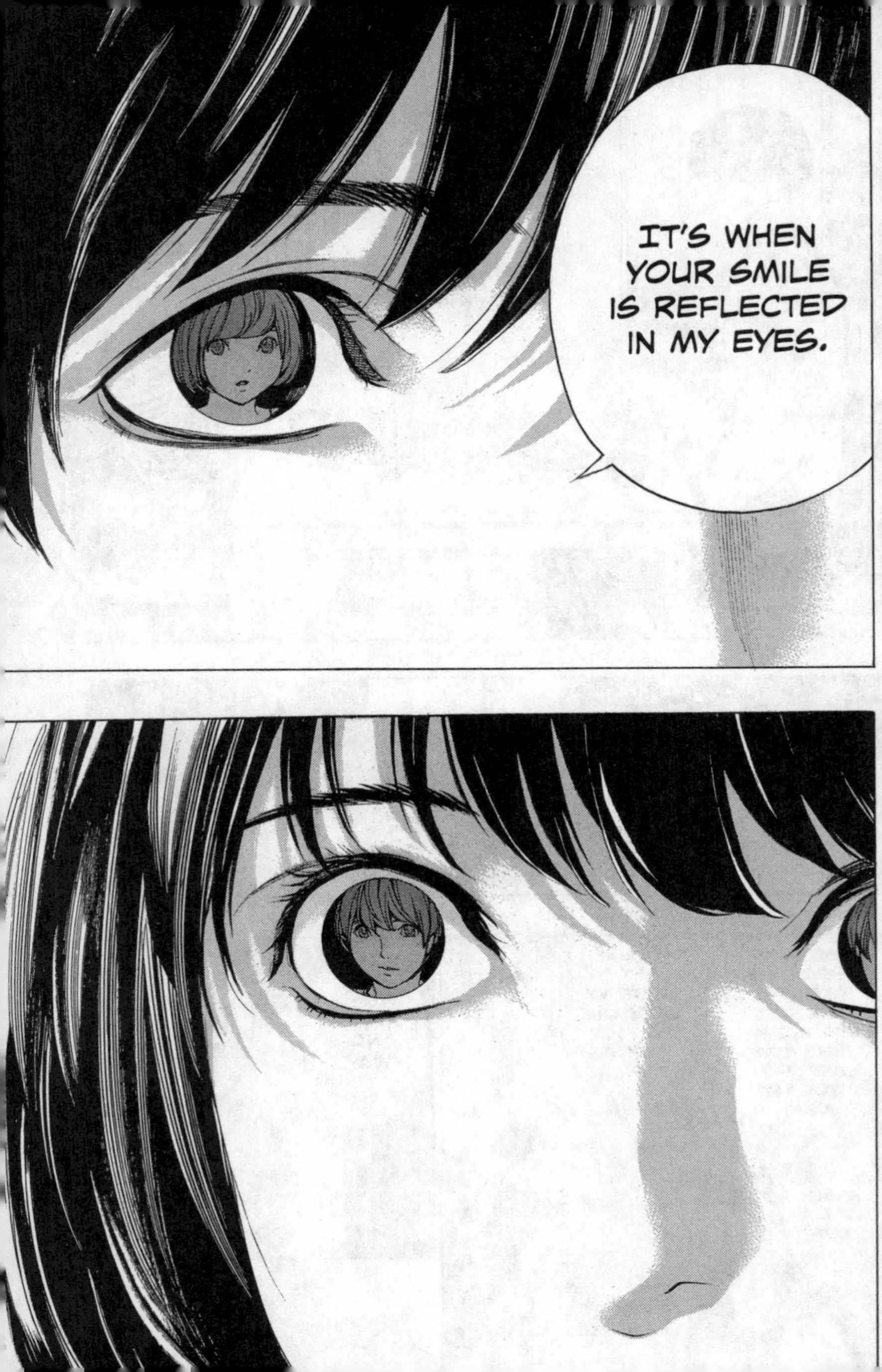
IT'S WHEN YOUR SMILE IS REFLECTED IN MY EYES.

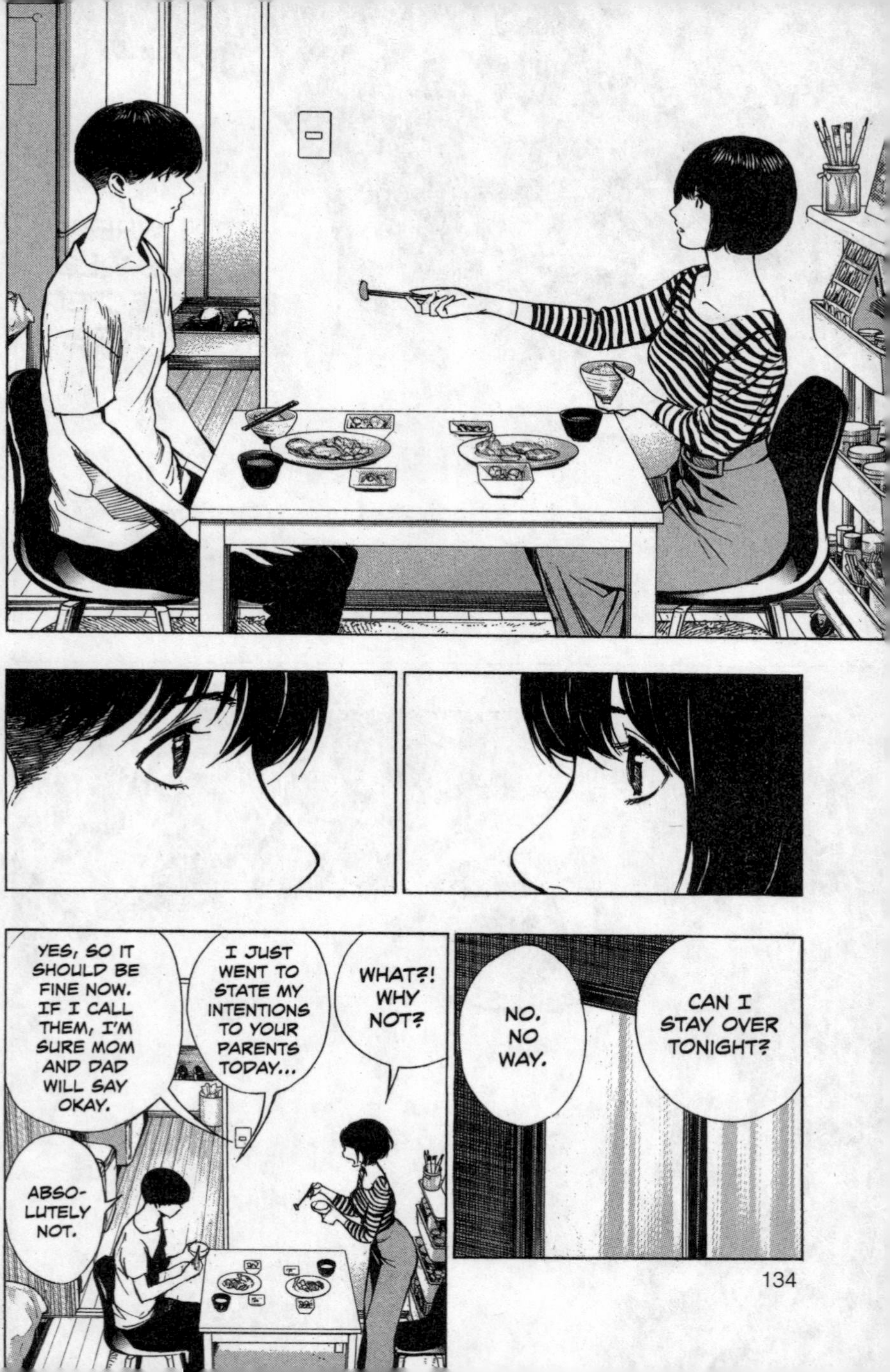
CAN I STAY OVER TONIGHT?
NO. NO WAY.
WHAT?! WHY NOT?
I JUST WENT TO STATE MY INTENTIONS TO YOUR PARENTS TODAY...
YES, SO IT SHOULD BE FINE NOW. IF I CALL THEM, I'M SURE MOM AND DAD WILL SAY OKAY.
ABSO-LUTELY NOT.

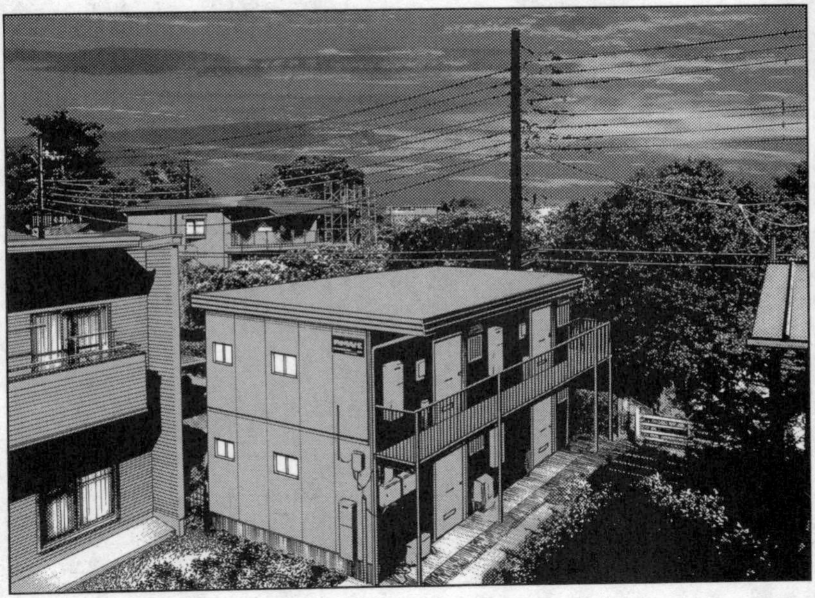

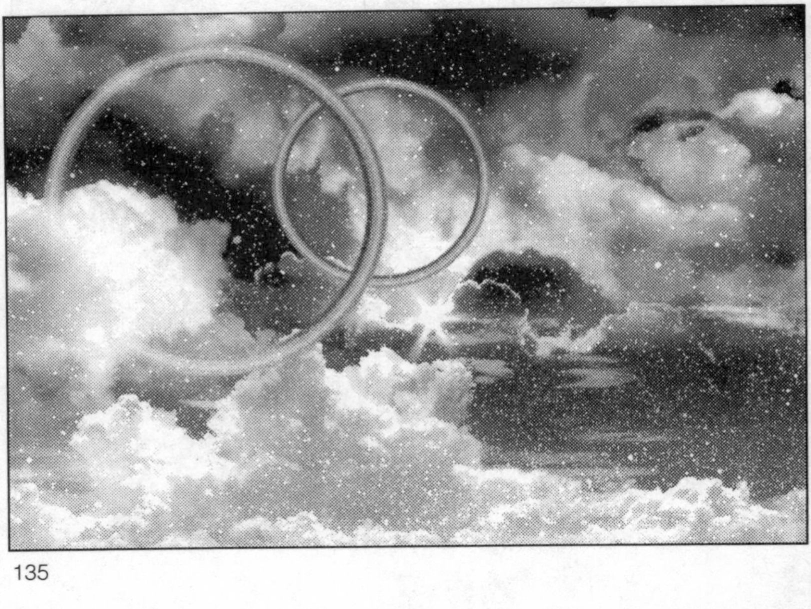

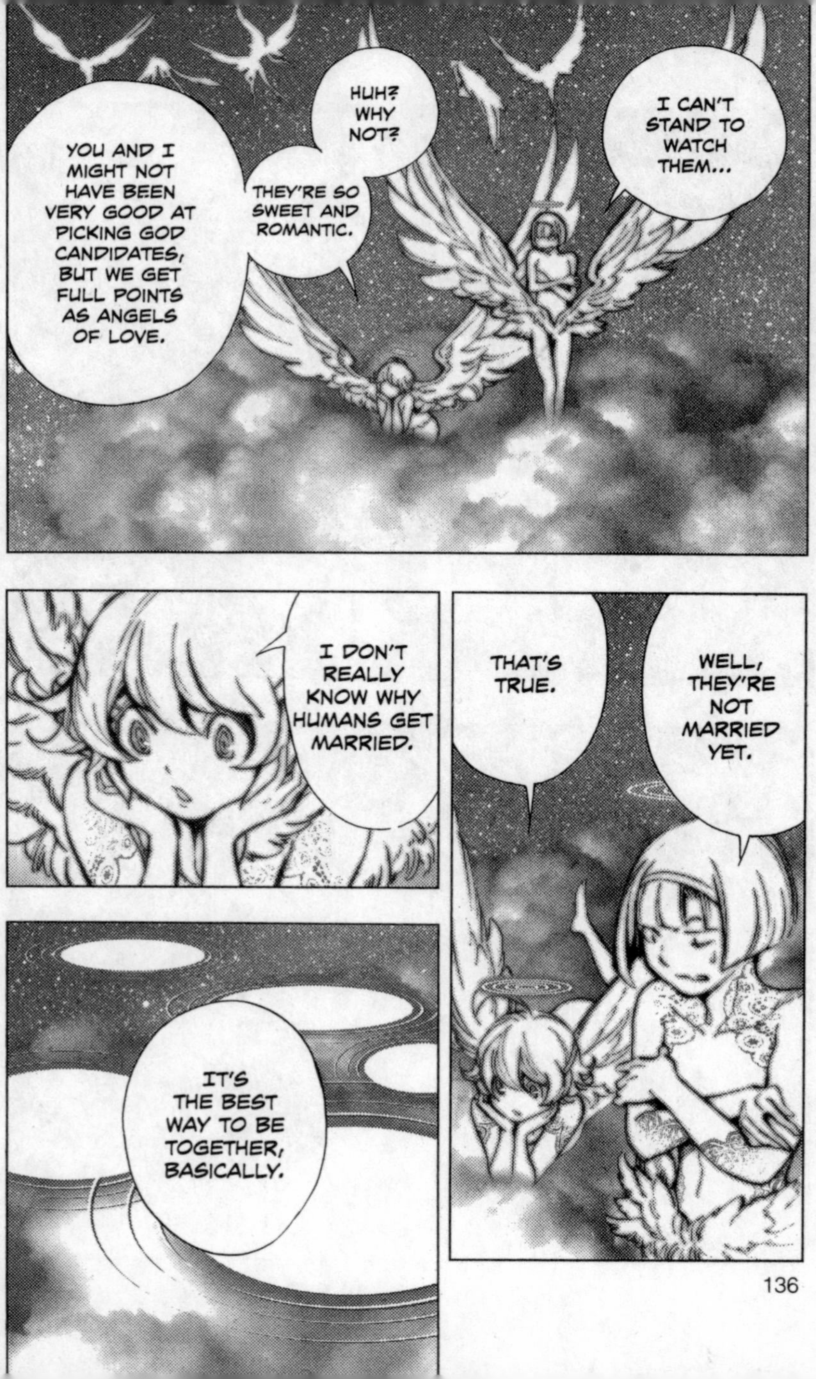
I CAN'T STAND TO WATCH THEM...
HUH? WHY NOT?
THEY'RE SO SWEET AND ROMANTIC.
YOU AND I MIGHT NOT HAVE BEEN VERY GOOD AT PICKING GOD CANDIDATES, BUT WE GET FULL POINTS AS ANGELS OF LOVE.
WELL, THEY'RE NOT MARRIED YET.
THAT'S TRUE.
I DON'T REALLY KNOW WHY HUMANS GET MARRIED.
IT'S THE BEST WAY TO BE TOGETHER, BASICALLY.

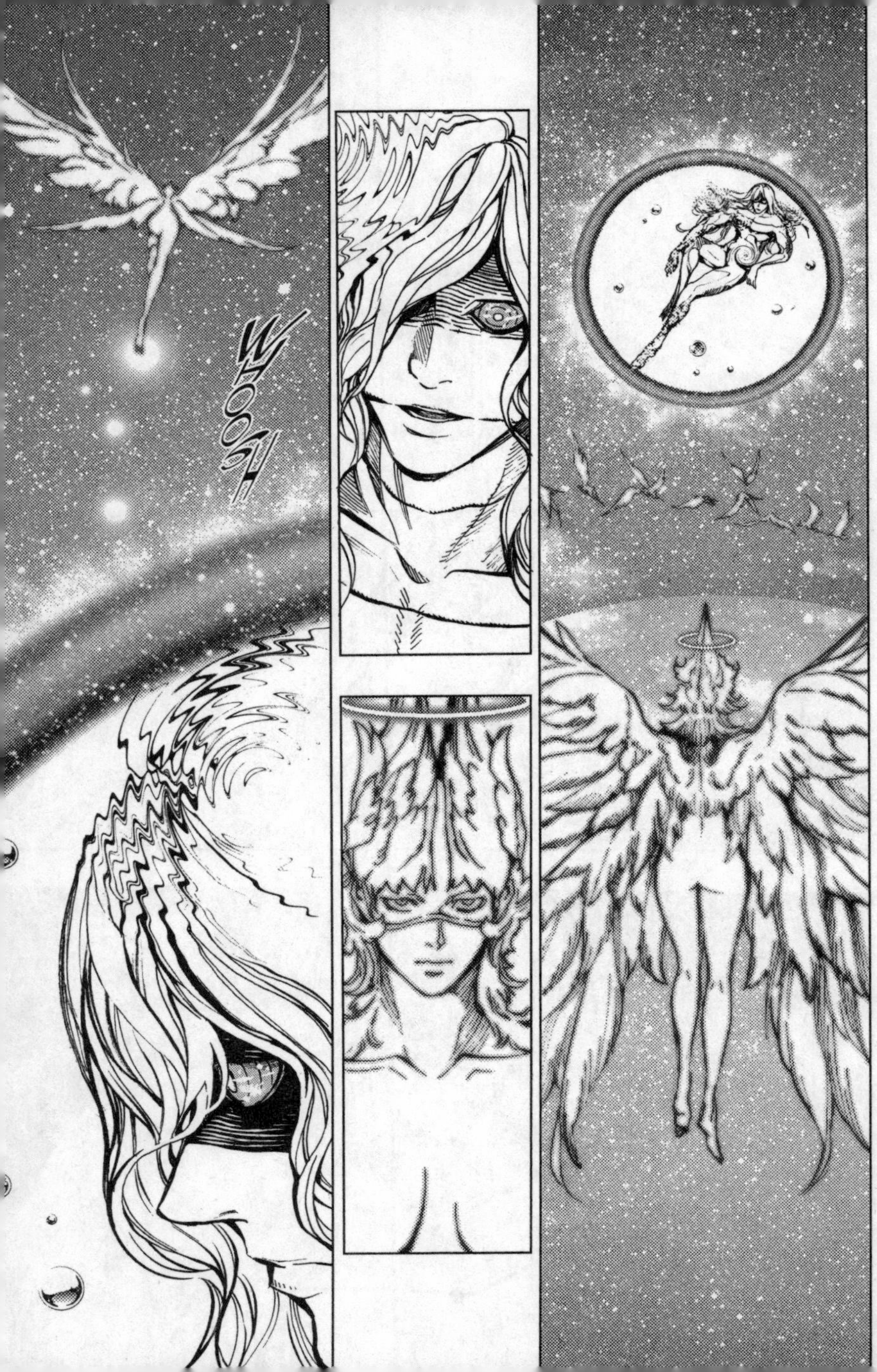
WHOOSH

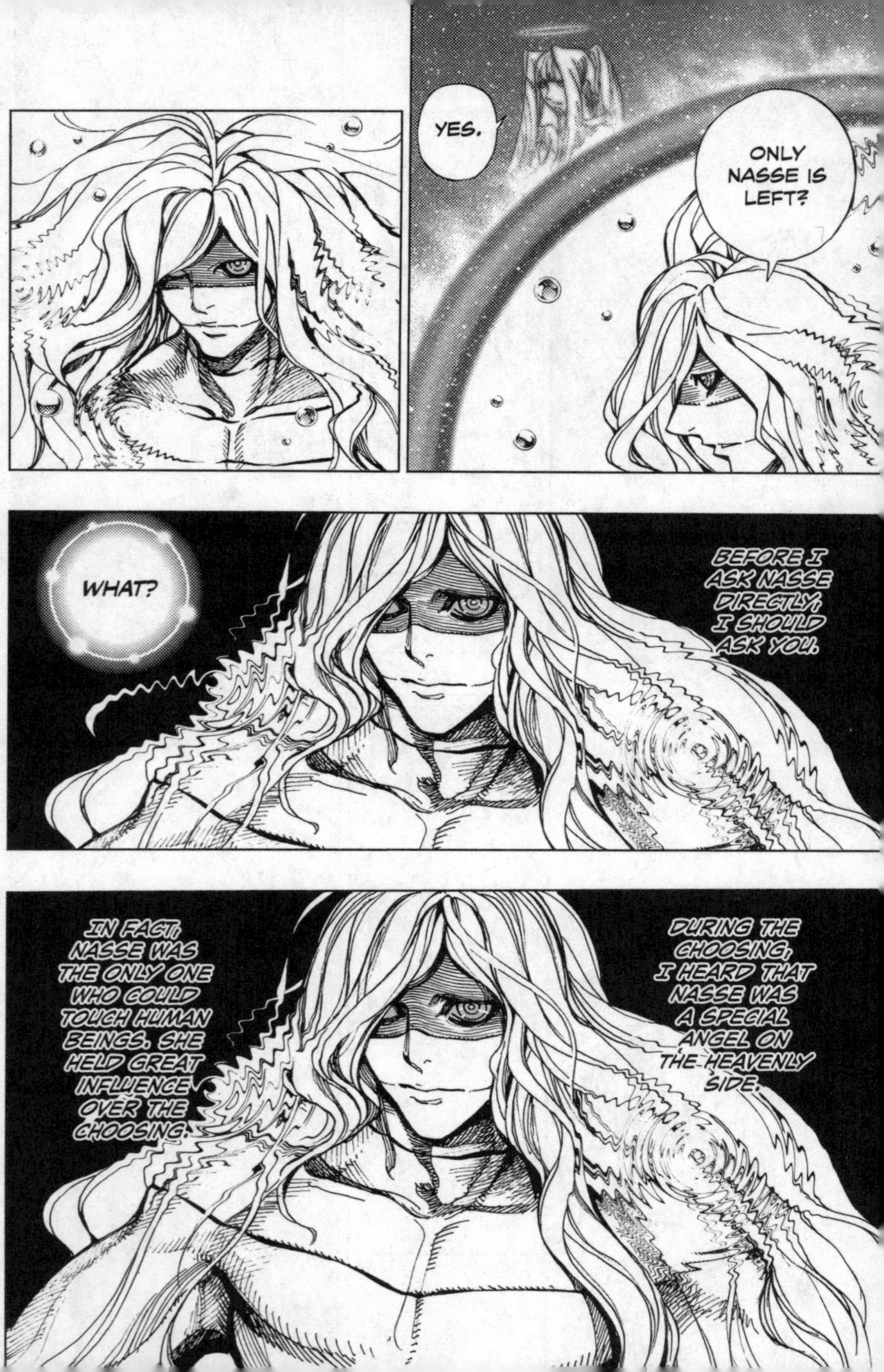
ONLY NASSE IS LEFT?
YES.
BEFORE I ASK NASSE DIRECTLY, I SHOULD ASK YOU.
WHAT?
DURING THE CHOOSING, I HEARD THAT NASSE WAS A SPECIAL ANGEL ON THE HEAVENLY SIDE.
IN FACT, NASSE WAS THE ONLY ONE WHO COULD TOUCH HUMAN BEINGS. SHE HELD GREAT INFLUENCE OVER THE CHOOSING.

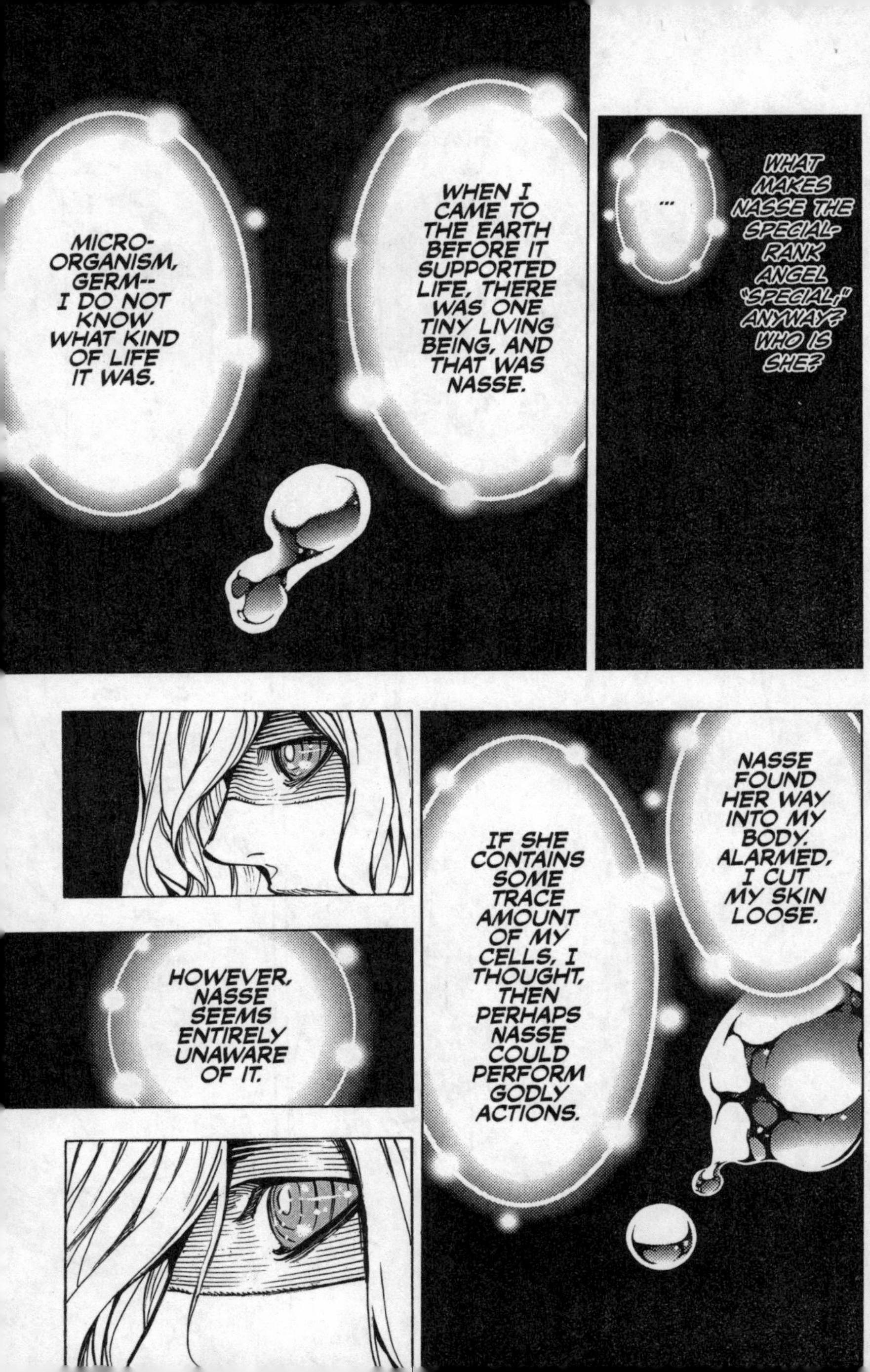
WHAT MAKES NASSE THE SPECIAL-RANK ANGEL "SPECIAL," ANYWAY? WHO IS SHE?
...
WHEN I CAME TO THE EARTH BEFORE IT SUPPORTED LIFE, THERE WAS ONE TINY LIVING BEING, AND THAT WAS NASSE.
MICRO-ORGANISM, GERM-- I DO NOT KNOW WHAT KIND OF LIFE IT WAS.
NASSE FOUND HER WAY INTO MY BODY. ALARMED, I CUT MY SKIN LOOSE.
IF SHE CONTAINS SOME TRACE AMOUNT OF MY CELLS, I THOUGHT, THEN PERHAPS NASSE COULD PERFORM GODLY ACTIONS.
HOWEVER, NASSE SEEMS ENTIRELY UNAWARE OF IT.

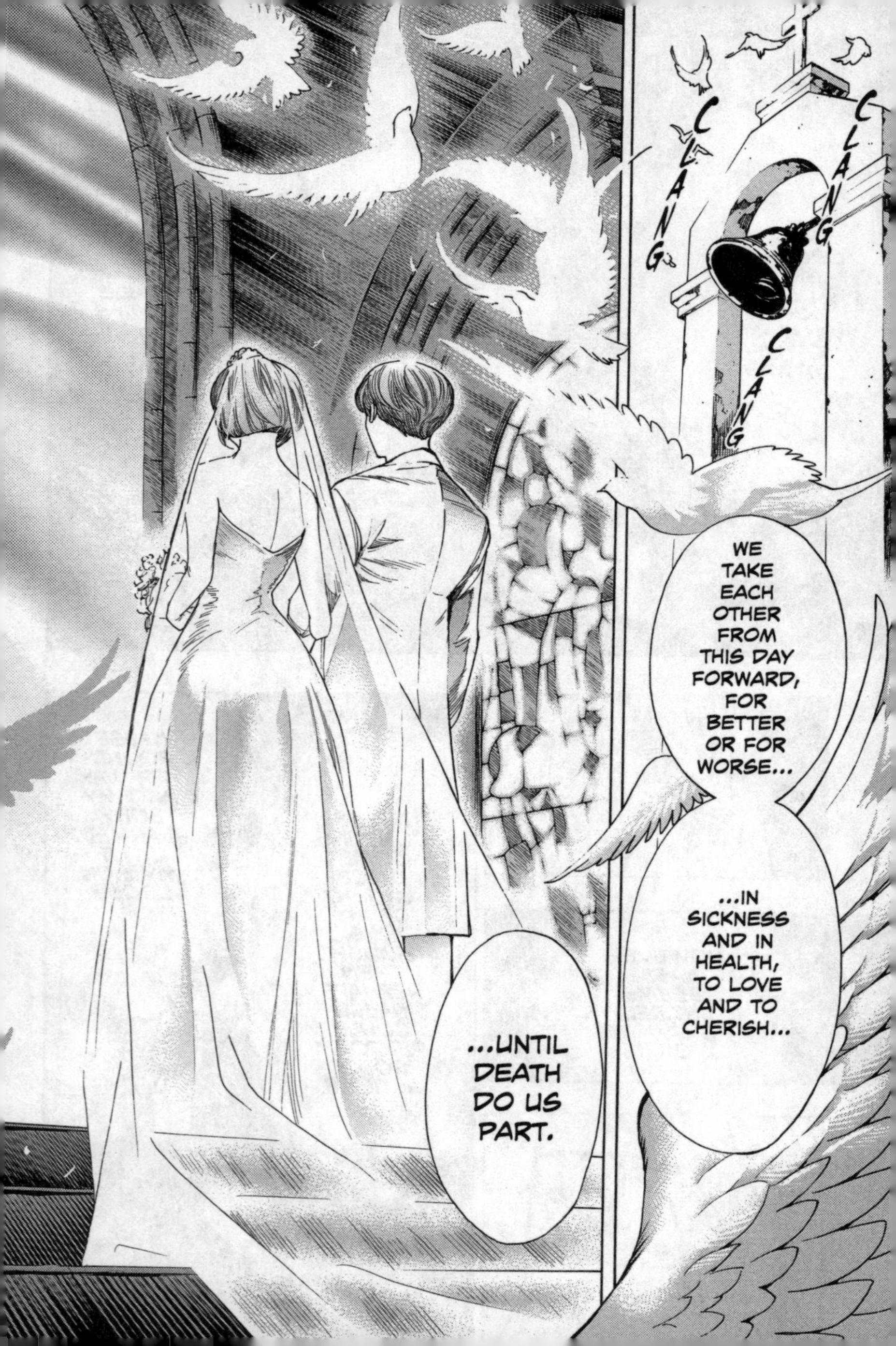
CLANG
CLANG
CLANG
WE TAKE EACH OTHER FROM THIS DAY FORWARD, FOR BETTER OR FOR WORSE...
...IN SICKNESS AND IN HEALTH, TO LOVE AND TO CHERISH...
...UNTIL DEATH DO US PART.

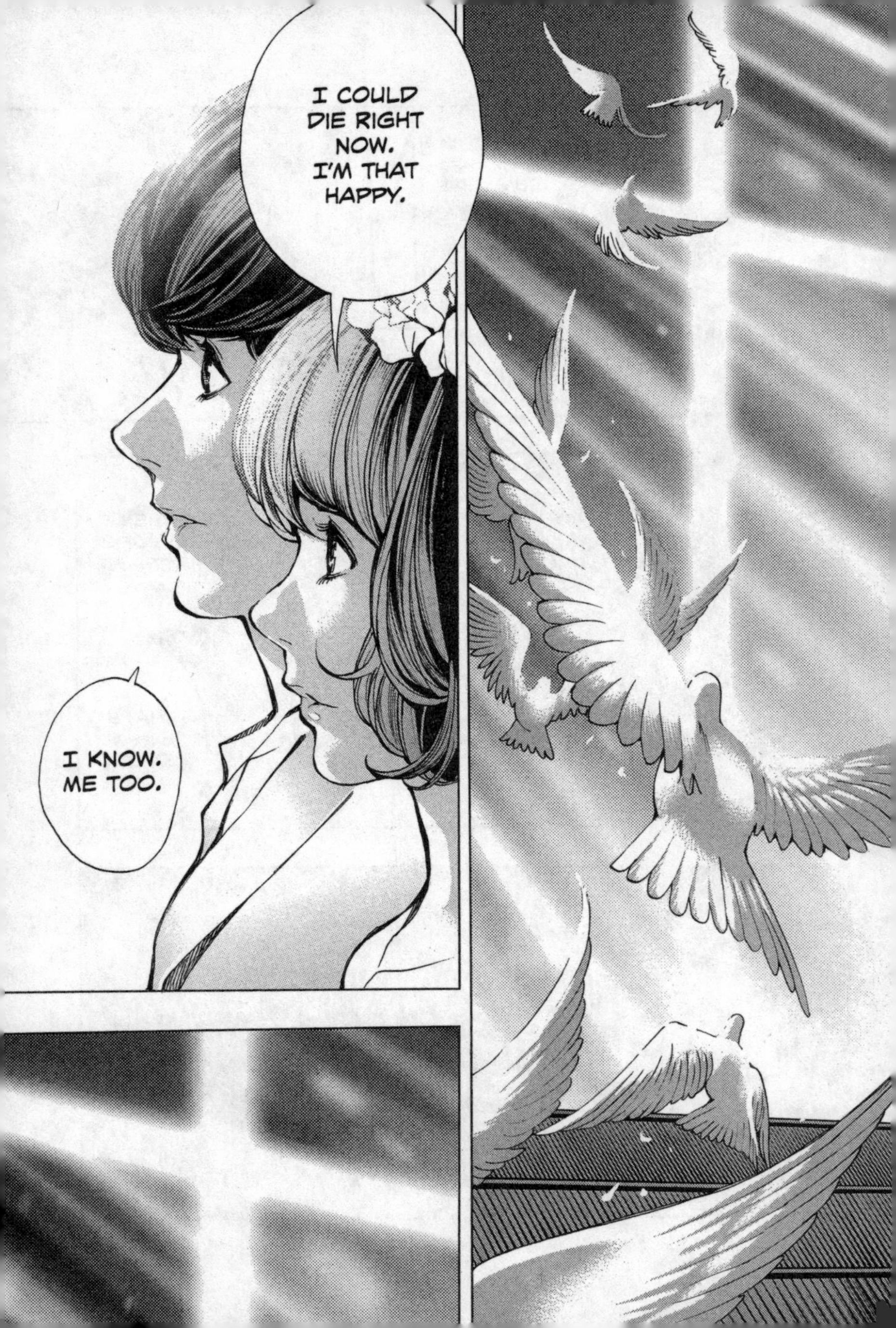
I COULD DIE RIGHT NOW. I'M THAT HAPPY.
I KNOW. ME TOO.

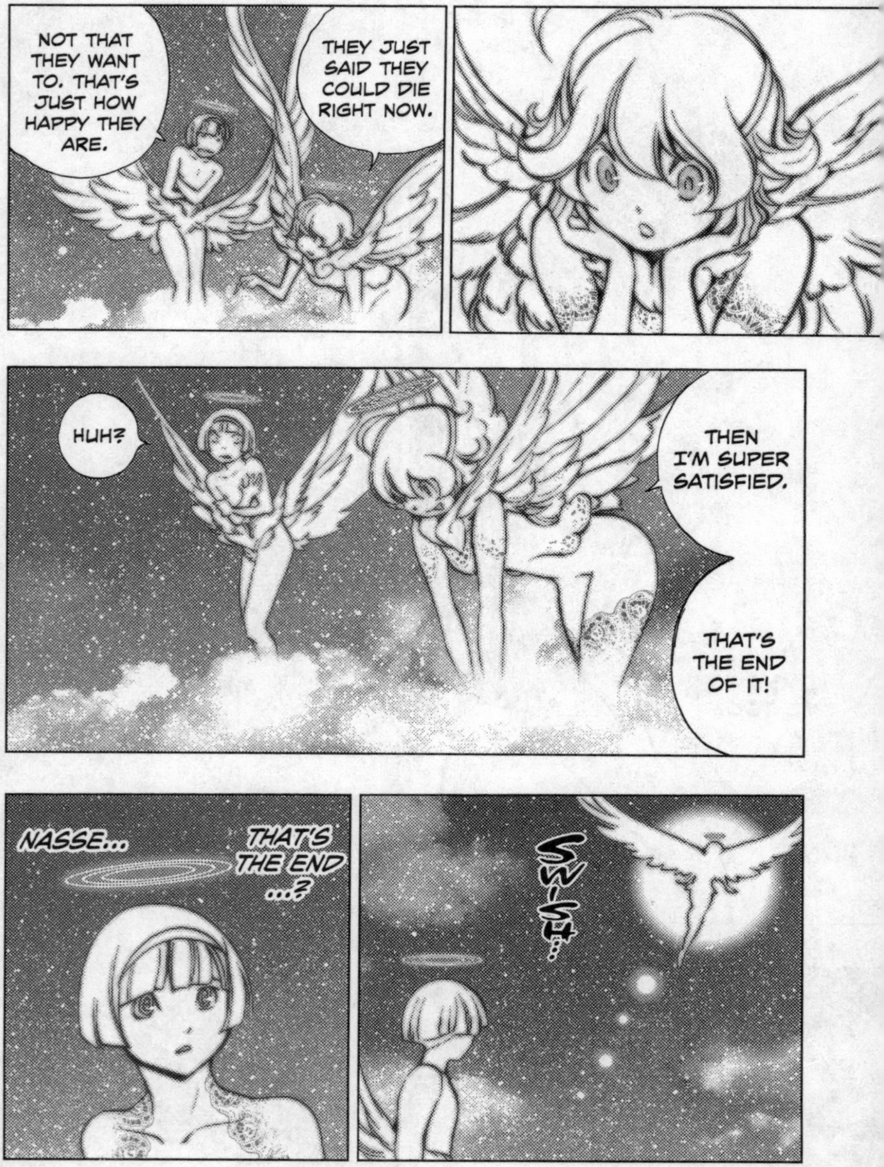
THEY JUST SAID THEY COULD DIE RIGHT NOW.
NOT THAT THEY WANT TO. THAT'S JUST HOW HAPPY THEY ARE.
THEN I'M SUPER SATISFIED.
THAT'S THE END OF IT!
HUH?
SW-SH...
THAT'S THE END ...?
NASSE...

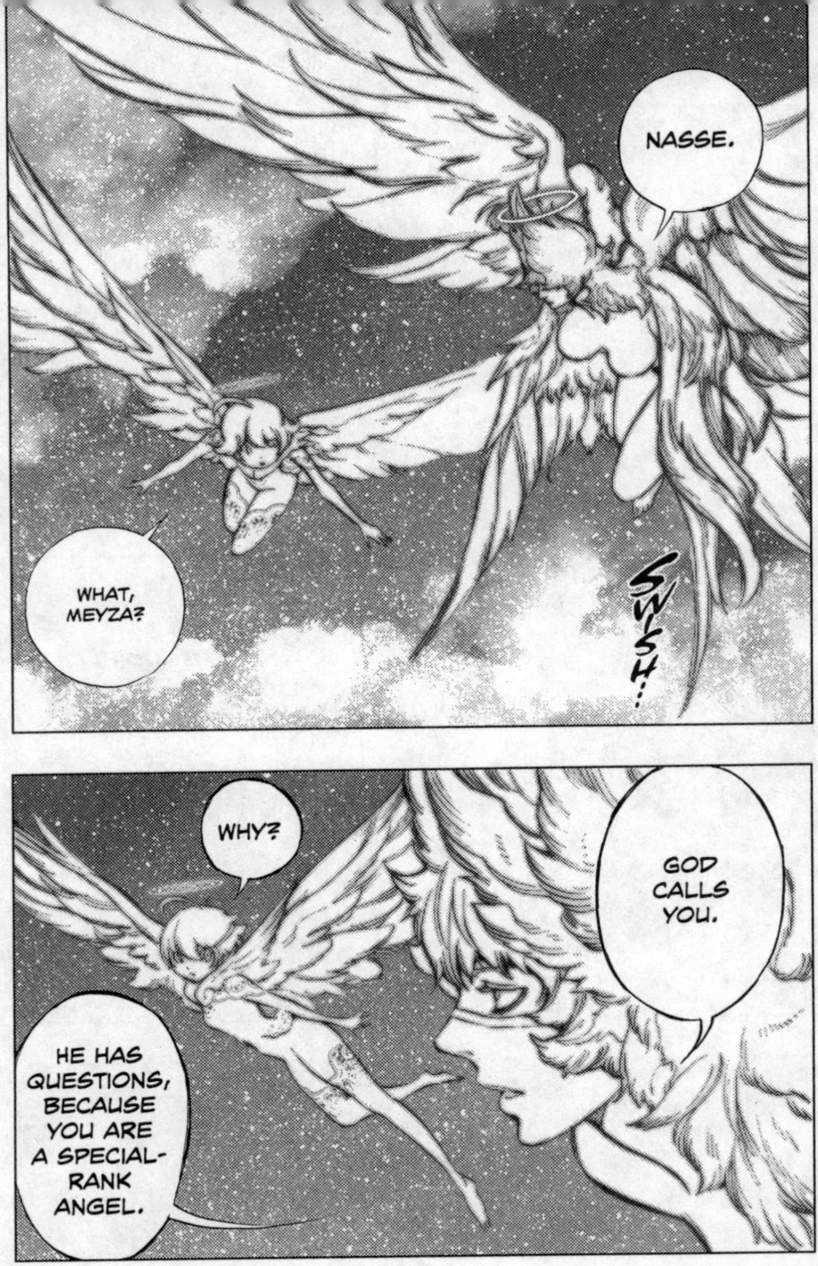
NASSE.
SWISH!!
WHAT, MEYZA?
GOD CALLS YOU.
WHY?
HE HAS QUESTIONS, BECAUSE YOU ARE A SPECIAL-RANK ANGEL.

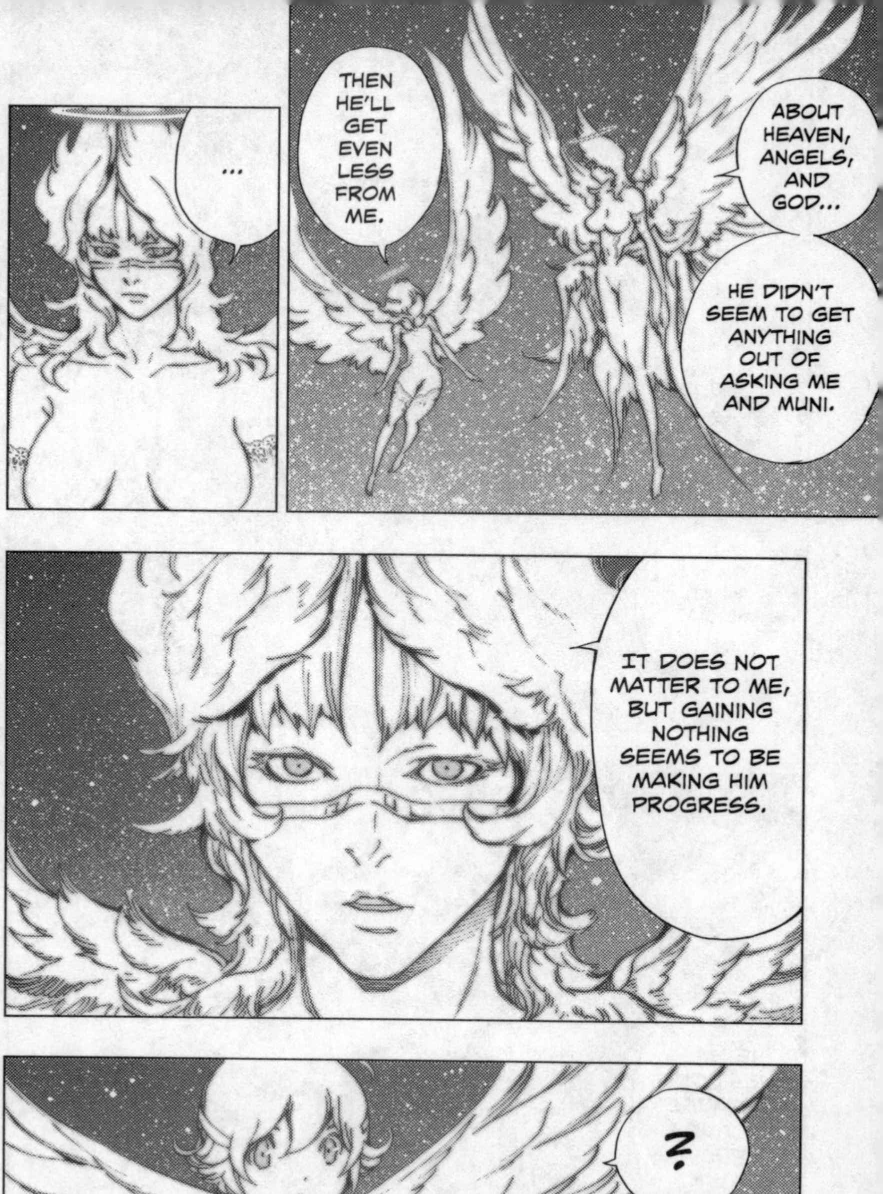
ABOUT HEAVEN, ANGELS, AND GOD...
HE DIDN'T SEEM TO GET ANYTHING OUT OF ASKING ME AND MUNI.
THEN HE'LL GET EVEN LESS FROM ME.
...
IT DOES NOT MATTER TO ME, BUT GAINING NOTHING SEEMS TO BE MAKING HIM PROGRESS.
?

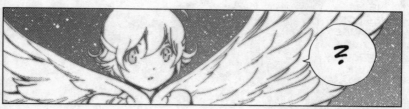

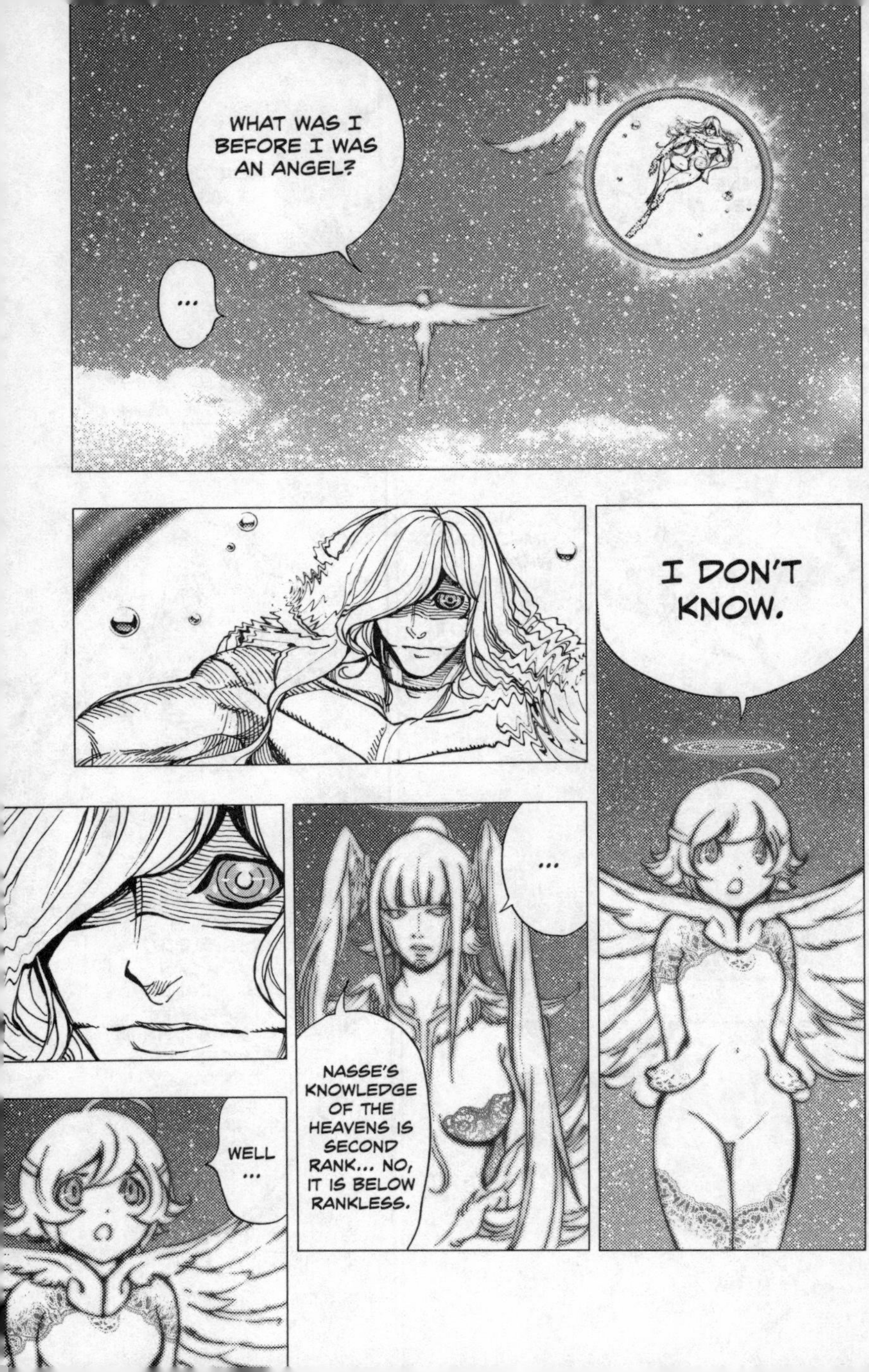
WHAT WAS I BEFORE I WAS AN ANGEL?
...
I DON'T KNOW.
...
NASSE'S KNOWLEDGE OF THE HEAVENS IS SECOND RANK... NO, IT IS BELOW RANKLESS.
WELL ...

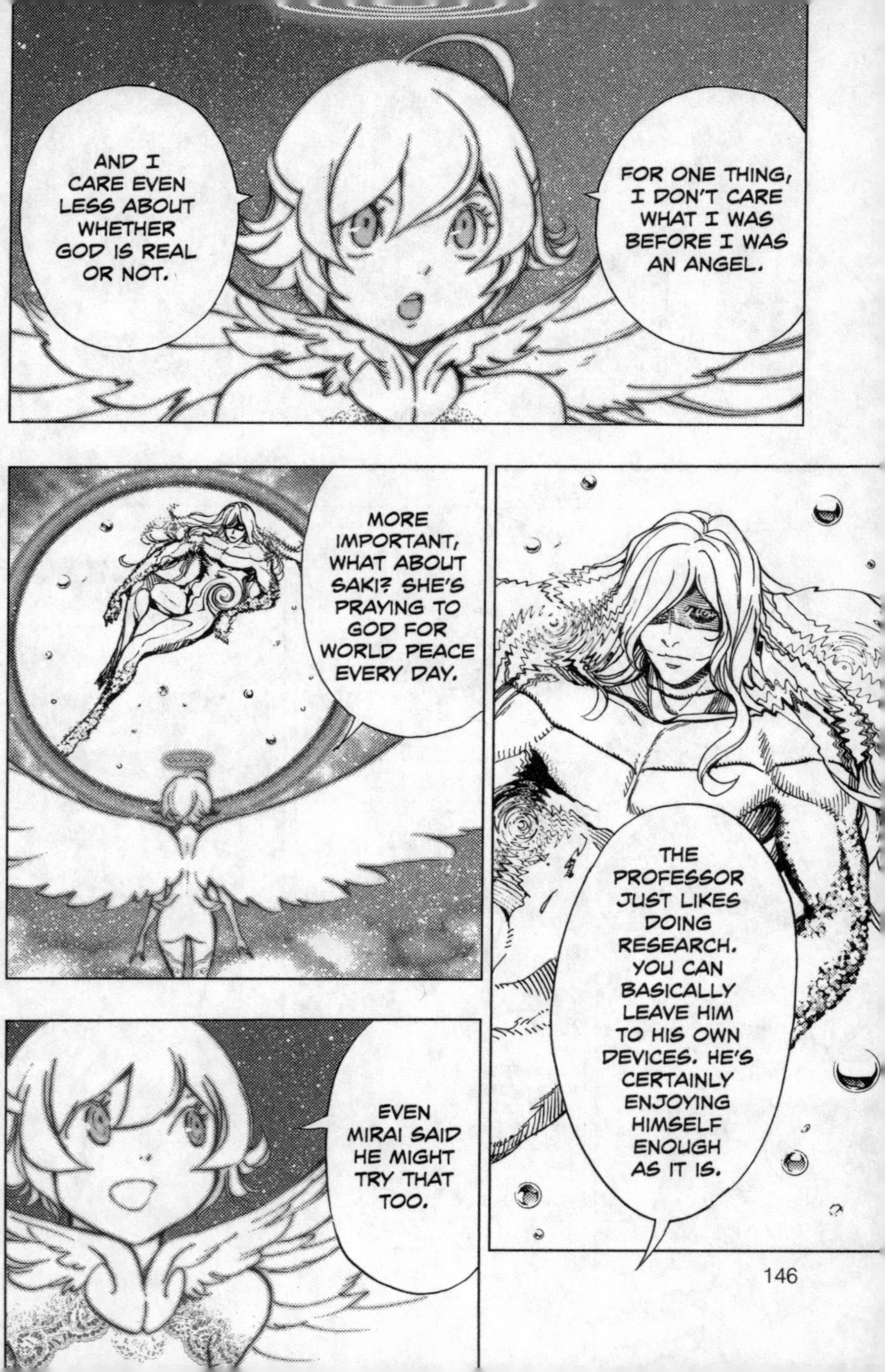
FOR ONE THING, I DON'T CARE WHAT I WAS BEFORE I WAS AN ANGEL.
AND I CARE EVEN LESS ABOUT WHETHER GOD IS REAL OR NOT.
THE PROFESSOR JUST LIKES DOING RESEARCH. YOU CAN BASICALLY LEAVE HIM TO HIS OWN DEVICES. HE'S CERTAINLY ENJOYING HIMSELF ENOUGH AS IT IS.
MORE IMPORTANT, WHAT ABOUT SAKI? SHE'S PRAYING TO GOD FOR WORLD PEACE EVERY DAY.
EVEN MIRAI SAID HE MIGHT TRY THAT TOO.

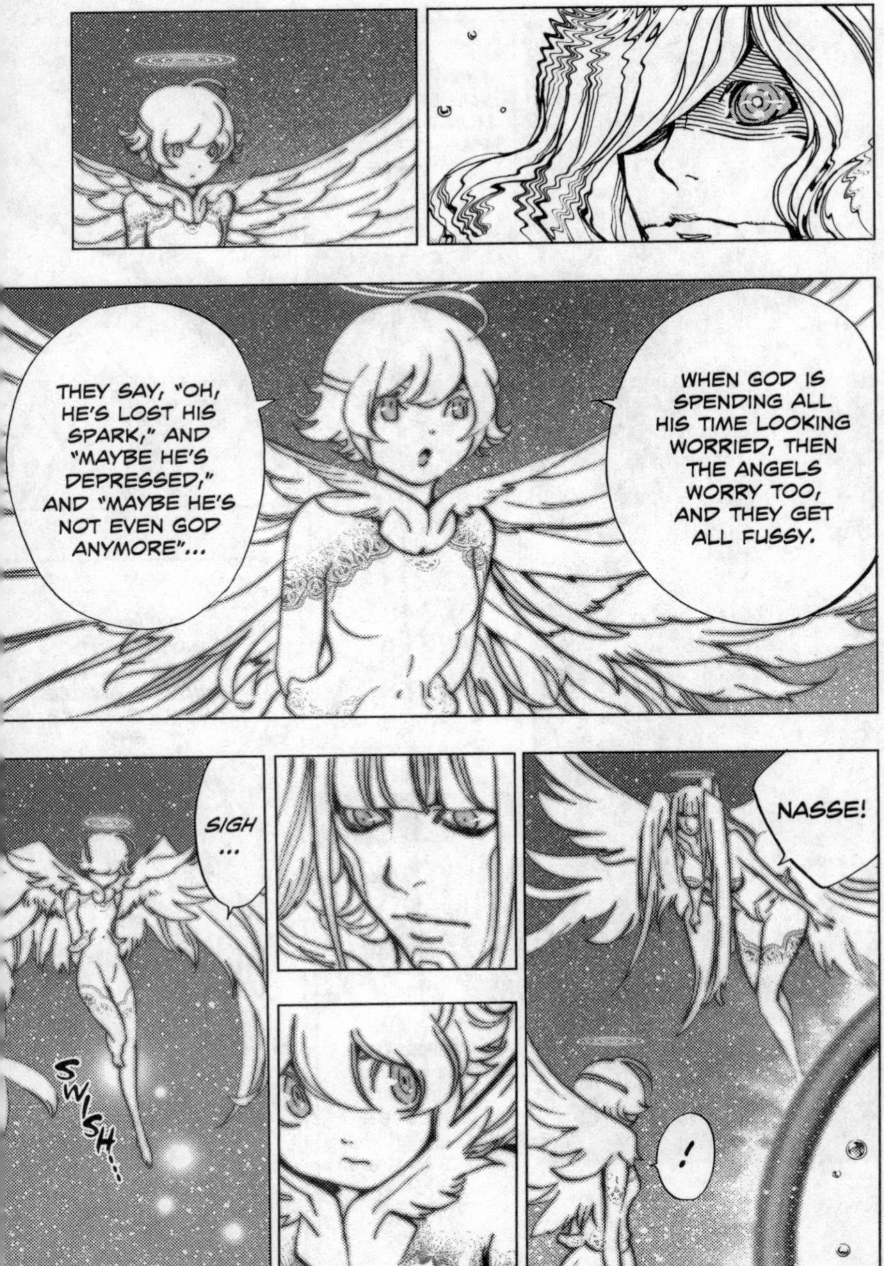
WHEN GOD IS SPENDING ALL HIS TIME LOOKING WORRIED, THEN THE ANGELS WORRY TOO, AND THEY GET ALL FUSSY.
THEY SAY, "OH, HE'S LOST HIS SPARK," AND "MAYBE HE'S DEPRESSED," AND "MAYBE HE'S NOT EVEN GOD ANYMORE"...
NASSE!
!
SIGH...
SWISH...

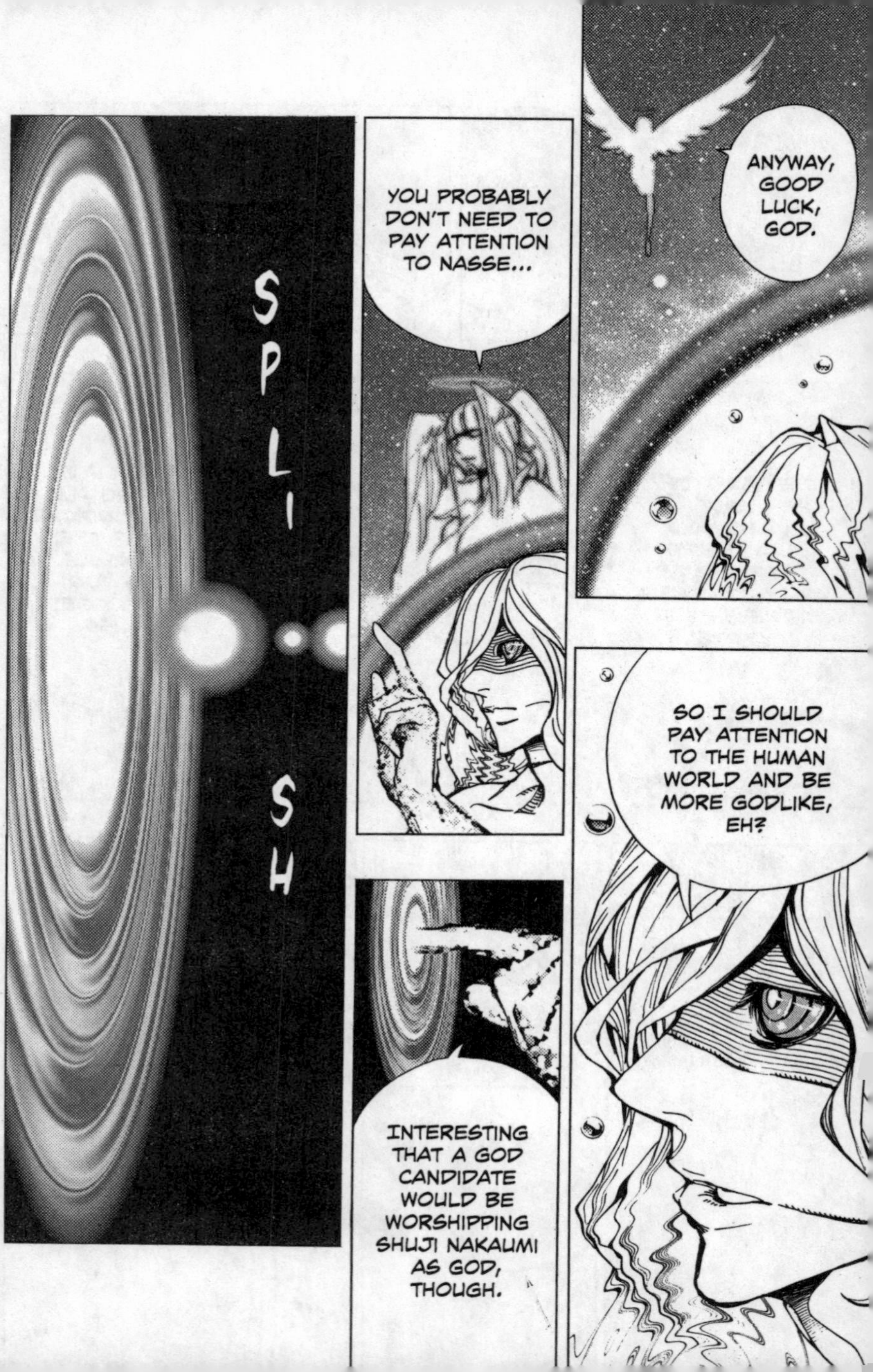
ANYWAY, GOOD LUCK, GOD.
SO I SHOULD PAY ATTENTION TO THE HUMAN WORLD AND BE MORE GODLIKE, EH?
YOU PROBABLY DON'T NEED TO PAY ATTENTION TO NASSE...
INTERESTING THAT A GOD CANDIDATE WOULD BE WORSHIPPING SHUJI NAKAUMI AS GOD, THOUGH.
SPLISH

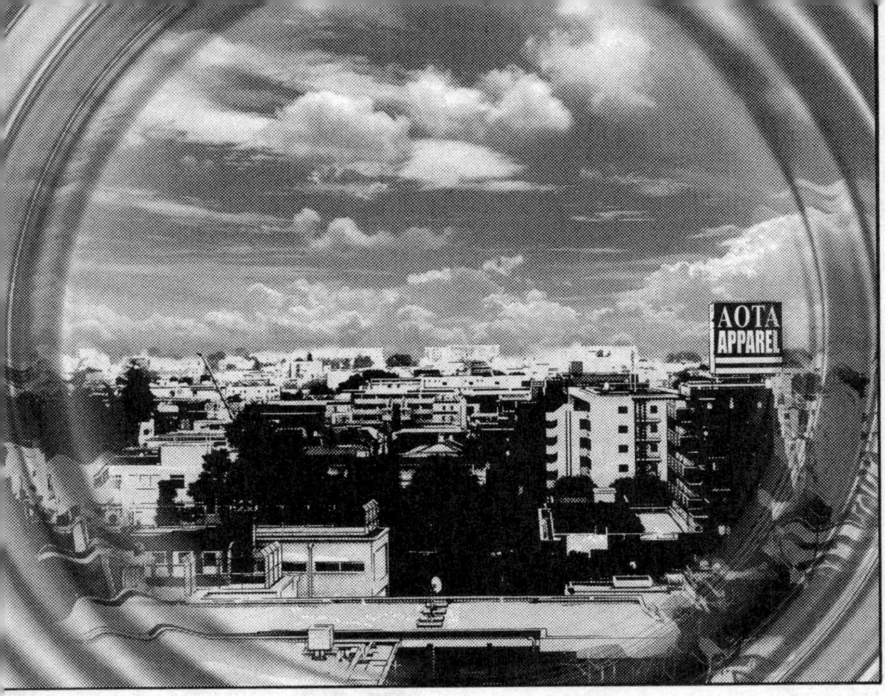
AOTA
APPAREL
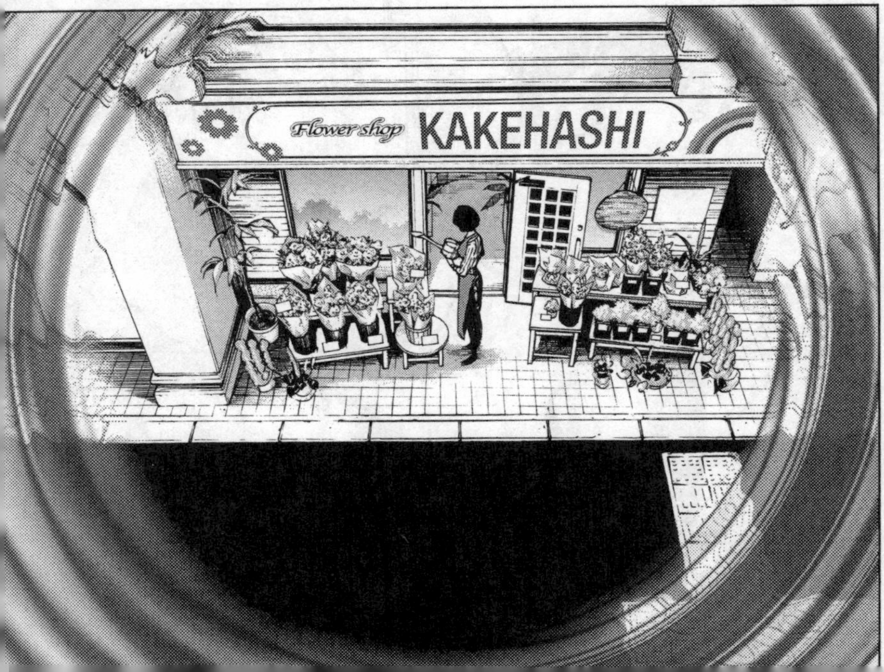
Flower shop KAKEHASHI

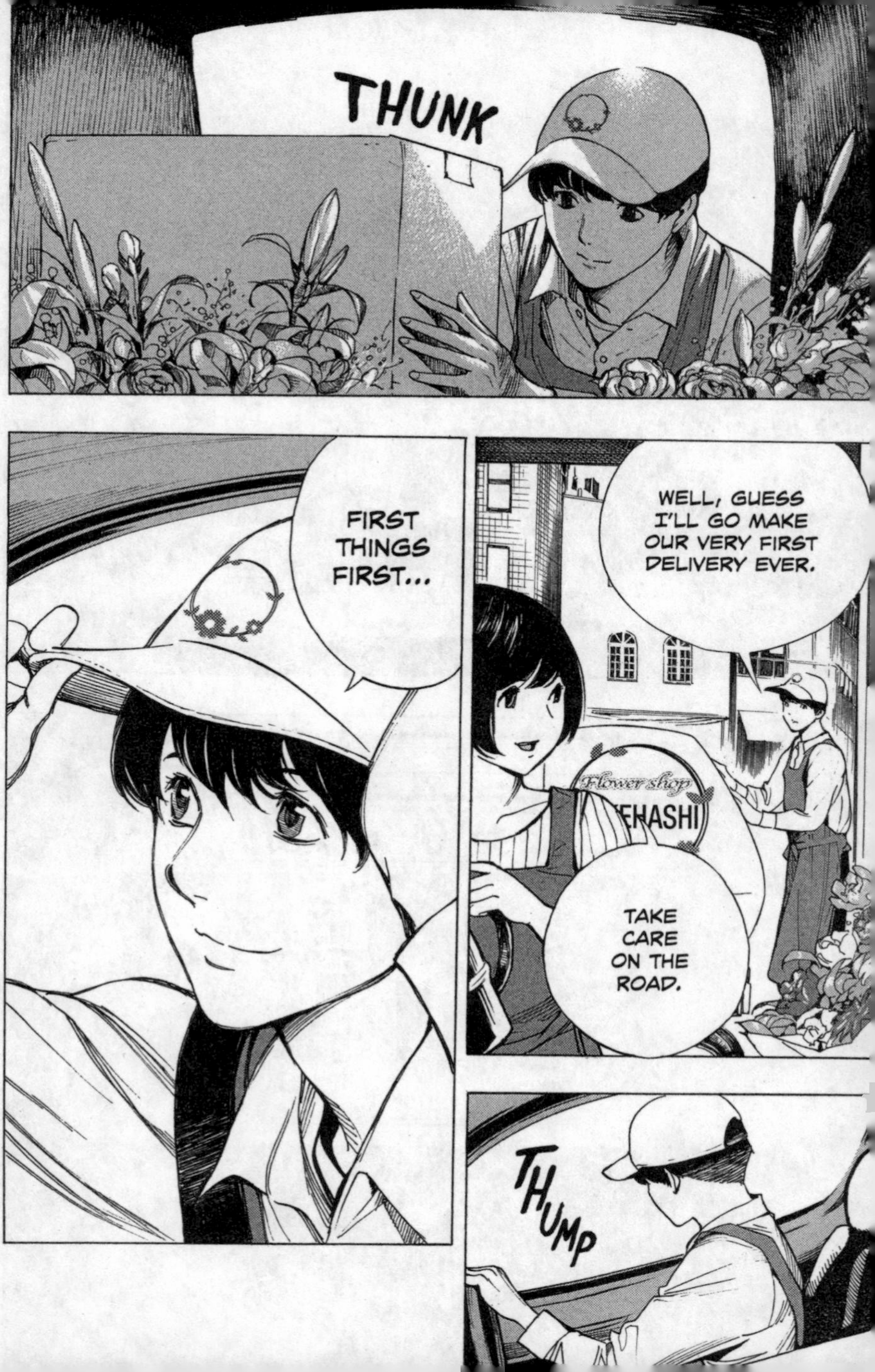
THUNK
WELL, GUESS I'LL GO MAKE OUR VERY FIRST DELIVERY EVER.
Flower shop
EHASHI
TAKE CARE ON THE ROAD.
THUMP
FIRST THINGS FIRST...

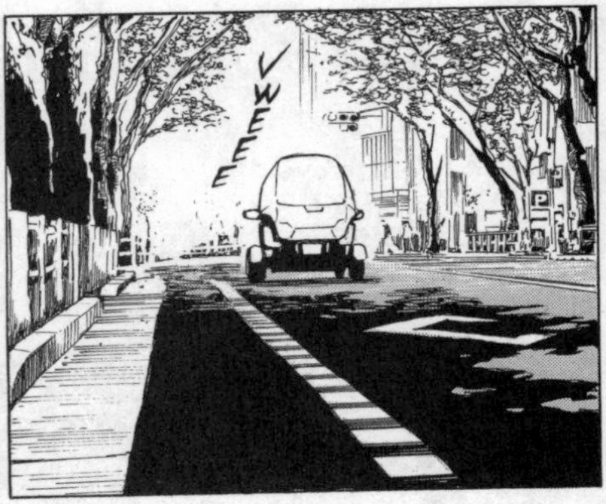
VWEEE

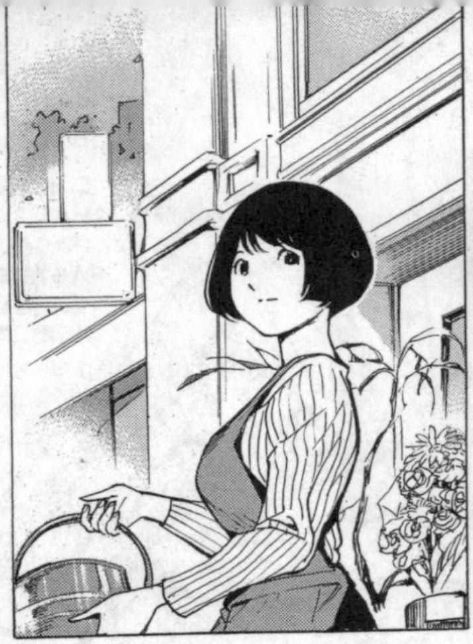

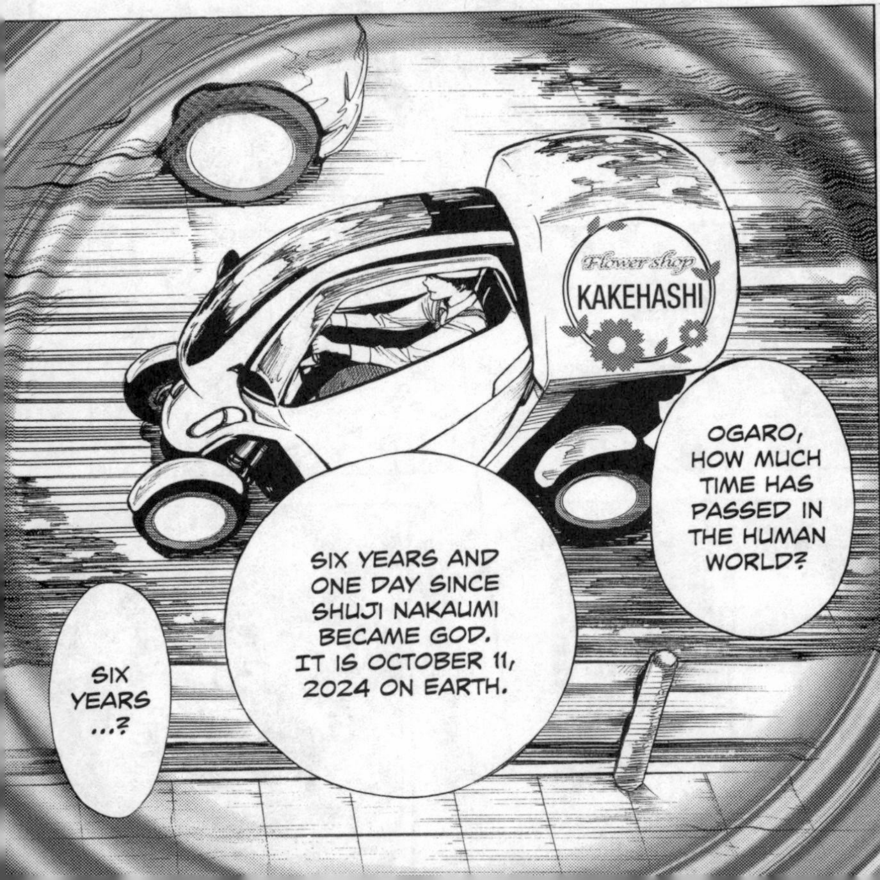
Flower shop
KAKEHASHI
OGARO, HOW MUCH TIME HAS PASSED IN THE HUMAN WORLD?
SIX YEARS AND ONE DAY SINCE SHUJI NAKAUMI BECAME GOD. IT IS OCTOBER 11, 2024 ON EARTH.
SIX YEARS ...?

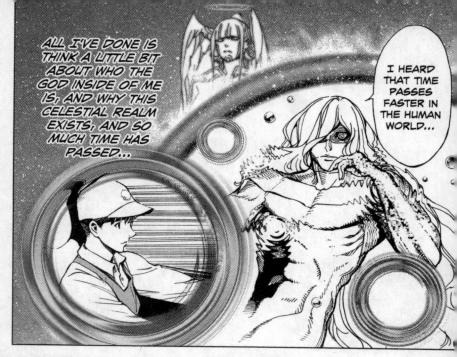

I HEARD THAT TIME PASSES FASTER IN THE HUMAN WORLD...
ALL I'VE DONE IS THINK A LITTLE BIT ABOUT WHO THE GOD INSIDE OF ME IS, AND WHY THIS CELESTIAL REALM EXISTS, AND SO MUCH TIME HAS PASSED...
SPLISH...
Professor Emeritus Yoneda Laboratory One

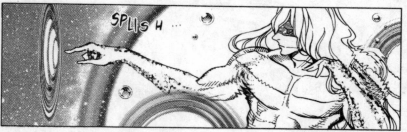

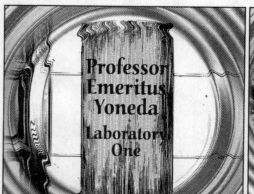

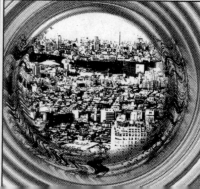

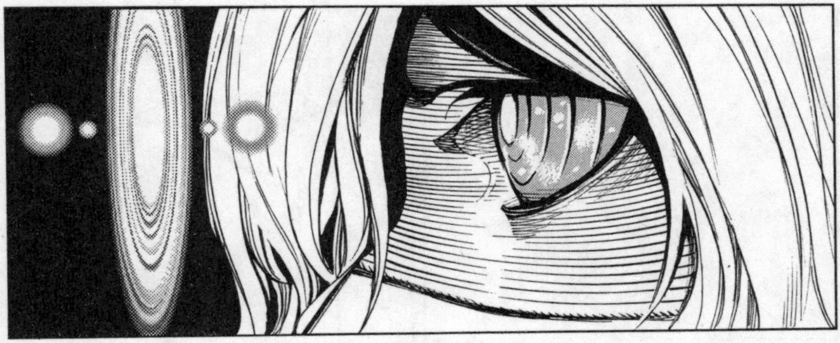
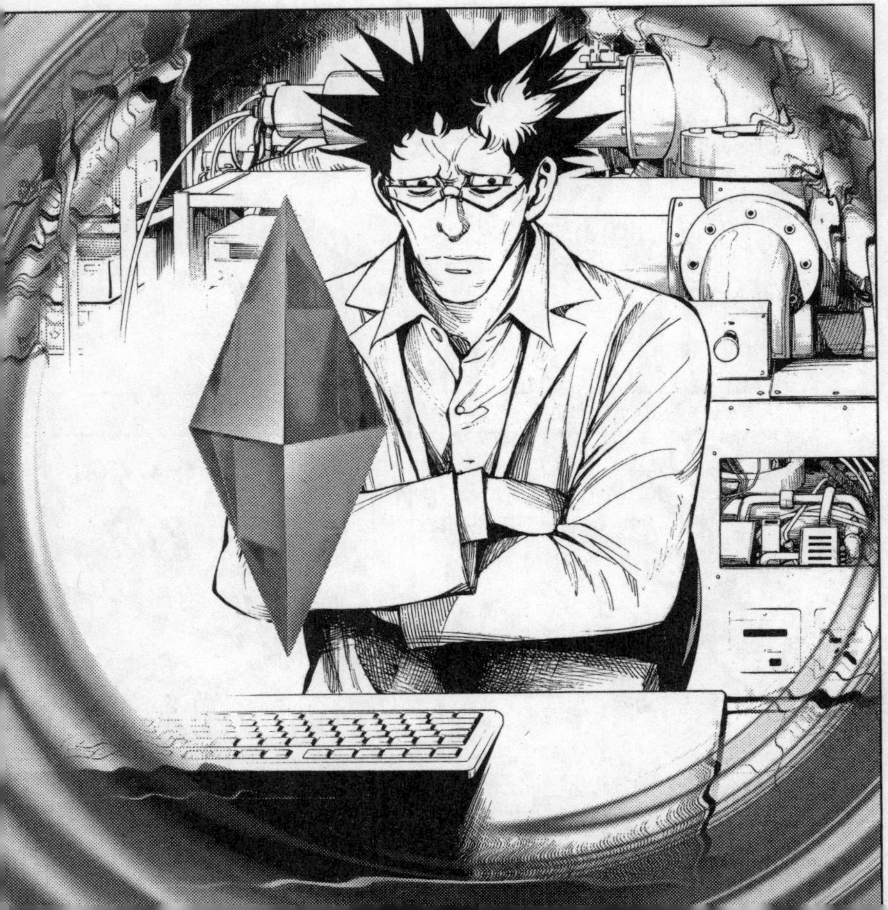

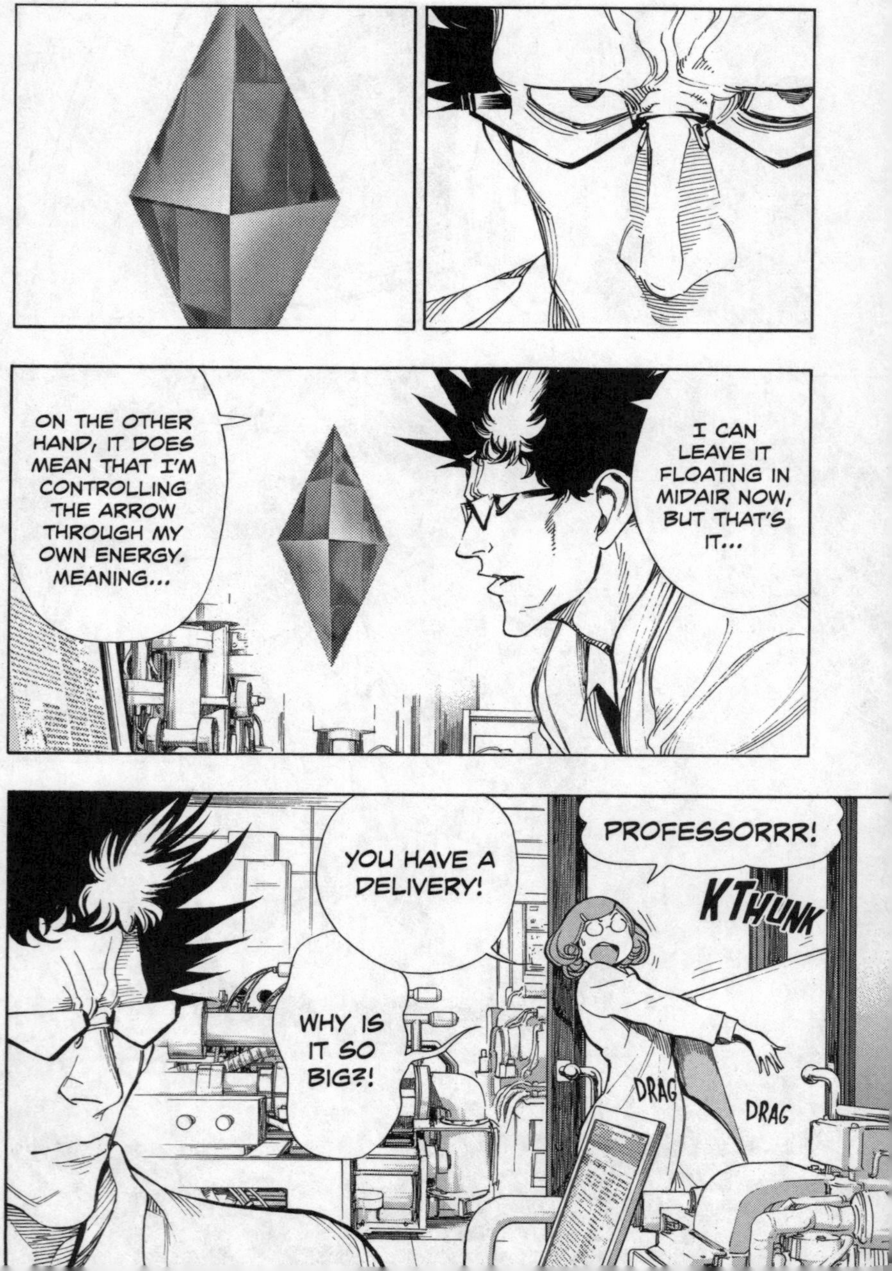
I CAN LEAVE IT FLOATING IN MIDAIR NOW, BUT THAT'S IT...
ON THE OTHER HAND, IT DOES MEAN THAT I'M CONTROLLING THE ARROW THROUGH MY OWN ENERGY. MEANING...
PROFESSORRR!
KTHUNK
YOU HAVE A DELIVERY!
WHY IS IT SO BIG?!
DRAG
DRAG

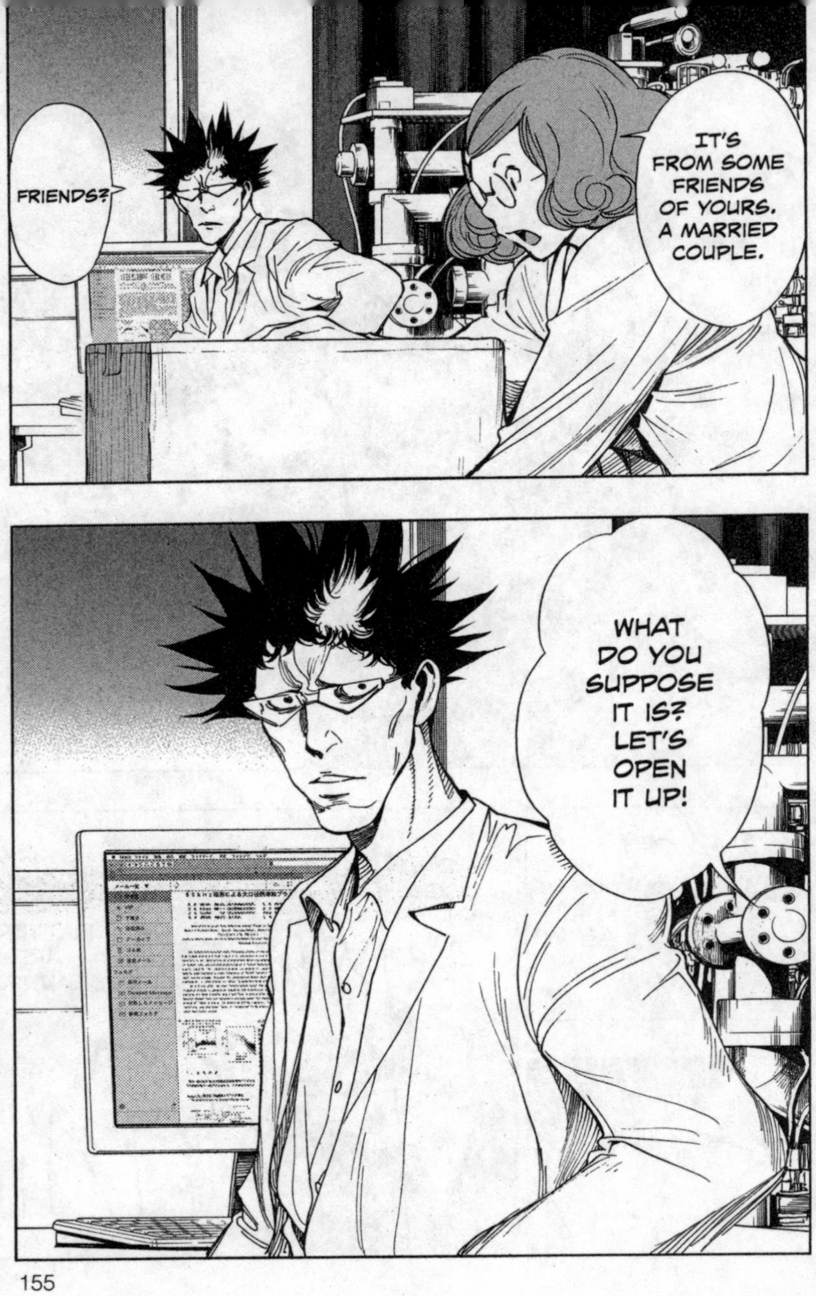
IT'S FROM SOME FRIENDS OF YOURS. A MARRIED COUPLE.
FRIENDS?
WHAT DO YOU SUPPOSE IT IS? LET'S OPEN IT UP!

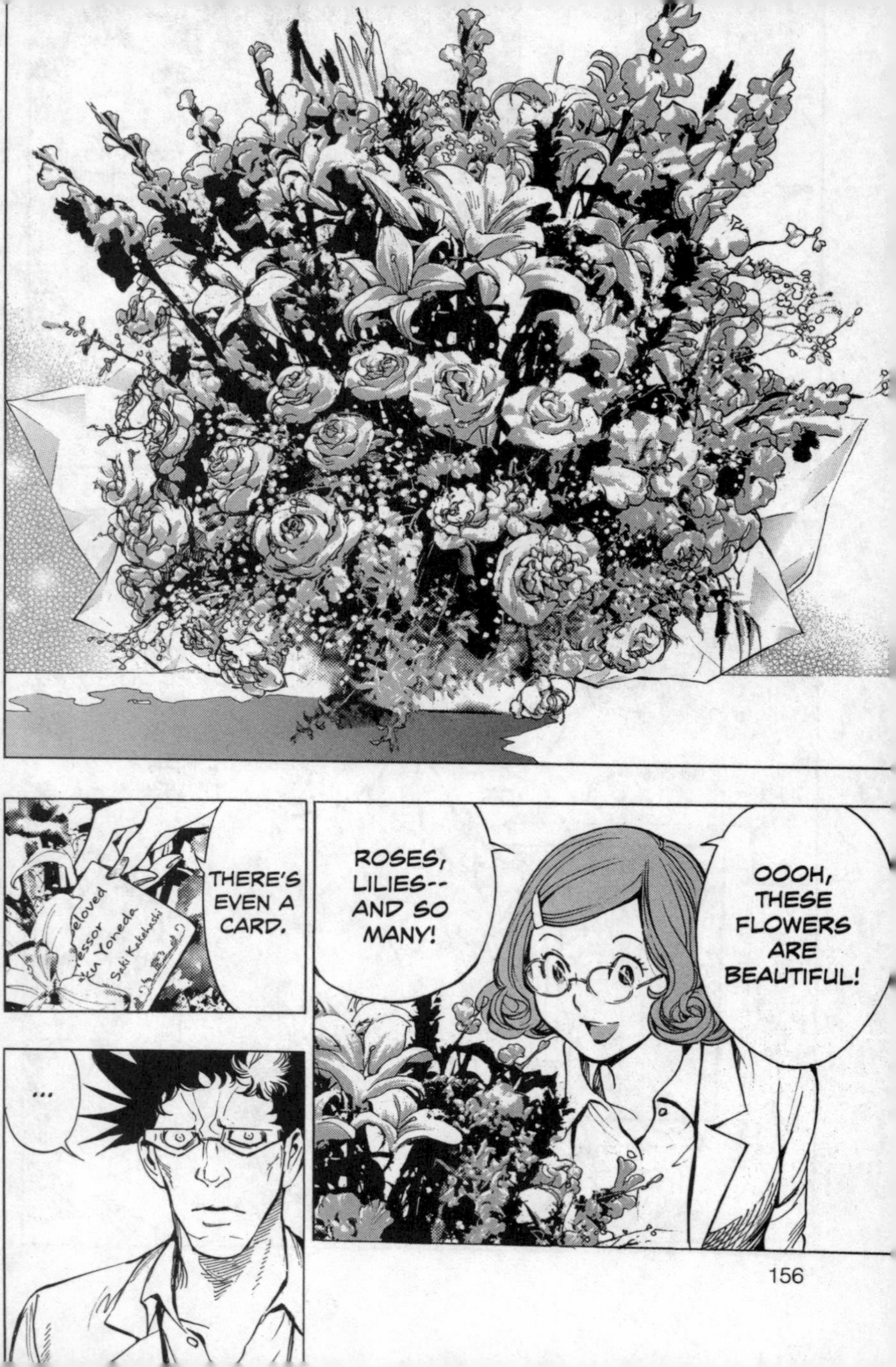
OOOH, THESE FLOWERS ARE BEAUTIFUL!
ROSES, LILIES-- AND SO MANY!
THERE'S EVEN A CARD.
Saki Kakehashi
...

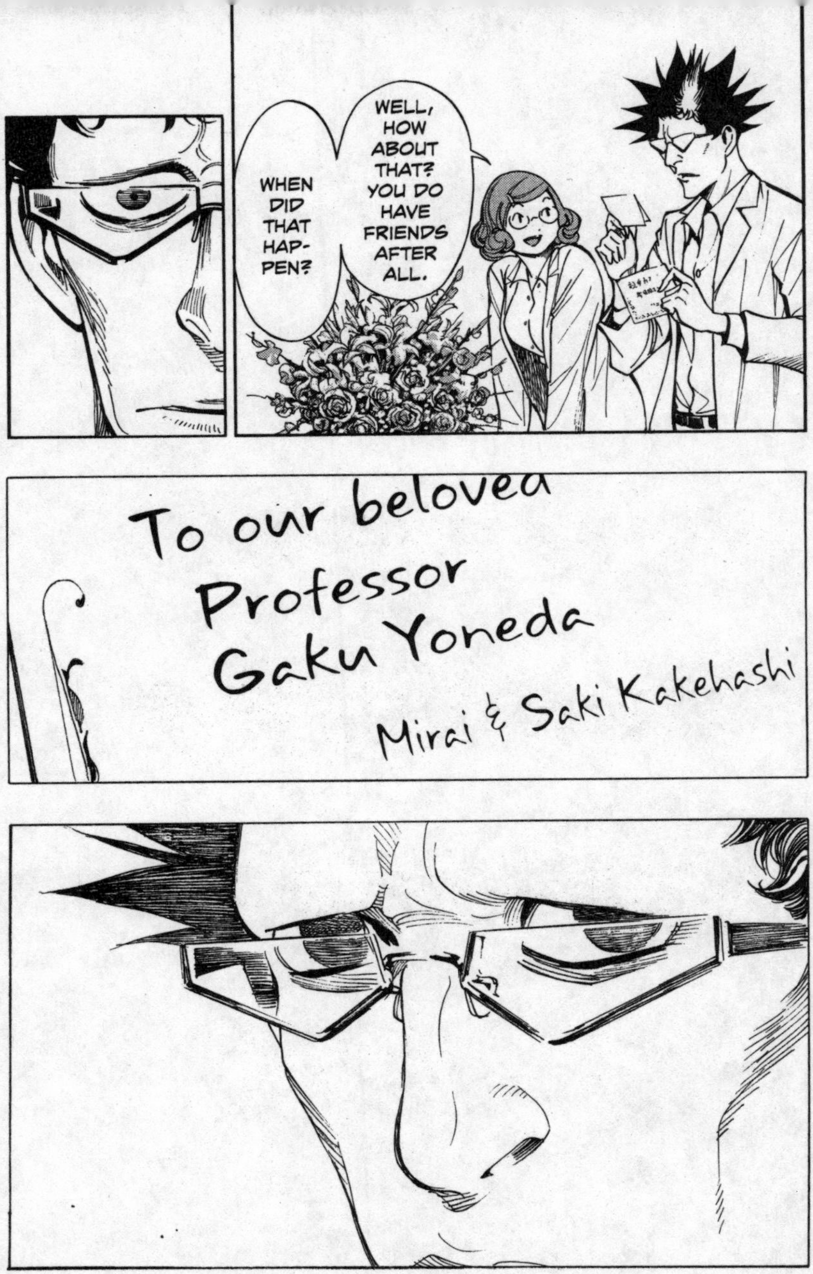
WELL, HOW ABOUT THAT? YOU DO HAVE FRIENDS AFTER ALL.
WHEN DID THAT HAP-PEN?
To our beloved Professor Gaku Yoneda
Mirai & Saki Kakehashi

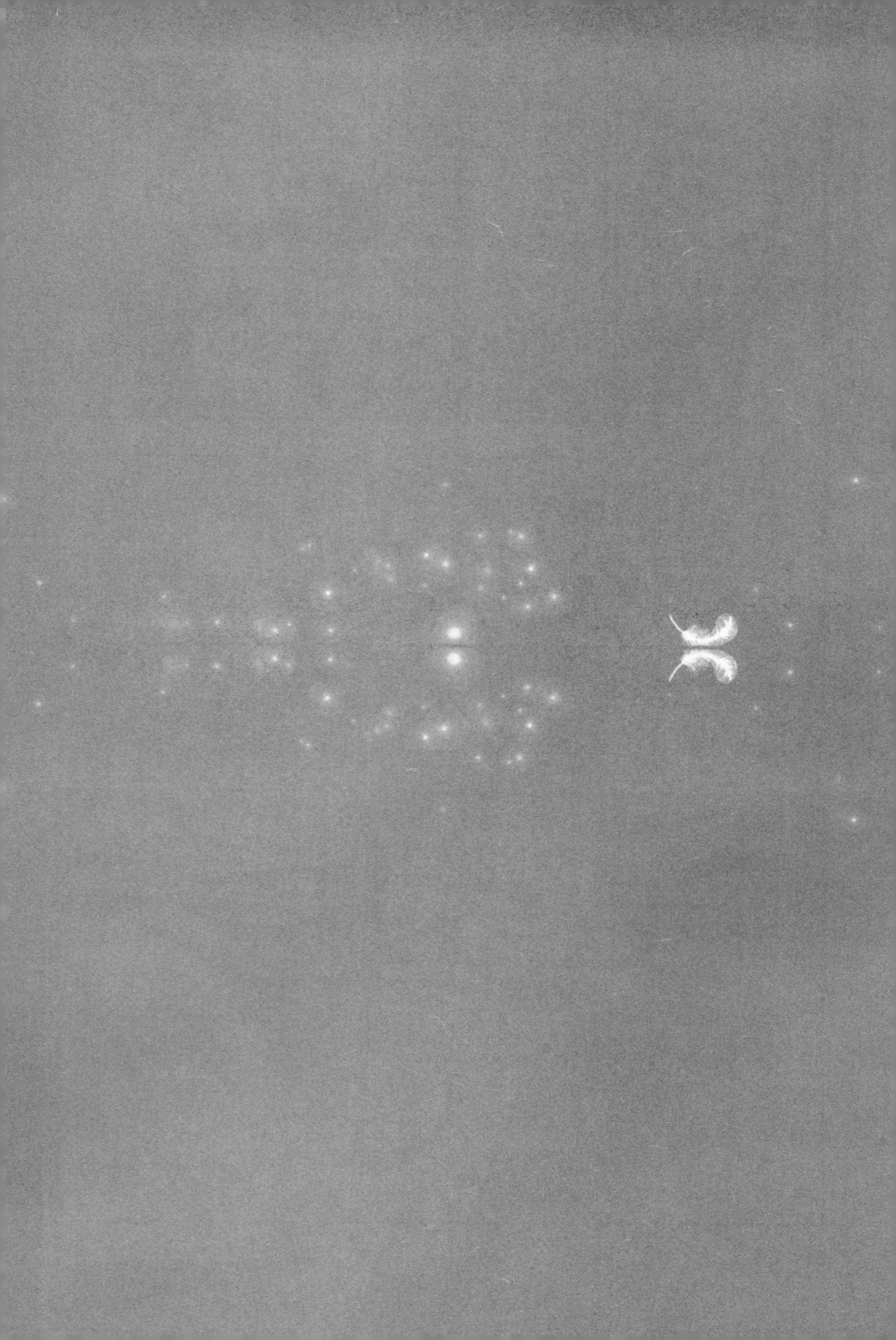

#58 The Final Arrow

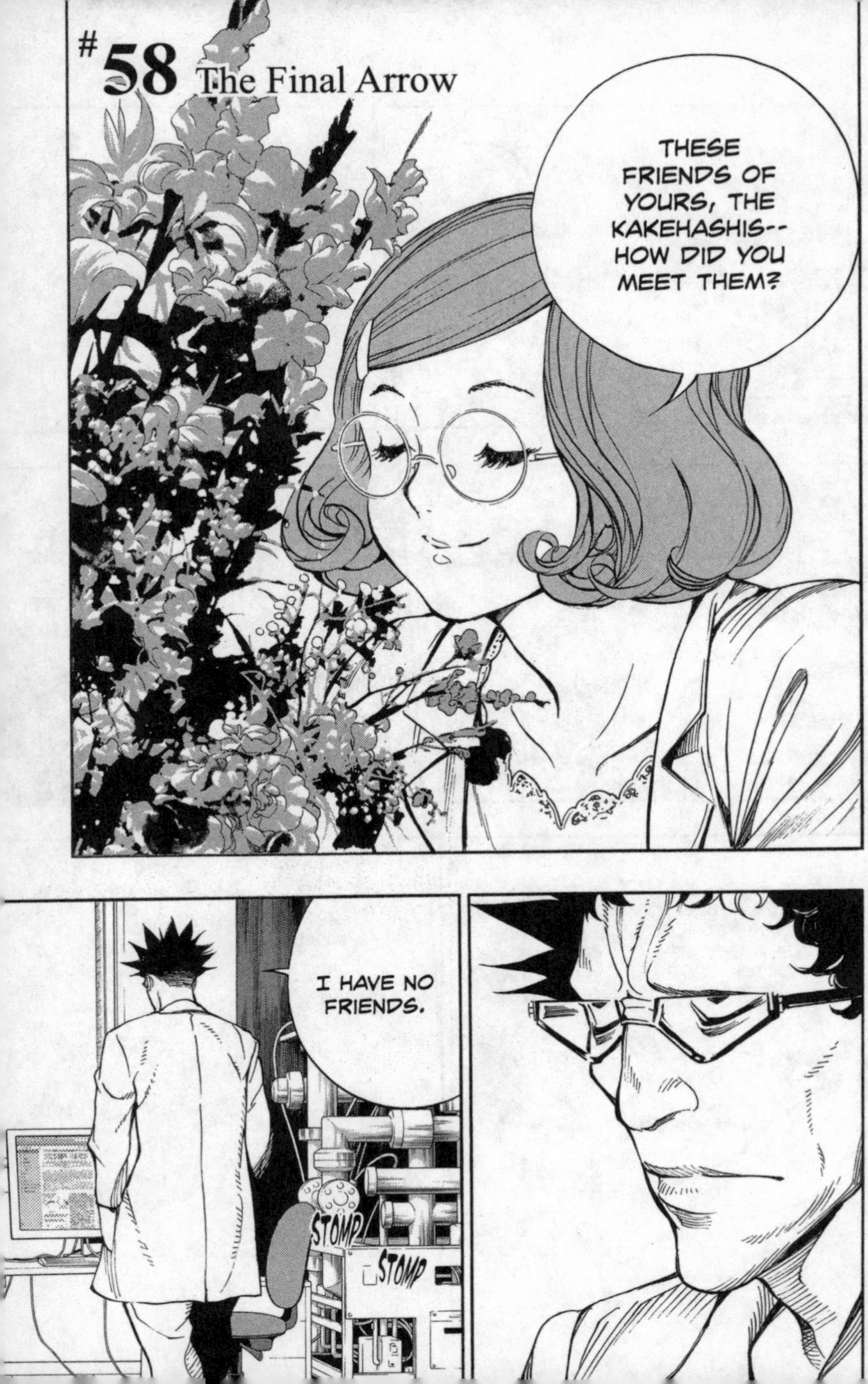
THESE FRIENDS OF YOURS, THE KAKEHASHIS-- HOW DID YOU MEET THEM?
I HAVE NO FRIENDS.
STOMP
STOMP

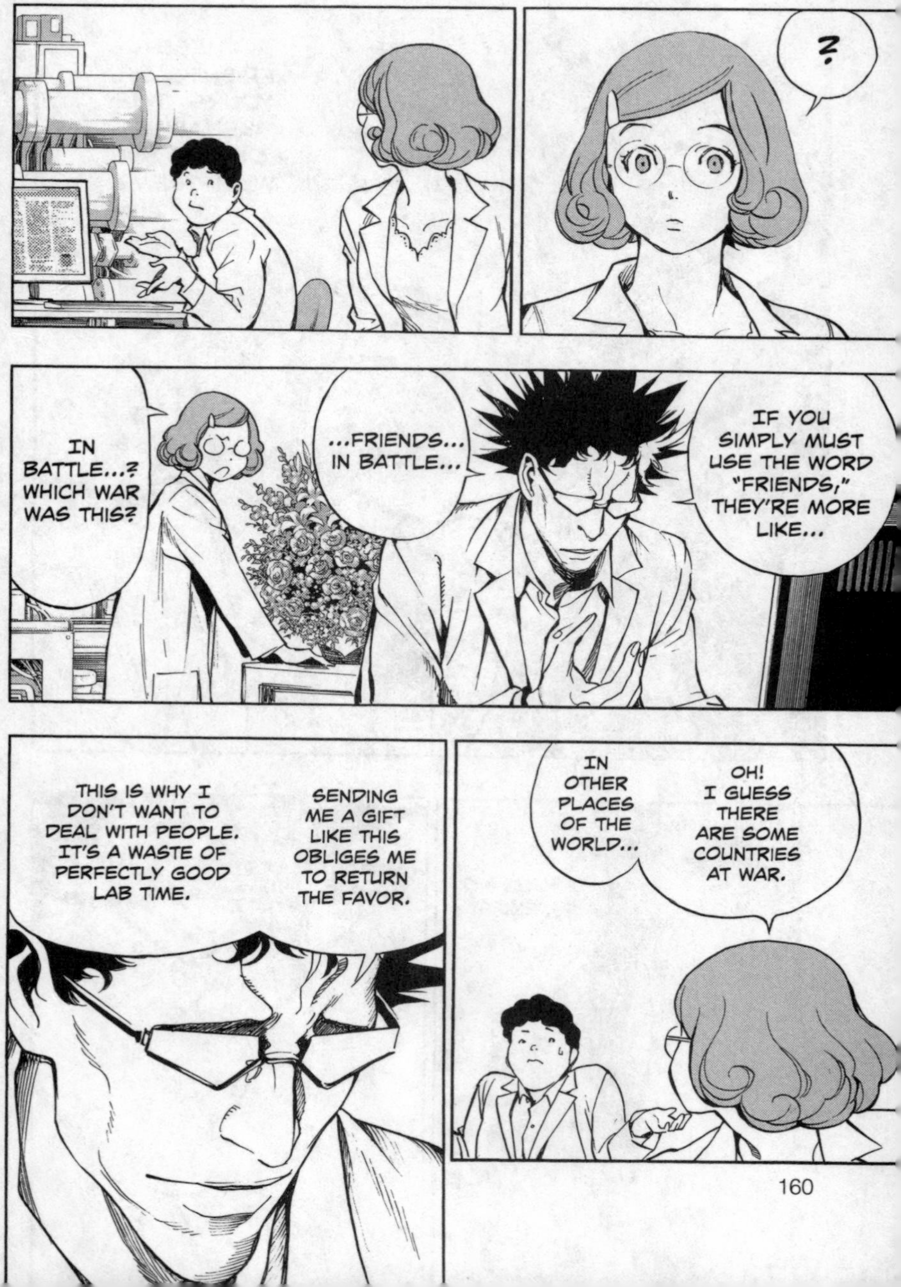
?
IF YOU SIMPLY MUST USE THE WORD "FRIENDS," THEY'RE MORE LIKE...
...FRIENDS... IN BATTLE...
IN BATTLE...? WHICH WAR WAS THIS?
OH! I GUESS THERE ARE SOME COUNTRIES AT WAR.
IN OTHER PLACES OF THE WORLD...
SENDING ME A GIFT LIKE THIS OBLIGES ME TO RETURN THE FAVOR.
THIS IS WHY I DON'T WANT TO DEAL WITH PEOPLE. IT'S A WASTE OF PERFECTLY GOOD LAB TIME.

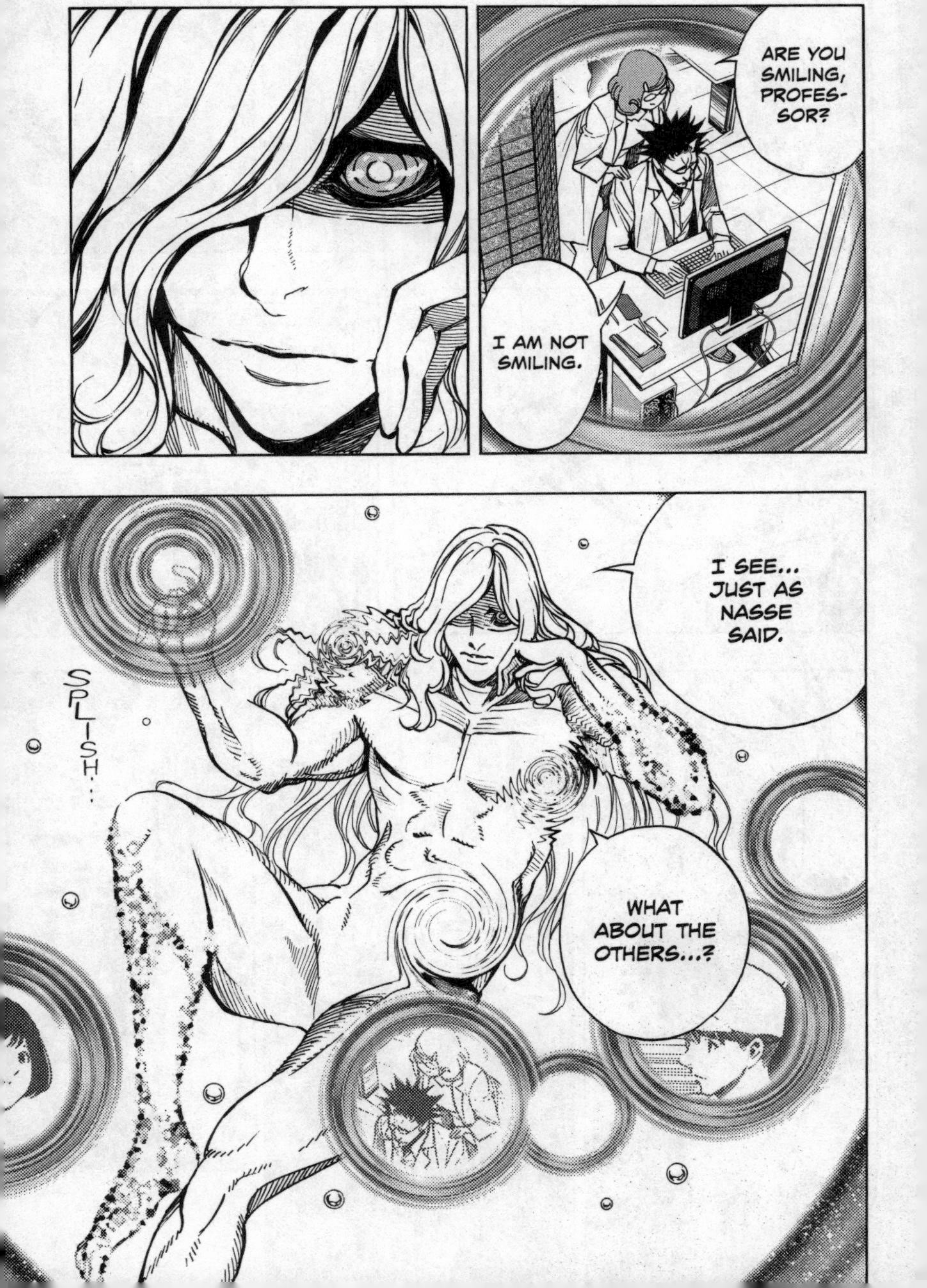
ARE YOU SMILING, PROFESSOR?
I AM NOT SMILING.
I SEE... JUST AS NASSE SAID.
SPLISH...
WHAT ABOUT THE OTHERS...?

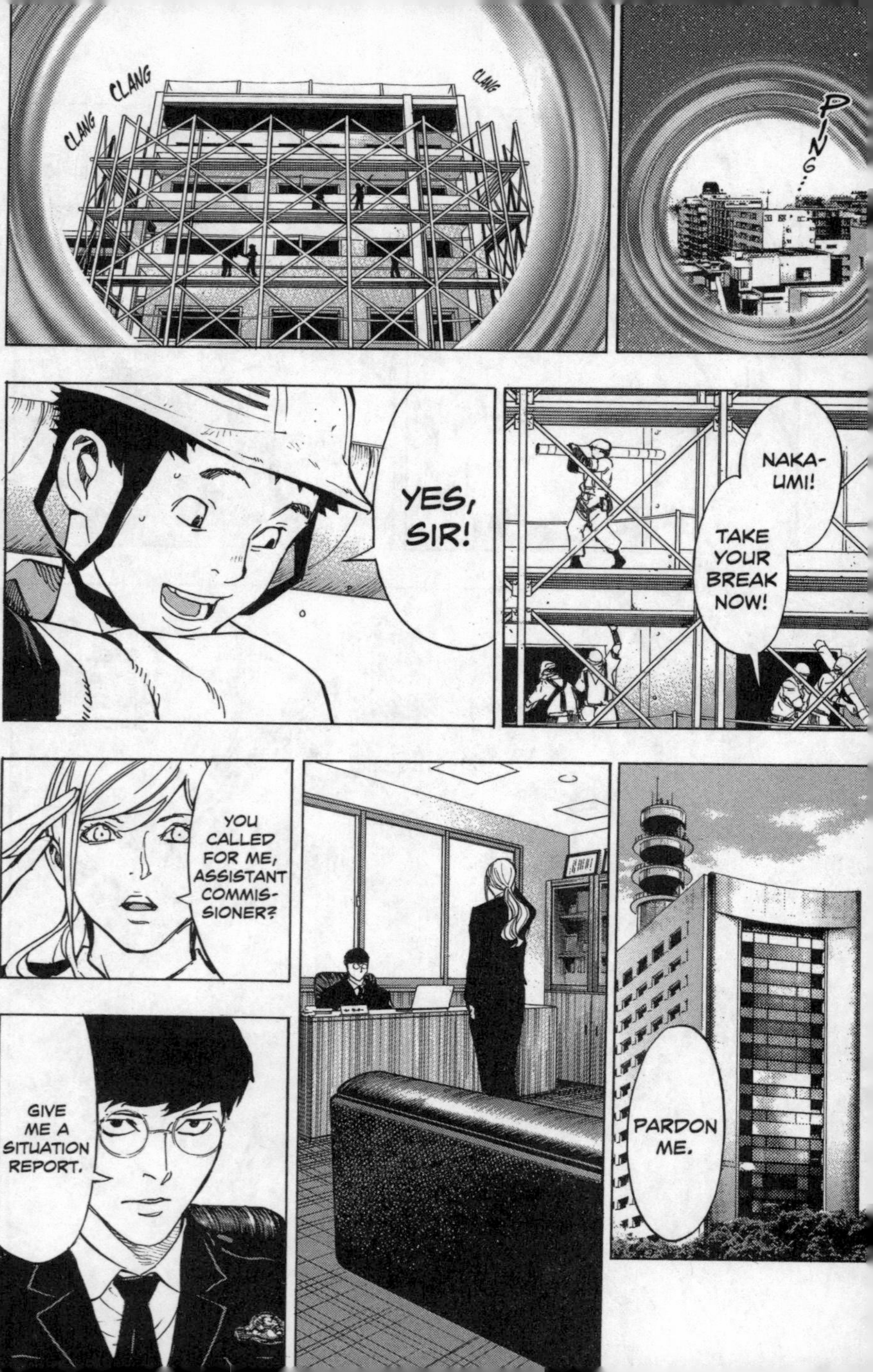
PING...
CLANG
CLANG
CLANG
NAKA-UMI!
TAKE YOUR BREAK NOW!
YES, SIR!
PARDON ME.
YOU CALLED FOR ME, ASSISTANT COMMISSIONER?
GIVE ME A SITUATION REPORT.

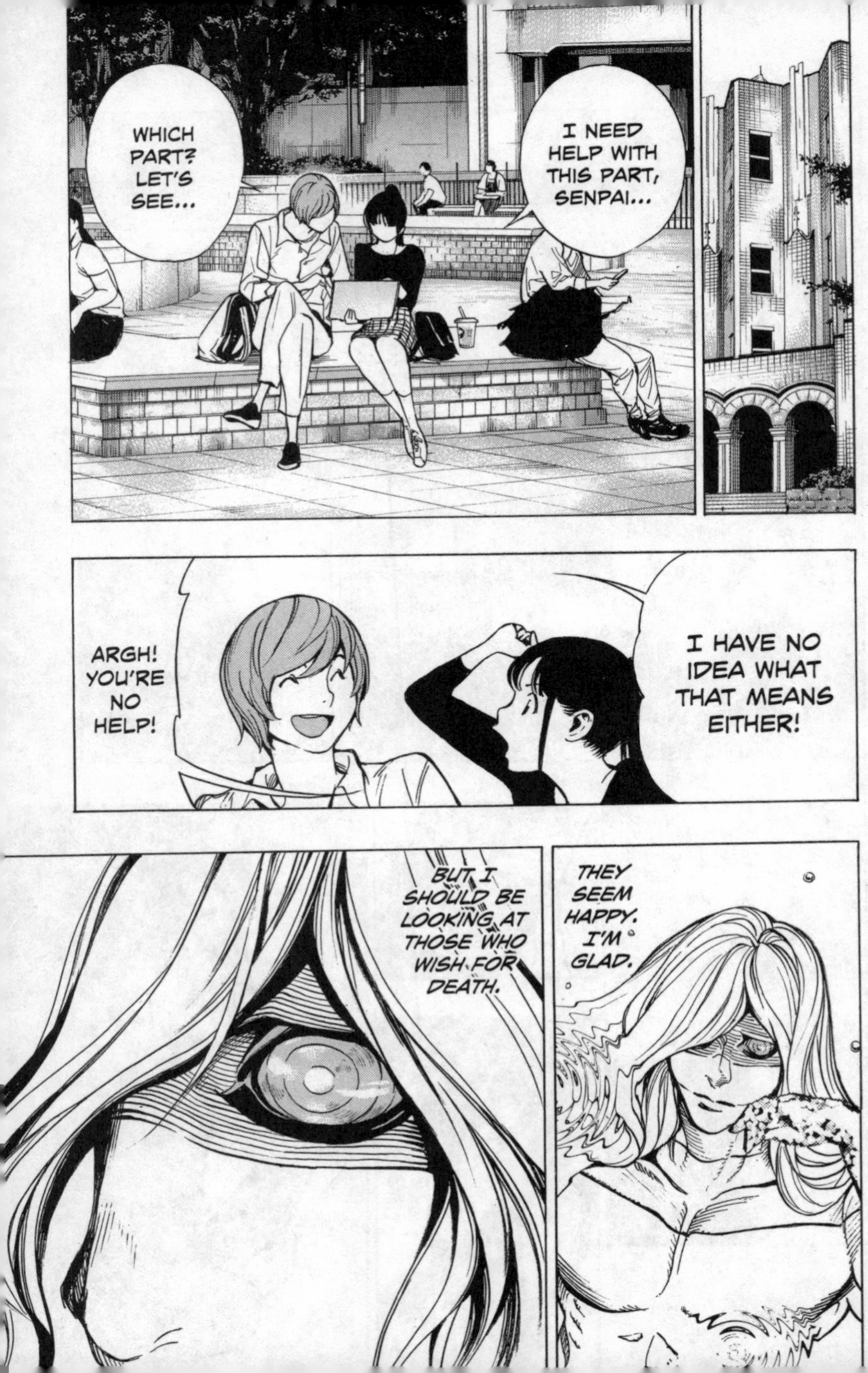
I NEED HELP WITH THIS PART, SENPAI...
WHICH PART? LET'S SEE...
I HAVE NO IDEA WHAT THAT MEANS EITHER!
ARGH! YOU'RE NO HELP!
THEY SEEM HAPPY. I'M GLAD.
BUT I SHOULD BE LOOKING AT THOSE WHO WISH FOR DEATH.

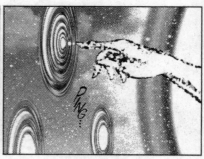

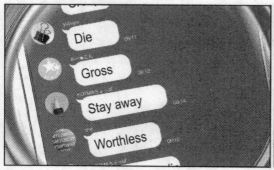

Die

Gross

Stay away

Worthless

Creep
Die
Gross
Stay away
Worthless
When will u die

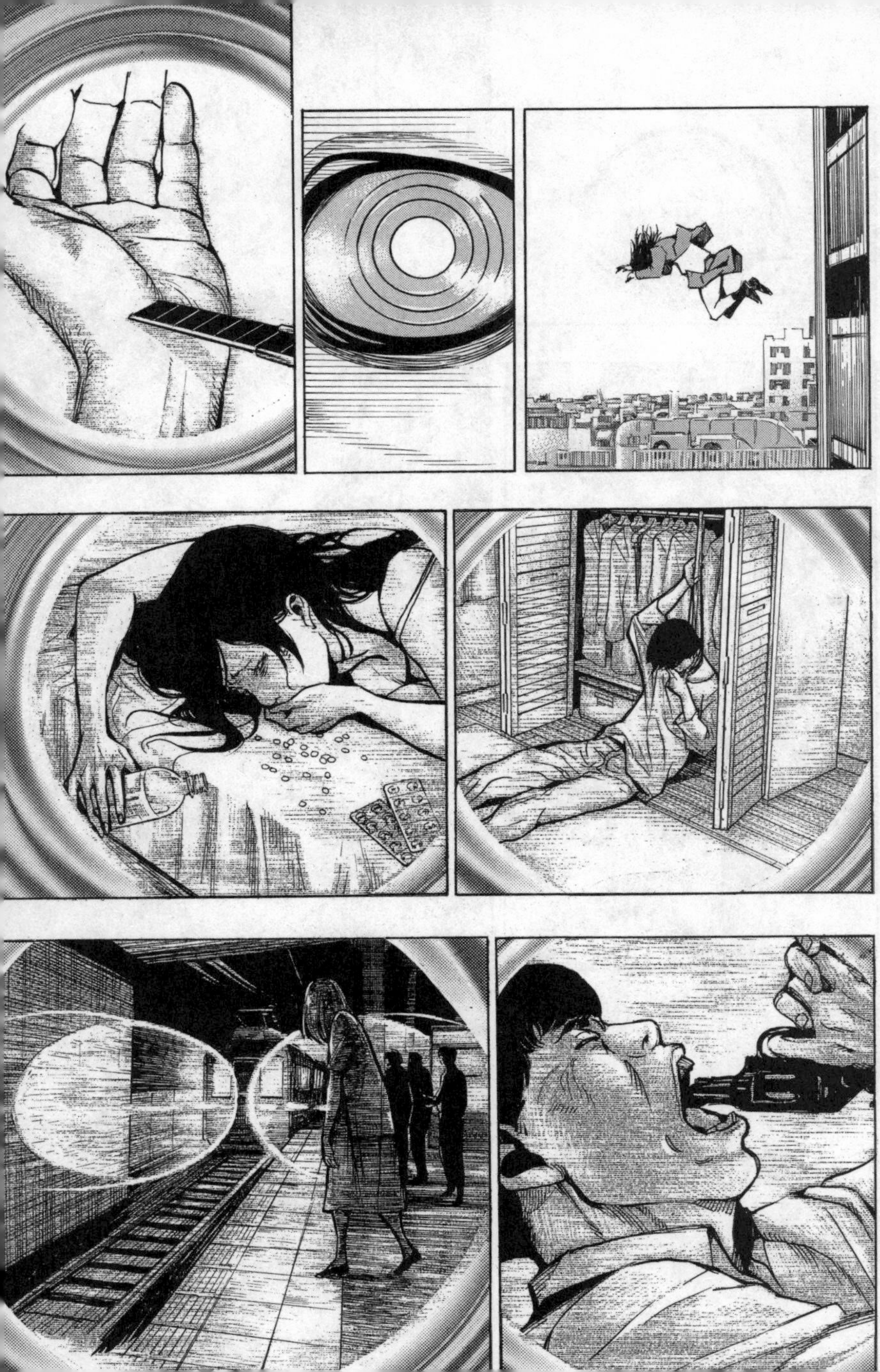

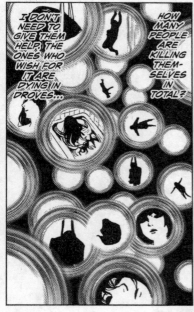

HOW MANY PEOPLE ARE KILLING THEM-SELVES IN TOTAL?
I DON'T NEED TO GIVE THEM HELP. THE ONES WHO WISH FOR IT ARE DYING IN DROVES...

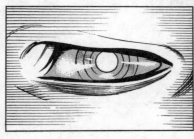

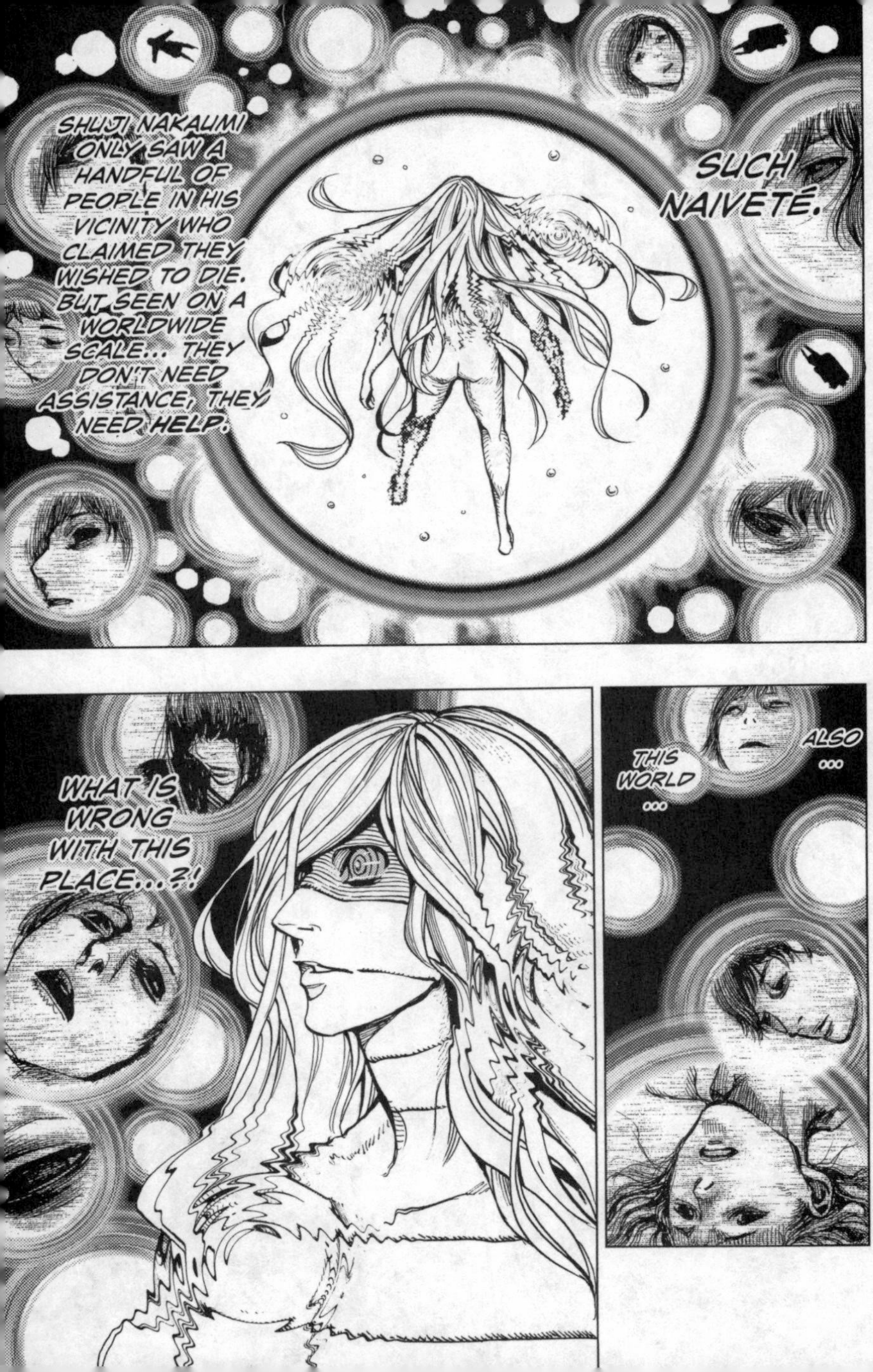
SUCH NAIVETÉ.
SHUJI NAKAUMI ONLY SAW A HANDFUL OF PEOPLE IN HIS VICINITY WHO CLAIMED THEY WISHED TO DIE. BUT SEEN ON A WORLDWIDE SCALE... THEY DON'T NEED ASSISTANCE, THEY NEED HELP.
ALSO ...
THIS WORLD ...
WHAT IS WRONG WITH THIS PLACE...?!

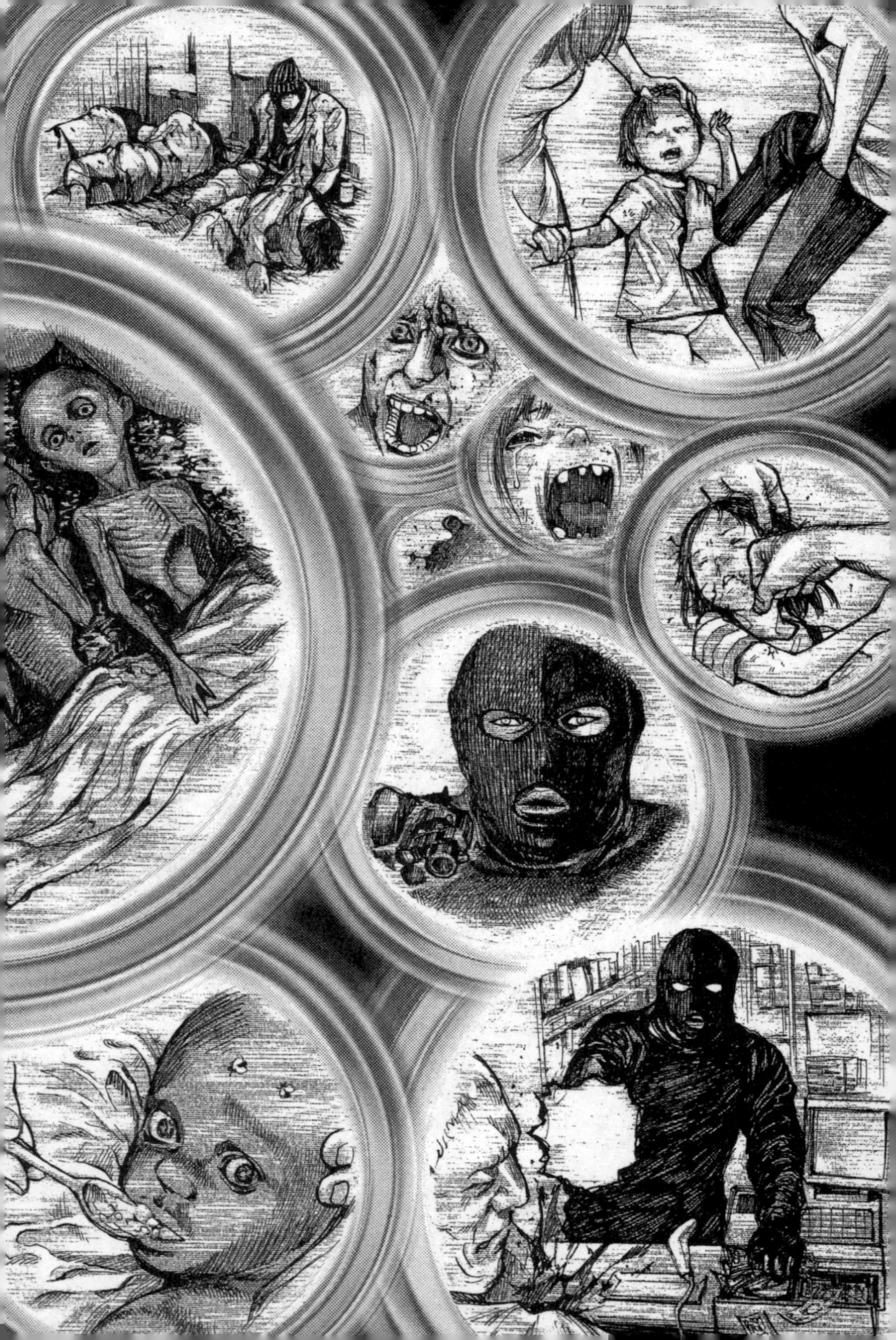

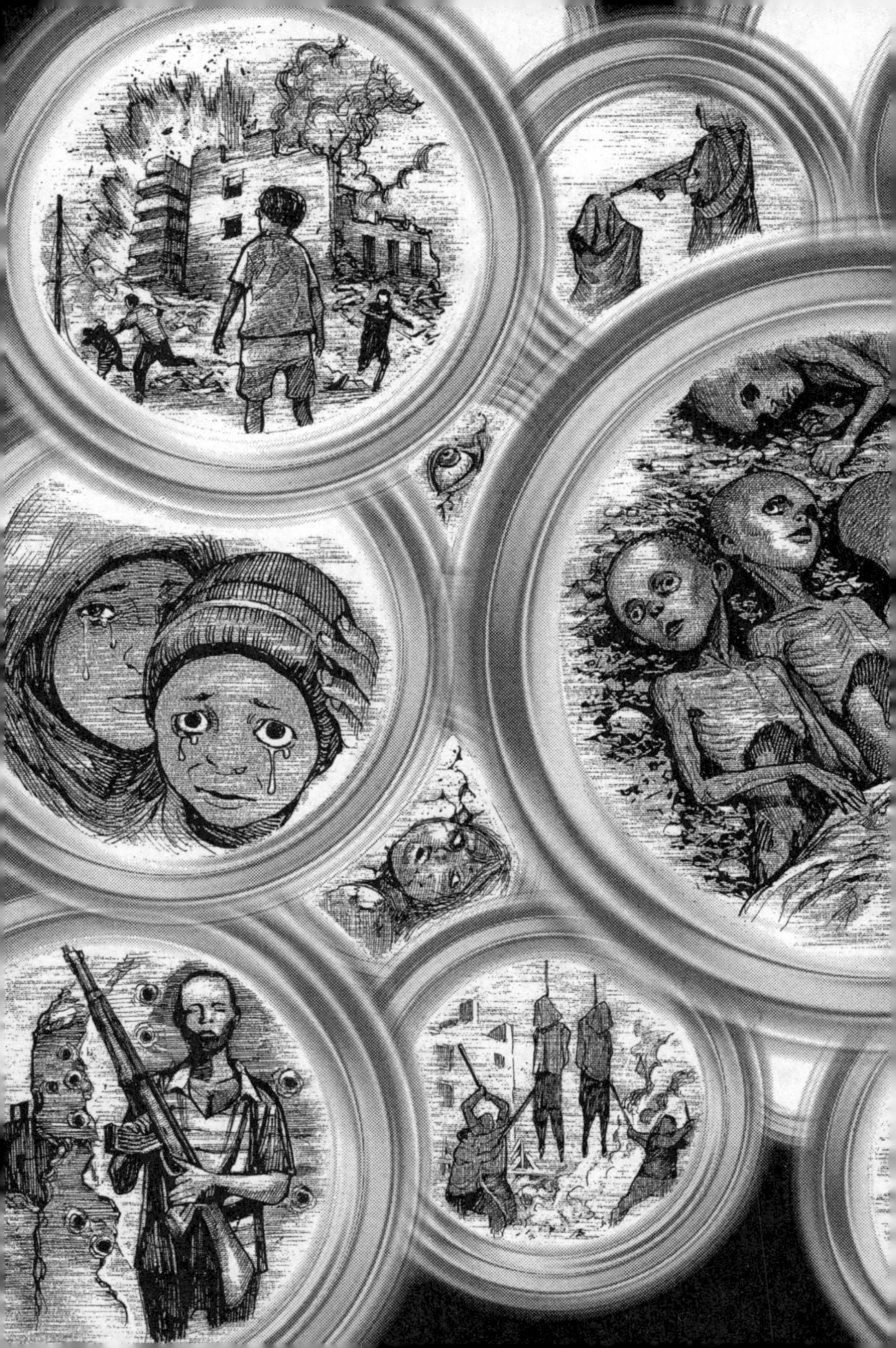

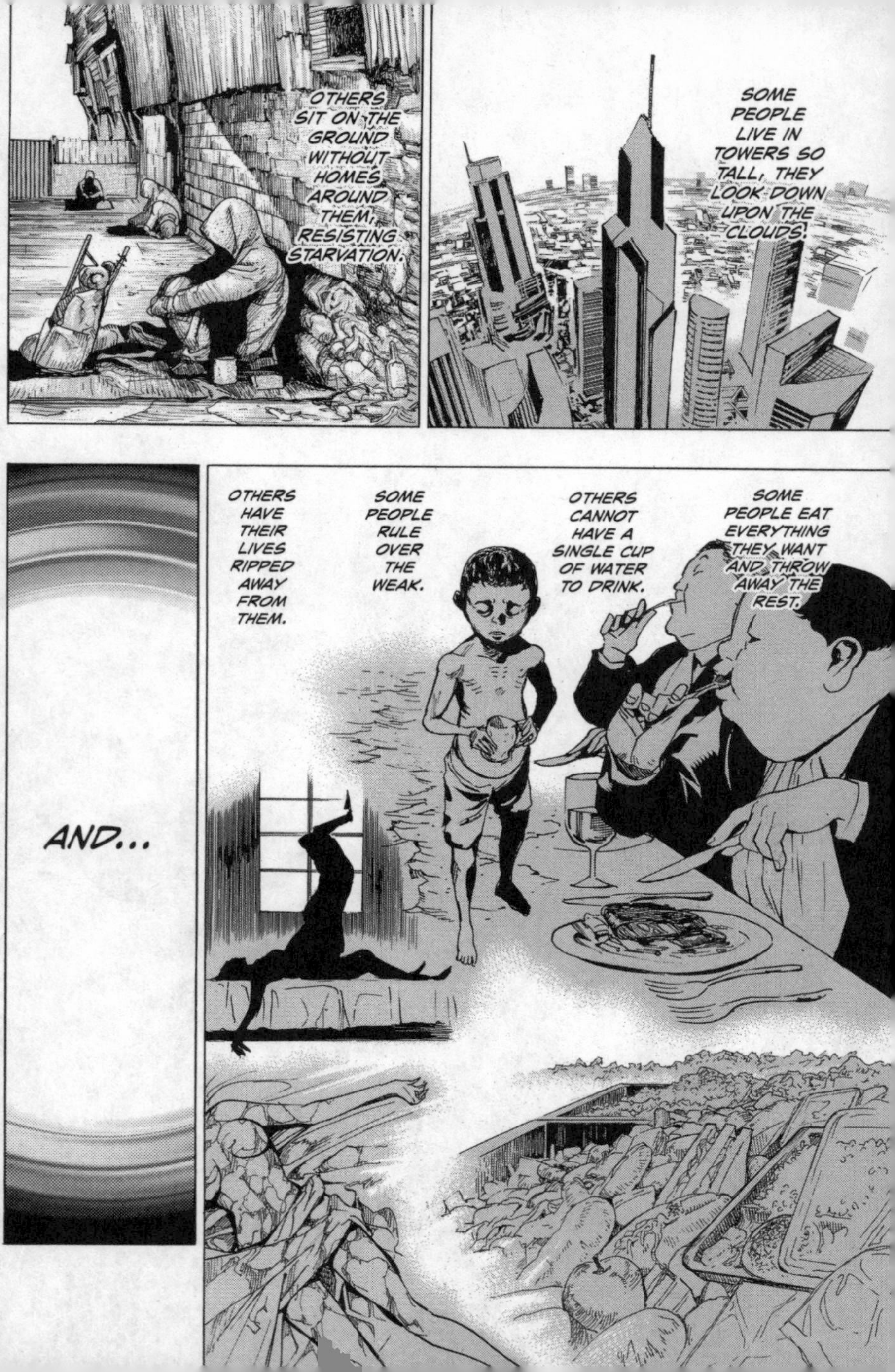
SOME PEOPLE LIVE IN TOWERS SO TALL, THEY LOOK DOWN UPON THE CLOUDS.
OTHERS SIT ON THE GROUND WITHOUT HOMES AROUND THEM, RESISTING STARVATION.
SOME PEOPLE EAT EVERYTHING THEY WANT AND THROW AWAY THE REST.
OTHERS CANNOT HAVE A SINGLE CUP OF WATER TO DRINK.
SOME PEOPLE RULE OVER THE WEAK.
OTHERS HAVE THEIR LIVES RIPPED AWAY FROM THEM.
AND...

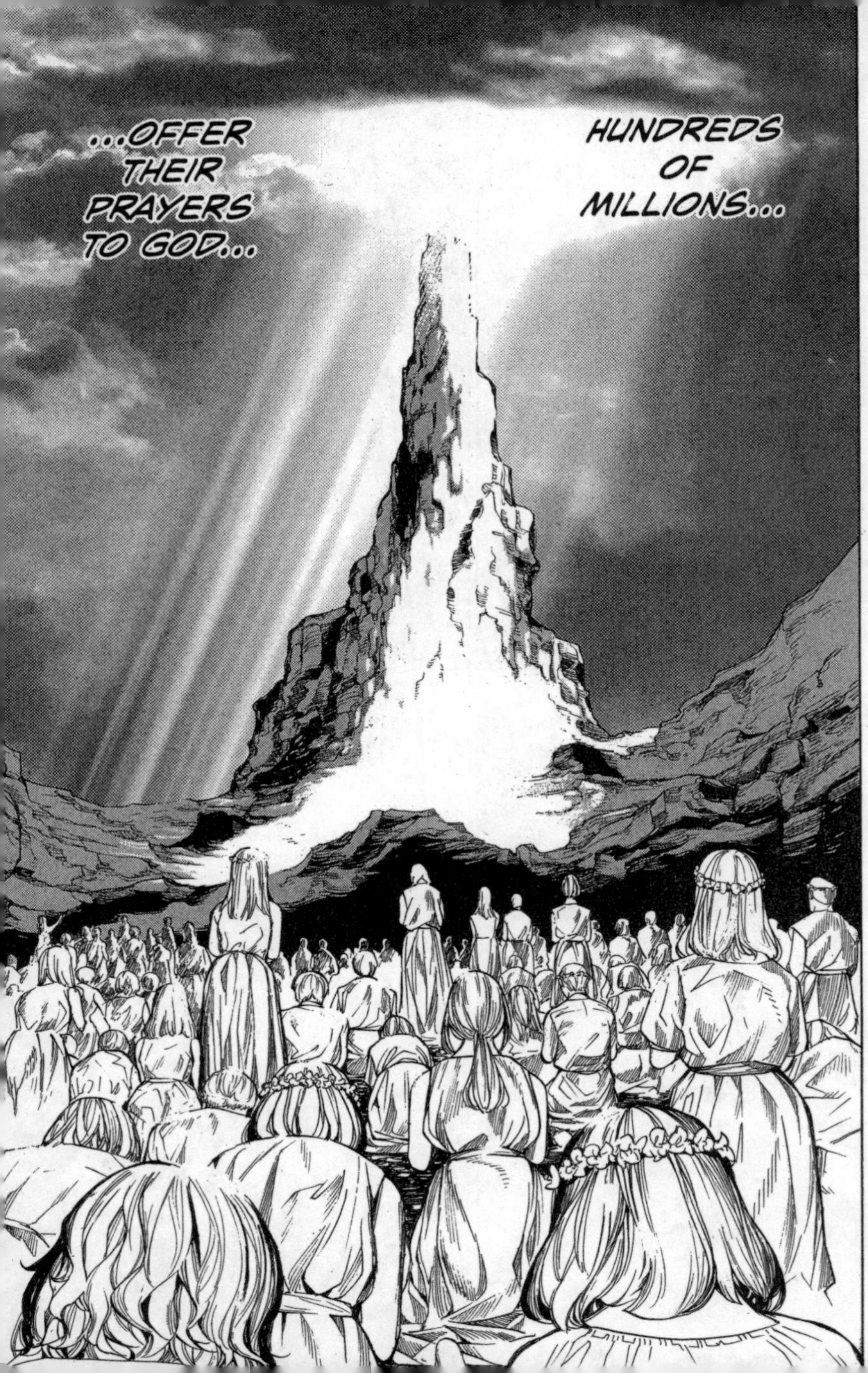
HUNDREDS OF MILLIONS...
...OFFER THEIR PRAYERS TO GOD...

...OF THE WORLD ... THIS IS THE NATURE ...

WHAT WAS THE PREVIOUS GOD DOING? WHY IS THERE A GOD?

...

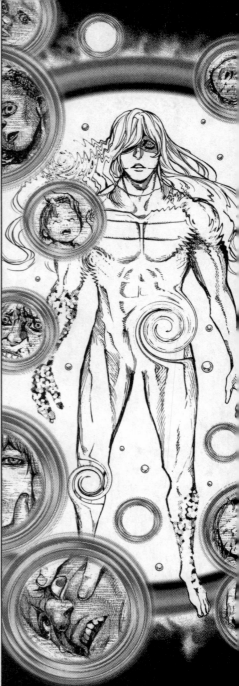

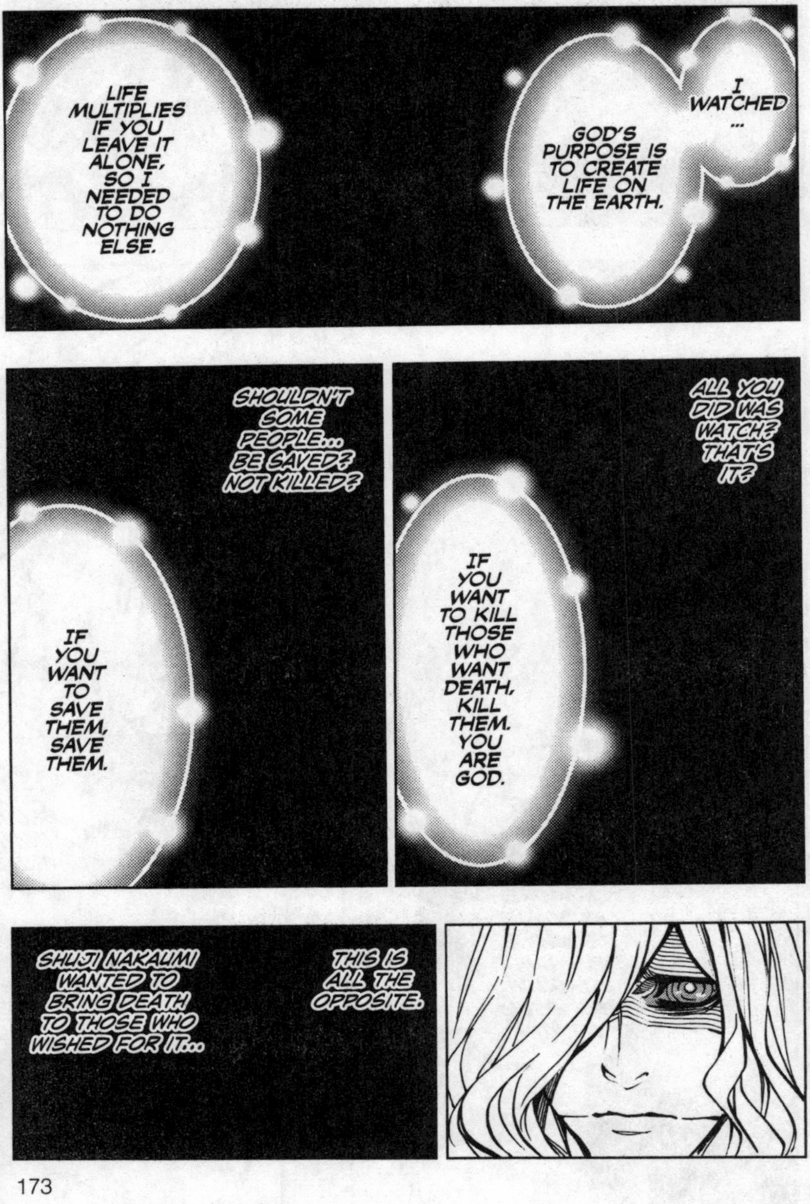
I WATCHED ...
GOD'S PURPOSE IS TO CREATE LIFE ON THE EARTH.
LIFE MULTIPLIES IF YOU LEAVE IT ALONE, SO I NEEDED TO DO NOTHING ELSE.
ALL YOU DID WAS WATCH? THAT'S IT?
IF YOU WANT TO KILL THOSE WHO WANT DEATH, KILL THEM. YOU ARE GOD.
SHOULDN'T SOME PEOPLE... BE SAVED? NOT KILLED?
IF YOU WANT TO SAVE THEM, SAVE THEM.
THIS IS ALL THE OPPOSITE.
SHUJI NAKAUMI WANTED TO BRING DEATH TO THOSE WHO WISHED FOR IT...

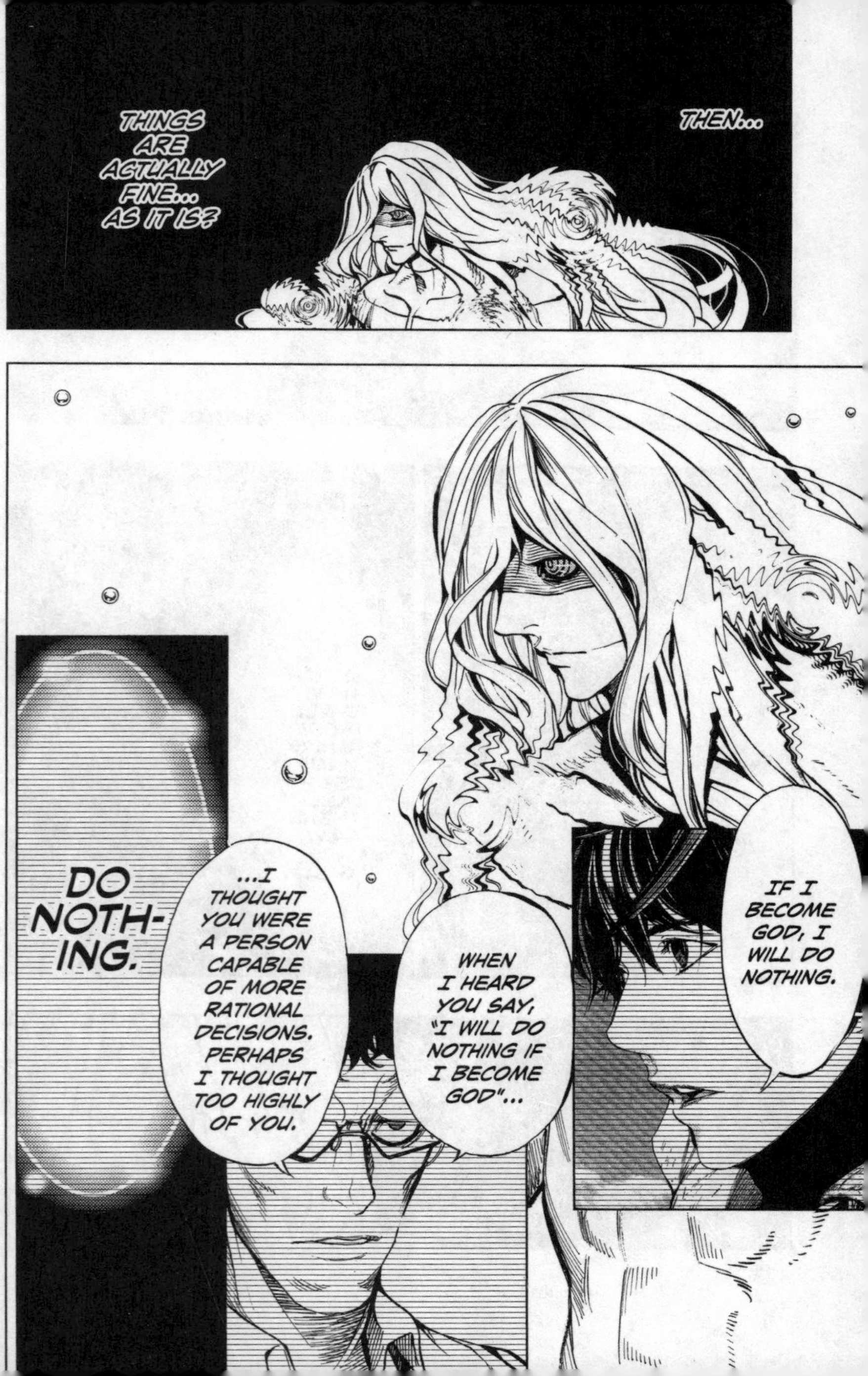
THEN...
THINGS ARE ACTUALLY FINE... AS IT IS?
IF I BECOME GOD, I WILL DO NOTHING.
WHEN I HEARD YOU SAY, "I WILL DO NOTHING IF I BECOME GOD"...
...I THOUGHT YOU WERE A PERSON CAPABLE OF MORE RATIONAL DECISIONS. PERHAPS I THOUGHT TOO HIGHLY OF YOU.
DO NOTH-ING.

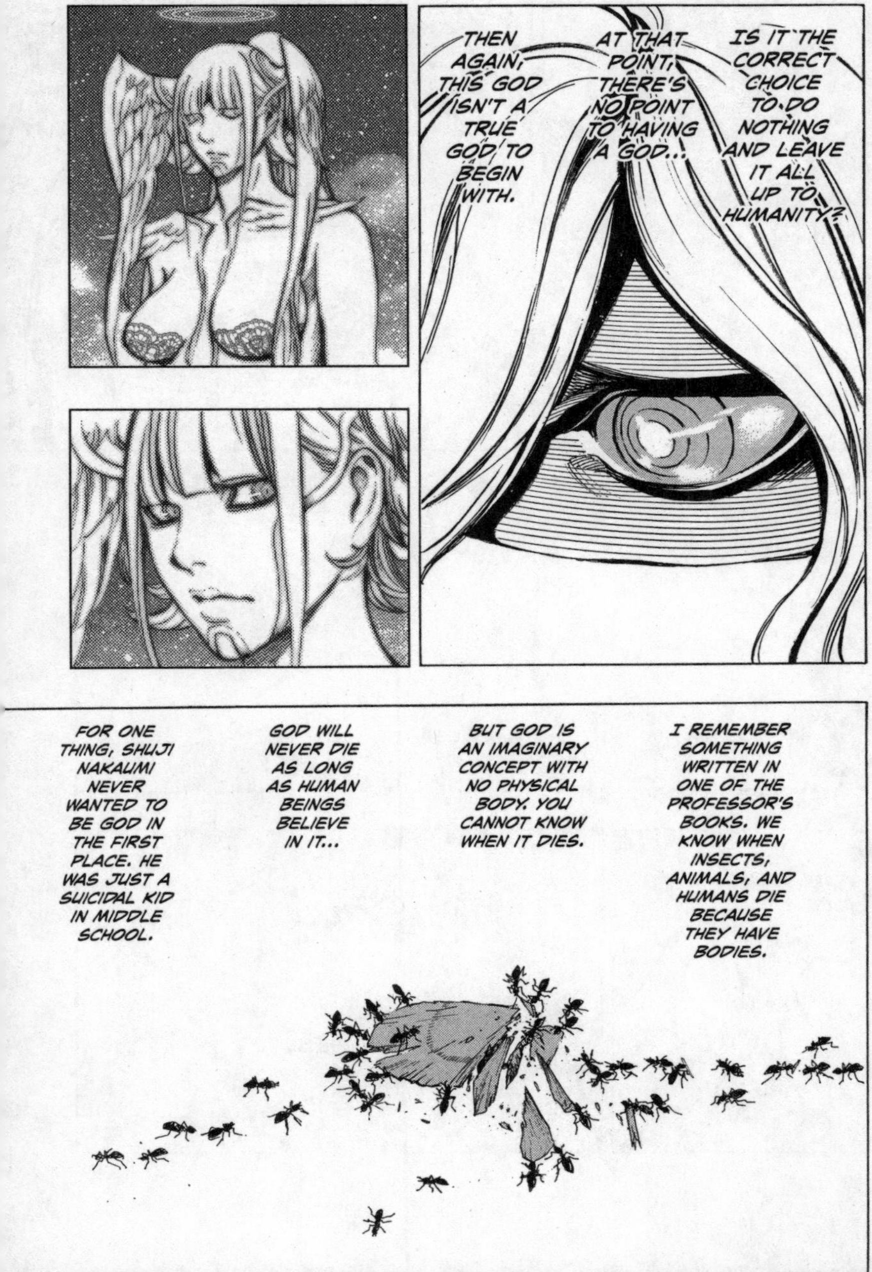
IS IT THE CORRECT CHOICE TO DO NOTHING AND LEAVE IT ALL UP TO HUMANITY?
AT THAT POINT, THERE'S NO POINT TO HAVING A GOD...
THEN AGAIN, THIS GOD ISN'T A TRUE GOD TO BEGIN WITH.
I REMEMBER SOMETHING WRITTEN IN ONE OF THE PROFESSOR'S BOOKS. WE KNOW WHEN INSECTS, ANIMALS, AND HUMANS DIE BECAUSE THEY HAVE BODIES.
BUT GOD IS AN IMAGINARY CONCEPT WITH NO PHYSICAL BODY. YOU CANNOT KNOW WHEN IT DIES.
GOD WILL NEVER DIE AS LONG AS HUMAN BEINGS BELIEVE IN IT...
FOR ONE THING, SHUJI NAKAUMI NEVER WANTED TO BE GOD IN THE FIRST PLACE. HE WAS JUST A SUICIDAL KID IN MIDDLE SCHOOL.

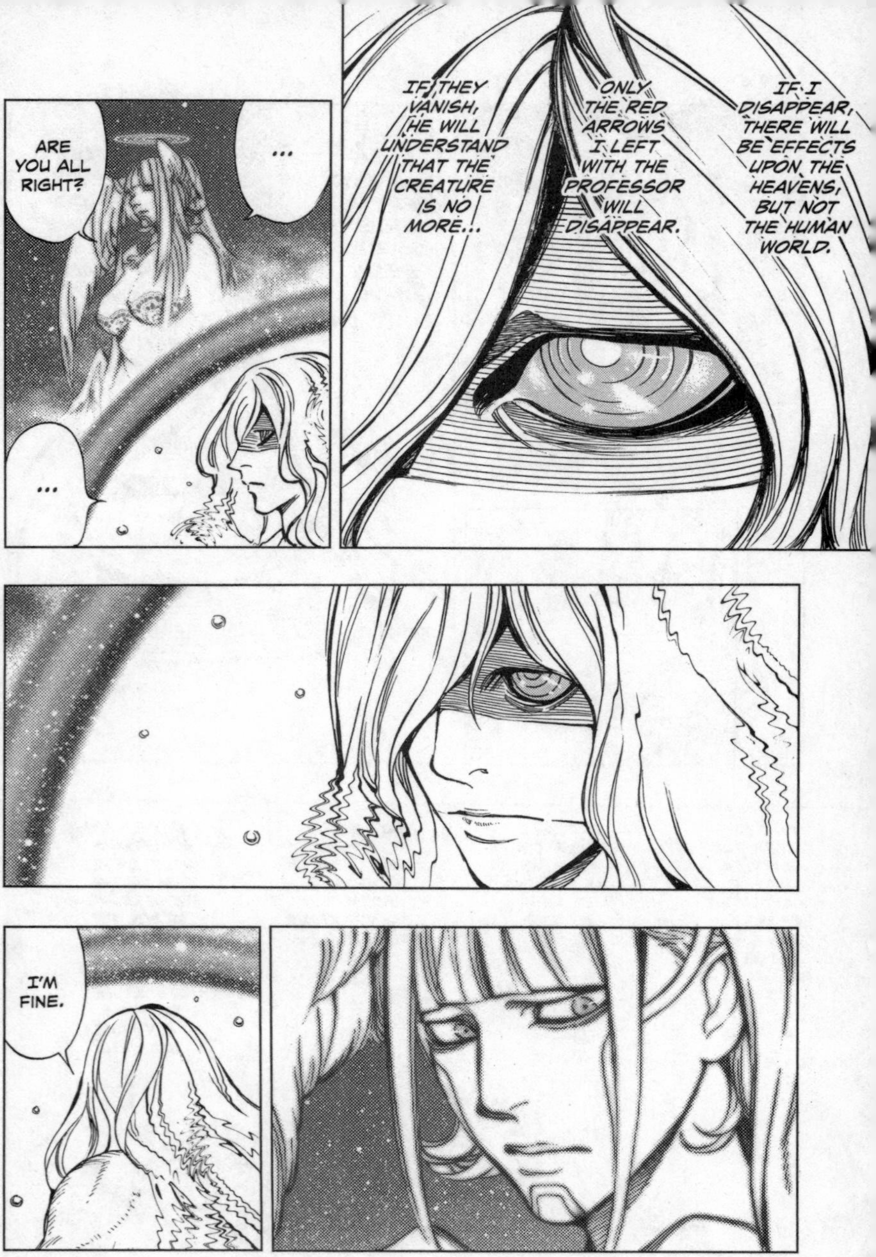
IF I DISAPPEAR, THERE WILL BE EFFECTS UPON THE HEAVENS, BUT NOT THE HUMAN WORLD.
ONLY THE RED ARROWS I LEFT WITH THE PROFESSOR WILL DISAPPEAR.
IF THEY VANISH, HE WILL UNDERSTAND THAT THE CREATURE IS NO MORE...
...
ARE YOU ALL RIGHT?
...
I'M FINE.

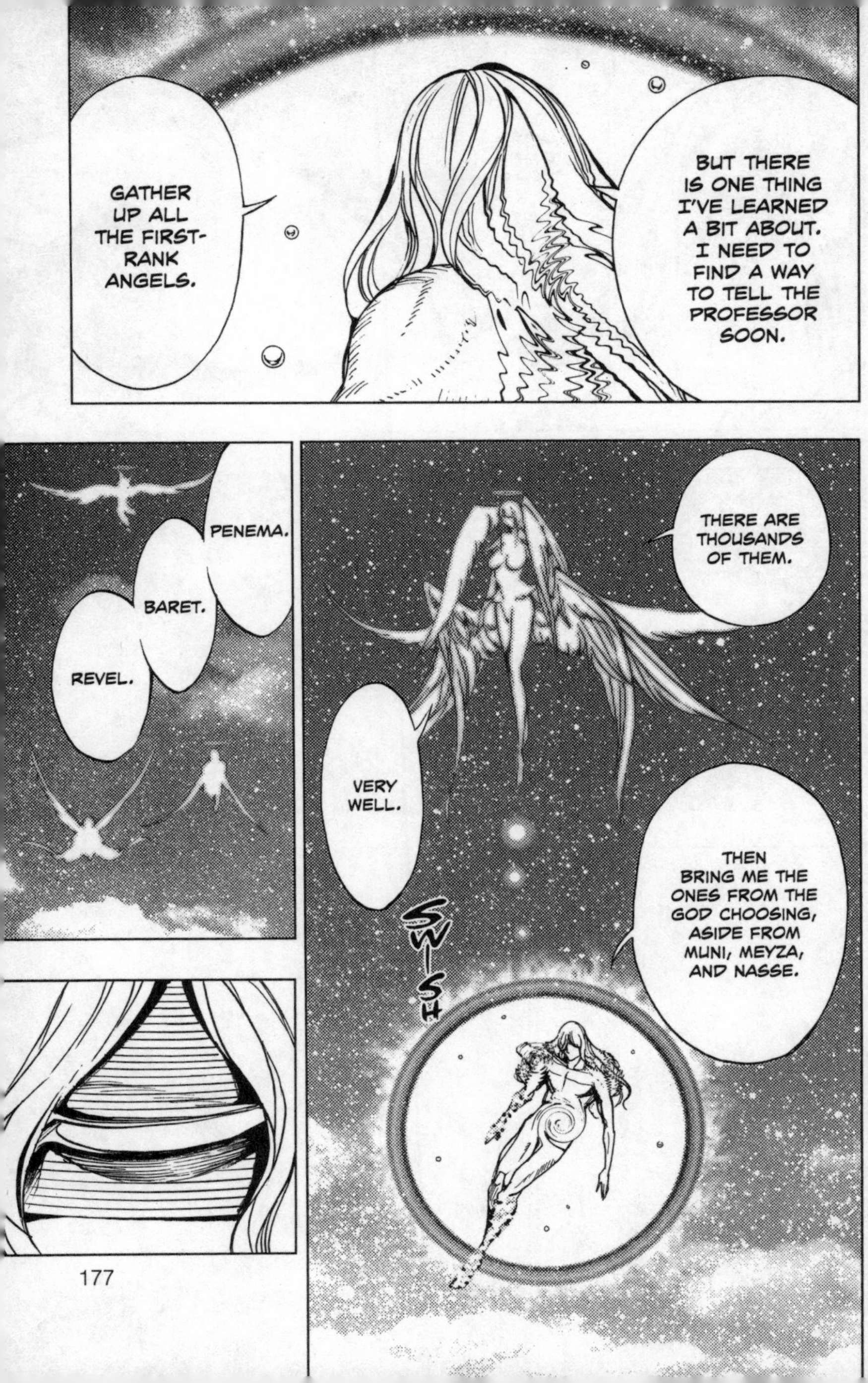
BUT THERE IS ONE THING I'VE LEARNED A BIT ABOUT. I NEED TO FIND A WAY TO TELL THE PROFESSOR SOON.
GATHER UP ALL THE FIRST-RANK ANGELS.
THERE ARE THOUSANDS OF THEM.
THEN BRING ME THE ONES FROM THE GOD CHOOSING, ASIDE FROM MUNI, MEYZA, AND NASSE.
VERY WELL.
SWISH
PENEMA.
BARET.
REVEL.

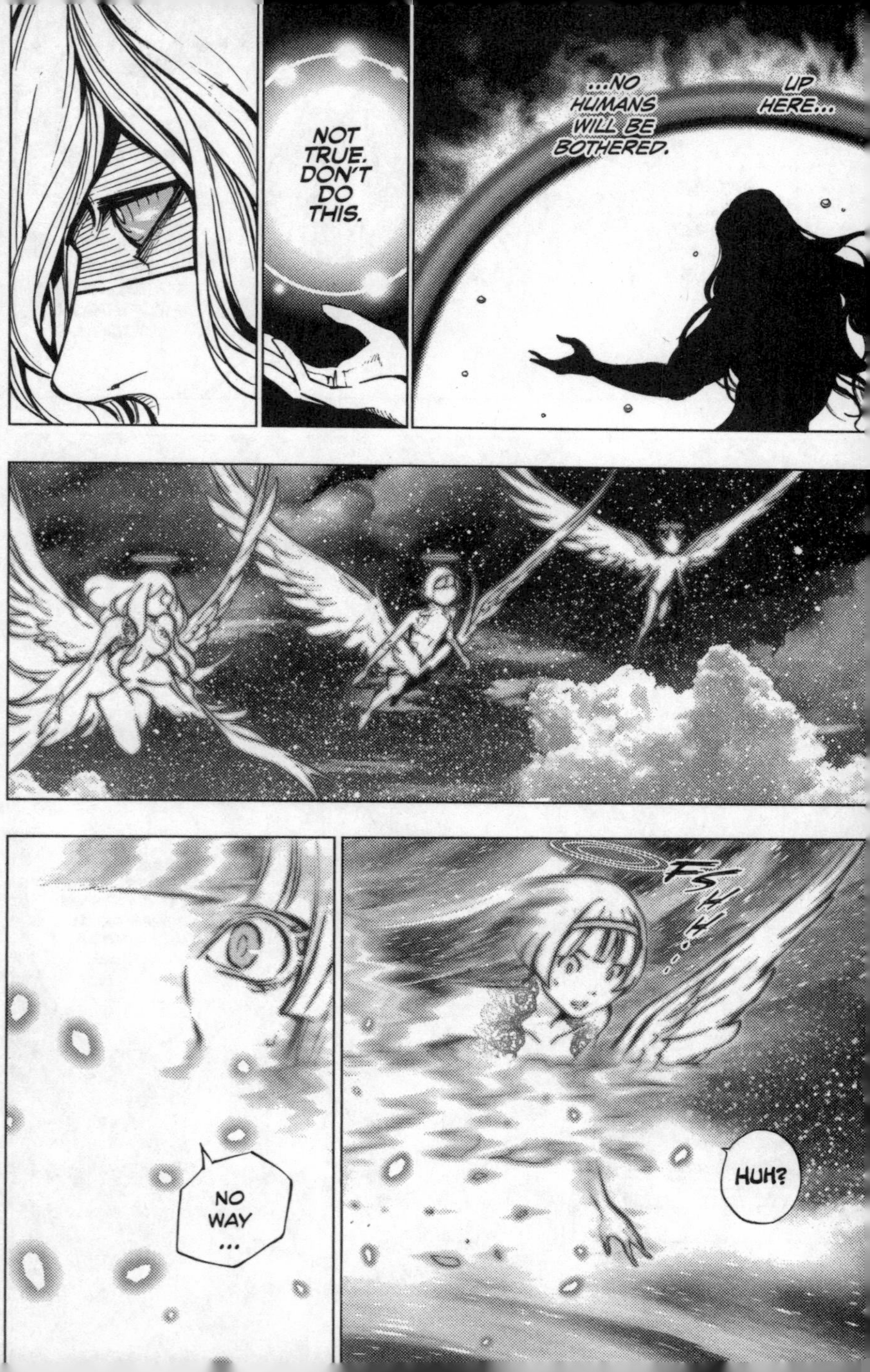
UP HERE...
...NO HUMANS WILL BE BOTHERED.
NOT TRUE. DON'T DO THIS.
FSHHH...
HUH?
NO WAY ...

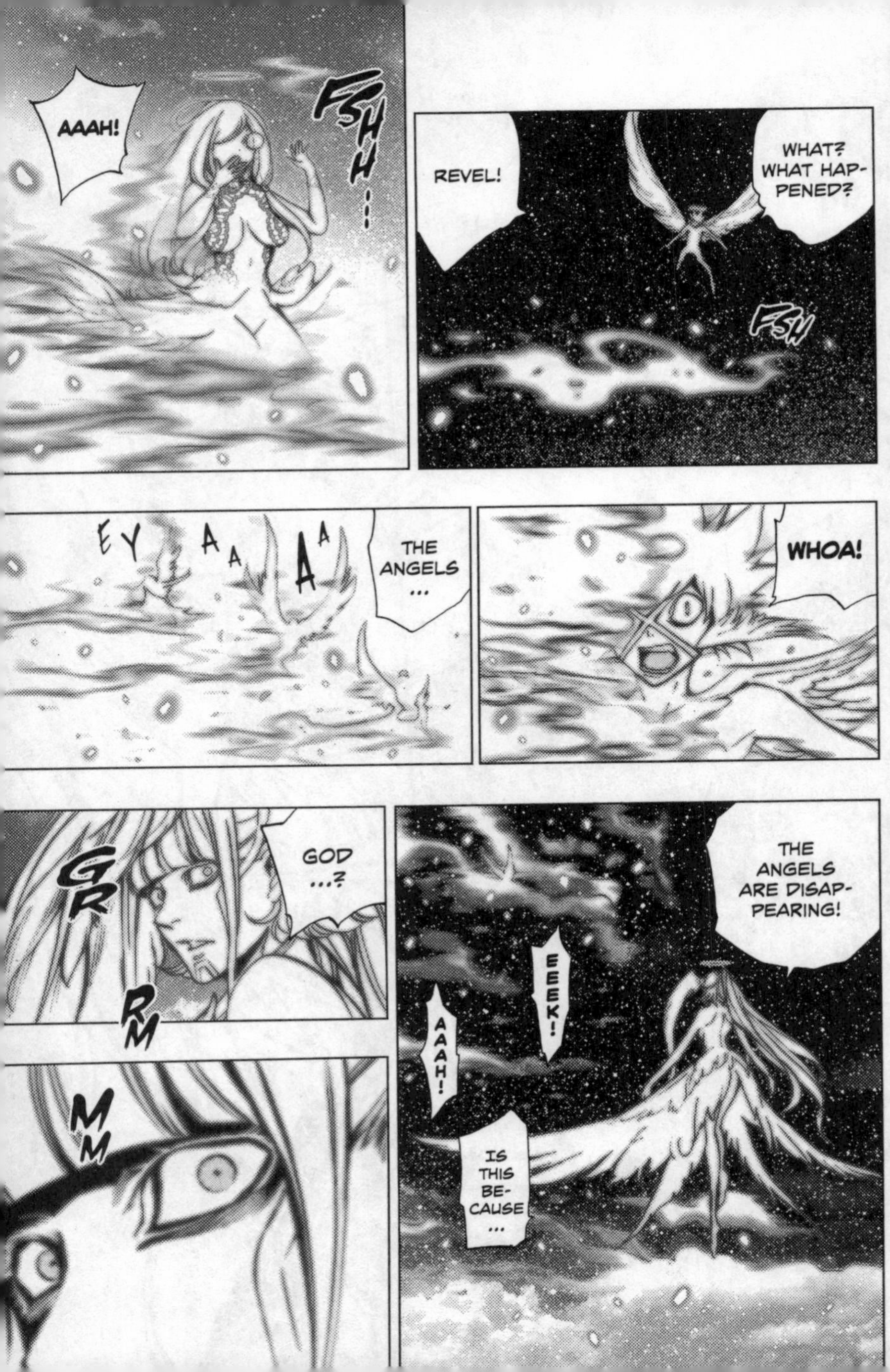
WHAT? WHAT HAPPENED?
REVEL!
FSH
FSHH...
AAAH!
WHOA!
THE ANGELS...
EYAAAAA
THE ANGELS ARE DISAPPEARING!
EEEK!
AAAH!
IS THIS BECAUSE...
GOD...?
GRRM
MM

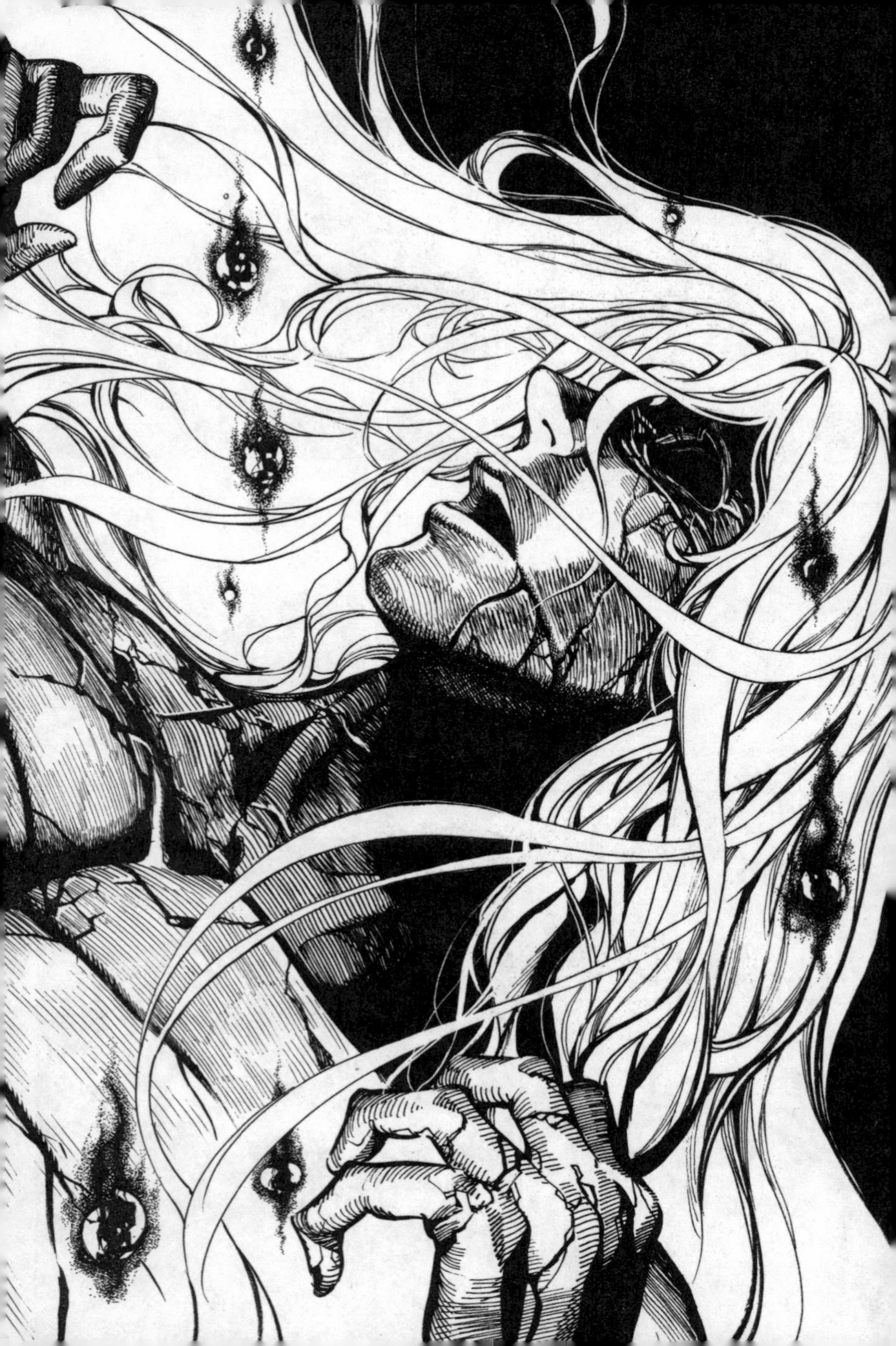

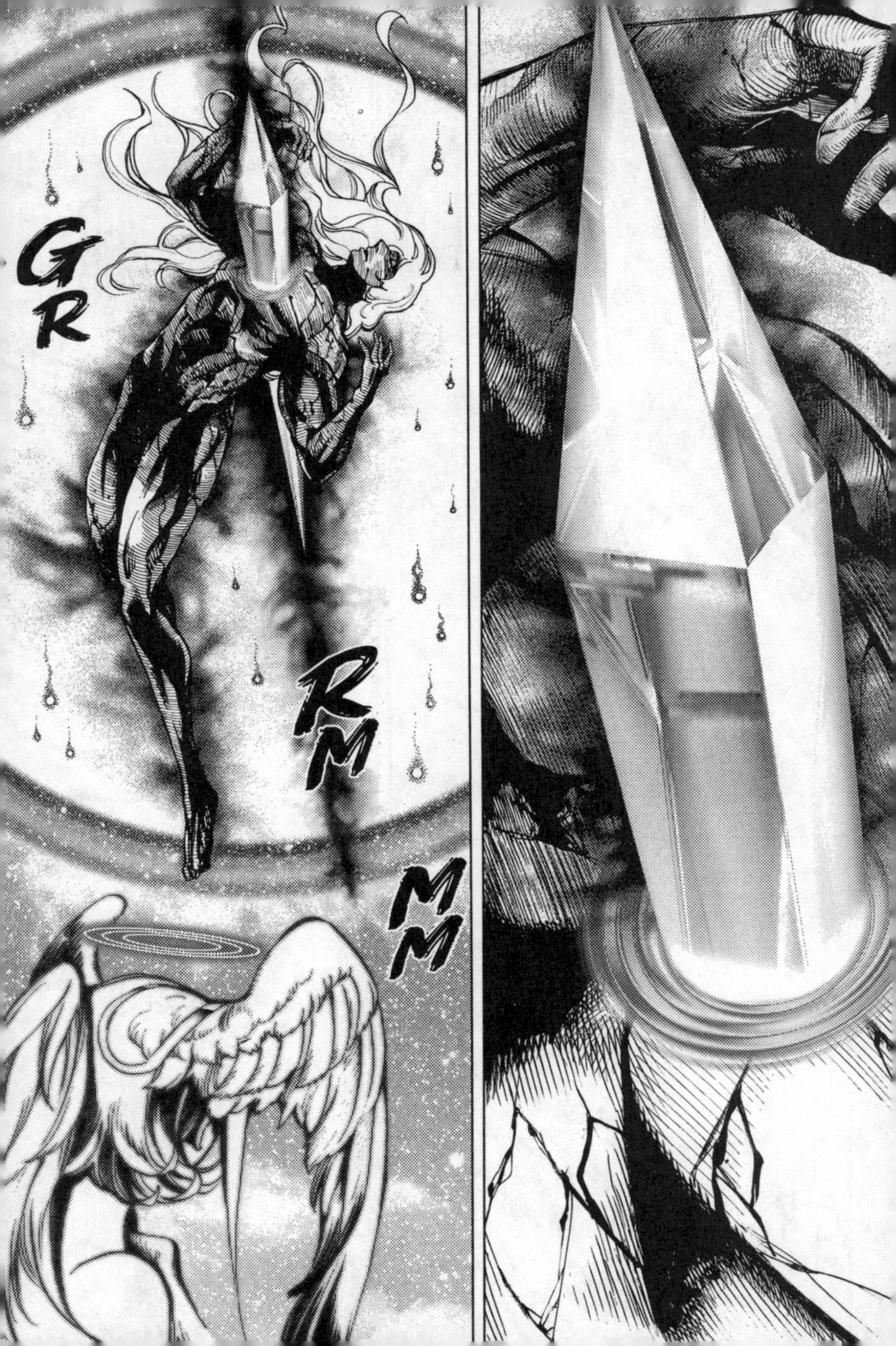
GRRMMM

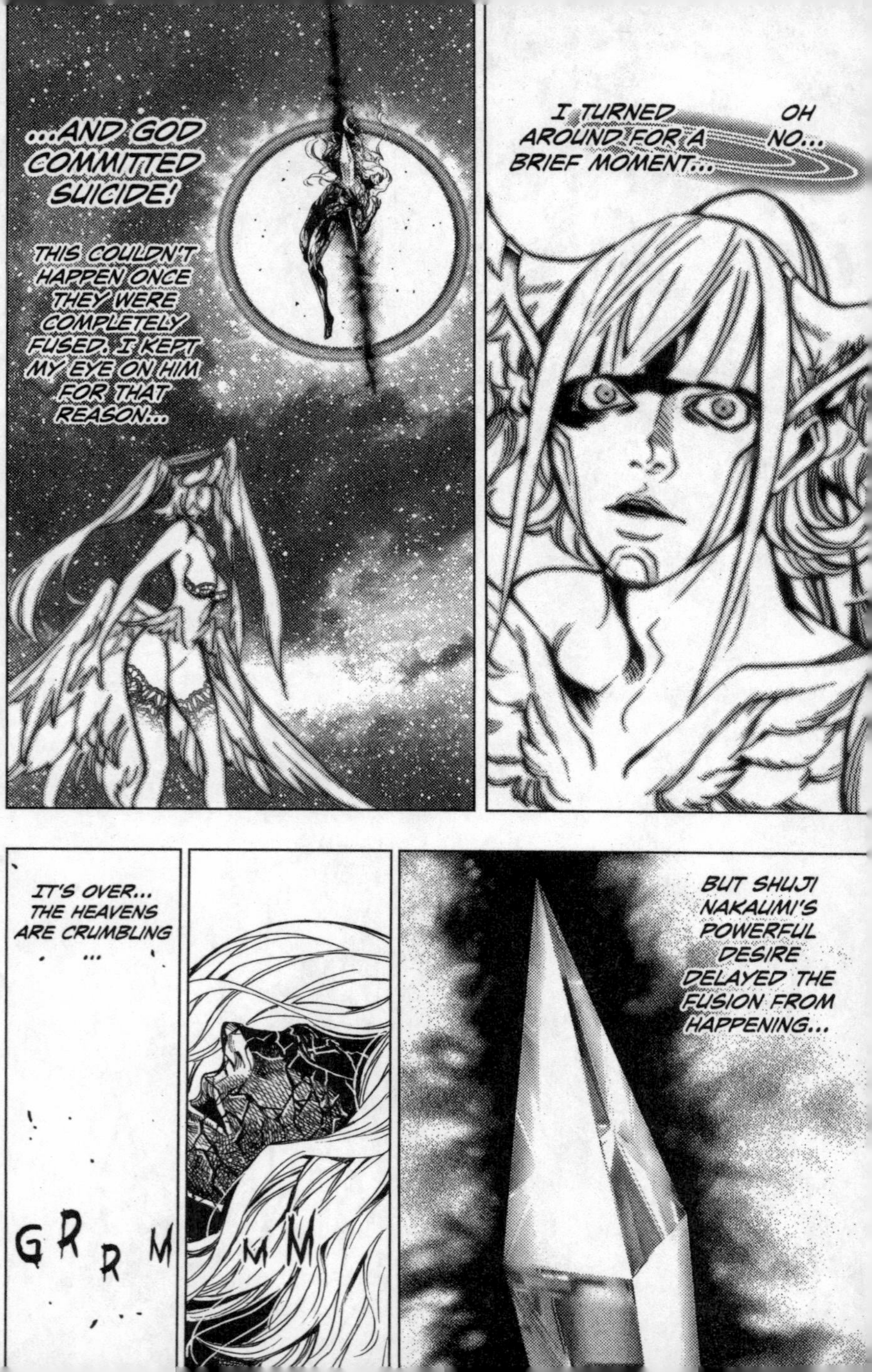
OH NO...
I TURNED AROUND FOR A BRIEF MOMENT...
...AND GOD COMMITTED SUICIDE!
THIS COULDN'T HAPPEN ONCE THEY WERE COMPLETELY FUSED. I KEPT MY EYE ON HIM FOR THAT REASON...
BUT SHUJI NAKAUMI'S POWERFUL DESIRE DELAYED THE FUSION FROM HAPPENING...
IT'S OVER... THE HEAVENS ARE CRUMBLING...
GRRMMMM

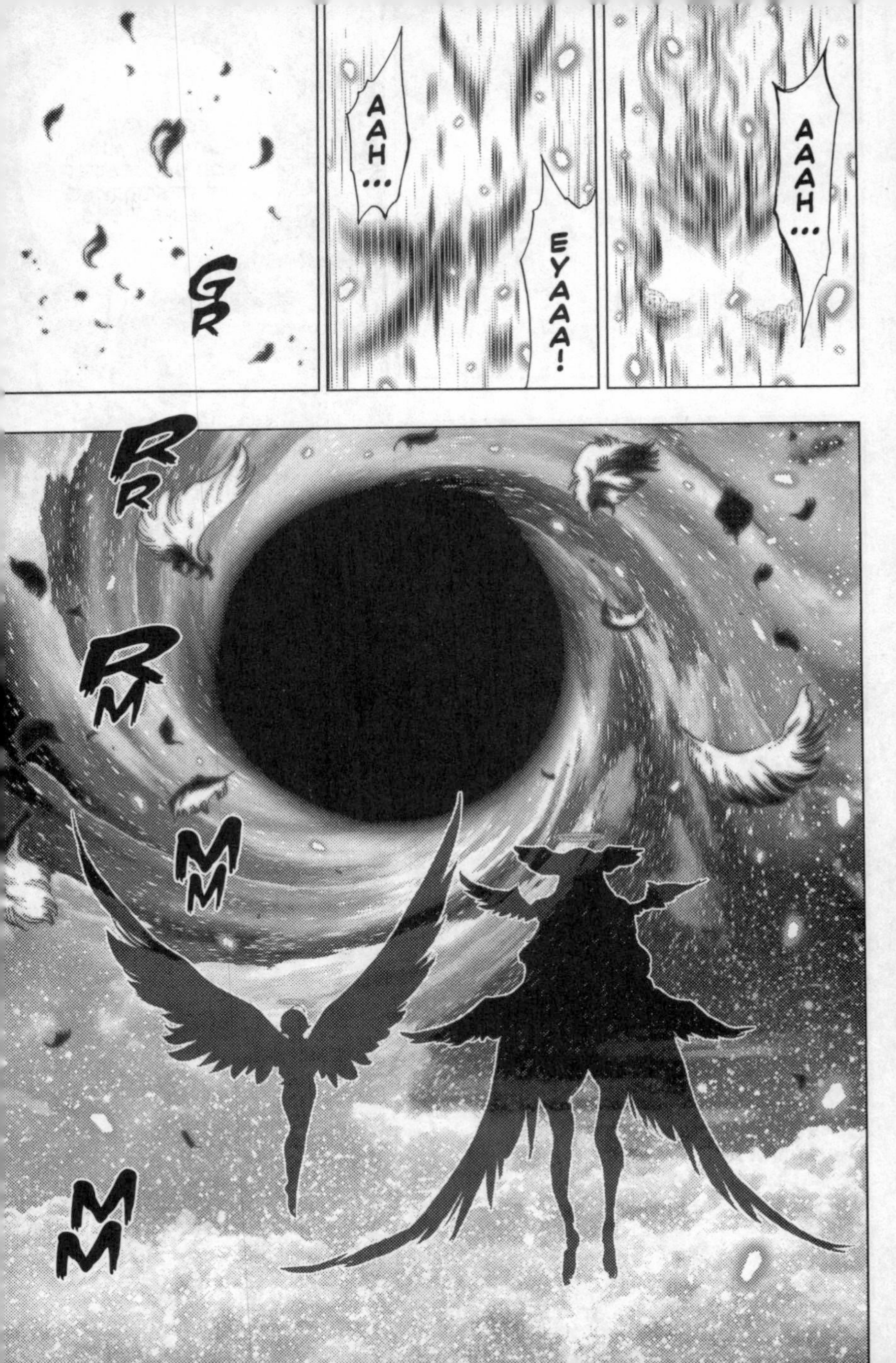
AAAAH...
EYAAAA!
AAH...
GR
RR
RM
MM
MM

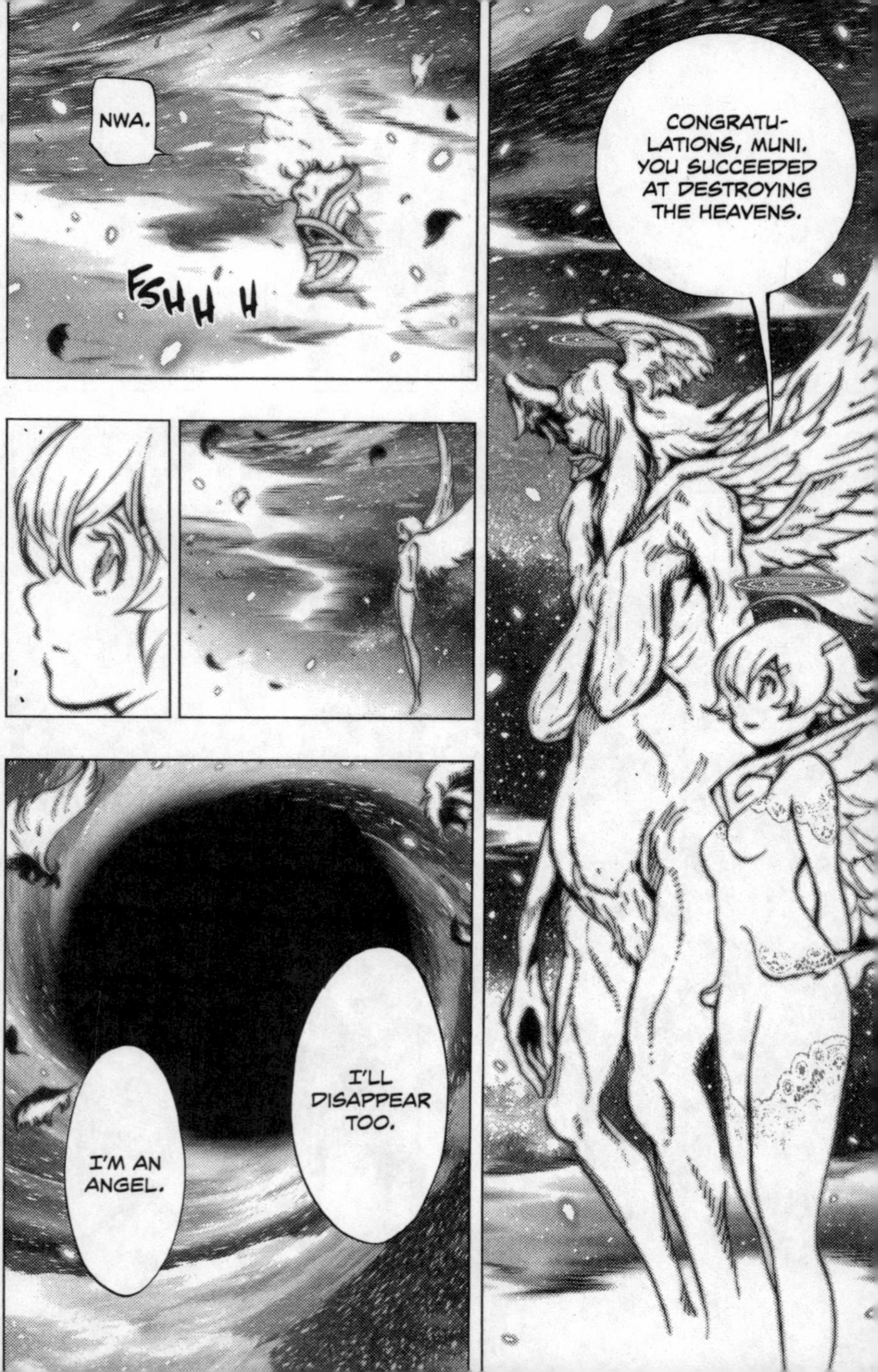
CONGRATULATIONS, MUNI. YOU SUCCEEDED AT DESTROYING THE HEAVENS.
NWA.
FSHHH
I'LL DISAPPEAR TOO.
I'M AN ANGEL.

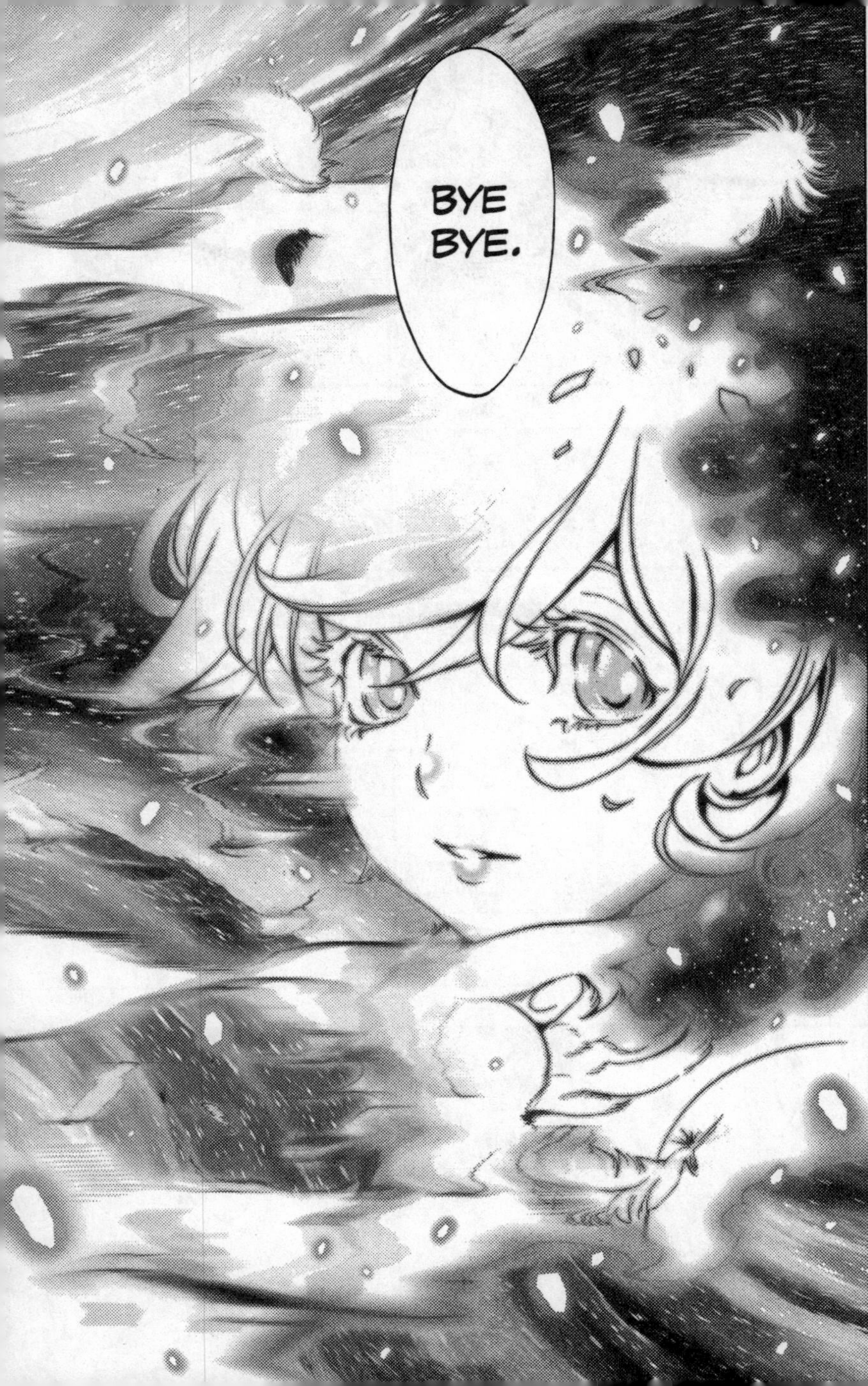
BYE BYE.

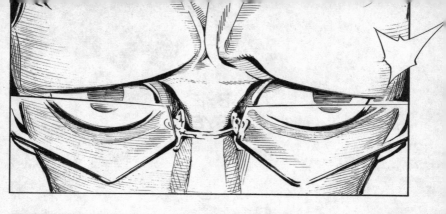

THE RED ARROW IS GONE...

PROFESSOR ...

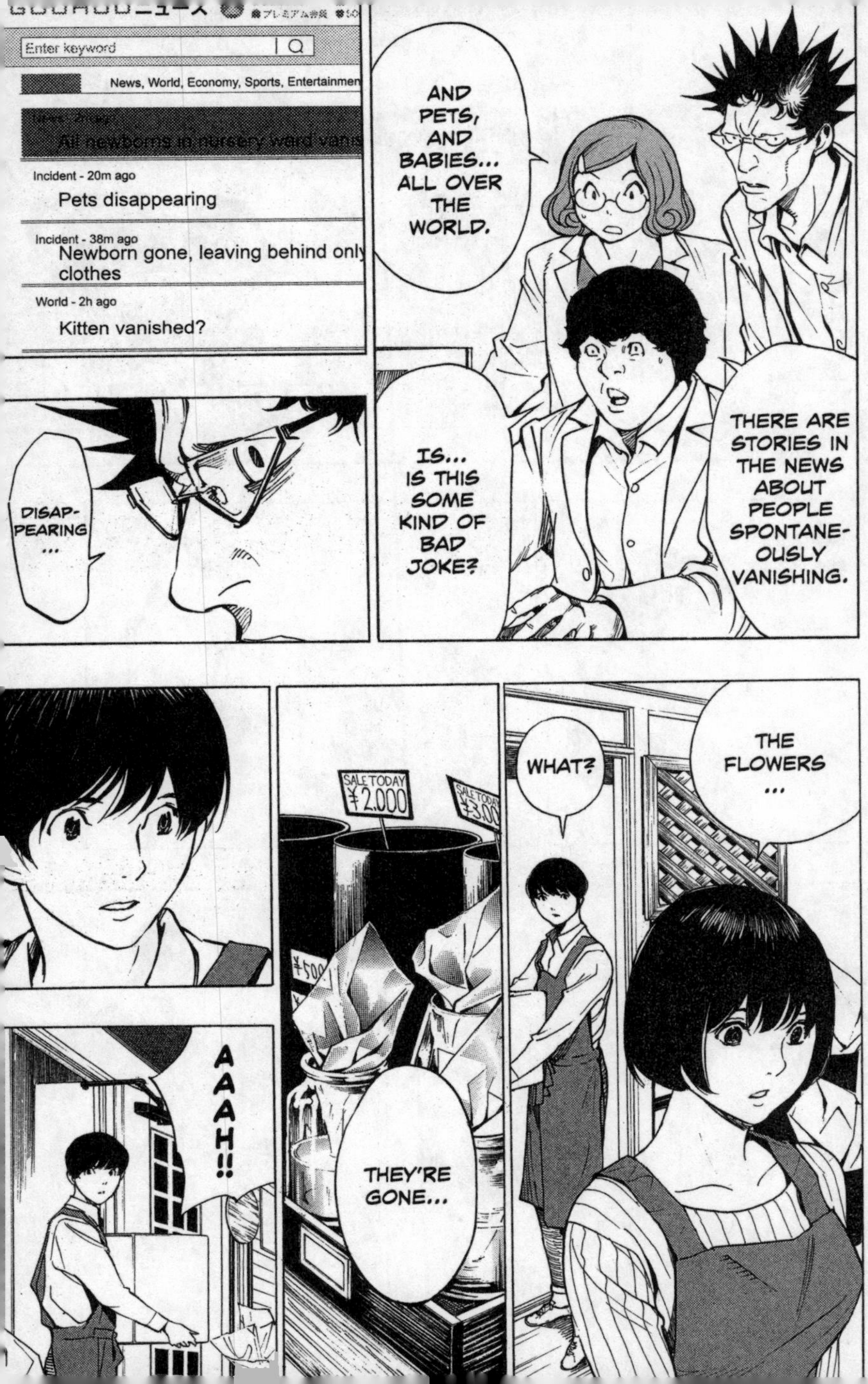
AND PETS, AND BABIES... ALL OVER THE WORLD.
THERE ARE STORIES IN THE NEWS ABOUT PEOPLE SPONTANE-OUSLY VANISHING.
IS... IS THIS SOME KIND OF BAD JOKE?
Enter keyword
News, World, Economy, Sports, Entertainmen
All newborns in nursery ward vanis
Incident - 20m ago
Pets disappearing
Incident - 38m ago
Newborn gone, leaving behind only clothes
World - 2h ago
Kitten vanished?
DISAP-PEARING...
THE FLOWERS...
WHAT?
SALE TODAY ¥2,000
SALE TODAY ¥3,00
¥500
THEY'RE GONE...
AAAAH!!

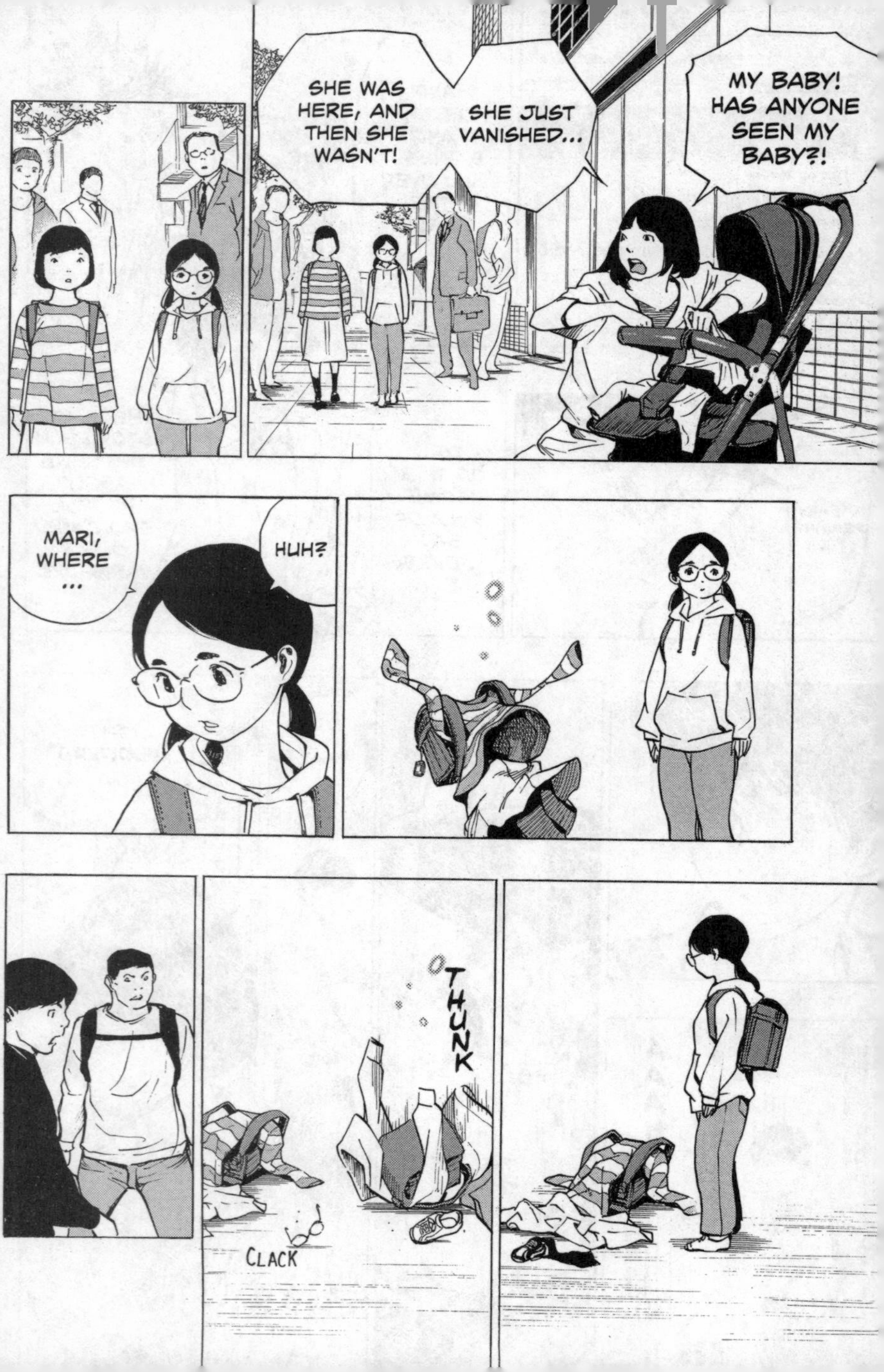
MY BABY! HAS ANYONE SEEN MY BABY?!
SHE JUST VANISHED...
SHE WAS HERE, AND THEN SHE WASN'T!
HUH?
MARI, WHERE ...
THUNK
CLACK

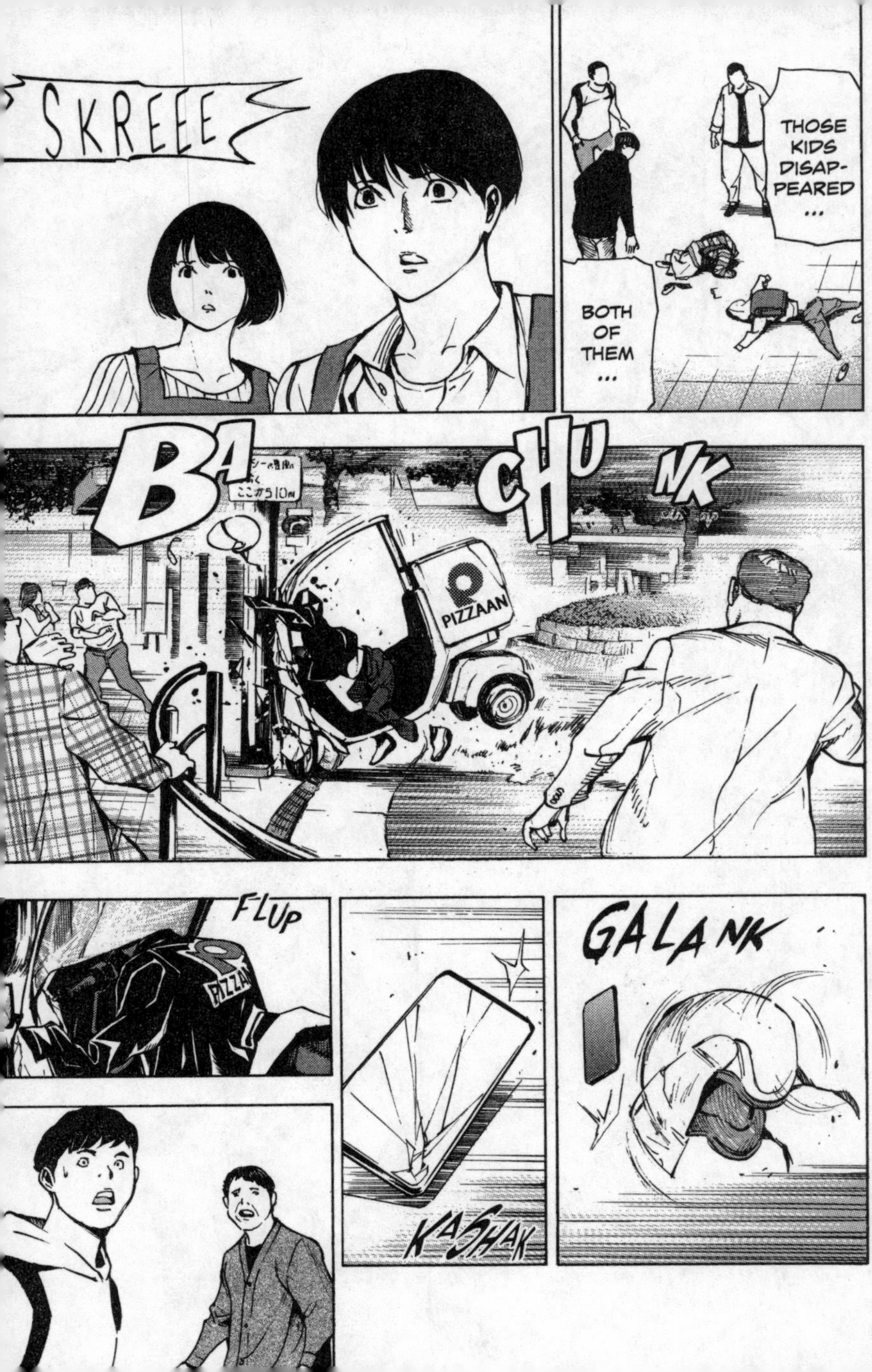
THOSE KIDS DISAPPEARED ...
BOTH OF THEM ...
SKREEE
BA CHU NK
PIZZAAN
GALANK
KASHAK
FLUP
PIZZAAN

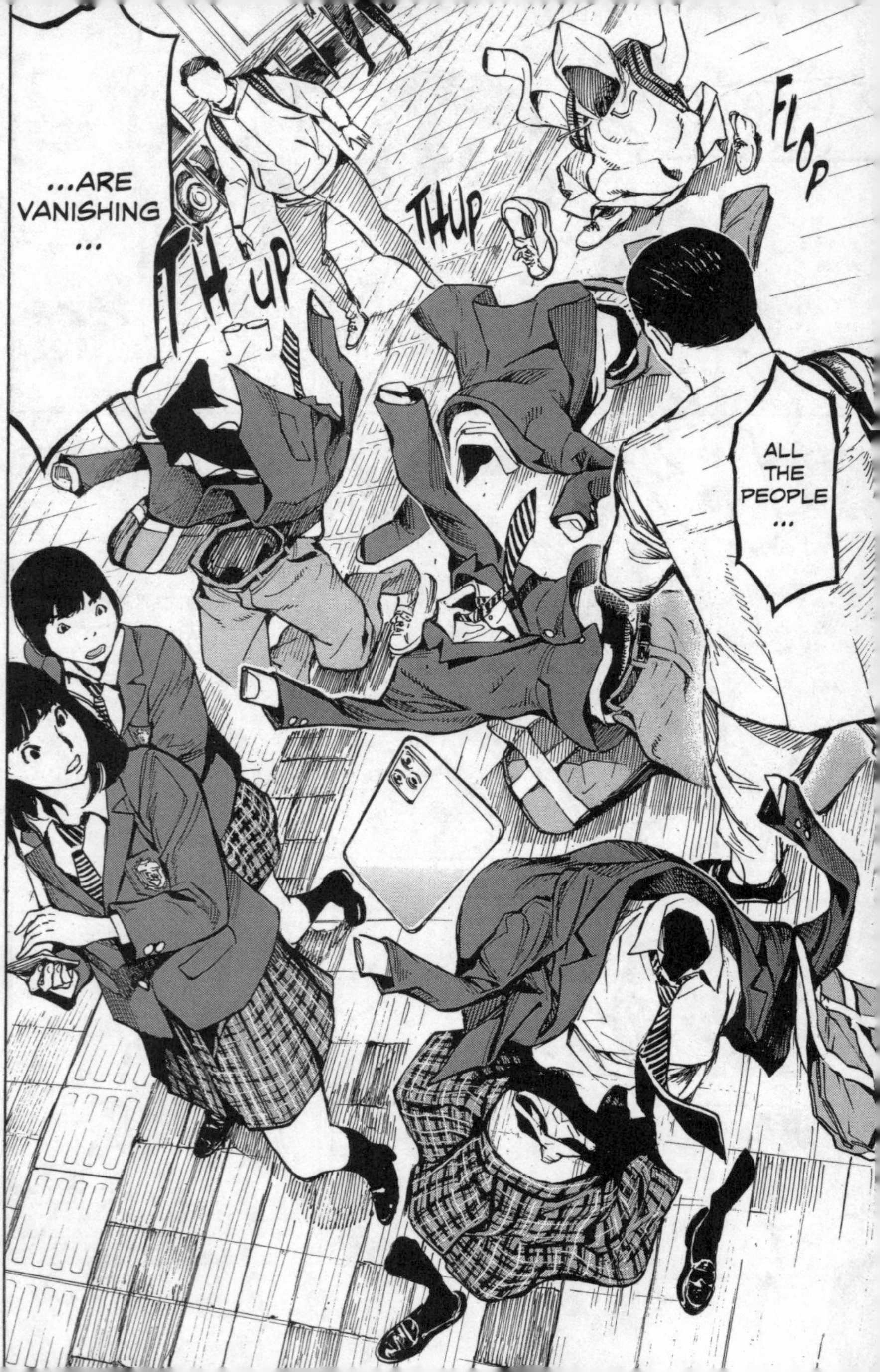
ALL THE PEOPLE ...
FLOP
THUP
THUP
...ARE VANISHING ...

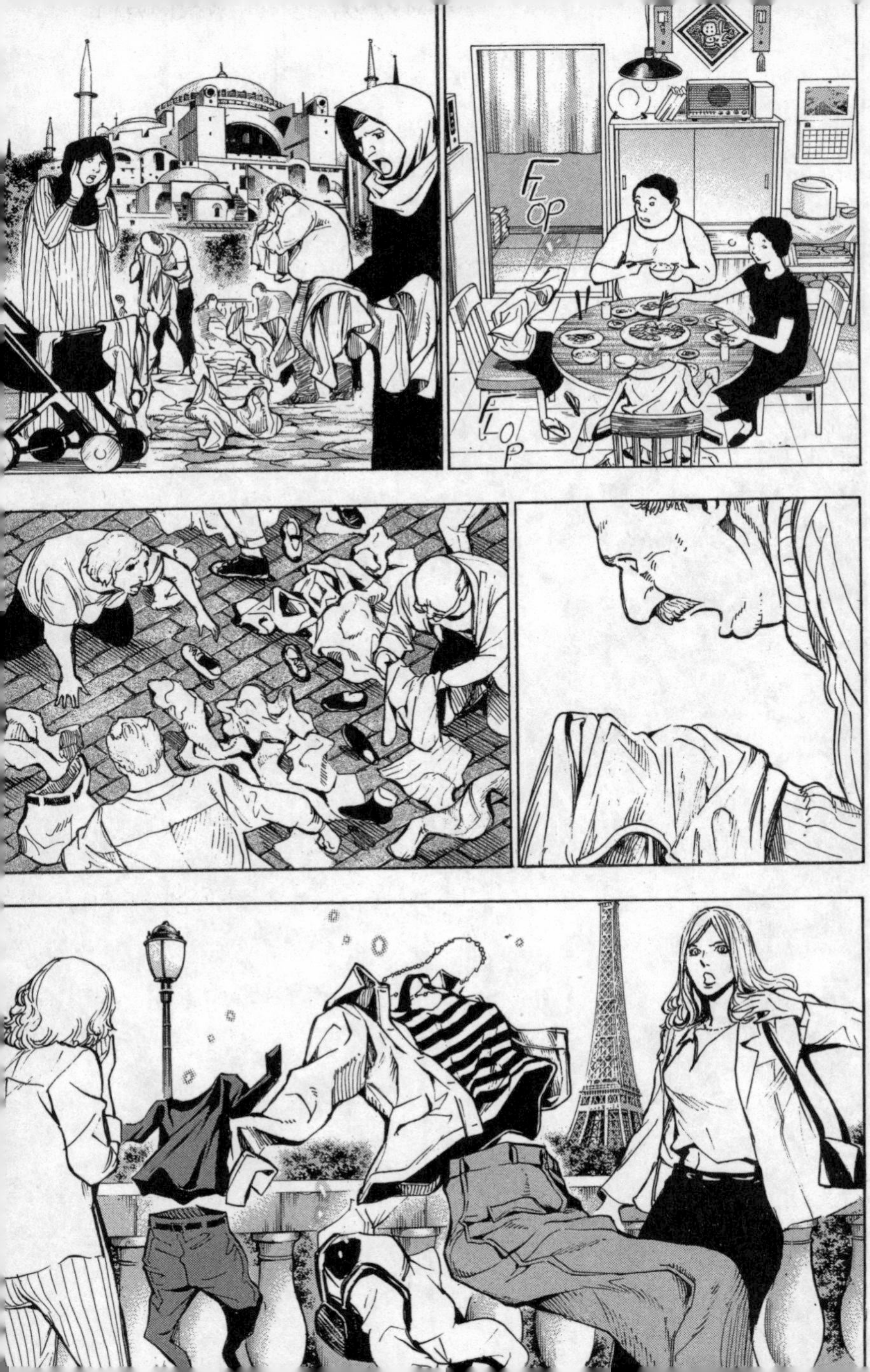
FLOP
FLOP

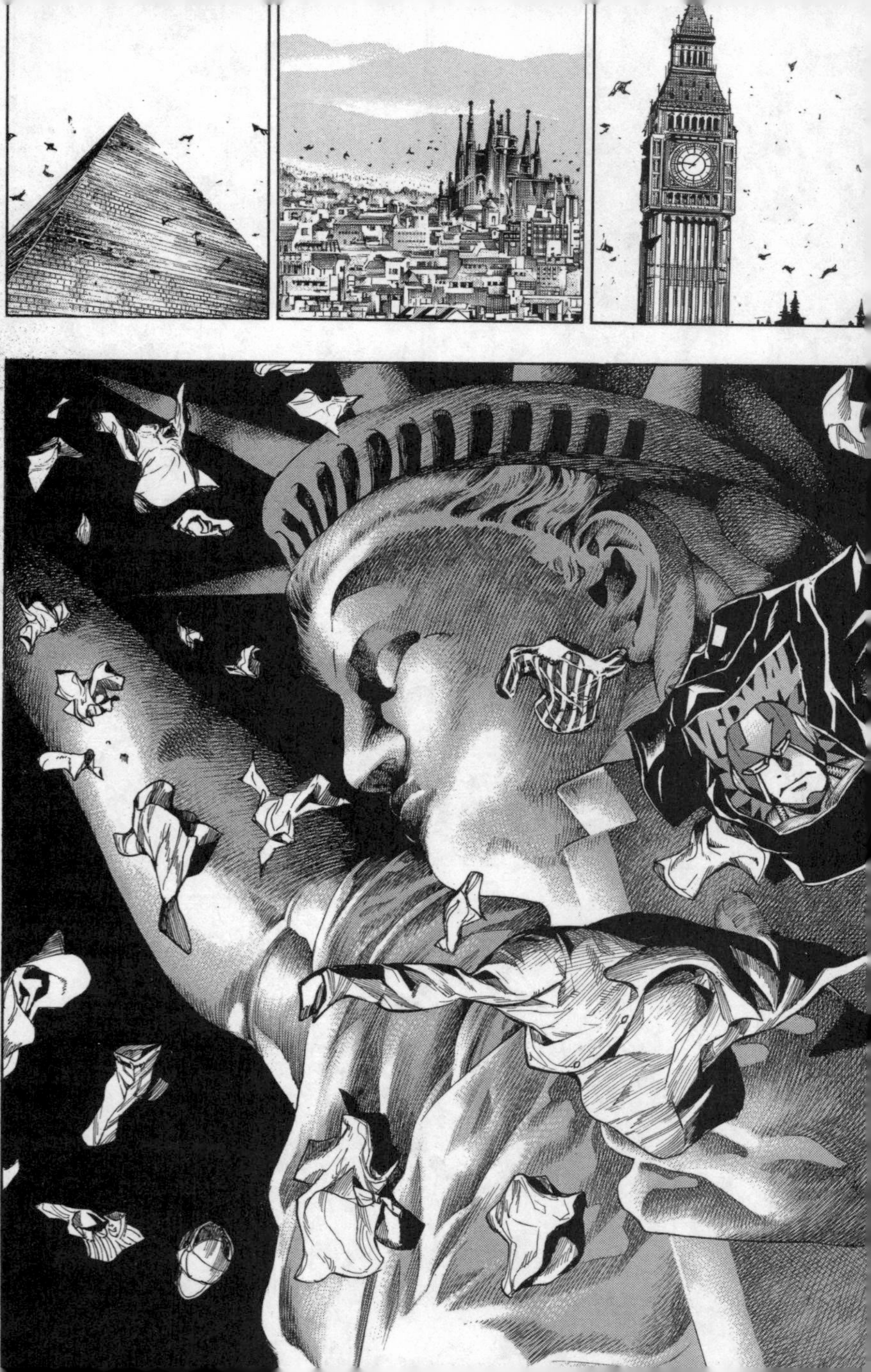

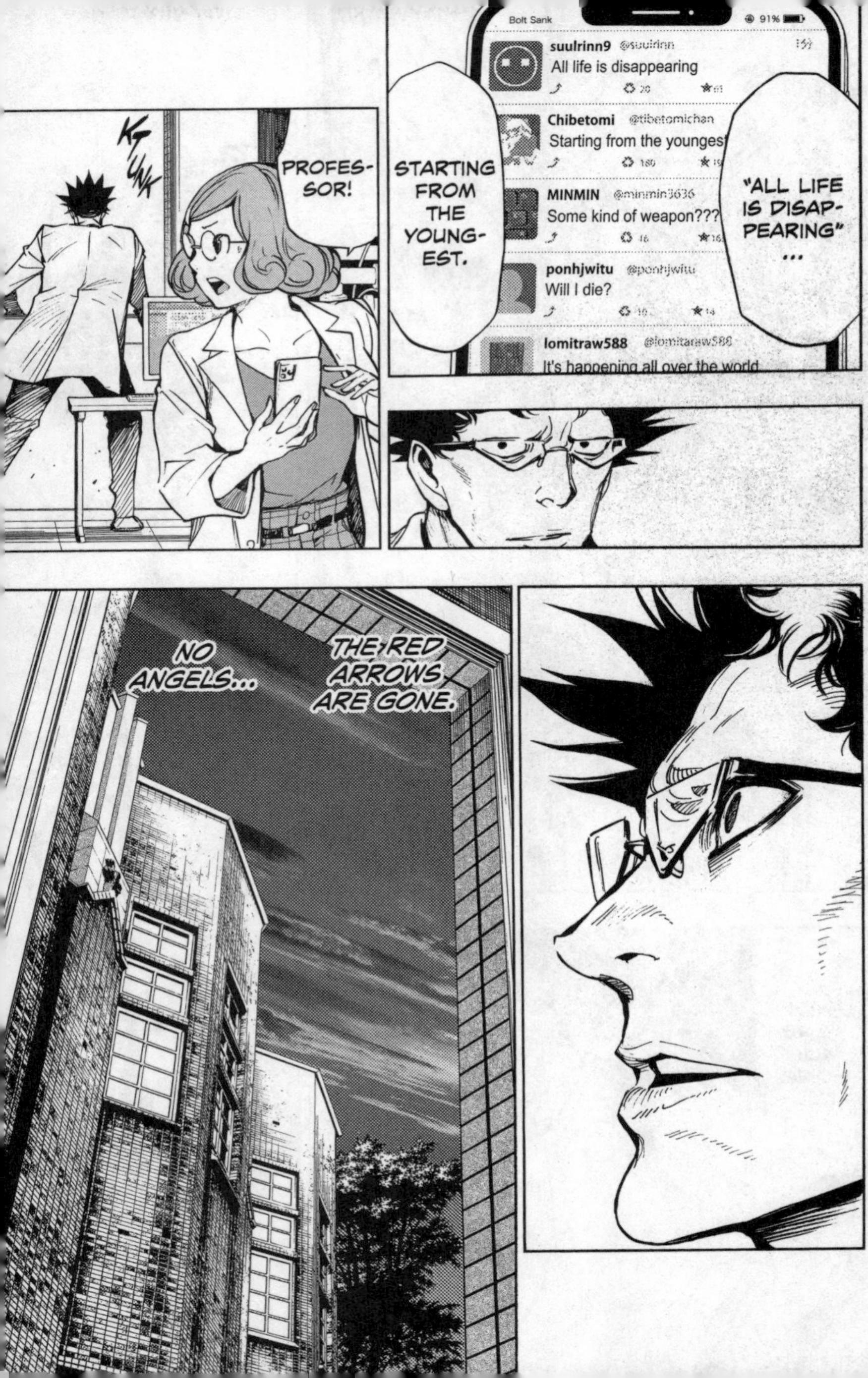

Bolt Sank
91%
suulrinn9 @suulrinn
All life is disappearing
Chibetomi @tibetomichan
Starting from the youngest
MINMIN @minmin3636
Some kind of weapon???
ponhjwitu @ponhjwitu
Will I die?
lomitraw588 @lomitraw588
It's happening all over the world
"ALL LIFE IS DISAPPEARING"...
STARTING FROM THE YOUNGEST.
KATUNK
PROFESSOR!
THE RED ARROWS ARE GONE.
NO ANGELS...

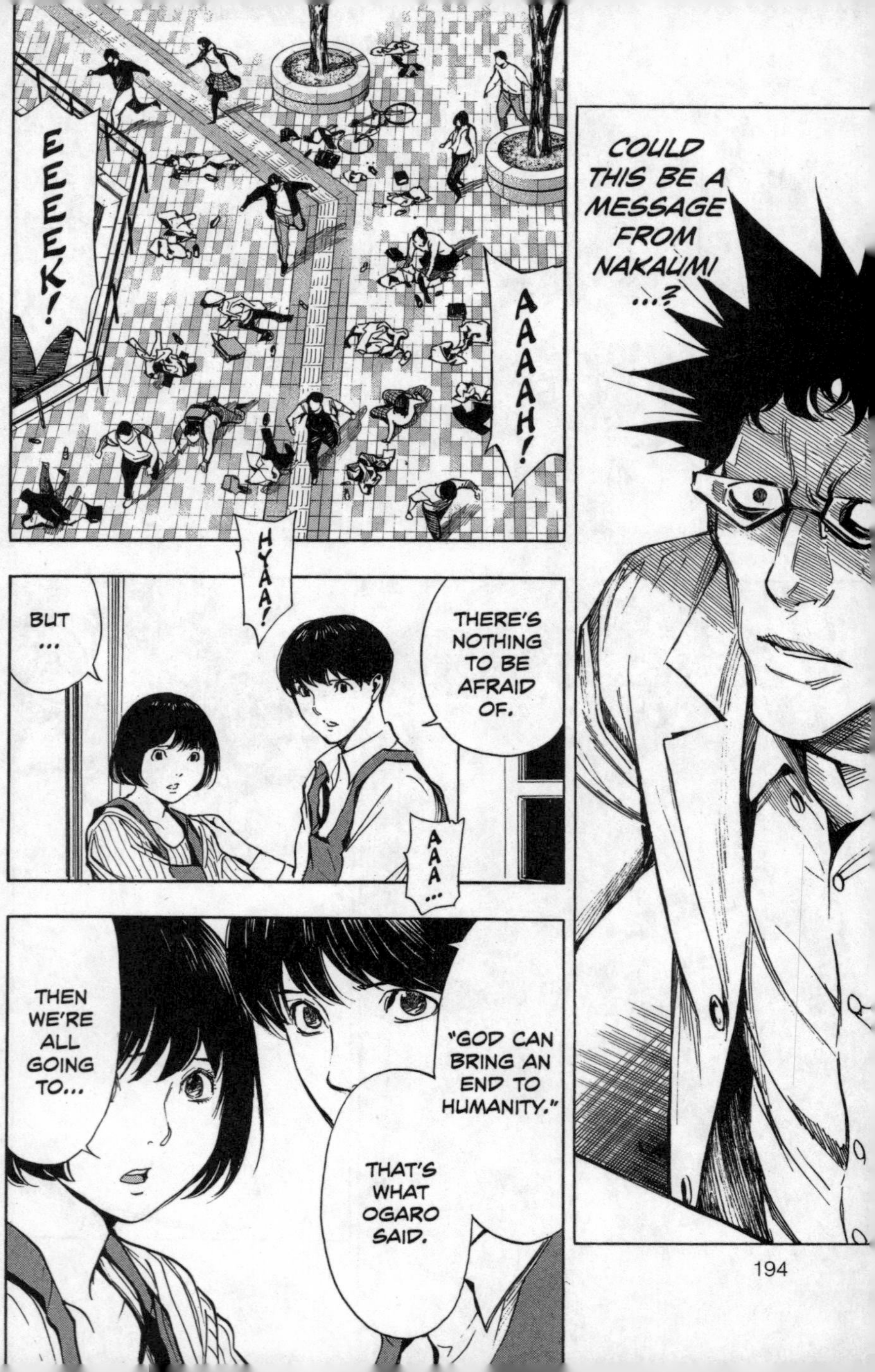
COULD THIS BE A MESSAGE FROM NAKAUMI ...?
AAAAAH!
EEEEEK!
HYAAA!
THERE'S NOTHING TO BE AFRAID OF.
AAA...
BUT ...
"GOD CAN BRING AN END TO HUMANITY."
THAT'S WHAT OGARO SAID.
THEN WE'RE ALL GOING TO...

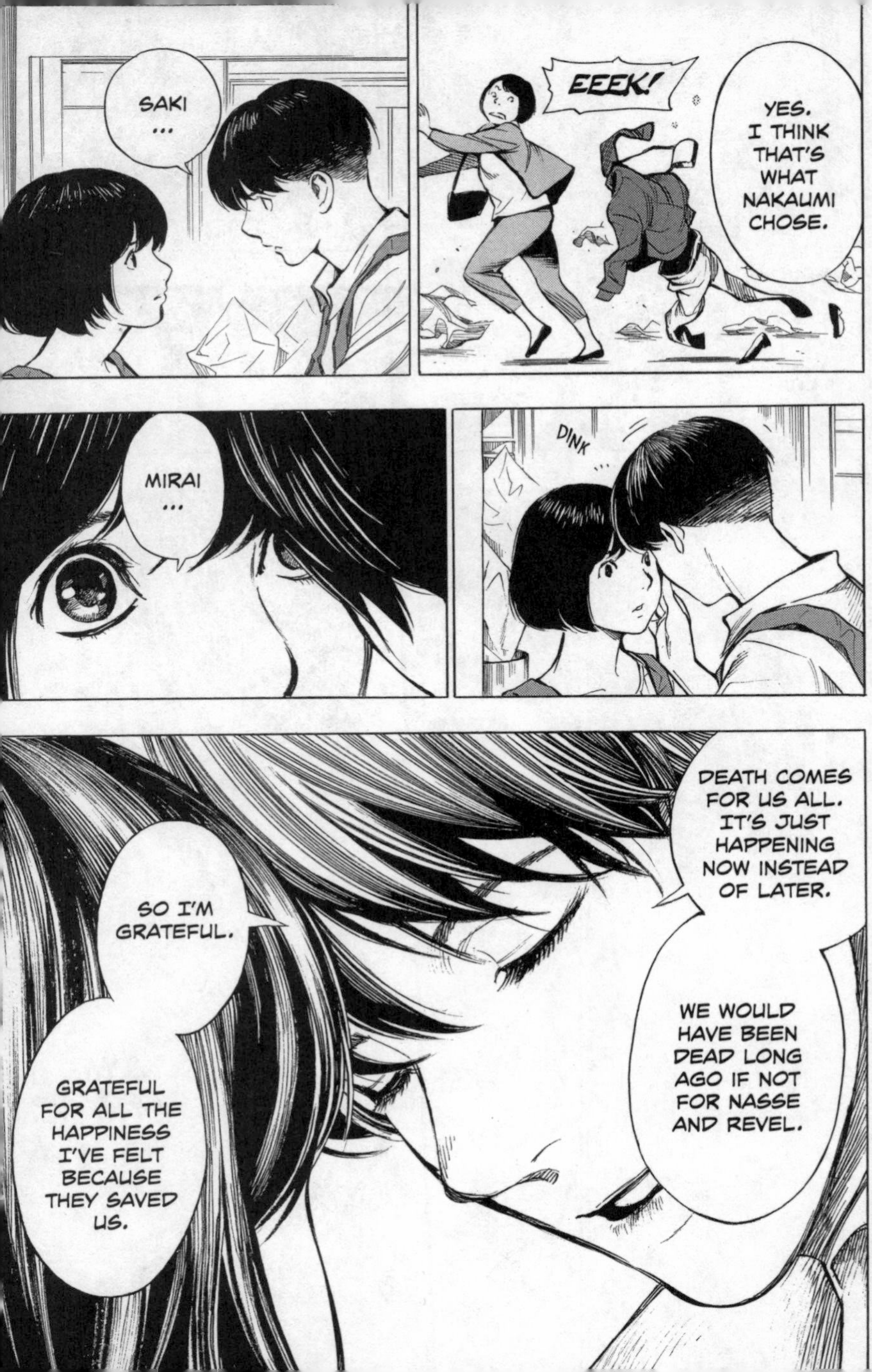
YES. I THINK THAT'S WHAT NAKAUMI CHOSE.
EEEK!
SAKI ...
DINK
...
MIRAI ...
DEATH COMES FOR US ALL. IT'S JUST HAPPENING NOW INSTEAD OF LATER.
WE WOULD HAVE BEEN DEAD LONG AGO IF NOT FOR NASSE AND REVEL.
SO I'M GRATEFUL.
GRATEFUL FOR ALL THE HAPPINESS I'VE FELT BECAUSE THEY SAVED US.

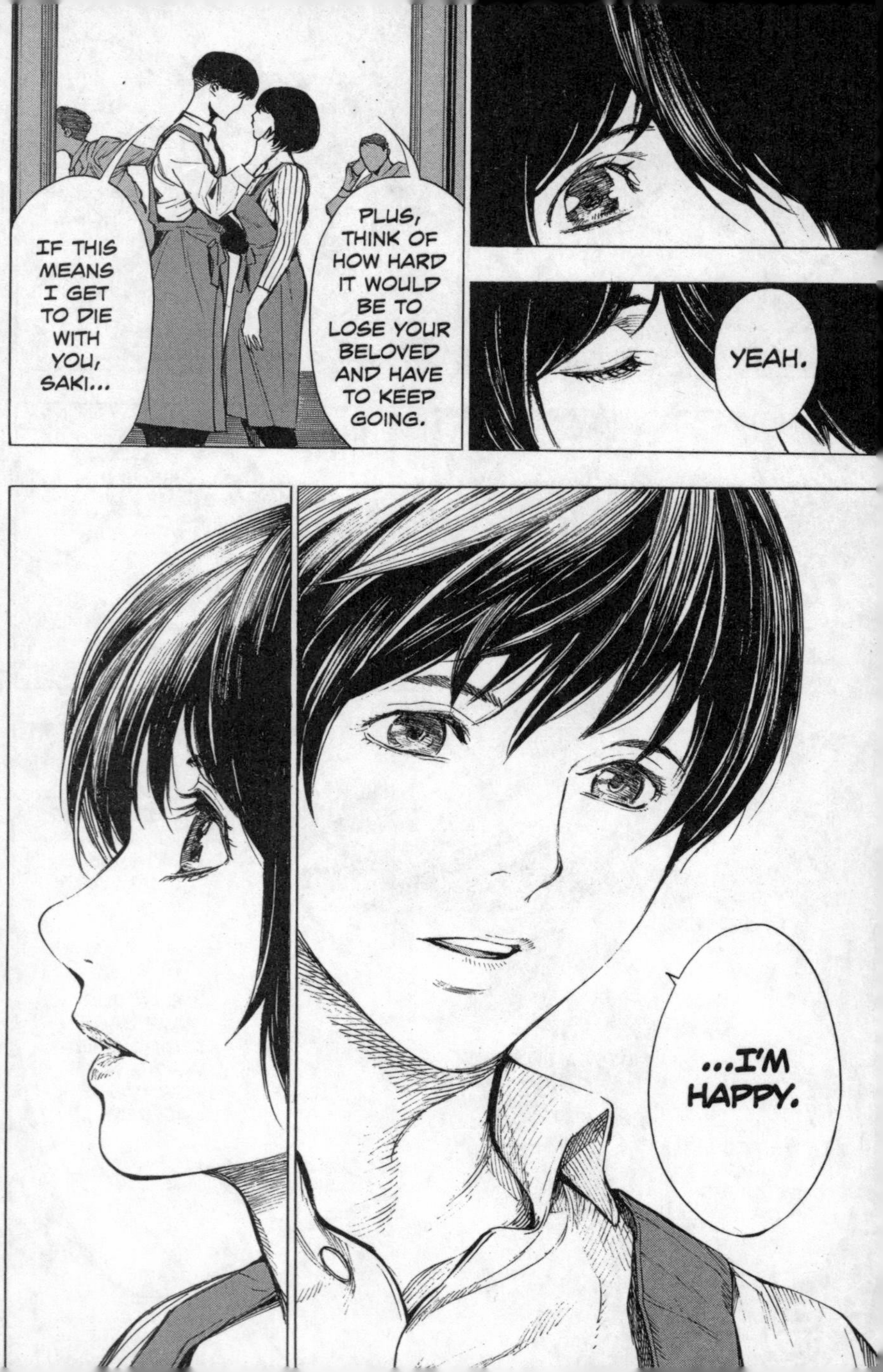
YEAH.
PLUS, THINK OF HOW HARD IT WOULD BE TO LOSE YOUR BELOVED AND HAVE TO KEEP GOING.
IF THIS MEANS I GET TO DIE WITH YOU, SAKI...
...I'M HAPPY.

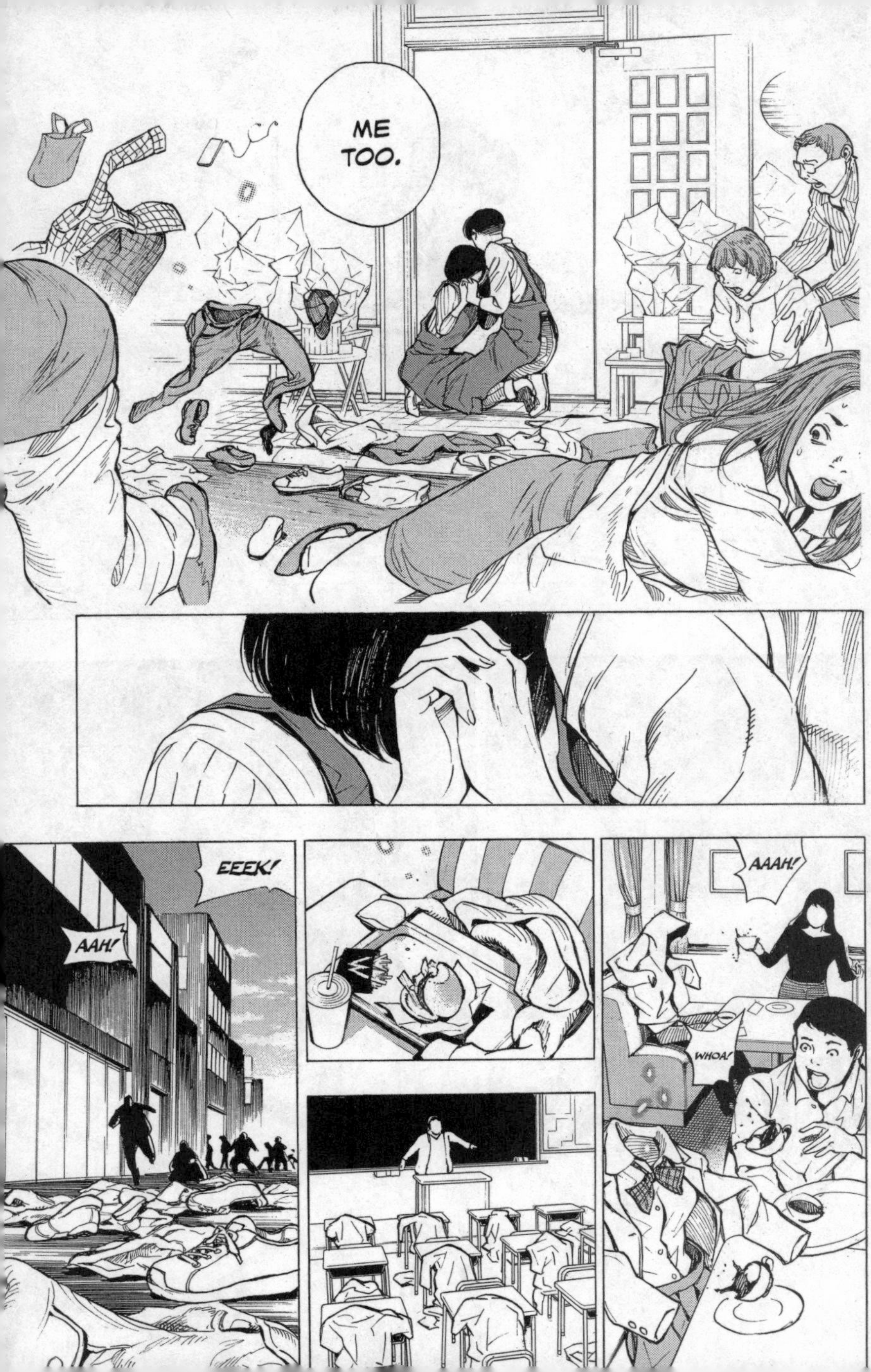
ME TOO.
AAAH!
WHOA!
EEEK!
AAH!

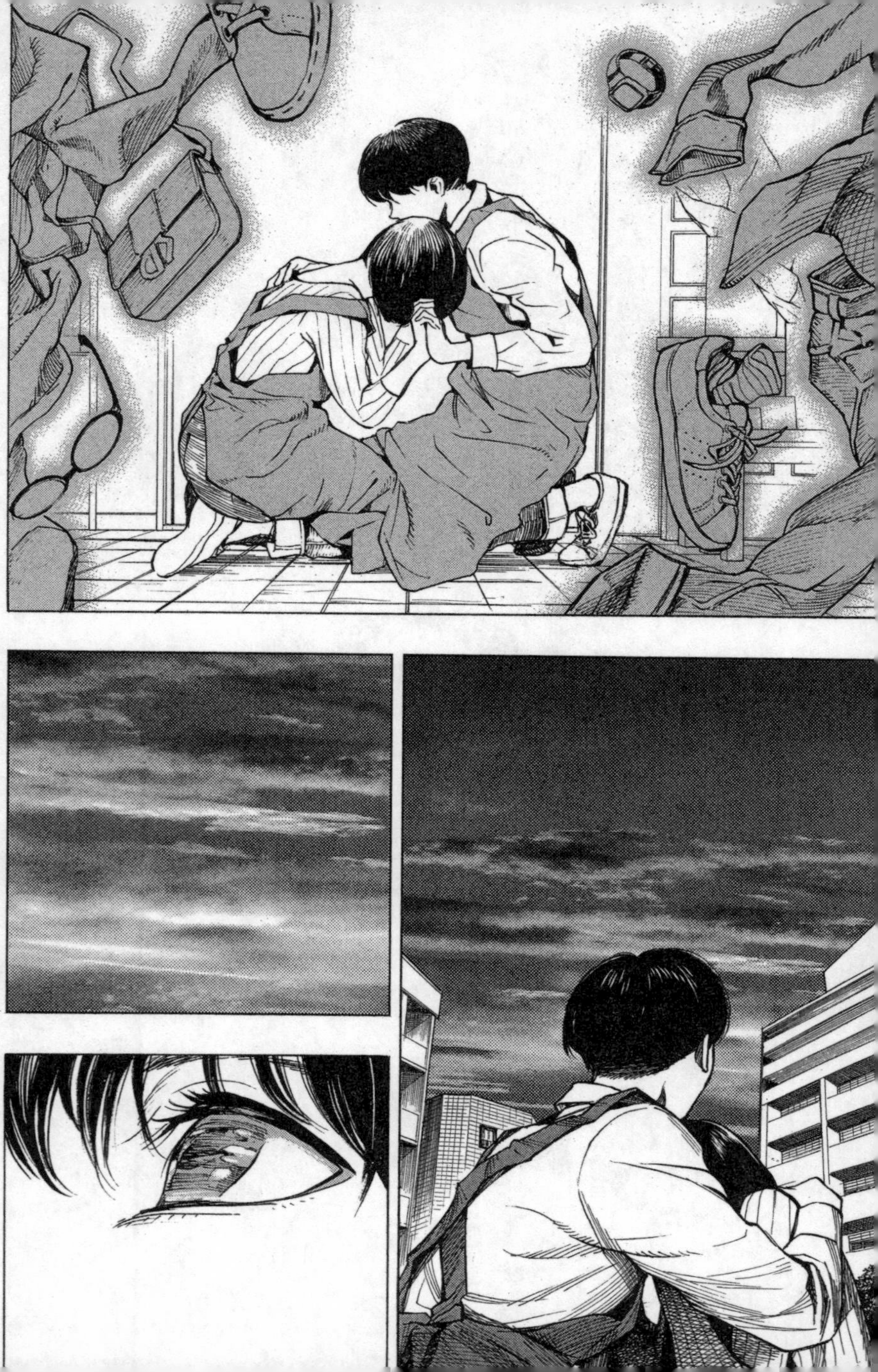

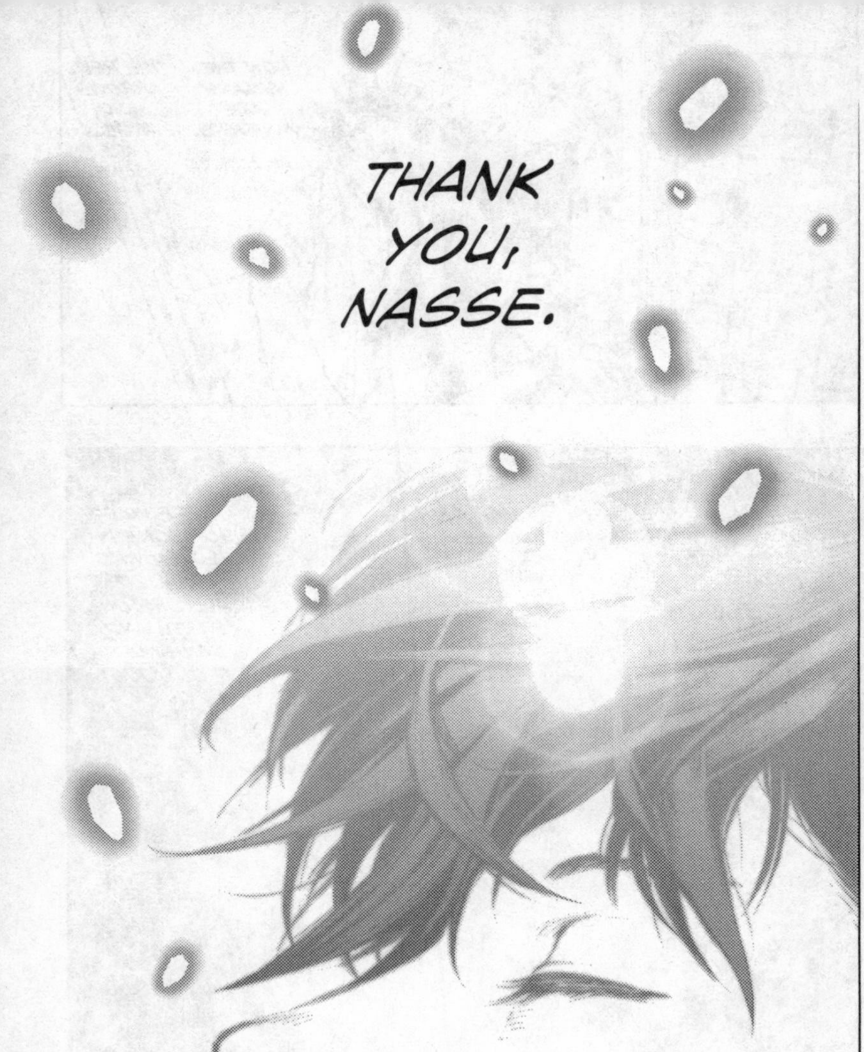
THANK YOU, NASSE.

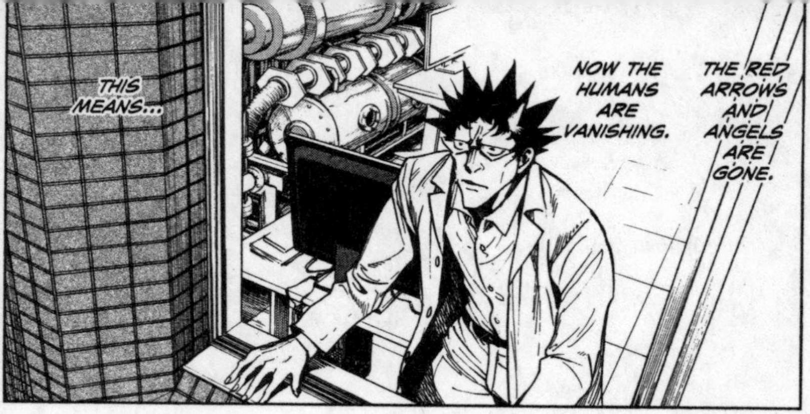
THE RED ARROWS AND ANGELS ARE GONE.
NOW THE HUMANS ARE VANISHING.
THIS MEANS...

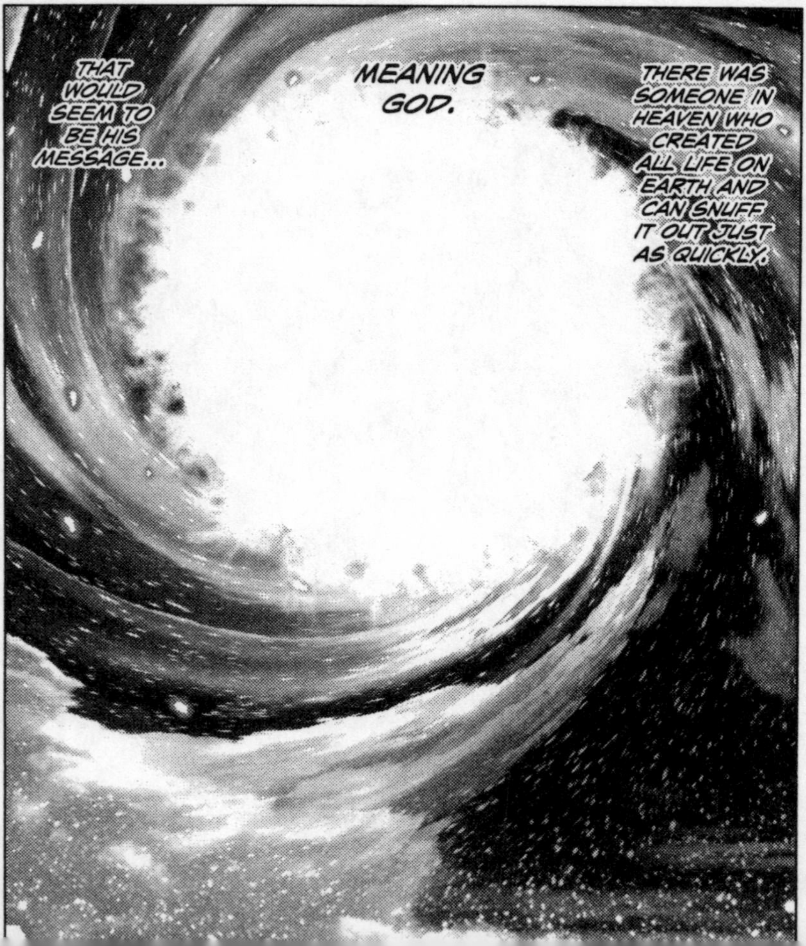
THERE WAS SOMEONE IN HEAVEN WHO CREATED ALL LIFE ON EARTH AND CAN SNUFF IT OUT JUST AS QUICKLY.
MEANING GOD.
THAT WOULD SEEM TO BE HIS MESSAGE...

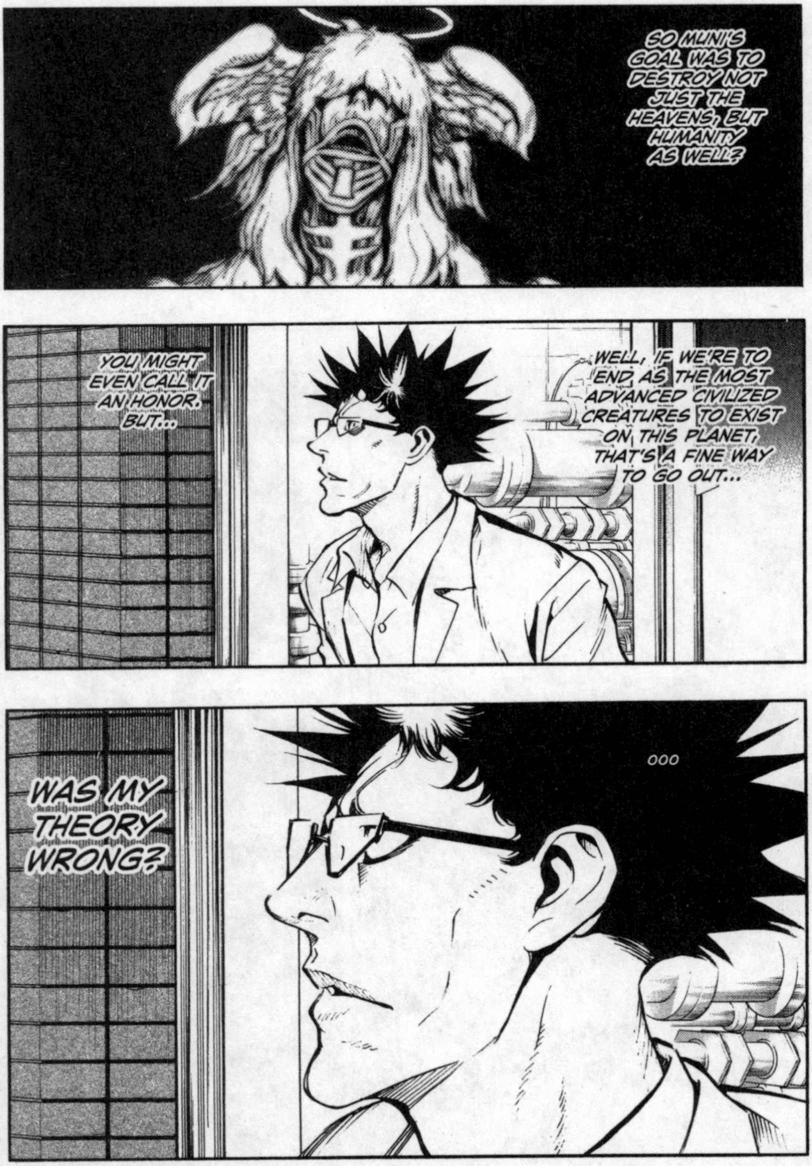
SO MUNI'S GOAL WAS TO DESTROY NOT JUST THE HEAVENS, BUT HUMANITY AS WELL?
WELL, IF WE'RE TO END AS THE MOST ADVANCED CIVILIZED CREATURES TO EXIST ON THIS PLANET, THAT'S A FINE WAY TO GO OUT...
YOU MIGHT EVEN CALL IT AN HONOR. BUT...
ooo
WAS MY THEORY WRONG?

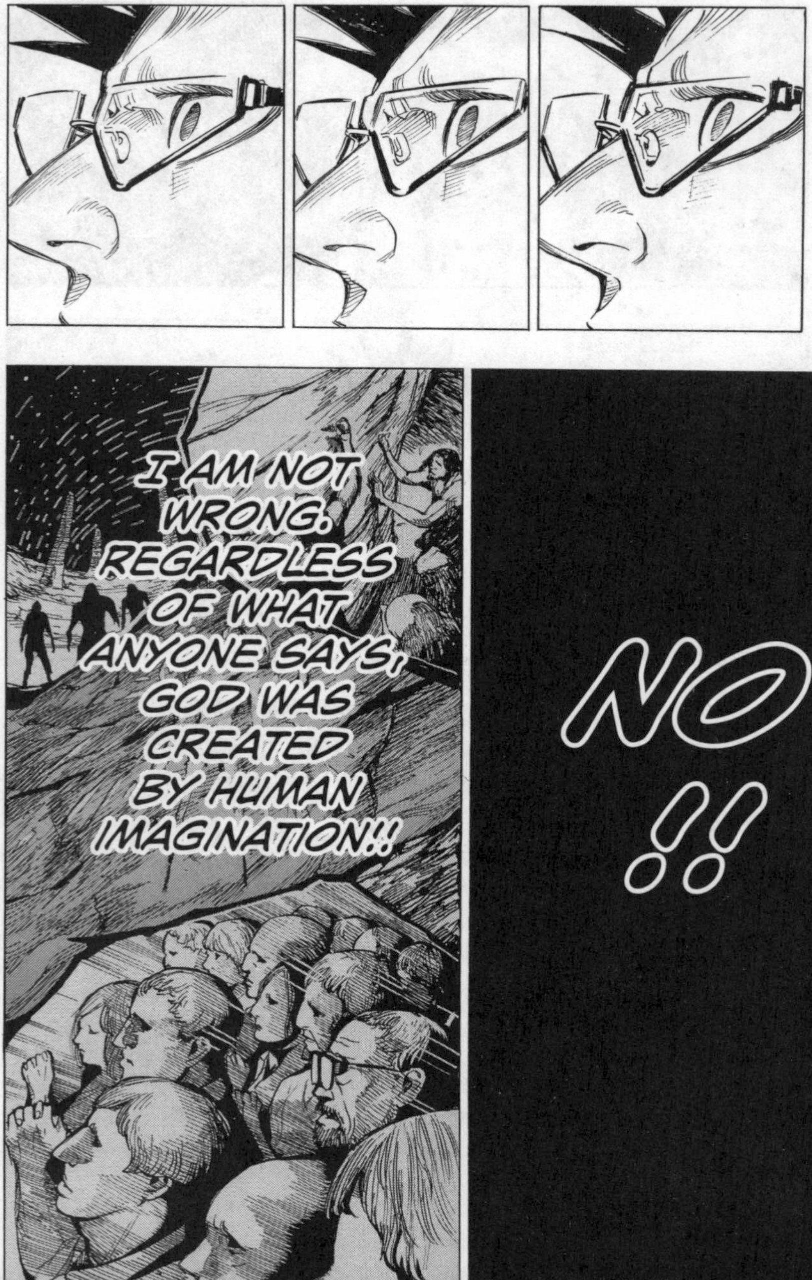
NO!!
I AM NOT WRONG. REGARDLESS OF WHAT ANYONE SAYS, GOD WAS CREATED BY HUMAN IMAGINATION!!

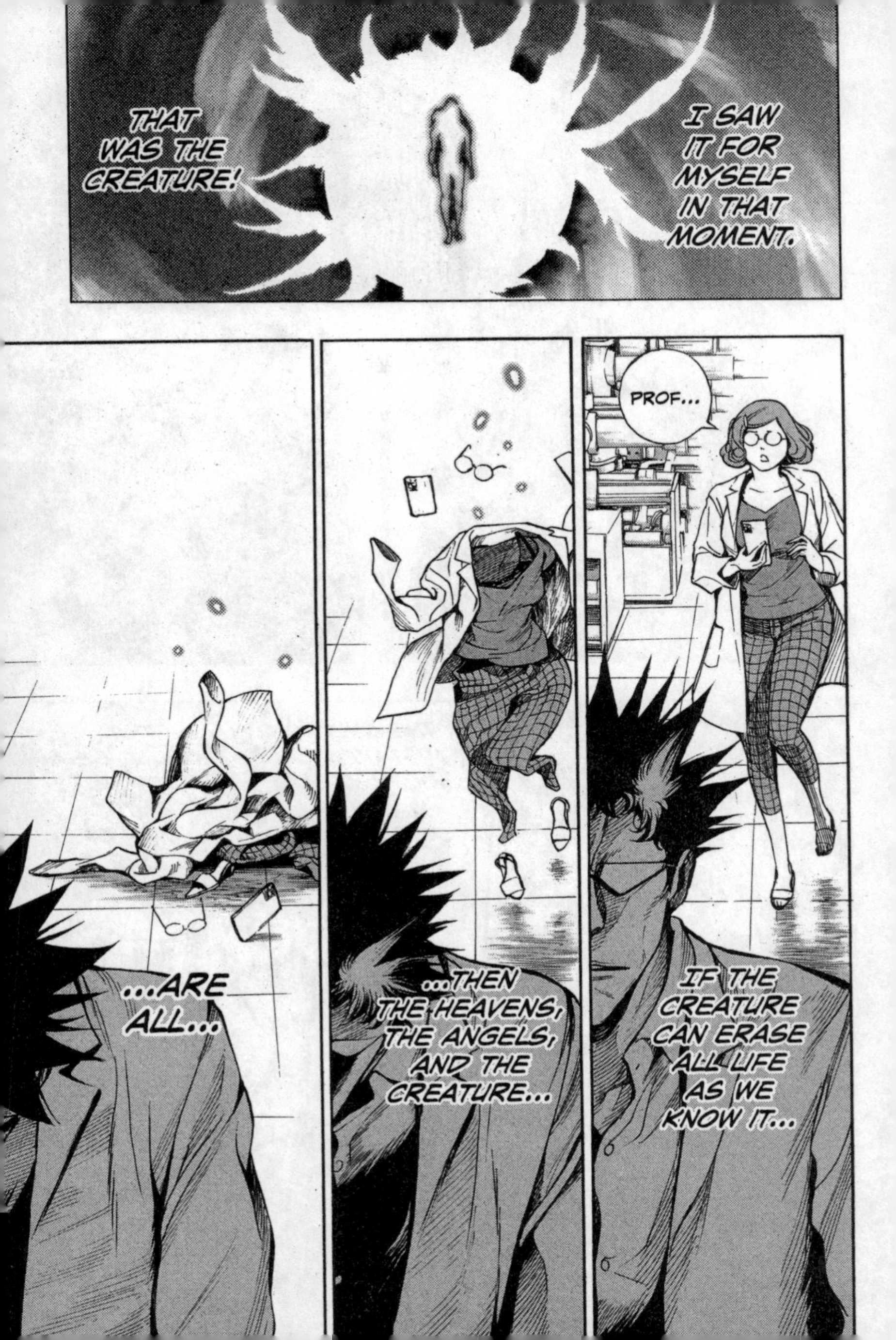
I SAW IT FOR MYSELF IN THAT MOMENT.
THAT WAS THE CREATURE!
PROF...
IF THE CREATURE CAN ERASE ALL LIFE AS WE KNOW IT...
...THEN THE HEAVENS, THE ANGELS, AND THE CREATURE...
...ARE ALL...

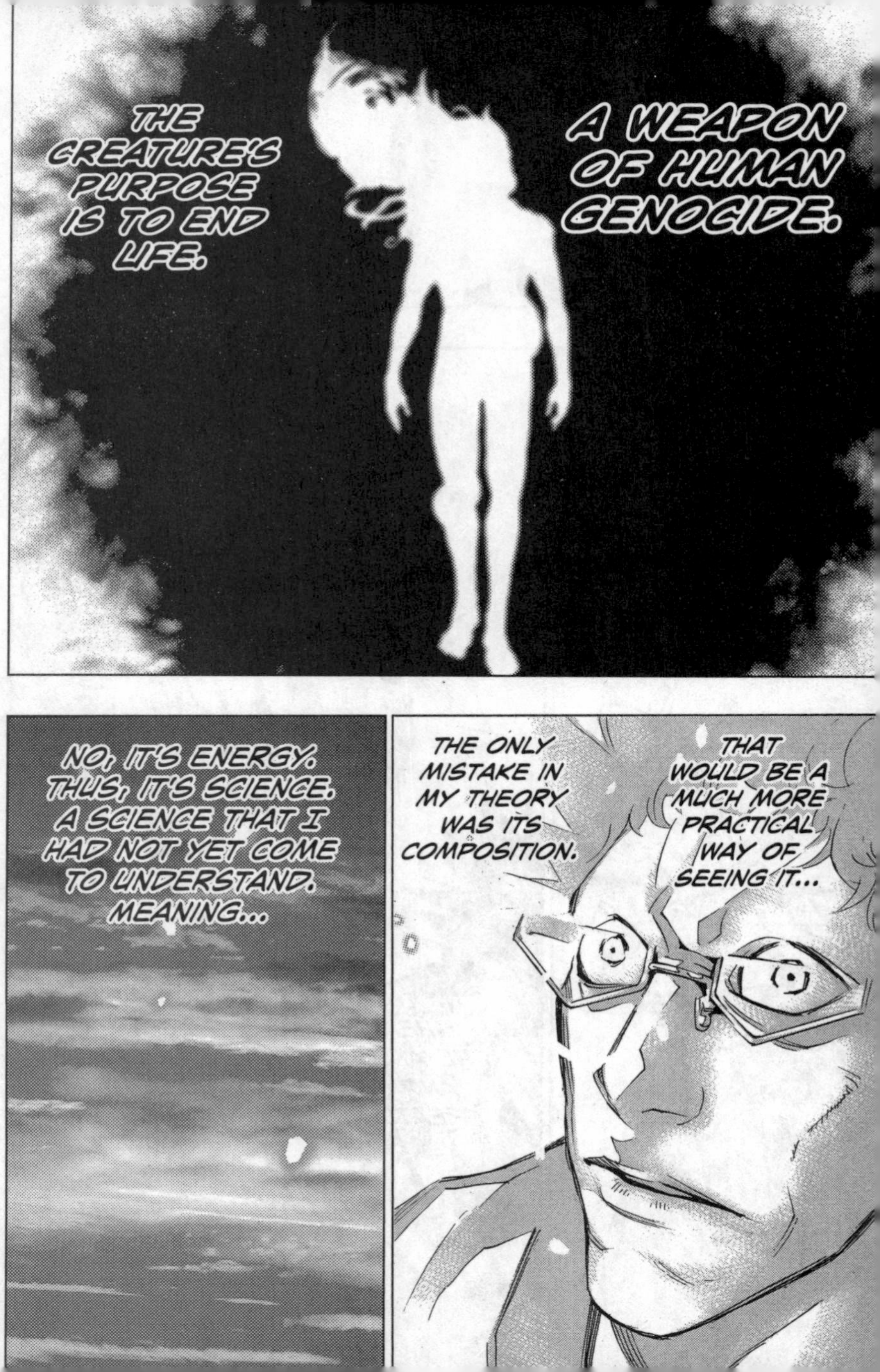
A WEAPON OF HUMAN GENOCIDE.
THE CREATURE'S PURPOSE IS TO END LIFE.
THAT WOULD BE A MUCH MORE PRACTICAL WAY OF SEEING IT...
THE ONLY MISTAKE IN MY THEORY WAS ITS COMPOSITION.
NO, IT'S ENERGY. THUS, IT'S SCIENCE. A SCIENCE THAT I HAD NOT YET COME TO UNDERSTAND. MEANING...

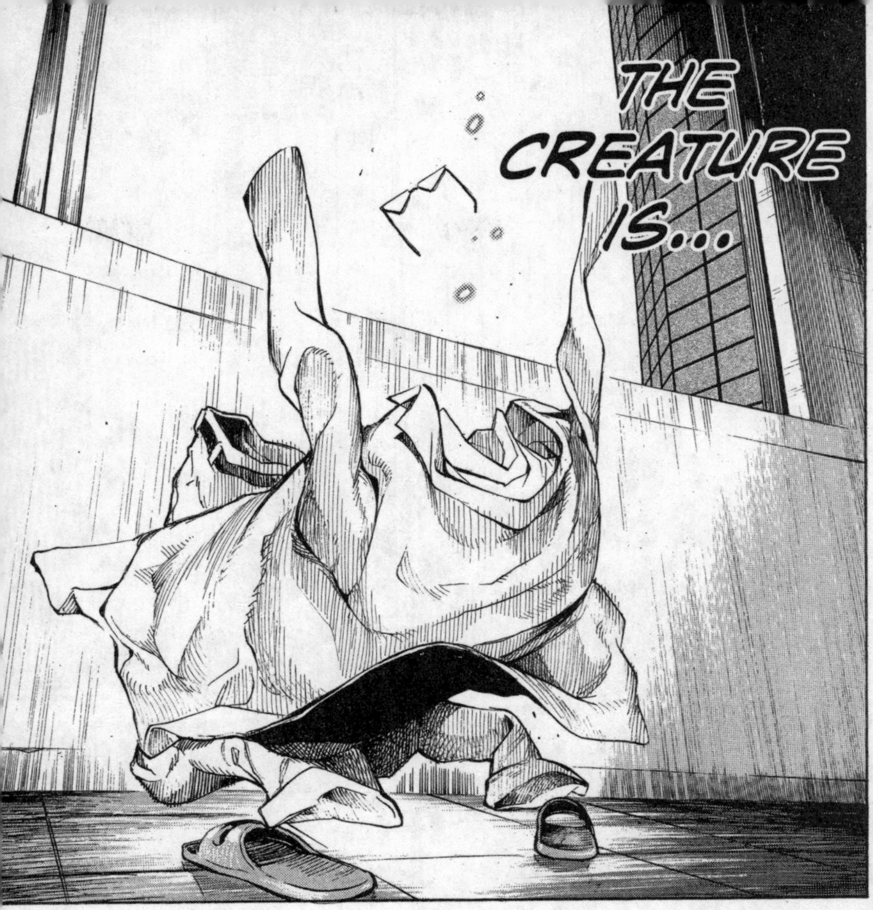
THE CREATURE IS...

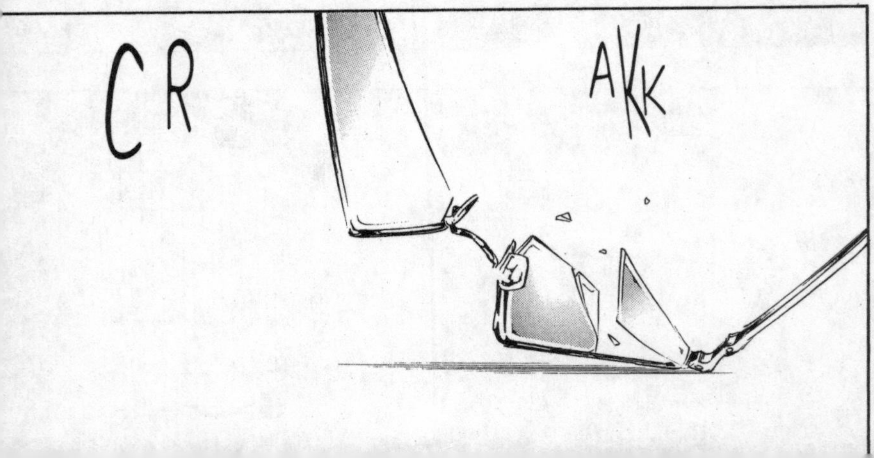
CRAKK

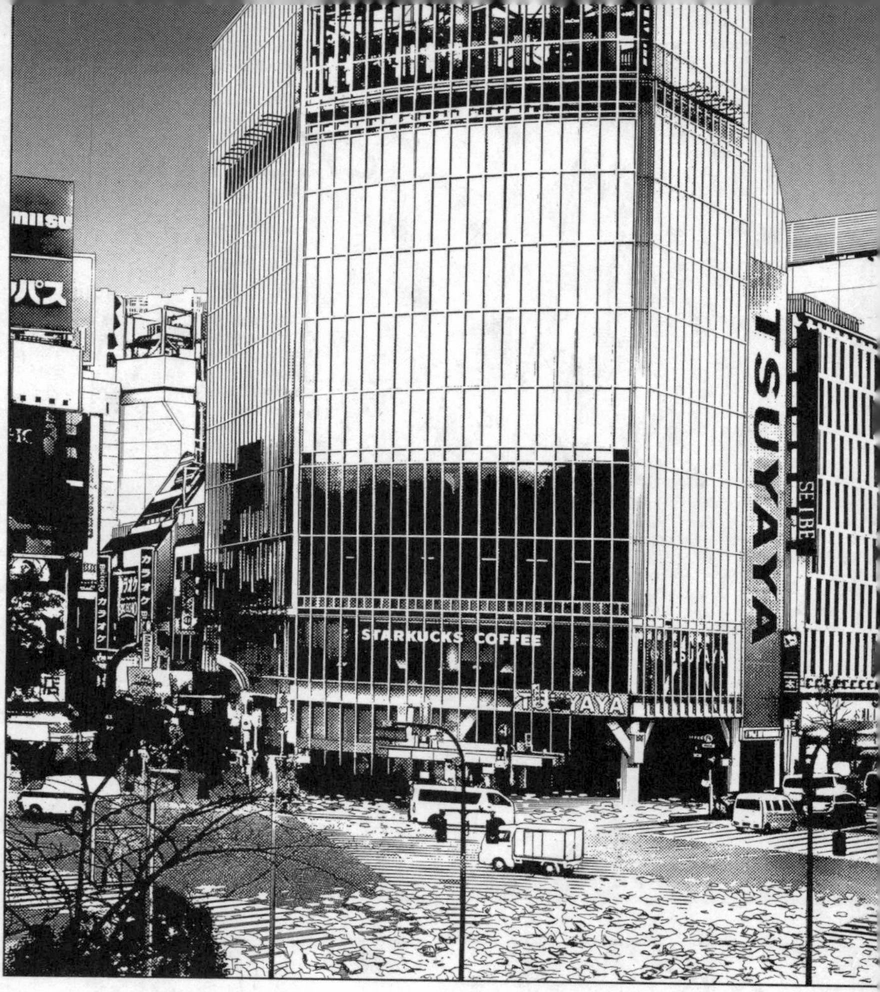
TSUYAYA
SEIBE
カラオケ
STARKUCKS COFFEE
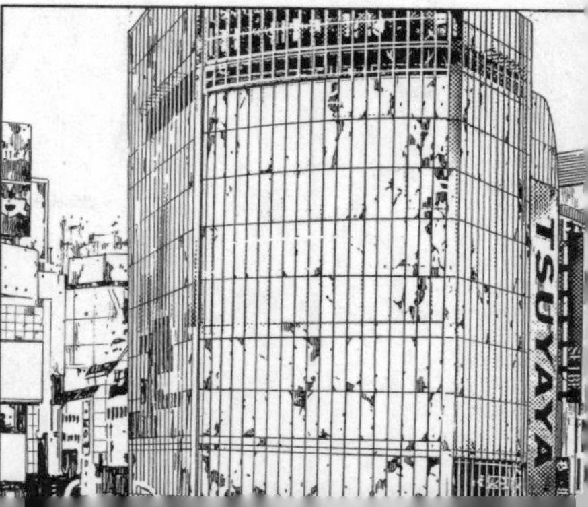
TSUYAYA
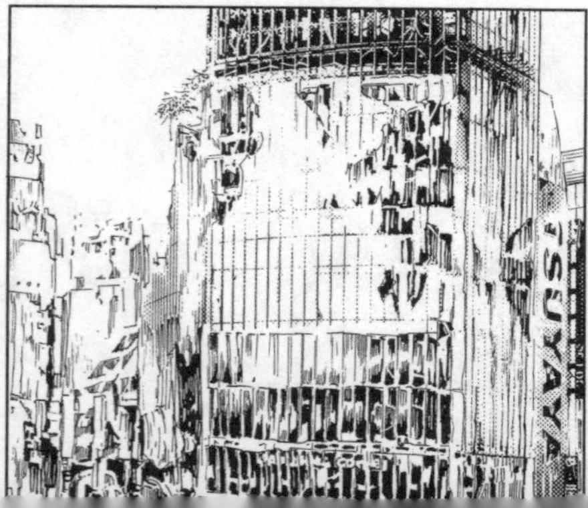
TSUYAYA

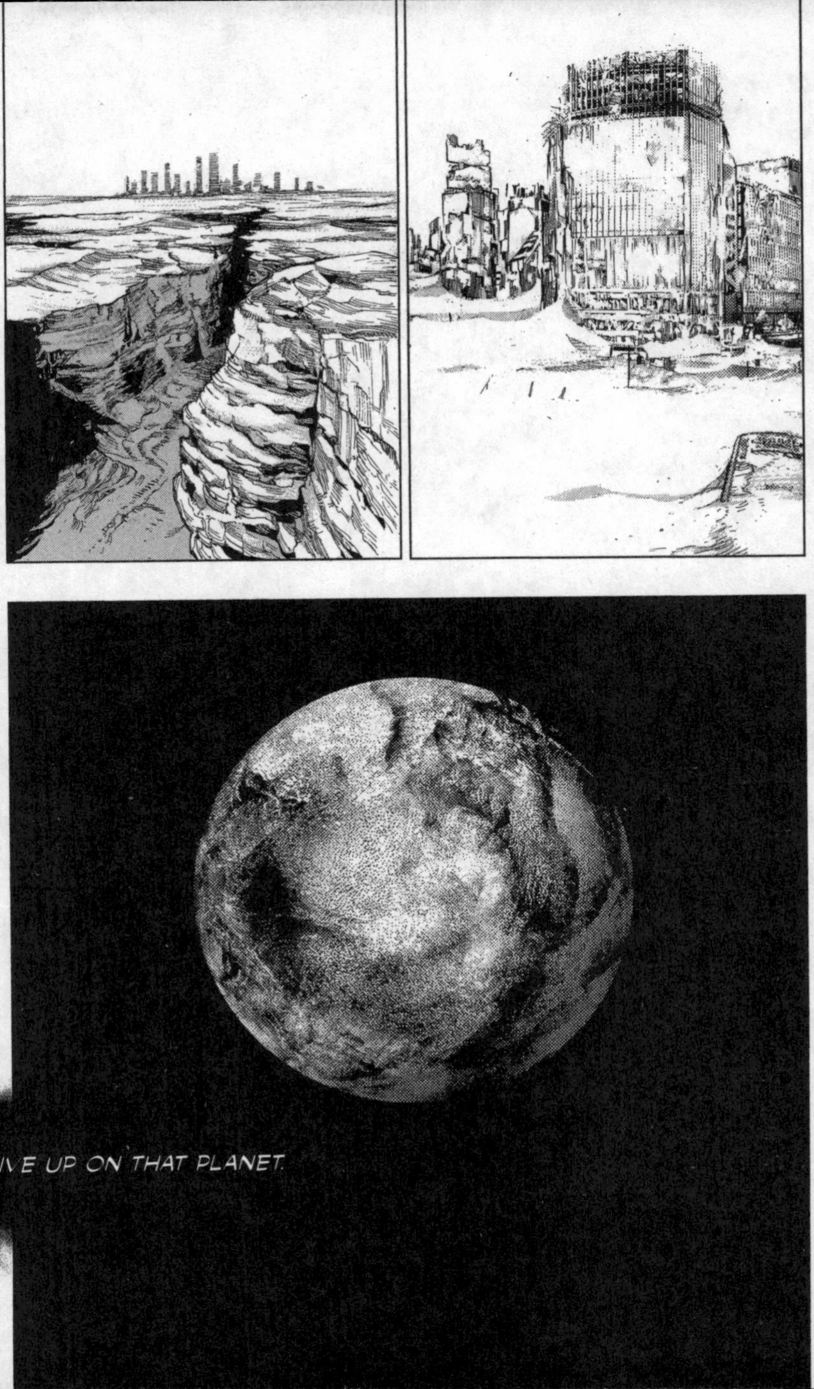
GIVE UP ON THAT PLANET.

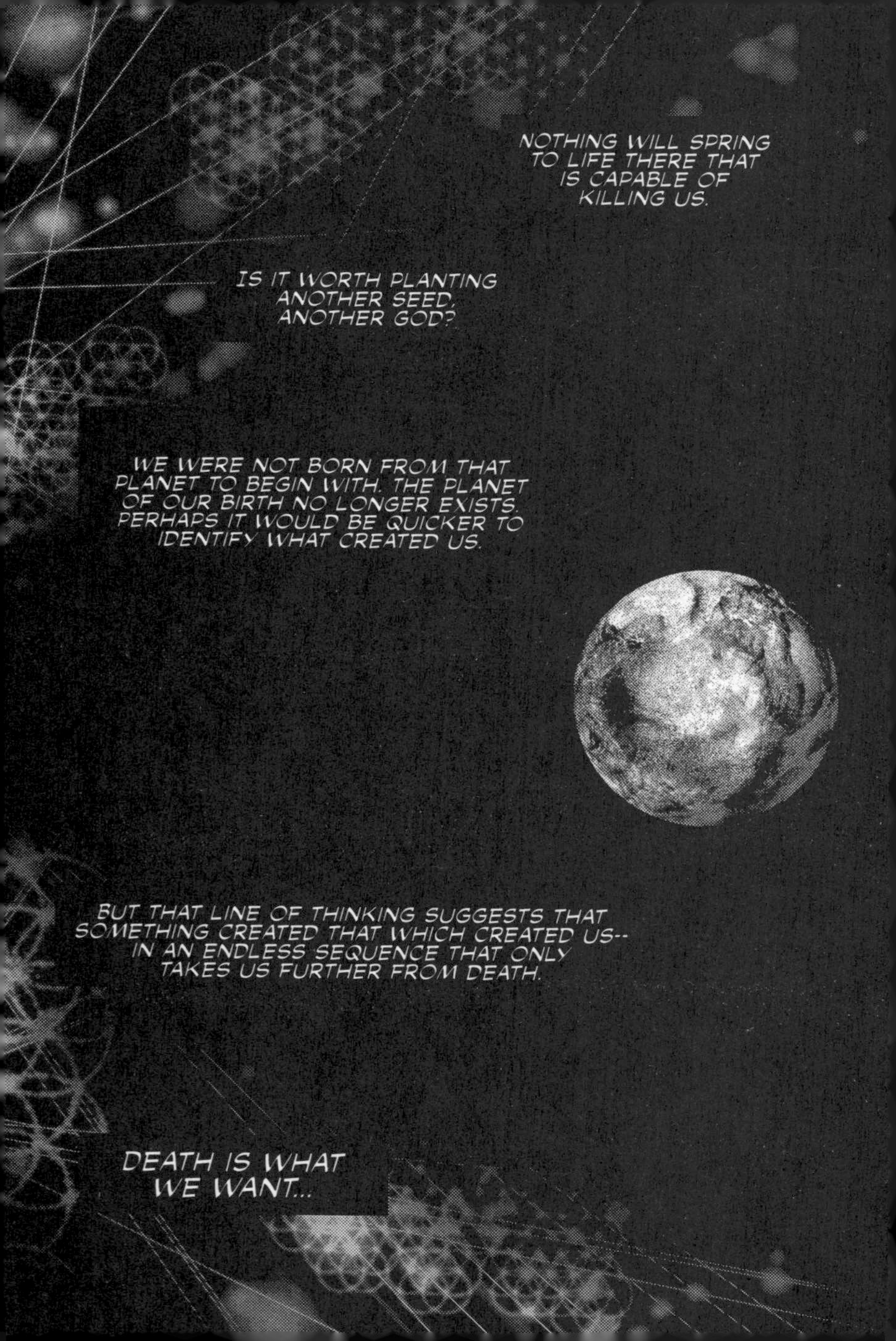
NOTHING WILL SPRING TO LIFE THERE THAT IS CAPABLE OF KILLING US.
IS IT WORTH PLANTING ANOTHER SEED, ANOTHER GOD?
WE WERE NOT BORN FROM THAT PLANET TO BEGIN WITH. THE PLANET OF OUR BIRTH NO LONGER EXISTS. PERHAPS IT WOULD BE QUICKER TO IDENTIFY WHAT CREATED US.
BUT THAT LINE OF THINKING SUGGESTS THAT SOMETHING CREATED THAT WHICH CREATED US-- IN AN ENDLESS SEQUENCE THAT ONLY TAKES US FURTHER FROM DEATH.
DEATH IS WHAT WE WANT...

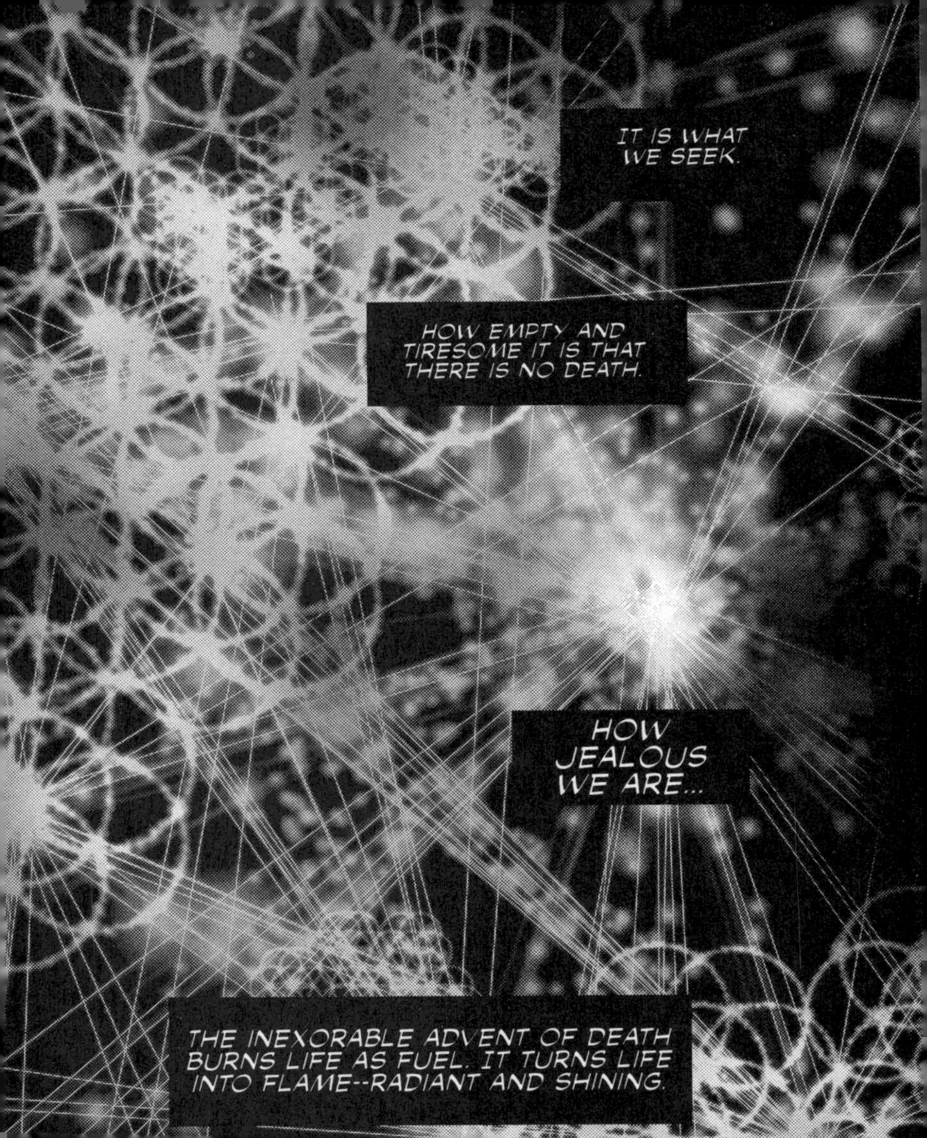
IT IS WHAT WE SEEK.
HOW EMPTY AND TIRESOME IT IS THAT THERE IS NO DEATH.
HOW JEALOUS WE ARE...
THE INEXORABLE ADVENT OF DEATH BURNS LIFE AS FUEL. IT TURNS LIFE INTO FLAME--RADIANT AND SHINING.

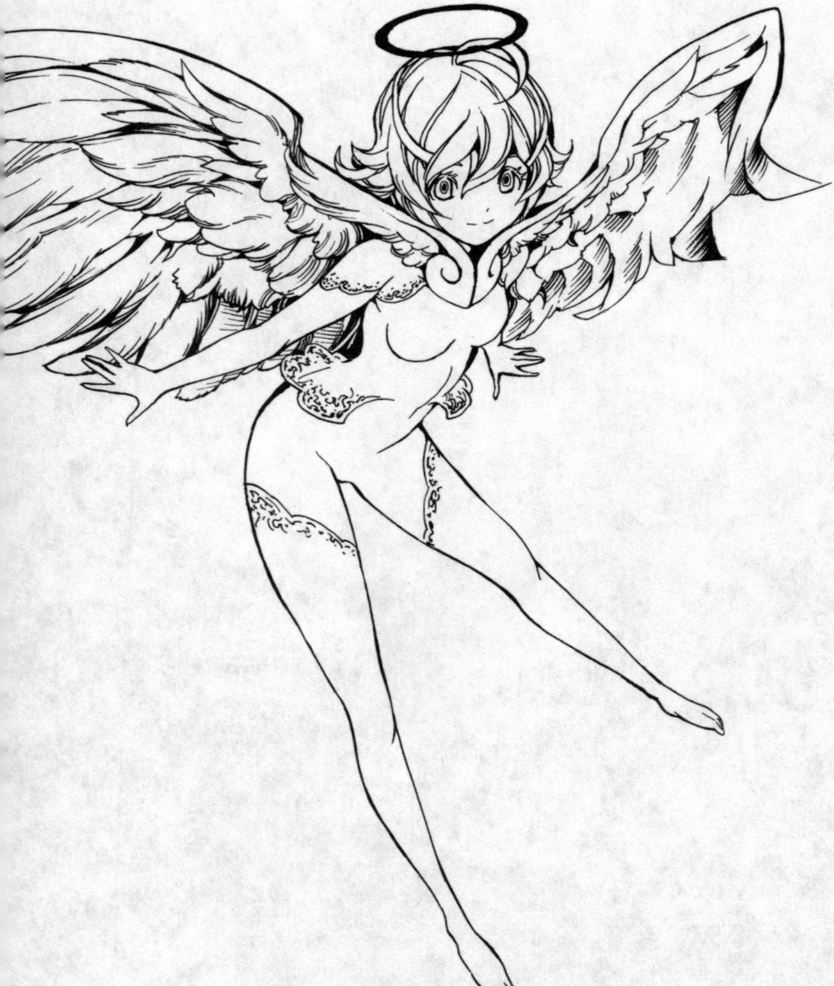

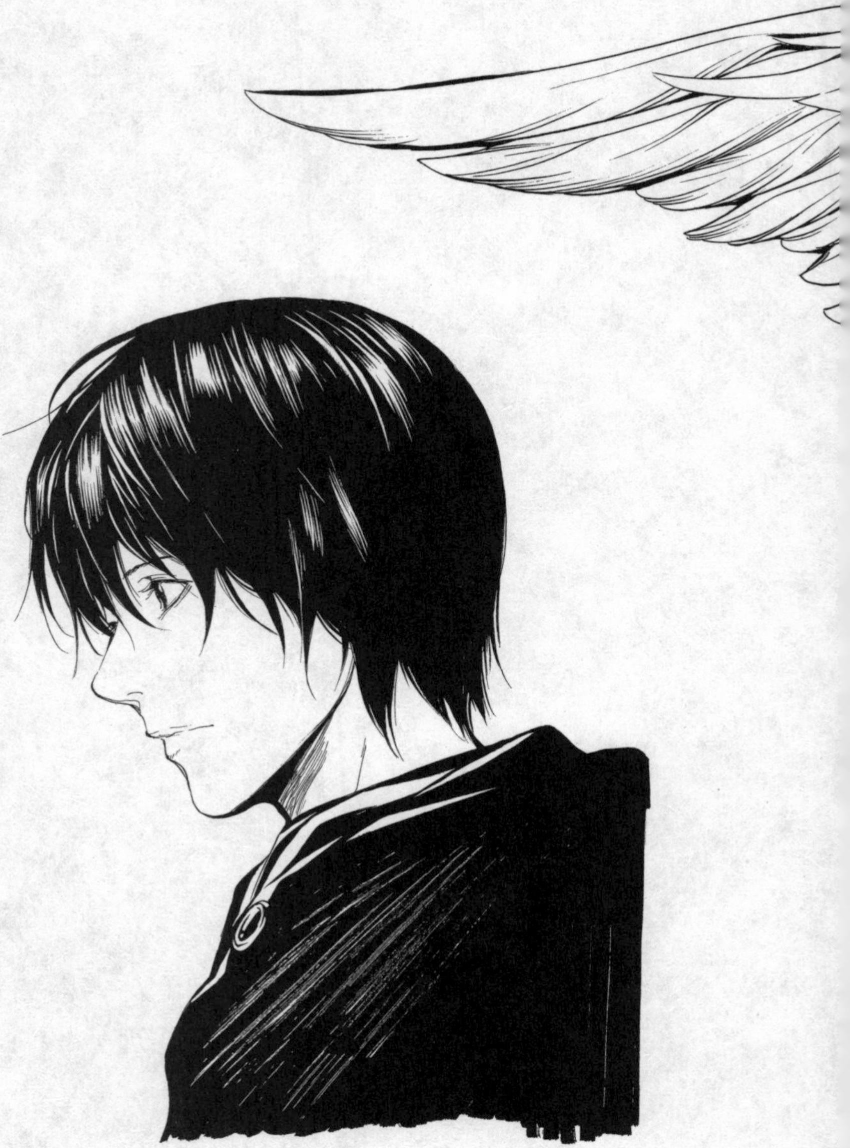

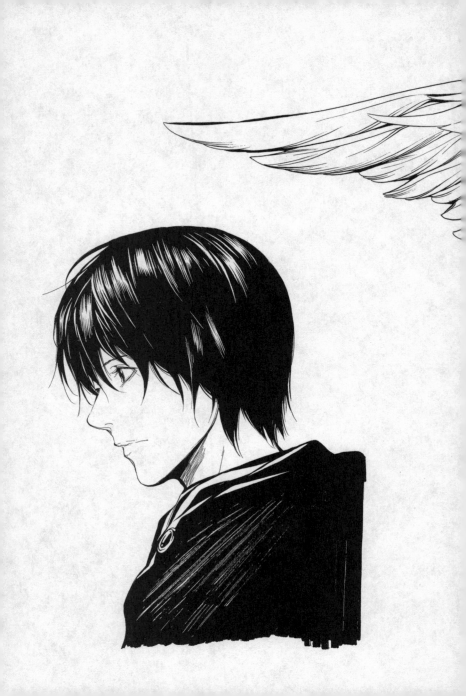

T sugu mi **Oh** b **a**

Born in Tokyo, Tsugumi Ohba is the author
of the hit series *Death Note* and *Bakuman*。

Ta **k** e **sh** i **Oba ta**

Takeshi Obata was born in 1969 in Niigata,
Japan, and first achieved international
recognition as the artist of the wildly popular
Shonen Jump title *Hikaru no Go*, which won the
2003 Tezuka Osamu Cultural Prize: Shinsei
"New Hope" Award and the 2000 Shogakukan
Manga Award. He went on to illustrate the smash
hit *Death Note* as well as the hugely successful
manga *Bakuman*。and *All You Need Is Kill*.

PLATINVM END

VOLUME 14
SHONEN JUMP Manga Edition

○

STORY **T**su**g**u mi **O**h b a
ART Ta **k** e **sh** i O ba **ta**

○

TRANSLATION Stephen Paul
TOUCH-UP ART & LETTERING James Gaubatz
DESIGN Shawn Carrico
EDITOR Alexis Kirsch

○

ORIGINAL COVER DESIGN Narumi Noriko

○

PLATINUM END © 2015 by Tsugumi Ohba, Takeshi Obata
All rights reserved.
First published in Japan in 2015 by SHUEISHA Inc., Tokyo.
English translation rights arranged by SHUEISHA Inc.

○

The stories, characters, and incidents mentioned in this
publication are entirely fictional.

No portion of this book may be reproduced or transmitted
in any form or by any means without written permission
from the copyright holders.

○

Printed in the U.S.A.

Published by VIZ Media, LLC
P.O. Box 77010
San Francisco, CA 94107

○

10 9 8 7 6 5 4 3 2 1
First printing, March 2022

viz.com

PARENTAL ADVISORY
PLATINUM END is rated M for Mature
and is recommended for mature readers.
This volume contains suggestive themes.

THE ACTION-PACKED SUPERHERO COMEDY ABOUT
ONE MAN'S AMBITION TO BE A HERO FOR FUN!

ONE-PUNCH MAN

STORY BY
ONE

ART BY
YUSUKE MURATA

Nothing about Saitama passes the eyeball test when it comes to superheroes, from his lifeless expression to his bald head to his unimpressive physique. However, this average-looking guy has a not-so-average problem—he just can't seem to find an opponent strong enough to take on!

Can he finally find an opponent who can go toe-to-toe with him and give his life some meaning? Or is he doomed to a life of superpowered boredom?

ONE-PUNCH MAN © 2012 by ONE, Yusuke Murata/SHUEISHA inc.

www.viz.com

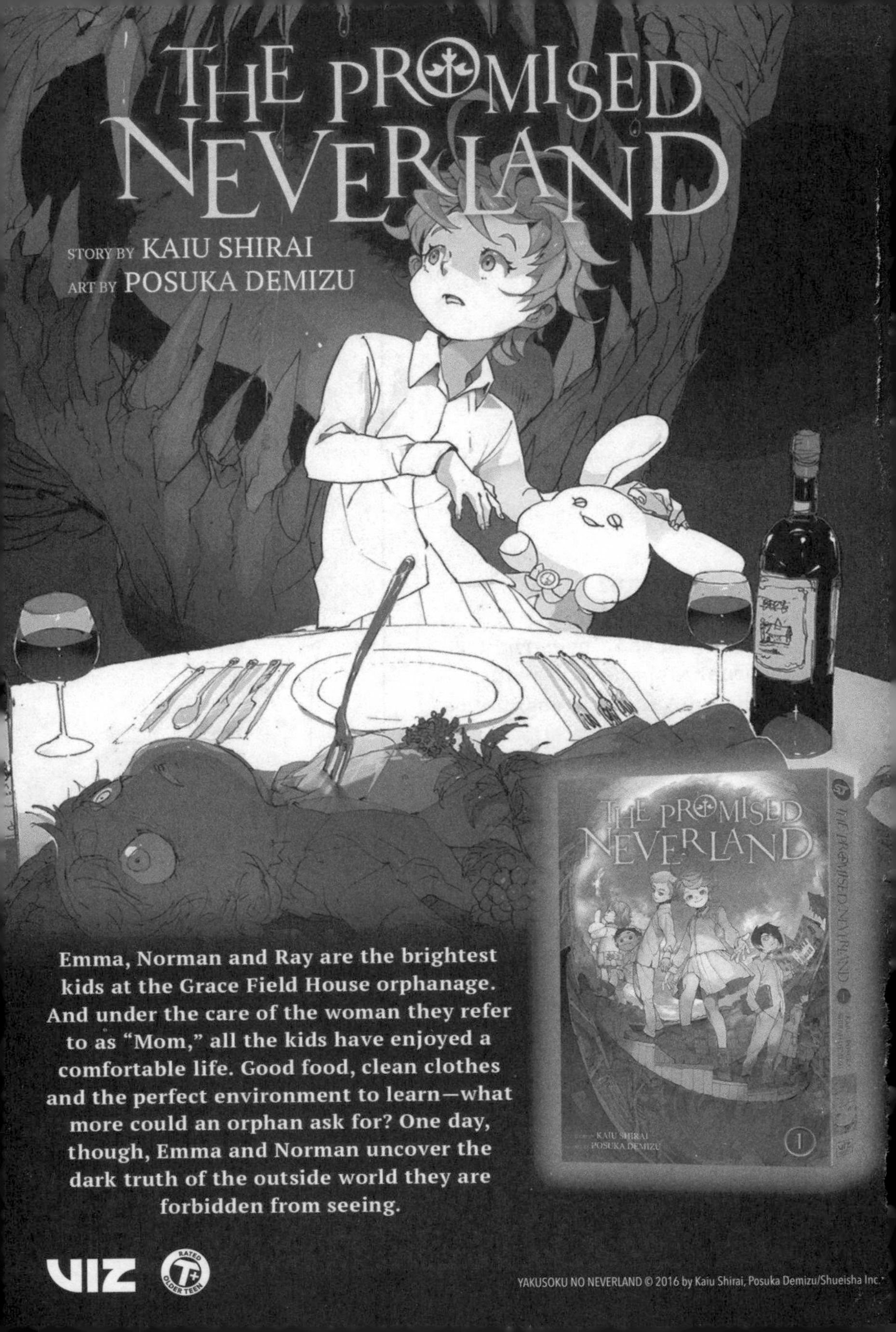
THE PROMISED NEVERLAND
STORY BY KAIU SHIRAI
ART BY POSUKA DEMIZU
Emma, Norman and Ray are the brightest kids at the Grace Field House orphanage. And under the care of the woman they refer to as "Mom," all the kids have enjoyed a comfortable life. Good food, clean clothes and the perfect environment to learn—what more could an orphan ask for? One day, though, Emma and Norman uncover the dark truth of the outside world they are forbidden from seeing.
VIZ
RATED T+ OLDER TEEN
YAKUSOKU NO NEVERLAND © 2016 by Kaiu Shirai, Posuka Demizu/Shueisha Inc.

YOU'RE READING THE

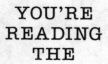

PLATINUM END
reads from right to left,
starting in the upper-right
corner. Japanese is read
from right to left, meaning
that action, sound effects,
and word-balloon order
are completely reversed
from English order.

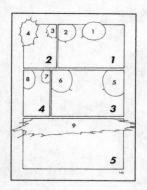